The Development of the Infant and Young Child Normal and Abnormal

Other books by the author

THE NORMAL CHILD: Some Problems of the Early Years and their Treatment. 1975, 6th Ed. London. Churchill Livingstone.

THE NORMAL SCHOOL CHILD: His Problems Physical and Emotional. 1964, London, Heinemann.

COMMON SYMPTOMS OF DISEASE IN CHILDREN. 1975, 5th Ed. Oxford, Blackwell Scientific Publications.

TREATMENT OF THE CHILD AT HOME: A guide for family doctors. 1971, Oxford, Blackwell Scientific Publications.

BASIC DEVELOPMENT SCREENING—0–2 years. 1973, Oxford, Blackwell Scientific Publications.

BABIES AND YOUNG CHILDREN: Feeding, Management and Care. (With C. M. Illingworth). 1972, 5th Ed. London, Churchill Livingstone.

LESSONS FROM CHILDHOOD: Some Aspects of the Early Life of Unusual Men and Women (with C. M. Illingworth) 1966, Edinburgh, Churchill Livingstone.

THE CHILD AT SCHOOL: A Paediatrician's Manual for Teachers. 1974. Oxford. Blackwell Scientific Publications.

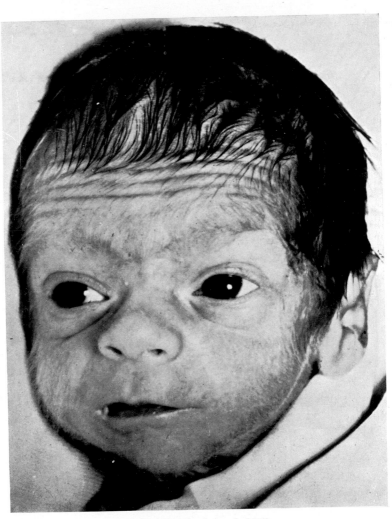

"What does the future hold?"
(A normal premature baby.)

to face title page

The Development
of the Infant
and Young Child
Normal and Abnormal

R. S. ILLINGWORTH

M.D. LEEDS, F.R.C.P., D.P.H., D.C.H.

Professor of Child Health, The University of Sheffield.
Paediatrician, The Children's Hospital, Sheffield, and the
Jessop Hospital for Women, Sheffield.

SIXTH EDITION

CHURCHILL LIVINGSTONE
EDINBURGH LONDON AND NEW YORK 1975

CHURCHILL LIVINGSTONE
Medical Division of Longman Group Limited

Distributed in the United States of America by Longman
Inc., 19 West 44th Street, New York, N.Y. 10036 and by
associated companies, branches and representatives throughout the world.

© Longman Group Limited 1975

First Edition	1960
Second Edition	1963
Third Edition	1966
Reprinted	1967
Fourth Edition	1970
Reprinted	1971
Fifth Edition	1972
Reprinted	1974
Sixth Edition	1975
Reprinted	1977

Translated into Japanese.

ISBN 0 443 01277 6

Printed in Hong Kong by
Dai Nippon Printing Co. (H.K.) Ltd.

PREFACE TO THE SIXTH EDITION

The interest in the development of the normal child is now wide-spread, and as a result, knowledge of his development is ever increasing; yet there is still a great deal to be learnt—and I expect there always will be. In preparing this edition I have gone through every word of the fifth edition, and brought it thoroughly up to date. I have paid heed to useful comments by reviewers of the fifth edition and attended to their suggestions.

A major problem is that of reference lists and their tendency to grow longer and longer with each successive edition. Rightly or wrongly I have deleted many references to articles written 15 or more years ago, retaining only older key references to particularly important articles: sometimes I have referred in the text to the authors of these older papers by name without including the references at the end of the chapter: occasionally I have deliberately included references in the list without mentioning them by name in the script, feeling that readers interested in a subject could look at the reference list for further reading. The time comes when research material becomes part of accepted knowledge and reference need no longer be made to the original paper. I realise that whatever one does about the problem of references lists, one provides grounds for criticism. I have added over a hundred new references to this edition, bringing it up to date to the end of 1974.

I have introduced a major new section on the philosophy of developmental testing and rewritten much of the chapter on prenatal factors which affect the child's development.

I have adhered strictly to my original aim in writing this book—to make it an essentially practical manual on the development of the child and on developmental assessment, excluding physical and emotional aspects. I have been criticised for not including more about advances in the scientific basis of development: I omitted much of this deliberately in order to adhere to my original aim of making it a simple practical manual which would be understood by anyone.

Plate numbers 74, 77, 79, 104, 105, 108, 110, 111, 112, 113, 114, 115, 122 are my own photographs. The others are by Alan Tunstill, Photographic Department, United Sheffield Hospitals.

Sheffield 1975

PREFACE TO THE FIRST EDITION

A thorough knowledge and understanding of the normal development of the infant and young child is just as fundamental to anyone concerned with the care of children, especially paediatricians, as is anatomy to the surgeon. Family doctor, paediatricians and others must know the normal, and the variations from the normal, before they attempt to diagnose the abnormal. I doubt whether a paediatrician will complete any out-patient clinic without having had to make at least one developmental assessment. Without such an assessment he is unable to make a proper diagnosis, to arrange proper treatment, and to help the parents or family doctor or school medical officer as much as he should.

The doctor inevitably has to assess the development of every baby which he sees in a well baby clinic, for otherwise he is not doing his job properly; he could not hope to diagnose the abnormal, to detect the early signs of cerebral palsy or of mental subnormality, of a hearing or visual defect, of subluxation of the hip, or of hydrocephalus, unless he were first conversant with the normal and then looked for the variations from the normal. In the hospital ward one does not carry out a developmental examination on an ill child with bronchopneumonia, and in a private house one does not assess the development of every young child with asthma; but in both places there are innumerable circumstances in which a developmental examination is essential, and without it the examination is seriously incomplete.

It is because I regard developmental assessment as an essential part of everyday practice that I wrote this book, in order to describe just what can be learnt about a child's development with a minimum of equipment in an ordinary mixed clinic, and not in a special room, at a special time, with special complicated equipment. Everyone dealing with children needs this knowledge. It is not just the province of an expert who does nothing else.

Because I am convinced that the best assessment must be based on a full consideration of prenatal, perinatal and environmental factors which affect development, and on a careful developmental history, I have written separate chapters on these matters. I have placed particular emphasis on the normal variations which occur in all fields of development, and on the reasons for these variations. I have repeatedly emphasised the difficulties in developmental assessment, and the reasons why assessments in infancy can never have a high correlation with intelligence tests in older children, and still less with success in later life. I have discussed in detail the reasons for the limitations in developmental testing. Perhaps the most important chapter is the last one—on the pitfalls in developmental assessment.

The limitations and fallacies must be known and understood. There is a rapidly increasing interest in the physiology and pathology of pregnancy in relation to the foetus, and attempts to correlate events in pregnancy with the development of the infant are liable to give entirely fallacious results unless the difficulties of developmental testing, its possibilities and its limitations, are fully understood. As in other kinds of research, one must avoid the mistake of making accurate analyses of inaccurate data.

This book does not attempt to discuss the normal physical and emotional development of the child. I have confined the book to the study of the infant and preschool child.

I wish to express my gratitude to Arnold Gesell and Catherine Amatruda, above all others, for giving me the privilege to work under them and for teaching me the fundamentals of child development, so that I could then continue to learn for the rest of my working life.

R.S.I.

CONTENTS

CHAPTER 1

THE NEED FOR KNOWLEDGE OF CHILD DEVELOPMENT

All those with responsibility for the care of children, whether child welfare doctors, general practitioners, paediatricians or others, require a thorough knowledge of the normal and of variations from it, in order that they can recognise the abnormal—and in particular mental and physical handicaps. They will need this knowledge on almost every day of their work.

Every parent feels a natural curiosity about the development of his children, and if with a previous pregnancy there had been an unfortunate experience, such as a miscarriage or stillbirth, or if the child born alive proved to be mentally or physically handicapped, there is all the more reason why he should be concerned about the wellbeing of subsequent children. Sometimes there is a potentially noxious factor during pregnancy, such as an infection, injury or illness, or there is a difficult delivery, and the child is ill at birth or shortly after, so that the parents are anxious to know whether he is developing normally or not. There may be a family history of mental deficiency, epilepsy or other handicap, which heightens their anxiety. The family doctor and others who are responsible for children need to be in a position to reassure them with a fair degree of confidence, based on the necessary knowledge.

A husband and wife, who are unable to have children of their own, may decide to adopt. They should be able to rely on a doctor to give a sound opinion as to whether the child offered to them for adoption is mentally normal or not. In my opinion the decision is of such momentous importance for the happiness of the parents and child, that the paediatrician should be the one to examine such babies. A thorough knowledge of child development, and in particular of all the factors which may have affected his development in the past and which may affect it in the future, is essential for a reasonable opinion to be possible. It is a double tragedy for a husband and wife, who have been unable after several years of marriage to satisfy their normal desire to have children of their own, to adopt a child who subsequently proves to be mentally defective.

It is a worse tragedy if a child who is in fact normal is said to be mentally defective or spastic and therefore unsuitable for adoption. Such a mistake is likely to cause serious psychological trauma and emotional deprivation, and may affect his whole life. At the time of writing this I saw a four year old who was in a foster home because a doctor had said three and a half years previously that the child was spastic and unsuitable for adoption. He was not, therefore, adopted.

1

In fact the child was normal. The result of the mistake was that the boy had to change homes and 'parents' when four years old, in order to be adopted. All too often babies are passed as suitable for adoption without any developmental examination at all, merely on clinical impression, and rejected without any expert examination or assessment.

On innumerable other occasions the doctor needs to call on his knowledge of child development. He is confronted with a child with an odd-looking face, or a skull of unusual shape or size and he wants to assess his attainments and the outlook for him. The baby may have a mild degree of hydrocephalus or craniostenosis, and the physician is asked by the surgeon for advice as to whether he should operate or not. The physician will be guided by the present attainments of the child in relation to the previous rate of development, and by the subsequently observed rate of progress.

The physician is anxious to know whether a child who was born many weeks prematurely, or with a severe degree of asphyxia, or who had cyanotic attacks or convulsions in the newborn period, or a subdural haematoma, is progressing satisfactorily. He is constantly confronted with the problem of convulsions, whether due to epilepsy or other causes, and knows the frequent relationship between convulsions and physical and mental handicaps. He sees children with congenital anomalies, such as cleft palate or congenital heart disease, and wonders whether there is additional mental retardation. He wants to follow up children born with haemolytic disease of the newborn. He wants to observe the rate of mental development of children with hypothyroidism under his care, as one of the checks on the adequacy of his treatment. He is anxious to know whether a head injury, or an attack of pyogenic meningitis, or of virus encephalitis, has left any permanent mental sequelae. He is repeatedly faced with the problem of children with cerebral palsy, and wants to assess their mental development, with particular regard to the type of education most suitable for them.

He is often asked to advise about babies and young children whose behaviour is bad, or who are backward in one or several fields of development. He is concerned about the young baby with severe feeding difficulties, such as difficulty in swallowing and excessive regurgitation. In all these he needs to eliminate mental and physical defects by his developmental examination.

The physician is constantly confronted with the child who is backward in all fields of development, and in whom mental deficiency is suspected. An incorrect diagnosis of mental deficiency is a tragedy, and the diagnosis must never be even hinted at until one is sure of one's ground. Early diagnosis, however, is important for many reasons. It may provide the pointer to curable conditions, such as developing hypothyroidism, or to certain other metabolic conditions, such as phenylketonuria, which are amenable to treatment; and it is desirable that the parents should be told about the position, so that they can face and plan the future.   I have asked innumerable mothers how soon they think that parents should be informed that their child is backward. Without exception they have answered that they should be told as soon as possible, so that they are not left to find out for themselves after months or even years of lingering doubts, often after visits to one doctor after another, in the effort to find someone who will tell them the truth.   The diagnosis, however, must be based on really sound evidence, for it is a shocking tragedy if parents are told that their child is mentally defective, when in fact he is normal.

It is important to distinguish backwardness of environmental origin from backwardness due to a low innate level of intelligence. In the former case a great deal can be done to help, and to raise the child's performance to a higher level. In the latter case the correct diagnosis should lead, amongst other things, to the avoidance of overprotection by the parents, and of efforts to push him beyond his capabilities. In addition, having decided that a child is mentally backward, one will try to give the parents the prognosis with regard to the likelihood of his learning to walk, talk, go to school and earn his living.

I should have thought that the rôle of developmental diagnosis was obvious and I may seem to have laboured the point by citing the above examples. Several writers, however, have belittled its value, and criticised any attempts to assess a child's development.   Many of these doubts are related to the firm conviction possessed by many that developmental tests in infancy have no predictive value.

CHAPTER 2

DEVELOPMENTAL TESTING
AND ITS VALUE

The Development of Mental Testing

I propose to give only a brief outline of the development of mental testing. For a more complete account the reader should refer to testbooks of Psychology.

STUDIES OF INDIVIDUAL CHILDREN

According to Goodenough[20] Tiedemann in Germany (1787) was the first to publish a detailed record of the development of one child, but it was not until Charles Darwin[11] in 1877 published a detailed account of the development of one of his own ten children that interest was aroused. Charles Darwin wrote: 'My first child was born on December 27th, 1839, and I at once commenced to make notes on the first dawn of the various experiences which he exhibited, for I felt convinced, even at this early period, that the most complex and fine shades of expression must all have had a gradual and natural origin'. He described the rooting reflex, hearing in the newborn period, the absence of tears in the first few weeks except when his coat sleeve accidentally caught his child's eye, the first co-ordinated movements of the hands at 6 weeks, the cephalocaudal sequence of development, the reciprocal kick, hand regard at 4 months, the first sign of anger (at 10 weeks), of humour (at 3 months), of fear, imitation and of enjoyment of the sound of the piano (at 4 months). He described the first association of a person with her name (at 7 months), the first signs of jealousy, love, curiosity, association of ideas, deceit, moral sense, inhibitions, laughter, shyness, sympathy and handedness. He had already published his famous and fascinating book *The Expression of the Emotions in Man and Animals*,[10] which incorporated some of these and many other observations on crying, sobbing, laughter and other emotions.

In 1893 Shinn[32] published one of the most complete records of a young baby's development. In 1931 Shirley[33] wrote an extremely full account of 25 children in their first two years.

DEVELOPMENTAL TESTS

The history of developmental testing was mentioned by Bayley.[4] According to her, Binet's original aim was to identify children who were unlikely to benefit from regular school instruction. She wrote that in 1912 Stern and Kuhlman suggested that a child's relative status

4

could be indicated by a ratio between his mental age and his chronological age—the intelligence quotient.

In the early part of this century Arnold Gesell, while studying mentally defective children, began to think about the early signs of mental deficiency and so set about the study of the normal infant. In 1925 he established 'norms' on a small series of children, seen at monthly intervals: later he revised the norms on a large number of children. A large series of books followed, of which I consider the most valuable today are *Developmental Diagnosis, The First Five Years of Life*, and *Biographies of Child Development*. These established 'norms' of development, describing the development of infants and children from just after the newborn period to the age of 5 years. The philosophy of development, the technique of developmental testing and the interpretation of results are all discussed in detail in his books. In 1933 Bayley established 'norms' on a large number of children. In 1954 Ruth Griffiths tested 571 children aged 14 days to 24 months—up to 31 children in one monthly period. In 1967 the Denver study was published, based on a sample of over 1000 children, a sample, however, which was 'selected' and not representative of the country as a whole.

I shall not attempt to review all the infant tests which have been described, but will refer to books by four authors—those of Charlotte Bühler,[7] Psyche Cattell,[9] Ruth Griffiths[21] and Haeussermann.[22]

Bühler's tests are of interest and importance because of her attempt to cover all fields of development and not merely sensorimotor skills. The tests are described in detail and are easy to apply. Cattell's tests are modified from those of Gesell. Her book had the merit of providing simple instructions for the application of the tests, but like Bühler she did not describe the philosophy of developmental testing or the importance of the history. This criticism applies still more forcibly to the book by Ruth Griffiths, whose tests are again modified from those of Gesell. No attention was paid to the history and environmental circumstances, the tests being entirely objective. I shall explain that in my view proper interpretation of development on this basis is impossible. In marked contrast to the above is the book by Haeussermann, which was concerned mainly with developmental testing of handicapped children. A full account of history taking and the interpretation of results made this a most valuable book.

THE PHILOSOPHY OF DEVELOPMENTAL TESTING

The approach of Psychologists and Paediatricians compared

I shall not in this chapter, nor, I hope, at any other time, make the mistake of using the words "most think that" or "everyone agrees that"—statements which under any circumstances are almost bound to be wrong: but I shall make certain generalisations about the attitudes of psychologists and paediatricians about developmental testing, for they are fundamentally different.

Neither psychologists nor paediatricians have been notably successful in making a widely accepted definition of intelligence, but paediatricians are apt to be more imprecise in the use of the term intelligence quotient and in the understanding of its significance. In an 'Exhibition' as part of a clinical meeting in a well-known children's hospital I saw a set of figures which purported to display the value of a phenylalanine-low diet for phenylketonuria: the IQ was said to be 58 at 4 weeks of age, before treatment, and 66 after two months of treatment: the scale used was that of Ruth Griffiths. Nothing could have provided a better demonstration of lack of understanding of developmental testing.

Paediatricians are apt to be imprecise in their use of the term mental subnormality. In this book I denote by that term a developmental quotient or intelligence quotient of under 70: but I shall emphasize the dangers of making that diagnosis in the early weeks and months.

Paediatricians and psychologists tend to advocate the use of tests whose significance has not been validated. These are often tests which would be extremely unlikely to be of developmental significance. For instance, there are some 73 primitive reflexes of which I am aware, all occurring in the early days or weeks of life: but as far as I have been able to determine, only about six of these have been shown as yet to be of importance for developmental assessment. Brazelton (1974) described a "neonatal behavioral assessment scale" involving 30 different tests and manoeuvres: but the examination is said to take 20 to 30 minutes, and is therefore unlikely to be used in a busy neonatal unit involving three or four thousand or more deliveries a year. The tests include several of questionable value, such as Galant's incurvation reflex (see Chapter 5). I am unaware of its importance in assessment. Brazelton does not say why he thinks these tests are of value. If tests are to be practical they should not take too long: if they are not to take too long they should be cut down to those which matter, leaving other tests for possible investigation by research workers and perhaps, therefore, for future validation. Ruth Griffiths included the following parameters for the child from one to three months:-

Kicks vigorously
Enjoys bath
Pushes feet against examiner's hands
Energetic arm movements

One would hardly have thought that these would be useful milestones for developmental assessment. Only careful observation, experience and long-term follow up will decide which tests are of value for developmental assessment and which are not. In subsequent chapters

I have tried to reduce testing to the minimum: and I have summarised those in a small book termed "Basic Developmental Screening" (1974) for practical every-day use.

Many psychologists and some paediatricians feel a particular attraction for centiles which define the proportion of infants achieving skills by certain ages. A reviewer of the fifth edition of this book,[5] referring to my preface in which I wrote that I had added some 56 new references, wrote that he "would have done without any of the 56 new references in exchange for two others"—meaning the Denver scale[15,16] and a Newcastle study[31]—because they showed the percentage of children achieving certain skills at certain ages. When I wrote the fifth edition I was fully aware of the above publications but did not think that it would be profitable to refer to them: but as others hold these papers in high esteem it is reasonable to discuss them here. The Newcastle study[31] gave the 3rd, 10th, 25th, 50th, 75th and 90th and 97th centile for four milestones, sitting unsupported, walking, saying single words and making sentences: the figures were as follows:

Milestones	Number	3	10	25	Centiles 50	75	90	97
Sits unsupported	3831	4·6	5·2	5·8	6·4	7·2	8·1	9·3
Walks	3554	9·7	10·7	11·8	12·8	14·2	15·8	18·4
Single words boys	1824	8·7	10·0	11·6	12·4	15·0	18·0	21·9
Single words girls	1747	8·6	9·8	11·5	12·3	14·6	17·3	20·1
Sentences boys	1653	17·5	19·1	21·4	23·8	26·8	32·5	36·0
Sentences girls	1575	16·2	18·4	20·4	22·9	25·0	30·8	36·0

The Denver scale gives the 25th, 50th, 75th and 90th centile for 105 items: these milestones are shown in a graphic form and the writers claim that "it vividly shows on the chart the range of normal variations". "It enables the examiner to determine whether he (the child) is within the normal range". The scale is designed to act as a screen for slow development, and to alert the examiner to the need to investigate the child further. The writers make it clear that they do not intend the scale to be used as an intelligence test. The scale includes gross motor, language, fine motor, adaptive and personal-social items: it was standardised on 1036 presumably normal children aged 2 weeks to 6 years who were thought to be respresentative of Denver children.

Though many may disagree, particularly, I think, psychologists, I think that the centile distribution of milestones of development is of little value.   It is definitely incorrect to say that the Denver scale chart shows at a glance whether a child's milestones are normal or not. It is probably never possible to draw the line between normal and abnormal.   The Newcastle study gave the age of 18·4 months for the 97th centile for walking without help; the Denver scale gave the age of 14·3 months for the 90th centile for the same skill.   But I have seen dozens of normal children who were unable to walk without help until after 14·3 months, and a considerable number who could not walk without help until 18·4 months.   The number of proved followed-up normal children who were unable to walk without support until after 2·0 years, seen by me personally, is now about twenty one.

It is true that the further away from the average a child is in anything (haemoglobin, blood urea, age of walking etc.,) the more likely he is to be abnormal: but it is totally wrong to say that figures on a chart showing the centile distribution of developmental milestones will show whether a child's performance is normal or abnormal.   The obvious reply to my doubts about the value of centiles for milestones of development is that I am inconsistent, for I advocate the use of centile charts for the weight, height and head circumference. It is not easy to answer this.   Measurements of the weight, height and head circumference are (or should be) accurate.   Though single measurements on a centile chart are of value, serial measurements are much more so: they enable one to see at a glance when there is a departure of the child's measurement from its position in relation to the marked centiles.   One is comparing a child's placing at one time with his previous or subsequent placing for the same measurement.   But in the case of developmental milestones serial measurements are useless, because developmental skills represent different aspects of development as the child grows older and cannot be compared with each other.   Admittedly an overall score, a developmental quotient, could be plotted serially, but it would perhaps be unwise because each DQ would be based on different milestones and parameters.   In the case of a centile chart for weight, height and head circumference, it would be incorrect to say that if a child's measurement is below the 90th or 97th centile it is necessarily abnormal.

It is important to distinguish studies, such as the Newcastle one in which the centiles are based on the age at which children first reached certain milestones, such as walking, from studies such as the Denver one, which are based on the ability of the child to pass certain tests at given ages—a very different matter: for in the latter case a child who passes a test might have been able to pass it a long time previously.

But it is in fact very difficult in the case of most milestones to say precisely when a certain milestone is reached. For instance, it is difficult to say accurately when a child first smiles at his mother in response to her overtures, first chews, or first says single words. As I explained elsewhere, a child trying to say the word dog is likely to say 'g' and later 'og' when he sees a picture of a dog, or hears a dog barking, or an imitation of a bark: it is difficult to decide at what age he should be regarded as first having said the word. Looking at the Denver figure one notes that some of the milestones would be difficult to define accurately: e.g., sits, head steady (50th centile 2·9 months): bears some weight on legs (50th centile 4·6 months), walks, well (12·1 months): stands holding on (5·8 months). One also notes that the 50th centile given by the Denver workers is in some milestones considerably different from that of the New Haven children examined by Gessell. For instance, "Rolls over"—Denver figure 2·8 months: turns to voice (5·6 months): the former is far earlier than the Gesell figures, and the latter much later; and the 50th centile given by the Denver study for sitting without support (5·5 months) is much earlier than that given by Gesell, and that given by the Newcastle team (6·4 months). I am not in favour of making accurate analyses of inaccurate data. I have many times seen an IQ score given to one place of decimals, and occasionally to two places of decimals. Considering the inaccuracy of many of the data on which such a score is based, I do not favour this. In the years since the papers from Denver and Newcastle were published, I have not felt the need to refer back to them except for the purpose of this paper: I have certainly not needed them to help me in the assessment of some hundreds of babies. I have not yet been able to think of the circumstances in which I should want the information.

Differences of Approach

Psychologists, rightly wanting scientific accuracy, rely almost entirely on objective tests: clinicians, one hopes, make a diagnosis on the basis of the history, the examination, special investigations where necessary, and the interpretation. Perhaps because I am a clinician, I favour the clinician's approach.

The History

This is discussed in more detail in Chapter 12. The history must include the following:-

(1) *Risk factors.* These are prenatal, natal and postnatal factors which increase the likelihood that a particular child has an abnormality—such as cerebral palsy, visual or auditory defect, mental subnormality or a degenerative disease of the nervous system. This depends on accurate history-taking. Having obtained a history of an important risk factor, such as maternal mental subnormality,

one must not be biased by it so that one assumes that the child is abnormal: it is just one factor which one uses in the interpretation of the whole examination.   If a parent has a predominantly hereditary condition such as schizophrenia or manic-depressive psychosis, the child is at risk of developing the same condition—but in these two cases there will be no means of telling whether the child will develop these or not, and for assessment for adoption, this is important.

(2) *Prematurity.*   It should be obvious that if a baby is born prematurely, he has missed a period of development in utero, and allowance must be made for it.   If, for instance, he was born three months prematurely, and he is assessed six months after birth, he must be compared not with an average six month old baby but with a three month old one.   In the following table I have shown the difference which correction to the real age makes in calculating the developmental quotient.

16 weeks after birth	Developmental level (weeks)	DQ
Full term	16	100
6 weeks premature (therefore real age = 10 weeks)	16	160
Full term	10	62
4 weeks postmature	16	?

It can readily be seen that if allowance is not made for prematurity, gross errors will be made in the case of the young child.   Ruth Griffiths and other psychologists failed to make such an allowance.   I am constantly being asked up to what age one has to allow for prematurity, and 'how long does it take for a premature baby to catch up?'.   These always seem to me to be particularly silly questions. As for the first question, it is surely obvious that the younger the baby the more important it is to allow for prematurity: an allowance of two months for development missed in utero matters a great deal in the early weeks: it would hardly be significant when he is 10 years old. As for the second question, the premature baby 'does not catch up'. He does not develop more quickly than full term children: he is not 'retarded' just because he missed two months development in utero.

It is uncertain whether allowance should be made for postmaturity. Postmaturity is rare now, because of the risks; it is so often associated with placental insufficiency that it may perhaps be incorrect to allow for postmature delivery.

Unusual familial patterns of development are common.   For instance, there may be a familial tendency to delayed motor maturation, so that sitting and walking are late, or there is delayed sphincter control or delayed speech.   This must be taken into consideration when assessing a baby, for it is unrelated to intelligence. It would be silly to give a child a low score because he was retarded in the age of walking, and nothing else, when other normal members of the family exhibited the same trait.

It is often important to enquire about the previous rate of development, by asking the parents about the child's previous milestones. There may be evidence that the child was a slow starter, or that after an illness the child has had a spurt in development and is catching up to the average. To ignore this one invites inaccuracy. In the same way one must ask about previous illness which may have affected development: for instance, an illness may have retarded weight bearing on the legs, and it would then be silly to give the child a low score for this, for it could have no bearing on his potential. One also asks about the child's management: a mother may keep her child off his legs in the mistaken belief that weight-bearing will cause knock-knee, bow legs or rickets. The child who has been deliberately kept off his legs should not be given a low score for defective weight bearing, because it is irrelevant in assessing his developmental quotient.

A child may be severely retarded by emotional deprivation. This is difficult to make an allowance for, because it is impossible to determine at one examination what degree of retardation it has caused: and one cannot say how reversible the effects will be, especially after the first year. The fact that the child suffered emotional deprivation must be noted and remembered, so that at subsequent examinations one can determine how much improvement, if any, there has been— so that some sort of estimate of his potential can be made.

A careful history of the child's past and present skills, taken from an intelligent mother, enables one to form a rough check of one's own objective findings against the mother's story. This may be of importance if the child is tired or non-cooperative at the time of examination. It enables one at least to guess what the child can achieve under better conditions.

The Examination

The psychologists' reliance on purely objective tests results in the use only of scorable items, commonly termed 'sensorimotor'—and they fully recognise this fact. Unfortunately gross motor development, such as sitting, weight bearing and walking, are the least important in developmental assessment (Chapter 14). Of far greater importance are the baby's alertness, responsiveness, interest in surroundings, determination and concentration—all items which cannot so far be scored. Arnold Gesell termed these 'Insurance Factors', and emphasised their importance. If a child were backward in everything else, and yet showed alertness, responsiveness and the other features mentioned, he would reserve an opinion about the child's potential, because he recognised that they were of greater importance than the scorable items on which the child had given a poor showing.

The Haeussermann approach, described in her book and in the book by Jedrysek et al[22,27], like Gesell, recognised the importance of non-scorable items; their books are a complete contrast to those of Ruth Griffiths, who paid no attention to anything but scorable objective tests. Jedrysek et al wrote 'Every moment of contact with the child is important. The very first observations of the child's behaviour are invaluable'. They gave no age norms, writing, concerning the child after infancy—'We feel strongly committed to the position that classification of a young child is often a deterrent to optimal development. Since the purpose of the manual is to assist the teacher who wants to promote each child's personal growth to maximal capacity, the authors have provided a systematic method for looking at the way a child is functioning, leaving the assignment of a scale to those professionals who sometimes need to make such a judgment'. Their method applies just as much to the infant as to the older child.

Apart from Gesell's 'insurance factors', there are other developmental items which are of great importance for assessment. The baby's vocalisations are of much significance: the experienced observer can tell much of the maturity of the baby by the quality of his vocalisations in relation to his age. Now that electronic methods of recordings vocalisations (including the nature of the cry) have been developed by the Scandinavian workers, there is good scope for research into the value of vocalisations for developmental assessment.

The persistence of primitive responses beyond the age at which they are usually lost is another feature which the experienced clinician uses in assessing a baby. Arnold Gesell paid particular attention to the age at which hand-regard (Chapter 9) is lost: it's persistence beyond the usual age is a feature of mental subnormality. The age at which mouthing, drooling and casting is lost is of much significance. Casting should have ceased by about 15 months: its persistence thereafter is an almost certain sign of mental subnormality.

Another item which is at present unscorable is the understanding of speech. Children understand the meaning of words long before they can articulate them (Chapter 9): a child may understand dozens of words before he can say any of them. There is scope for an important developmental test here.

A major criticism of the psychologists' approach is the failure of their scoring method to indicate *how* a child responds rather than *whether* he responds to a particular test. For instance, there are numerous stages in the maturation of the grasp, from the crude palmar grasp to the late grasp between the tip of the forefinger and the tip of the thumb. These stages are observed by the clinician who can 'date' the child's development by the maturity of his grasp.   Another example is the response to sound.   The average baby at 3 or 4 months turns his head slowly to sound: but at 6 months the response is a rapid one and he begins to turn to a source of sound below the ear; later he turns to sound above the ear.   It is not enough merely to record that he turns to sound: one has to note the maturity and rapidity and nature of the response.   In other words one wants to know not just *whether* he can achieve a particular skill, but *how long* he has been able to do it and with what maturity he can do it.   Failure of an examiner to note this denies him much valuable information.

There is abundant scope for research into more refined methods of testing.   Now that psychologists are developing more and more sophisticated methods of studying the performance of babies from birth onwards, it is to be hoped that they will develop ways of applying their methods to the assessment of the child's maturity and development and therefore to determining something about his potential.   Having developed the method of testing by electronic and other sophisticated apparatus they have a great opportunity for applying their tests for assessment.

The psychologists' approach is different from that of the clinician in another important way.   The psychologist pays little or no attention to the physicial examination, whereas the clinician examines the child as a whole.   To give a gross example, it is silly to give a low score for weight-bearing at 6 months, as the Ruth Griffiths method would, if the child has paralysed legs as a result of a meningomyelocele. It is silly to give a low score for manipulative tests if the child is spastic, or to give a low score for motor development if he is hypotonic. (Chapter 14).   Allowance must be made for a physical handicap which explains a poor performance on tests.

I have explained elsewhere that the size of the baby's head depends mainly on the growth of the cranial contents (Chapter 8). If there is a brain defect, resulting in failure of normal brain growth, the head is likely to be small (microcephaly).   It follows that measurement of the maximum head circumference and its relation to the size of the baby must be part of the routine examination.   If there is already some doubt as to whether the baby's development is normal or not, the feature of an usually small head, as shown on the centile chart, is an important additional point which may indicate mental subnormality. In my opinion no developmental examination can be complete without this measurement—yet psychologists ignore it.   As I have stated elsewhere, it is not only the maximum circumference which matters, but the shape of the head.   The physical examination of the baby cannot be omitted if one is going to give a reasonable opinion about a baby's development.   I decry reliance on purely objective tests because it denies one vital information which is of the utmost relevance in assessment.

The clinician, having taken the history of all relevant factors, and having conducted a full physical and developmental examination, may sometimes conduct some special investigations (such as the protein-bound-iodine): and he then interprets his findings. He knows that some fields of development, notably gross motor development (sitting, walking, etc.) are much less important than others (Chapter 14), and therefore knows to avoid the mistake of adding up the score in the various fields of development, dividing by a number corresponding to the number of tests used, and then giving an overall score—as Ruth Griffiths did. He makes an allowance for physical handicap—not, for instance, giving a low score for speech if the child is deaf; he considers all factors, such as emotional deprivation or illness which may have affected the development: he considers the various patterns of development (Chapter 14): he makes due allowance ance for prematurity: he considers all the points mentioned in this chapter, puts all the varied information into his cerebral computer, and emerges with his assessment. To the psychologist this is distressingly unscientific: to the clinician it is the only rational approach to assessment, and any other method introduces unnecessary inaccuracies because of the omission of vitally important information.

PREDICTIVE VALUE

The Gesell View on Developmental Testing

I have summarised elsewhere the rationale of Arnold Gesell's philosophy of development.[24] I wrote: 'It would seem reasonable to suppose that if careful detailed observation were made of the course of development of a sufficiently large number of babies, record being made of the age at which various skills were learned, it should be possible to establish some relationship between records so obtained and their subsequent progress through childhood. Though it is impossible to say what is 'normal', there is no difficulty in defining the 'average', and it should be easy to determine the sequence and rate of growth of the average child and to note the frequency with which deviations from the usual growth pattern occur as a result of known or unknown factors. Having determined the developmental pattern of average children, it should be possible to determine whether an individual child has developed as far as the average one of his age, taking into account all factors which might have affected his development. By making further examinations at intervals in order to assess his rate of development, and by taking into account all possible factors in the child and his environment which might affect the future course of his development, one ought to be able to make a reasonable prediction of his future progress provided that one knows the frequency of abnormal growth patterns. Arnold Gesell and his staff at the Yale Clinic of Child Development made such studies for 40 years or more, and they were convinced that such prediction is in fact possible'.   By 1930 Gesell estimated that he and his staff had examined more than 10,000 infants at numerous age periods.   He wrote that 'attained growth is an indicator of past growth processes and a foreteller of growth yet to be achieved'.   He emphasised the 'lawfulness of growth',and said that 'where there is lawfulness there is potential prediction'.   He constantly called for caution in attempting to predict a child's future development, because of all the variables concerned.   To use his words: 'Diagnostic prudence is required at every turn', and 'so utterly unforeseen are the vicissitudes of life that commonsense will deter one from attempting to forecast too precisely the developmental career of any child'.   Gesell followed one group of 30 infants up to adolescence.   He wrote: 'In no instance did the course of growth prove whimsical or erratic.   In only one case within the period of 10 years was there a marked alteration of trend, namely, from a low average to a high average level'.   Elsewhere[18,19] he wrote: 'By methods of developmental diagnosis supplemented with clinical experience, it is possible to diagnose in the first year of life nearly all cases of amentia, of cerebral injury, many sensory and motor defects, and severe personality deviations'.

Many years later, one of Gesell's former staff, L. Bates Ames[1], expressed her conviction of the value of infant testing.   She emphasized that developmental examinations are not tests of intelligence— though there is a fairly close relationship between the developmental quotient, an index of the infant's development and therefore maturity to date, and subsequent intelligence.   She added 'There is no question that infant behaviour tests are of considerable predictive value.   The correlation between a child's test response in early infancy and later on, as late as 10 years of age or in the teens, is often surprisingly close.'   Thirty-three children were examined in infancy by Gesell tests, and 44 in their pre-school years.   All were retarded at 10 years, mostly on the WISC scale.   21 of the 33, examined at the mean age of 33 months, had scores in infancy within 10 points of the 10 year IQ score, and 16 of these fell within 5 points of the final score.   Only 5 of the 33 scored less at 10 years than in infancy.   For all the 76 pre-school examinations, 58 (76 per cent) had scores within 10 points of the 10 year score.   She concluded that 'if the complexity of what the infant or pre-school developmental quotient represents is kept in mind, if clinical judgements are taken into account, and if it is remembered that the DQ and the IQ are different even though related measures, it can be shown that infant and pre-school examinations are highly predictive of behaviour which comes later.'

Views of Others

There is a considerable body of opinion which strongly favours the view that developmental tests in the first few years have no predictive value.

In 1933 Bayley[3] described her well known study.   She carried out

200 sensorimotor test items on 61 infants, and followed 49 of the children for 3 years. The longer the time interval between any two tests, the lower was the correlation. She concluded that behaviour in the early months had little predictive value with regard to future intelligence. She thought that the tests 'measure different functions rather than a unit function of intelligence'. She added: 'There was no evidence for a general factor of intelligence during the first three years, but the findings indicate instead a series of developing functions or group of functions, each growing out of but not necessarily correlated with previously matured behaviour patterns'.

Elsewhere she wrote that 'in general, tests are of great value in judging and diagnosing a child's current status, but they are of very little use in predicting what the child's I.Q. will be a few years later. It seems evident that the very nature of intelligence in children under two or three years of age is such that the tests in these early ages will have little if any predictive value'.

Wittenborn[38] attempted to determine the value of the assessment of infants in Gesell's clinic for the purposes of adoption, by means of a follow-up examination with Binet tests at the age of 5 years or more. His conclusion was as follows: 'We find no means of refuting an hypothesis that the infant examination has no useful predictive validity. Although we cannot prove that the hypothesis of no predictive validity is true, it describes our data'.

Lewis and McGurk[30] tested 20 infants on the Bayley scales at 3, 6, 9, 12, 18 and 24 months, and at 24 months gave them comprehension and vocabulary items from the Peabody picture vocabulary tests. They studied the stability of a particular infant's scores in the different tests, and the "predictability of his standing on one test from his standing on another". There was no consistency in either. Elkind[13], discussing this, wrote 'that is to say, it is not possible to make a reliable prediction, from a score an infant attains on a particular test at 3 months, as to what his score might be on the same test in 6 months, a year, or two years'. He added that predictive value increases as the child gets older; and added that 'infant tests measure primarily sensorimotor functions, while tests at later age levels are based upon verbal and reasoning skills'. He added that 'these negative conclusions must be qualified in one important respect. Infant tests can often reveal children who are at the extremes, those who are exceedingly advanced, or who are exceedingly slow. Where infant tests fall down is in the middle range of intellectual ability where finer discriminations are necessary'. Lewis and McGurk concluded 'any measure of organ systems gives, for the most part, an index of current function, not innate capacity. IQ tests assess current intellectual functioning, and not innate intellectual capacity'.

In contrast to the views cited above, other workers have been less definite in their condemnation of infant testing. Some of them found quite good correlations between early and later tests.

Cattell[9], in her chapter on the statistical basis of her tests, which were based on those of Gesell, found that tests at three months had relatively slight predictive value, particularly if the score were low: but if a child had a high score at three months there was an appreciably better than average chance of his having a high rating on the Stanford-Binet scale at 2 or 3 years.   The ten children with a rating below 88 had scores varying between 76 and 150 at 3 years.   Of the 10 infants receiving the highest rating at 3 months, only one fell below 100 in the 3 year follow-up period.   Tests at 6, 9 and 12 months gave higher coefficients of 0·88, 0·86 and 0·89 respectively.

Escalona and her colleagues[14] examined 58 infants between the age of 3 and 33 weeks using the Cattell and Gesell tests, and again at 6 to 9 years, using the Wechsler scale.   For infants tested at 20 weeks and above, both Cattell and Gesell scores showed slightly positive relationships to the later intelligence range, but clinical appraisal as distinct from purely objective tests significantly predicted differences in later intelligence.   When infant assessments were examined for their ability to distinguish between subjects who would later be of average or above average intelligence, clinical appraisal (but neither of the objective tests alone) achieved this discrimination at a highly significant level (0·002).

Drillien[12] demonstrated the predictive value of developmental tests (mainly Gesell) in her extensive follow up of premature babies. She found, as others have, that it is easier to predict mental dullness in infancy than mental superiority.   Of 16 children found at 5 years to be unsuitable for education at an ordinary school (I.Q. less than 70), 12 were given the same level at 6 months and at each subsequent examination.   No child scored higher than very dull at any test at any age.   Of 16 found to have an I.Q. of 70–79 at school age, 12 were rated at this level or lower from 6 months.

In a comparison between test scores at 20 months and 10 years in 639 full term children,[37] the Cattell scores at 20 months gave r = 0·49 at 10 years.   A combination of Cattell scores, paediatricians' rating, social quotient, perinatal stress score and parental socioeconomic status yielded a multiple R of 0.58 with the 10 year I.Q. score.   For children with a Cattell score of below 80 at 20 months, a combination of infant test scores and paediatricians' ratings yielded a multiple R of 0·80 with the score at 10 years.   The majority of children with a low Cattell or paediatricians' rating at 20 months had serious school difficulties at the age of ten.

In a critical letter concerning the predictiveness of developmental tests, Knobloch[29] discussed the function of infant testing, and described follow-up studies by Pasamanick and his colleagues at Johns Hopkins Hospital, which indicated that in fact these tests, properly carried out, have considerable predictive value.   In one study quoted by her, fifty negro children were examined in infancy and re-examined at 7 years of age by different examiners unaware of the initial findings.   The correlation between the two examinations was 0·5. Correlations of 0·5 to 0·75 were obtained in another study of 100 infants examined at several ages between 16 weeks and 18 months. She described another follow-up study of 300 infants examined at the Johns Hopkins Hospital at 14 weeks, with re-examination at 3 years by an examiner who had no knowledge of the findings at the initial examination; the correlation was 0·5 in those without intellectual impairment, and 0·75 in those with such impairment.   Between 40 weeks and 3 years 50 per cent. of the 300 infants varied less than 10 points, and 75 per cent. less than 15 points.

Hindley[23] compared the Griffiths scores on 80 babies at six months and 18 months with Stanford Binet scores at three and five years; the intercorrelations varied from 0·32 between scores at six months and five years, and 0·78 between scores at three and five years.   He suggested that later scores may reflect the cumulative effect of environment and the gradual emergence of inherited differences of ability.

Ausubel[2] summed up the position as follows: 'Developmental norms are valuable because they provide a standard or frame of reference for evaluating and interpreting the status or current behaviour of an individual.   They can be abused if the range of variability is overlooked: if expectations for *all* children are geared to group averages: if substantial parallelism is expected between component rates of growth: if they are unwarrantedly applied to individuals who could not be included in the sampling population: and if individual guidance depends on normative comparisons alone to the exclusion of information regarding individual patterns.   They are also abused if they are regarded as inevitable and immutable products of maturation or as necessarily desirable.   But because an instrument is subject to abuse is no reason for declaring it valueless or urging its abolition as some over-zealous but misguided exponents of the 'clinical' approach have suggested'.

Comments on the Literature

The evidence on which so many writers have proclaimed the lack of predictive value of developmental tests in the early years does not seem to be adequate, and there is plenty of evidence for the contrary view, namely that properly used, developmental tests are of considerable value.

No one should expect developmental tests when repeated to give a constant value.   The variability of I.Q. test results in older children is well known.   Burt's[8] comments on I.Q. prediction are particularly apt.   The following were his words: 'Since genetic constitution merely determines growth-tendencies, and since the child's observable progress and performance are the result of innumerable factors, both internal and external, we could never hope, even with the most precise specification of the newborn infants' equipment of genes, to make infallible predictions about his ultimate level.   No competent psychologist has ever supposed that an I.Q. can be exactly ascertained, much less that it will remain immutable for each individual child'.

In the previous chapter I have set out the philosophy of developmental testing, and tried to describe some of the fundamental differences in the approach of the psychologist and the clinician.   The psychologist relies on objective tests of scorable items, but ignores features of the baby's behaviour which the clinician regards as of great importance: the psychologist ignores the 'risk' factors, the fact that the baby was born prematurely, environmental and familial factors which profoundly affect the baby's development, the physical examination and particularly the head size, and other important data. In some cases workers used the Gesell tests; but there is a great difference between using Gesell's tests and Gesell's method.   Before Gesell or a member of his staff examined a child a social worker had visited the home and had gone into the social and family background in detail.   A full developmental history was taken in the clinic, the child being examined physically and developmentally, and then at the ensuing staff conference the whole child was discussed and a clinical assessment was reached, or else it was decided that further observation was required and the child was seen at a later date before a decision was made.

In some papers the figures given do not correspond with the opinions expressed by the writers.   For instance, I have tried several times to understand Wittenborn's figures and hope that I have not misinterpreted them; but they do not seem to indicate quite such a low level of prediction as he claimed.   Of 30 children who were placed for adoption after the developmental examination, 14 were given a developmental quotient below 100, 8 of these had a subsequent Binet score below 100.   Of 16 infants given a D.Q. of 100 or more, 14 had a Binet score of 100 or more.   In another study he scored the educational and occupational status of the adopting parents of 30 children and related them to the Binet score of the children.   None of the infants placed in families with high educational and occupational scores had I.Q. results below 110, while more than half placed with families with low scores had I.Q. scores below that figure.   This was exactly what Gesell's clinic tried to achieve.   An attempt was made to match the infant's developmental potential with that of the adopting parents, and Wittenborn's figures, if they can be considered valid in view of the mode of selection, seem to indicate that the developmental assessment was in fact quite successful.

Wittenborn stated that his failure to prove the value of developmental tests in infancy corresponded exactly with the findings of Cattell.   But Cattell's findings, to which reference has been made, indicated that there was a good correlation between her tests in infancy and those carried out in later years.

Knobloch[2], discussing Wittenborn's findings, remarked that it is unsatisfactory to use adopted infants for the purpose of assessing the validity of infant tests because of the difficulties of the early environment, differences in foster homes, and sometimes because of the effect of institutional care. She added that Wittenborn failed to discuss the purpose of the developmental examination and had not indicated that any poor placements were made on the basis of failure to diagnose neurological or intellectual deficits.

In many studies the babies were 'selected' and not representative of the population. In some centres 'norms' were based on the performance of children of members of the University staff. The average I.Q. of Bayley's cases at the age of 9 was 129.

Wittenborn's cases were so selected that it is difficult to know what attention should be paid to them. Defective children had already been excluded before they came to Gesell's clinic for assessment for suitability for adoption. Wittenborn noted this, but made the strange comment that 'one could suppose for the most part these children are identified without the aid of infant examination'! Wittenborn then selected a group of those already selected children, and added some highly selected infants of members of the staff of Yale University Clinic. It seems that only 114 of the group of 310 were assessed at the age of five or later, the remaining 196 not being examined. The reader is left to conclude (without evidence) that those not followed up would have fared the same as those who were followed. It is difficult to provide evidence that those followed up are truly representative of the whole. One can imagine that some parents may not be willing to bring their children because they are backward, or who were in some way different from children of parents who were pleased to co-operate in the study.

The 'selection' of children for study is of great importance, for the various studies described, on which so many have based their conviction that developmental tests have no predictive value, have excluded the very children in whom a confident prognosis can be most readily given—the mentally defective ones. Terman and Merrill[31] remarked that the I.Q. of dull children is much more constant than it is in normal or supernormal children. Goodenough[18] wrote: 'Inasmuch as radical changes in the treatment of backward and feebleminded children are more likely to depend upon the results of mental tests than is the case with children of normal or superior intelligence, the greater dependability of the intelligence quotient at the lower levels is a matter of considerable importance for those actively concerned with the welfare of children'. Gesell[19] wrote that 'Practically every case of mental deficiency can be diagnosed in the first year of life, excluding, of course, the small number of exceptional cases which occur from secondary causes in later infancy or early childhood'. Thomas reviewed the difficulties of early developmental assessment and of evaluating studies of developmental prediction. He mentioned amongst other things the problems of sampling, of the population base rates and of clinical impressions.

I have always been unhappy about the exclusion of mentally subnormal children—yet most, if not all studies, have done this. I feel that if one is establishing norms for the whole population, norms against which any individual child can be compared, the sample should not exclude any child. One could hardly determine the mean haemoglobin of all children in a village or town if one began by excluding all anaemic children, and included only those from better social circumstances.

Personal Studies

I cannot agree that it is only the severe cases of mental deficiency which can be diagnosed in infancy. In a study at Sheffield[25] we followed up 135 children who were considered at any time in the first two years of life to be mentally retarded, however slightly. Cases of mongolism, cretinism, hydrocephalus and anencephaly were excluded. In 10 of the children the mental retardation was of postnatal origin, and in the others it was of prenatal or natal origin. Apart from these exclusions, the cases were in no way selected, in that we included all children thought by me or my staff to be backward—even though one or two very shortly after the initial assessment were subsequently thought to be normal. The initial diagnosis was based on a clinical assessment in the Out-patient Department, using some of the Gesell tests, with full consideration of the developmental history and other data. All but 2 of the survivors were traced and re-examined, using for the most part Terman and Merrill tests at the age of 5 years or later. All but 5 of them were retarded. In 77 the initial diagnosis was made in the first year, and in 59 it was made in the second year. A total of 34 had died. In all 10 in whom autopsies were performed, gross anomalies of the brain were present. Of the 101 survivors who were traced, 59 on follow-up examinations were seriously subnormal (I.Q. score below 50), 24 had an I.Q. score of 50 to 75, 13 had an I.Q. score of 76 to 94, and 5 had an I.Q. score of 100 or more. Of 67 who were thought to be severely retarded in infancy, 55 on follow-up examination were found to be seriously subnormal. Of 20 who were regarded as only slightly retarded in infancy, only 2 on follow-up examination were found to be seriously subnormal. I shall refer later to the 5 who were found to have an I.Q. score of 100 or more.

The figures indicate that mental retardation can be confidently diagnosed in the first two years, apart from the obvious forms such as mongolism. For practical purposes this is the most important function of developmental tests.   It does not matter much whether a baby has a developmental quotient of 110 or 130: but it matters a great deal for purposes of adoption if his developmental quotient, being 70 or less, suggests that the child is going to be mentally retarded in later years.

At the Children's Hospital, Sheffield, infants were examined every week for the purpose of assessment for suitability for adoption.[26] They were seen by me personally in their first year, usually at the age of six months.   On the basis of tests described in this book they were graded as follows:

Grade 1   ..   Possibly above average.
      2   ..   Average.
      3   ..   Possibly below average.
      4   ..   Inferior.

When they reached school age they were examined by School Medical Officers (who knew nothing of my grading), I.Q. test scores being made on the basis of Terman and Merrill and other methods.   The following were the mean I.Q. scores at school age for each of the grades allotted in infancy.

The total number of children followed up and tested at school age was 230.   Five additional babies could not be followed because of emigration or because they could not be traced: otherwise the series was complete.   Table 1 shows the grades allotted in infancy and the mean I.Q. at age 5 to 8 years.

TABLE 1

Grading in infancy in relation to I.Q.
at school age (1)

Grading alotted in infancy	Total	Mean I.Q. at 5–8 years
1	69	111·5
2	92	108·0
3	54	94·9
4	15	76·0

Table 2 shows the scores allotted in infancy to children who proved later to have a high or low I.Q. score.

TABLE 2

Grading in infancy in relation to I.Q. at school age (2)

Grade in first year	1 Total 69	2 Total 92	3–4 Total 69
I.Q. at school			
Below 80	1(1·5%)	1(1·1%)	
Over 120			1(1·4%)

Only one child placed in Grade 1 subsequently had an I.Q. below 80 (actually 79), and one placed in Grade 2 (actually 69). One child in Group 3 had an I.Q. of 132. The differences between Groups 2 and 3 and 3 and 4 were significant at the 0·1 per cent level.

It should be noted that in the earlier part of the investigation above the assessment was rendered more difficult by the fact that the infants had been in an institution for the first six months or more of their life, and came direct from it, so that there was the factor of emotional deprivation which would have retarded their development. It was not possible to decide how much retardation had been caused by this factor and how much of it would be reversible. The institution was subsequently closed, the infants being placed in foster homes at the age of 9 or 10 days.

The figures support the contention that mental inferiority can be diagnosed more easily than mental superiority. One is more likely to underestimate potential than to overestimate it.

I have little evidence from my own work that mental superiority can be diagnosed with reasonable confidence in infancy. Some of the workers quoted have adduced evidence to that effect. But the fact that mental retardation can be diagnosed in infancy indicates that developmental tests, in this important practical matter at least, do have a definite predictive value.

Knobloch[28,29,31a] rightly pointed out that the principal function of developmental tests in infancy is the detection of abnormal neurological conditions and of subnormal developmental potential. She added that these tests are not intended to detect mental superiority or precise I.Q. scores later. Although a small percentage may be considered superior, the question of whether they remain so depends on their later experiences. She added that: 'As clinicians we would feel that an examination which would allow us to make the following statement is an eminently acceptable and useful tool. This infant has no neurologic impairment, and his potential is within the healthy range: depending on what his life experiences are between now and 6 years of age, he will at that time have a Stanford-Binet I.Q. above 90, unless qualitative changes in the central nervous system are caused by noxious agents, or gross changes in milieu alter major variables of function,' and: 'The studies that we have done indicate that when care is taken to eliminate bias and the infant examination is used as a clinical neurological tool by a physician adequately trained in its use, good correlations are obtained. These studies have not been challenged by the critics of infant evaluation: they have merely been ignored'.

In Chapter 19 I have put together the common errors in developmental diagnosis—errors made by many of us who attempt to assess the developmental status of infants and young children.

Developmental Prediction. What We Can and Cannot Do

Everyone who attempts to assess the development of babies should be fully conversant with the limitations of developmental prediction. Below I have summarised what we can hope to do, and what we must not expect to be able to do.

What we can do (but not necessarily in the earliest weeks), is as follows:–

1. We can say how far a baby has developed in relation to his age, and we can therefore compare him with the average performance of others at that age; and we can say something about his rate of development. By so doing we can say something about his developmental potential.

2. We can diagnose moderate or severe mental subnormality.

3. We can diagnose moderate or severe cerebral palsy.

4. We can assess muscle tone.

5. We can diagnose moderate or severe deafness.

6. We can diagnose moderate or severe visual defects.

7. We can diagnose subluxation or dislocation of the hips.

8. We can diagnose neurological defects in infancy.

9. As a result of our developmental and neurological examination, we are in a better position to give genetic counselling.

What we cannot do is as follows:–

1. We cannot draw a dividing line between normal and abnormal. All that we can say is that the further away from the average the child is in anything, the more likely he is to be abnormal.

2. We cannot make accurate predictions of his future intelligence and achievements, because these will be profoundly affected by environmental and other factors in the future.   There never will be a high correlation between developmental assessment in infancy and subsequent intellectual achievement.

3. We cannot eliminate the possibility that he will undergo mental deterioration in future months or years.

4. If he has suffered severe emotional deprivation before we assess him, we cannot assess at one examination the extent of the damage which he has suffered, or its reversibility.

5. If he is backward and has not microcephaly, we cannot be sure that he is not a slow starter (delayed maturation).

6. If he was a low birth weight baby, and we do not know the duration of gestation, we cannot tell in retrospect by clinical means whether we should allow for prematurity or not—though the motor nerve conduction time will guide us in this.

7. We cannot make a sensible prediction for a full term baby at birth or in the first four weeks unless there are grossly abnormal signs; and still less can we make a valid assessment of a prematurely born baby until after due correction for prematurity he has reached at least

four to six weeks of age. For instance, if he were born eight weeks prematurely, it would be rash indeed to assess him until at least 12 to 14 weeks after delivery.

8. We cannot rely on diagnosing mild cerebral palsy or mild mental subnormality in the early weeks.

9. If we find abnormal neurological signs in the first few weeks we cannot be sure unless they are gross that they will not disappear; and if they disappear, we cannot be sure that when he is older, at school age, the finer tests of coordination and spatial appreciation then available will not show that there are in fact some residual signs, such as clumsiness. The older the infant, the less likely it is that abnormal signs will disappear, and after the first year it is unlikely that they will be anything but permanent.

10. We cannot eliminate in infancy the possibility that the child will subsequently display specific learning disorders, or difficulties of spatial appreciation.

11. We cannot translate into figures Gesell's 'insurance factors'—the baby's alertness, interest in his surroundings, social responsiveness, determination and powers of concentration—features which are of much more predictive value than the readily scorable items, such as gross motor development or sphincter control.

12. We cannot say what he will do with his talents or with what we have termed his developmental potential. This will depend on a wide variety of factors, such as his personality, his determination, ambition, willingness to work hard, ability to profit from mistakes, the quality of his home and of his education, opportunity, the right choice of subject for study or of career, his creativity and originality. We have instead to try to determine what talents he has: we cannot say what he will do with them.

13. We cannot prove, in any but exceptional cases, that a child's mental or neurological deficits are due to birth injury rather than to prenatal causes.

14. We cannot normally predict mental superiority.

Finally, it must be remembered that there are many aspects of ability (Vernon[36]); they include verbal, numerical, spatial, perceptual, memorising, reasoning, mechanical and imaginative qualities. It would hardly be likely that tests in infancy would detect these with a high degree of reliability.

We should constantly bear in mind the purpose of developmental examination. It is not to predict the child's future intelligence or success. The purpose is to determine whether the baby is developing normally for his age, and whether he has any mental, physical, neurological or sensory handicaps, so that if possible appropriate treatment can be given. When assessing a child for adoption, we want in particular to diagnose cerebral palsy or mental deficiency. All these we can do; but we do not need to be able to say whether in later years his I.Q. will be 110 or 120; this we cannot do.

Summary

Correlations between developmental tests in infancy and subsequent intelligence test scores and future achievements cannot be high and never will be, largely because the child's intelligence and future performance will be profoundly affected by environmental and other factors.

We can say how far the child has developed in relation to his age and to the average performance of others at that age.

We can diagnose moderate or severe mental subnormality, cerebral palsy, visual or auditory defects and neurological abnormalities in the early weeks; but we cannot diagnose the mildest cases of mental backwardness or cerebral palsy or of hearing or visual defects. We cannot eliminate the possibility of mental deterioration. We cannot usually be sure that abnormal neurological signs in early infancy will not disappear. We cannot score some of the most important features of a baby's performance. · We cannot say what a child will do with his talents. We need research into the relevance of tests and aspects of the examination with regard to assessment of his development.

REFERENCES

1. AMES, L. B., in HELLMUTH, J. (1967) *Exceptional Infant.* Seattle: Special Child Publications.
2. AUSUBEL, D. P. (1958) *Theory and Problems of Child Development.* New York. Grune and Stratton.
3. BAYLEY, N. (1933) Mental Growth during the First Three Years. *Genet. Psychol. Monogr.*, **14**, 1.
4. BAYLEY, N. (1958) Value and Limitations of Infant Testing. *Children*, **5**, 129.
5. Book Review (1973) *Archives of Disease in Childhood.* **48**, 166.
6. BRAZELTON, T. B. (1964) Neonatal Behavioral Assessment Scale. *Clinics in Developmental Medicine. No. 50.* London. Heinemann.
7. BUHLER, C. (1935) *From Birth to Maturity.* London. Kegan Paul.
8. BURT, C. (1959) General Ability and Special Aptitudes. *Educ. Res.*, **1**, 3.
9. CATTELL, P. (1947) *The Measurement of Intelligence of Infants and Young Children.* New York. The Psychological Corporation.
10. DARWIN, C. (1872) *The Expression of the Emotions in Man and Animals.* London. Murray.
11. DARWIN, C. (1877) A Biographical Sketch of an Infant. *Mind*, **2**, 285.
12. DRILLIEN, C. M. (1961) A Longitudinal Study of the Growth and Development of Prematurely and Maturely Born Children. *Arch. Dis. Childh.*, **36**, 233.
13. ELKIND, D. (1973) Infant Intelligence. *Amer. J. Dis. Child.* **126**, 143.
14. ESCALONA, S. K., MORIARTY, A. (1961) Prediction of Schoolage Intelligence from Infant Tests. *Child Development*, **32**, 597. *Bull. Menninger Clin.*, **14**, 117.
15. FRANKENBURG, W. K., CAMP, B.W., VAN NATTA, P. A., DEMERS-SEMAN, J. A., VOORHEES, S. F. (1971) Validity of the Denver Developmental Screening Test. *Child Development.* **42**, 475, 1315.
16. FRANKENBURG,W. K., DODDS,J. B. (1967) The Denver Developmental Screening Test. *J. Pediat.* **71**, 181.
17. GESELL, A. AMATRUDA, C. S., CASTNER, B. M., THOMPSON, H. (1930) *Biographies of Child Development.* London. Hamish Hamilton.

18. GESELL, A., AMATRUDA, C. S. (1947) *Developmental Diagnosis*. New York. Hoeber.
19. GESELL, A. (1948) *Studies in Child Development*. New York. Harper.
20. GOODENOUGH, F. L. (1950) *Mental Testing*. London. Staples.
21. GRIFFITHS, R. (1954) *The Abilities of Babies*. London. University of London Press.
22. HAEUSSERMANN, E. (1958) *Developmental Potential of Preschool Children*. London. Grune and Stratton.
23. HINDLEY, C. B. (1965) Stability and change in abilities up to five years; group trends. *J. Child. Psychol. Psychiat.*, **6**, 85.
24. ILLINGWORTH, R. S. (1975) *The Normal Child* London. Churchill.
25. ILLINGWORTH, R. S., BIRCH, L. B. (1959) The Diagnosis of Mental Retardation in Infancy. A Follow-up Study. *Arch. Dis. Childh.*, **34**, 269.
26. ILLINGWORTH, R. S. (1971). The predictive value of developmental assessment in infancy. *Develop. Med. Child. Neurol.* **13**, 721.
27. JEDRYSEK, E., KLAPPER, Z., POPE, L., WORTIS, J. (1972). Psychoeducational evaluation of the Preschool Child. A Manual Utilising the Haeussermann Approach. New York. Grune and Stratton.
28. KNOBLOCH, H. (1959) Pneumoencephalograms and Clinical Behavior *Pediatrics*, **23**, 175
29. KNOBLOCH, H. PASAMANICK, B. (1963) Predicting Intellectual Potential in Infancy. *Amer. J. Dis. Child.*, **106**, 43.
30. LEWIS, M., McGURK, H. C. (1972) Evaluation of Infant Intelligence. *Science*, **178**, 1174.
31. NELIGAN, G. and PRUDHAM, D. (1969) Norms for 4 standard developmental milestones by sex, social class and place in family. *Develop. Med. Child Neurol.* **11**, 413.
31a. PASAMANICK, B., KNOBLOCH, H. (1974) Infant Intelligence. *Amer. J. Dis. Child* **127**, 759.
32. SHINN, M.W. (1893) *Notes on the Development of a Child*. California. Univ. of California Press.
33. SHIRLEY, M. M. (1931) *The First Two Years*. Minneapolis. University of Minnesota Press.
34. TERMAN, L. M., MERRILL, M. (1937) *Measuring Intelligence*. Boston: Houghton, Mifflin.
35. THOMAS, H. (1967) Some problems of studies concerned with evaluating the predictive validity of infant tests. *J. Child Psychol. Psychiat.*, **8**, 197.
36. VERNON, P. E. (1969) *Intelligence and Cultural Environment*. London. Methuen.
37. WERNER, E. E., HONZIK, M. P., SMITH, R. S. (1968) Prediction of intelligence and achievement at 10 years from 20 months pediatric and psychologic examinations. *Child. Development*, **39**, 1063.
38. WITTENBORN, J. R. (1957) *The Placement of Adoptive Children*. Springfield. Thomas.

CHAPTER 3

PRENATAL AND PERINATAL FACTORS WHICH AFFECT MENTAL DEVELOPMENT

The number of prenatal factors known or thought to be related to a child's mental and physical development is steadily increasing, and it is difficult for anyone to keep abreast of the literature. In the table I have put together the known factors, and have included factors which do not have a direct bearing on the subject of this book, mental development, partly because I thought that a comprehensive list would be useful, and partly because many factors have an indirect bearing on the child's development.

Factors in Parents	*Effect on Child*
Before conception—upbringing of parents; desire for child; desire for child of given sex; method of punishment of parents in their childhood; love and security in their childhood; number of years married before conception.	Psychological
Mode of upbringing, intelligence, personality.	Management
Genetics.	Hereditary disease Intelligence Personality Multiple pregnancy Tendency to prematurity or postmaturity.
Social factors (i) Poverty	Greater abortion rate, stillbirth rate, prematurity rate, perinatal and infant mortality. Lower birth weight. More toxaemia. More congenital anomalies.
(ii) Nutrition	Effect on maternal fetus (rickets), and therefore on delivery. Low birth weight. Possible damage to fetal brain.
Folic acid deficiency	Folic acid deficiency

Factors in Parents	Effect on child
Twins—nutritional deprivation in utero	Lower I.Q.
(iii) Social class	Lower class—more parity, shorter gestation, lower birth weight.
(iv) Older mother	Higher stillbirth rate, perinatal mortality, prematurity rate, more mongolism. C.N.S. anomalies. Multiple pregnancies, Klinefelter's syndrome. Congenital dislocation of hip. Hare lip with cleft palate. Congenital heart disease. Pulmonary haemorrhage. Tetany.
(v) Older father	Achondroplasia Apert's syndrome Fewer live born males Certain mongols Congenital deafness C.N.S. anomalies (not spina bifida) More stillbirths
(vi) Parity. First born	Pyloric stenosis Patent ductus Hydramnios
(vii) Close spacing of births	More infant mortality Lower I.Q. Psychological Contact with mother less
(viii) Smoking	Low birth weight Higher stillbirth rate Child smaller in later years: less good ability.
(ix) Illegitimacy	Higher infant mortality and prematurity rate. Psychological.
(x) Lower maternal intelligence	Low birth weight
(xi) Lower maternal height	Lower intelligence
(xii) Marriage in adolescence	More divorce and therefore effect on child

Factors in Parents	Effect on child
Seasonal factors:	
Spring and Summer conceptions	More spina bifida, more tetany
Winter conceptions	More mental subnormality C.D. hip.
Seasonal factors	Mongols, spina bifida Anencephaly Schizophrenia
Conceptions in Summer (Lapland)	More multiple pregnancy More births More boys
Geographical factors:	Anencephaly Multiple pregnancy (e.g. West Africa).
Racial factors:	Polydactyly Spina bifida etc.
Infections in pregnancy:	
Rubella	Cataract, deafness (may be progressive), mental deficiency, congenital heart disease, hepatitis, purpura, bone changes, encephalitis, arterial disease, choroidoretinitis, low birth weight, failure to thrive, glaucoma, oesophageal atresia, later diabetes mellitus. Child excretes virus for a year after birth.
Smallpox	Abortion
Smallpox vaccination	Abortion, death of fetus
Chickenpox	Congenital anomalies Prematurity
Herpes simplex	C.N.S. anomalies
Coxsackie	Encephalitis, myocarditis
Serum hepatitis	Abortion

Factors in Parents	*Effect on child*
Influenza virus	Abortion, prematurity Anomalies.
Cytomegalovirus	Mental deficiency Choroidoretinitis Prematurity Hepatosplenomegaly Thrombocytopenia
Poliomyelitis	Abortion
Measles	Pneumonia Abortion
Other infections: Listeriosis	Pneumonia Meningitis
Toxoplasmosis	Abortion Prematurity Hydrocephalus Choroidoretinitis Hepatosplenomegaly Mental deficiency
Leptospira	Anomalies
Mycoplasma	Pneumonia
Syphilis	Congenital syphilis
Infection in late pregnancy:	Congenital syphilis, malaria, T.B., trypansomiasis, herpes simplex, hepatitis, poliomyelitis, pneumonia, virus pneumonia, chickenpox, smallpox.
Endocrine: Maternal diabetes	Large baby, pulmonary haemorrhage, hypoglycaemia, tetany, hypomagnesaemia, renal vein thrombosis, large heart, congenital deformities, respiratory distress syndrome, limb deformities, sacral agenesis.

Factors in Parents	*Effect on child*
Paternal diabetes	Large baby
Hyperthyroidism	Hyperthyroidism
Hypothyroidism	Thyroid deficiency
Hyperparathyroidism	Tetany, hypomagnesaemia
Hypoparathyroidism	Tetany, fractures, low birth weight.
Aldosteronism	Abortion
Cushing's syndrome	Adrenal insufficiency
Prolactin and oestrin	Breast enlargement, vaginal bleeding, enlargement of clitoris
Irradiation:	Childhood cancer, leukaemia, microcephaly

Drugs:
Thalidomide   Mixed anomalies
Phenmetrazine
Pyrimethamine
Dichlorophenol (defoliant)
Trimethoprim
Antimitotics
Ethionamide (T.B.)
Imipramine
Tolbutamide
Salicylates
Amphetamine
Chlorambucil
Iron in first trimester
Antacids in first trimester
Phenothiazines   Jaundice
Sulphonamides
Novobiocin
Sparine
Vitamin K excess
Nitrofurantoin
Salicylates
Ristocetin
Primaquine

Antiepileptic drugs Salicylates Chlorothiazide Quinine Tolbutamide Chloroquine Anticoagulants (coumarins, not heparin)	Coagulation defects Haemorrhage
Dicophane (D.D.T.)	Tumours
Mercury	Minamata disease.
Lead	Abortion
Streptomycin Kanamycin Gentamicin Vancomycin Neomycin Thalidomide Quinine	Deafness
Chlorpromazine Chloroquine	Blindness
Antidiabetic drugs	Hypoglycaemia
Phenytoin, other anti-epileptic drugs	Cleft palate, hypoplasia of distal phalanges, diaphragmatic hernia.
Imipramine Thalidomide Abortifacients Ergot	Limb deformities
Penicillin	Sensitisation
Tetracycline	Yellow teeth, enamel defects
Chloramphenicol	Circulatory collapse
Isoniazid	Lethargy
Hexamethonium	Ileus

Factors in Parents	Effect on child
Reserpine	Nasal congestion
Iodine deficiency	Thyroid deficiency
Iodine, antithyroid drugs	Goitre
Radioactive iodine	Radiation hazard
Bromides	Rashes
Ammonium Chloride	Acidosis
Phenothiazines	Extrapyramidal signs
Magnesium sulphate	Depression of C.N.S.
Diazepam	Hypothermia
Anaesthetics, analgesics	Respiratory depression
Local anaesthetics (spinal)	Bradycardia
Muscle relaxants	Paresis
	Ataxia
Oxytocin	Cerebral damage
	? jaundice
Corticosteroids	Low birth weight
	Cleft palate
Vitamin D excess	Hypercalcaemia.
Vitamin A excess	Cleft palate
	Syndactyly
Gonadotrophins	Multiple pregnancy
Androgens, progestagens, contraceptive pill	Virilisation
Stilboestrol	Carcinoma of vagina in adolescence
Electrolyte imbalance	Electrolyte imbalance
Lithium	Hypotonia
Drug addiction:	Drug dependence

Factors in Parents	*Effect on child*
Heroin	Effect for up to 6 months: low birth weight, irritability, fits, tremors, vomiting, high pitched cry, salivation, respiratory distress.
Cannabis	Visceral and limb deformity
Morphine	Fits, irritability, low birth weight
Methadone	Low birth weight, respiratory depression, fits, irritability (effects for up to 4 weeks).
Methedrine	Irritability, sneezing
Barbiturates	Cleft lip and palate, respiratory depression, (1–2 days after birth).
Alcohol	Hypoglycaemia, low birth weight, craniofacial anomalies, congenital heart disease, mental subnormality.
Alcohol withdrawal	Irritability, tachycardia, poor weight gain
Nicotine (withdrawal)	Irritability, tachycardia, poor weight gain
Male Anaesthetists	More girls
Female anaesthetists	More abortions, stillbirths
Conditions in Utero:	
Little amniotic fluid	Torticollis, talipes, renal agenesis, pulmonary hypoplasia
Hydramnios	Anencephaly, bulbar palsy, oesophageal atresia, achondroplasia, meningocele, pulmonary hydroplasia, genitourinary defects, cleft palate, congenital chloride diarrhoea.
Position in utero	Torticollis, facial palsy, craniotabes, dislocation of hip.

Abnormal placentation	Prematurity, anomalies
Retroversion	Anomalies, cerebral palsy
Toxaemia, A.P.H. (early)	Low birth weight, prematurity, stillbirths, myopia, tics, overactivity, mongolism, hypoglycaemia, hypocalcaemia, hypomagnesaemia, pulmonary haemorrhage.
Bleeding from placental vessels	Anaemia
Premature rupture of membranes	Stillbirth, infection
Relative infertility before and after birth of defective child	Mental defect, cerebral palsy
Hyperbilirubinaemia	Jaundice
No nausea or vomiting	Higher perinatal mortality
Mother's weight gain	Weight of fetus
Phenylketonuria	Mental defect, anomalies, growth retardation
Malabsorption	Fetal rickets
Osteomalacia	Fetal rickets
Chronic renal insufficiency	Tetany
Acetonuria	Damage to brain
Intrauterine sucking	Bullae on hand

Immune reactions

Antibodies to measles, smallpox, chickenpox, mumps, poliomyelitis, influenza, diphtheria, tetanus	Passive immunity
Platelet agglutinins	Purpura
Leucocyte isoagglutinins (after multiple transfusion)	Leucopenia

Factors in Parents	Effect on child
Rhesus incompatibility	Haemolytic disease
Autoimmune disease	Thrombocytopenia Thyrotoxicosis Myasthenia

Factors related to prematurity:

Age under 20, over 34 Smoking Low maternal I.Q. Illegitimacy Toxaemia Multiple pregnancy Genetic factors T.B., infectious disease Thyrotoxicosis	Prematurity
A.P.H., premature rupture of membranes Artificial induction of labour	

Factors related to postmaturity:	Drop in birth weight Increased mortality Damage to brain

Other factors:

Preparation of mother for breast feeding	Mode of feeding
Psychological stress	Anomalies, low birth weight, relation to schizophrenia. Effect of mother's attitude on child. Congenital pyloric stenosis
Obstetrical skill	Birth trauma
Trauma to abdomen	Fetal death
Semen: Abnormal sperm Drugs—methotrexate Delayed fertilisation of ovum (old sperm)	Abortion, stillbirth Anomalies Anomalies
Coitus early in ovulatory cycle	More male fetus

Factors in Parents	*Effect on child*
Schizophrenia developing in mother within a month either side of conception	More female fetus
Schizophrenia developing in mother during month after delivery	More male fetus

Some of these will now be picked out for special mention.

Preconception Factors

The parents' own childhood, upbringing and management are likely to have a profound effect on their children. Children subjected to corporal punishment are apt when they grow up to apply similar methods to their own children. Children who are happy and loved and wanted are more likely themselves to have happy children than are those who had an unhappy cruel childhood. A couple's desire for a child or for a child of a certain sex, and the number of years of married life before the child is conceived, are likely to affect their management of their child and so his development.

Genetic Factors

Genetic factors include those concerned with hereditary disease, intelligence, personality, multiple pregnancy and a tendency to premature or postmature delivery. It should be noted that if a mother gives birth to one or even more abnormal children, the cause of the fetal defect is not necessarily genetic; it could be an abnormality in the uterus or placenta or other environmental factors operative in the pregnancy.

Sir Francis Galton in 1869[38] was one of the first to study the genetics of intelligence. He made the observation that 977 eminent men had 535 eminent relatives, as against a total of 4 eminent relatives among 977 ordinary men. Terman and Oden[87] followed up 1528 children with an intelligence quotient of 140 or more. 348 of their children had a mean I.Q. of 127·7. The number with an I.Q. of 150 or more was 28 times that of unselected persons.

The genetic factor of intelligence—'intelligence A', as distinct from 'intelligence B', which is intelligence A modified by environmental factors—has been studied by comparing the intelligence of children placed in foster homes with that of their real and adopting parents[44,81] There was no correlation between the child's I.Q. and that of the true mother at first, but there was increasing correlation with advancing age—presumably because of genetic factors. The genetic aspect of intelligence has also been investigated by the well known method of studying identical twins reared apart, though an obvious fallacy of such studies lies in the possibility that similar foster parents might be chosen for identical twins.

The genetic aspect of mental deficiency is of great importance when one is assessing infants with regard to suitability for adoption. Severe mental subnormality occurs equally in the social classes, but mild mental subnormality is more common among the children of the poor than the well-to-do; to put it another way, the intelligence of a mildly retarded child is more likely to approximate to that of the parents than is that of a severely retarded one.

Before one can give genetic advice in a case of mental deficiency full investigation is essential in order that one can detect metabolic and other forms of mental deficiency with a known genetic pattern. For instance, if a child is found to have one of the recessive forms of mental deficiency, such as phenylketonuria or Tay-Sach's disease, the risk of another child being affected is 1 in 4, while for nonspecific forms of mental deficiency the risk is of the order of 1 in 30. Chromosomal studies are necessary before one can give genetic advice in the case of mongolism. The overall risk of a mongol being born is 0·15 per cent, rising to 2·5 per cent for a mother of 45 years; but if a mother under 25 has a chromosomal translocation, there is a 2 in 3 chance that her child will be a mongol or carry the translocation. In the unlikely case of a mongol becoming pregnant, there is an approximately one in two chance that the child will be normal.

The outlook for a child of a mentally defective parent is not as gloomy as was once thought. Skodak[80] studied 16 children whose mothers were feeble-minded, with a mean I.Q. of 66·4, and found that the mean I.Q. of the children was 116·4. In my own study of babies seen for adoption purposes, 22 children of certified mentally defective mothers had a mean I.Q. of 100·1.

Hereditary conditions related to development include gross anomalies of the central nervous system and epilepsy. According to Fraser[36] and others the risk of a child being born with a gross anomaly of the central nervous system when the parents are normal is 0·6 per cent. When the parents are normal the risk of their having a child with hydrocephalus alone is 1 in 1,000, and of having a child with hydrocephalus and spina bifida is 1 in 3,000. It has been found in Sheffield that the risk of a subsequent child being affected with hydrocephalus, spina bifida or anencephaly is about 1 in 15. If two affected infants are born, the risk is even greater[54]. The risk of a normal parent having an epileptic child is 0·4 per cent; if one is affected, the risk of another being abnormal is 2·4 per cent. The risk of an affected parent having an affected child is 2·5 to 5·0 per cent. About 3·2 per cent of parents, siblings or children of epileptic patients have fits.

Hereditary factors are also concerned with the child's personality, though the inherited characteristics are profoundly affected by his environment.

Kernicterus

Kernicterus is a preventable disease and in its fully developed form, with athetosis and deafness, should no longer be seen; but lesser degrees of brain damage such as slight intellectual or hearing impairment are likely to continue to result from hyperbilirubinaemia.   The level of indirect bilirubin which causes the damage is uncertain; it is thought that the low birth weight baby is likely to be damaged by a lower level than the full term baby.   Other variables are fetal anoxia, the duration of time over which the serum bilirubin is raised and the degree of completeness of replacement transfusion and early feeding—for early feeding of premature babies appears to reduce the depth of jaundice.

In studies of fully developed kernicterus, Gerrard[39], found that of 19 children, only 6 had an I.Q. score of 85 or more.   Gerver and Day[40] found that the mean I.Q. of 68 children with kernicterus due to haemolytic disease was 11:8 points below the average.   Day and Haines[24] studied 68 babies who had had a replacement transfusion. The degree of jaundice was significantly related to the level of intelligence; and the level of intelligence in turn was related to the degree of prematurity and its cause.   It is not merely the degree of jaundice which is relevant to the child's future: it is the duration of the high serum bilirubin which is significant.   Camp[13] followed up 51 children aged 3 to 15 who had had neonatal jaundice without evident neurological damage, and compared them with 49 controls who had had no visible jaundice.   The controls had a significantly higher intelligence quotient.

It would be wrong to think that brain damage by jaundice is an all or none phenomenon.   In the milder cases there may be merely a slight reduction in intelligence: in the slightly more severe cases an additional hearing loss; and in only the severest cases the full picture of kernicterus.

Minor degrees of hearing impairment, including high tone deafness, are unlikely to be detected before later years of childhood unless specially looked for.   There may be other defects.   Stewart, Walker and Savage[83] followed up 150 children who had had haemolytic disease and found significant visuomotor perceptual defects. The more severely affected children exhibited more emotional tension, more dominance and less conscientiousness than others.

Social Factors

Poverty and defective maternal nutrition increase infant and child morbidity, premature delivery and maternal toxaemia and anaemia.   Studies in Aberdeen[7] showed the important influence of social factors on obstetrical complications. They indicated the need for caution in ascribing abnormalities in the infant to birth injury unless due consideration has been given to social class differences in their relation to the events of pregnancy.

Experimental work has shown that maternal malnutrition in pregnancy may damage the fetal brain. It reduces brain cell mitosis and the number of brain cells and reduces the number of axon terminals from each neurone[1]; it causes a reduction in the DNA content of the animal brain, the number of brain cells, the brain weight, the myelin lipids—cholesterol, cerebroside and sulphatide, thought essential for brain function, and alters the enzyme system in the brain, affecting the succinate dehydrogenase, fructosediphosphate aldolase and the acetylcholinesterase.

Animal studies have also shown that prenatal factors may modify behavioural development[1].

Human brain growth starts at the end of the second trimester, and ends 18 to 24 months after birth. It is said that the cerebellum is more affected by malnutrition than other parts of the brain.

In the case of twins the smaller of twins may have had an inadequate share of the placenta, so that fetal malnutrition resulted.

The age of the mother has a bearing on fetal development. The older the mother, the greater is the incidence of anomalies of the central nervous system, mongolism, mental retardation, premature labour and dizygotic twins.

The age of the father is also relevant. Advanced paternal age is associated with an increased incidence of achondroplasia, craniostenosis with syndactyly (Apert's syndrome), mongolism associated with fusion of chromosomes 21 and 22[67], osteogenesis imperfecta, congenital deafness and certain forms of congenital heart disease[25,63].

Other Factors

The possibility that abnormalities of the spermatozoa may be related to perinatal disease was discussed by Spector[82]. It has been shown in Sweden that abnormal spermatozoa may be related to abortions, premature delivery and congenital malformations. The possibility that drugs taken by the father may affect the spermatozoa and so the fetus cannot be ignored.

Lanman[50] wrote a most interesting and comprehensive review of experimental work concerning possible changes in spermatozoa and ova when fertilisation occurs late in the cycle. There is abundant evidence that this leads to abnormalities in animals. It would be extremely difficult to determine whether this applies to human beings, as well it might.

It has been suggested[49,46] that more mentally defective children are born in the first three months of the year than at other times. Lander et al.[51] investigated the month of birth of 10,705 mental defectives, and found that significantly fewer were born in September than controls—mainly because fewer mongols were born in that month: the critical first three months of formative intrauterine life are therefore in the hot summer months.   The highest number of defectives were born following hot summers, perhaps due to lower protein intake in hot months, but possibly to other factors, such as the amount of exercise taken in the early weeks of pregnancy.   There have been similar studies concerning time of birth and the incidence of anencephaly, spina bifida, cerebral palsy, congenital dislocation of hip and other conditions.   It should be noted that some of these studies refer to the date of birth whereas it is obvious that the date of conception is more relevant, and that is not easy to obtain accurately in retrospect.

A useful Australian study provided further evidence.   Abnormalities were charted in terms of time of conception over a 16 year period. The abnormalities included hydrocephalus, anencephaly, spina bifida and mongolism.   They showed a fairly regular periodicity such as would be consistent with the waxing and waning of infectious disease epidemics.   Mongolism showed a clustering with regard to time and place of conception.

There is an inverse relationship between the *size of the family* and the intelligence of the child.   The size of the family may also affect the child's development in other ways.   This and the spacing of births will certainly affect his psychological development.   Surveys have shown that the eldest, the youngest and the only children are usually more intelligent than intermediate ones.[58].   This cannot be due to genetic factors, for obvious reasons, and is presumably due to environmental factors, such as the amount of contact which the child has with adults and the amount of attention which his mother is able to give him.   When two-child families are considered, the mean I.Q. score is higher when there is a longer interval between births.   The relatively lower mean I.Q. scores in twins (to be discussed later) may be due to similar factors.

Cigarette Smoking

There is a significant relationship between smoking, the stillbirth rate and fetal weight.   The more the mother smokes, the lower the mean birth weight[78].   At school age the mean weight of sons of mothers who smoked heavily was significantly less than that of sons of non-smokers.   The effect on the weight of girls was not quite statistically significant[32].

Low Birth Weight Babies

The smaller the baby at birth, especially if he is small for dates, the greater is the risk of cerebral palsy and mental subnormality.

There have been numerous studies of the intellectual development of prematurely born babies.   Dann, Levine and New[21] studied 100 infants who weighed 100 g. or less at birth. On follow-up examination the mean I.Q. was 94·8 as compared with a figure of 106·9 for their siblings; 59 per cent had eye defects. McDonald[59] followed up 1066 children with a birth weight of 4 lbs. (1800 g) or less assembled by the Medical Research Council between 1951 and 1953 while investigating the relationship of oxygen therapy to the development of retrolental fibroplasia. 13·6 per cent of the surviving singletons and 5·9 per cent of the twins or triplets had cerebral palsy, an I.Q. below 50, blindness or deafness. Many of the children who had died were known to have had defects. Of 206 children who weighed less than 3 lbs. at birth, 33 per cent had a defect. In another study[15], 51 children with undifferentiated mental deficiency had a significantly lower birth weight than 51 children who had an I.Q. of over 110, matched for sex, age, area of residence and social factors.

Heimer et al.[43] observed the incidence of neurological handicaps at the age of 30 months in 318 premature babies seen at King's County Hospital, Brooklyn. The incidence of neurological abnormalities was as follows:

	Total Babies	Percentage Handicapped
Less than 1,251 g.	39	39
1,251–1750 g.	104	24
1,751–2100 g.	175	13

The incidence of abnormalities was higher in boys. The incidence of abnormalities was higher where there had been a low body temperature or an infection. In a study of 241 prematurely born babies[77], it was found that the prognosis depended more on the birth weight than the duration of gestation.

Drillien, in a series of publications later brought together into one volume[30], described a detailed follow-up of prematurely born children in Edinburgh. The series included 110 children weighing 3 lbs. (1,360 g.) or less at birth; 72 were over five years of age. Over a third of those of school age were unsuitable for education in a normal school; over a third of those in an ordinary school were educationally retarded, and less than a third were doing work appropriate to their age. Seventy per cent of those of school age showed restlessness, overactivity and other behaviour problems. Of 51 with siblings, 76 per cent were inferior intellectually to their full term born siblings. The I.Q. score fell steadily with decreasing birth weight. Twins scored less than singletons. She suggested that neurological damage might have been caused by dehydration from starvation, hyperbilirubinaemia or disturbance of the acid base balance. The possible effect of social grouping was described because of the increased incidence of premature births in the lower social classes; but she found that in all social groupings the small premature babies fared less well than their full term siblings or controls compared with full term babies. Twice as many with a birth weight below 4½ lbs. were working below their intellectual capacity. She quoted the findings of the National Maternity Survey of 1946, in which it was found that 9·7 per cent of premature babies secured grammar school places, as compared with 22·0 per cent of full term controls. There was also an excess of disturbed behaviour in all birth weight groups when there was a history of severe complications of pregnancy, such as toxaemia or abnormal delivery. In a later study of 300 children whose birth weight was 2000 g or less, she found fewer sequelae. She noted that the outcome was related to the cause of the low birth weight, particularly if there were adverse factors in early pregnancy. An American study[56,57] traced 133 low birth weight babies and followed them for 10 years; 91 had a birth weight below 1500 g: 66 per cent had handicaps, 50 per cent of them severe: 85 per cent of the smallest infants were later handicapped. Others have shown that the mean birth weight of undifferentiated mentally subnormal children was appreciably less than that of controls.[16]

In another study of 856 infants weighing less than 2·0 kg at birth[16], 44 at the age of one year showed spastic diplegia. A follow-up period of one year is not, however, sufficient in my experience: mild degrees of spastic diplegia may readily pass unrecognised until the child is much older.

Takkunen et al.[86] followed 110 infants weighing 1,750 g or less at birth. Forty-one per cent had neurological defects. The mean I.Q. score was 94·8. Forty-nine per cent were assessed as 'immature for ordinary school'.

Others have written about the improving outlook for these babies[34,35]. Fitzhardinge studied 118 infants born between 1960 and 1966: there was a notably high mortality of 67 per cent, though all were of 31 weeks' gestation or less: 32 of 39 survivors were followed for 5 years or more: 10 were normal: an E.E.G. was done on 25, and it was abnormal in sixteen: the mean I.Q. of the boys was 88 and that of the girls 92. In a further study of 96 full term small for dates babies, one had cerebral palsy, six had fits, and 25 were 'clumsy'.

Douglas in his survey of children born in 1948 followed over 400 prematurely born children for 8 years and over 350 for 11 years[28]. In all respects the prematurely born babies fared less well than the controls. The teachers' comments concerning powers of concentration, attitude to work and discipline were unfavourable as compared with comments on controls. These differences were ascribed in part to adverse home conditions, lack of parental care and low educational aspirations. He found that those prematurely born children in whom there had been no good obstetrical cause for the prematurity, and for whom the small size could not be explained by the size of their parents, scored outstandingly less than others who were born prematurely.

In an investigation of 417 low birth weight children and 405 full term children, examined at 8 to 10 years, it was found[91] that the former fared less well in a wide variety of psychological tests, including 10 subtests of the Wechsler intelligence test for children. The disabilities were not due to social class or maternal attitudes and practices. There was significant impairment in scholastic work at the age of thirteen.

Francis-Williams and Davies[35a] carried out Wechsler, Gestalt and reading tests on 105 school children who weighed 1500 g or less at birth. The mean I.Q. of the 72 whose birth weight corresponded with the duration of gestation was 99·2: but that of the 36 who were 'small for dates' was 92·0. One fifth of all the low birth weight children had learning disorders, with a performance score significantly below their verbal score on the I.Q. tests.: the reason for this is as yet unknown, but it accords with the findings of others.

It is difficult to assess these reports because of the possibility of other factors. Defective concentration, over-activity and other features may be due in part to the lower mean level of intelligence of prematurely born children. There is a higher incidence of prematurity in the lower social classes, and in these classes there is also a lower overall mean I.Q. than in the upper classes. Baird[7], in his study of 363 primiparae in Aberdeen, found a striking excess of low intelligence scores in women who gave birth to premature babies. It was only when the birth weight of a baby was 3400 g or more that there was an excess of mothers of superior I.Q. and a deficiency of those with a low I.Q. Amongst those giving birth to premature babies there was a striking excess of small women, and amongst those there was an excess of women of sub-average I.Q. Knowing the association between prematurity and maternal illness such as toxaemia, one wonders whether the mother's illness may have been responsible for the subsequent psychological features in the child. Severe maternal illness may lead to undesirable factors in the management of the child, such as overprotection. This in turn may be aggravated by anxiety occasioned by the greater incidence of infections in the prematurely born child in the first 2 years of his life.

It may be that the outlook for a prematurely born child depends on the cause of the premature labour. This is pure conjecture, but one feels that the outlook might be better for a child born prematurely as a result of artificial induction of labour on account of dysproportion than it is for a baby born prematurely as a result of antepartum haemorrhage, toxaemia or other conditions which might have caused anoxia or other damage to the fetus.

One may conclude that the smaller the premature baby at birth, the greater the likelihood that he will have cerebral palsy or mental retardation, but the reason for this fact is not clear.   There are many variables which make it difficult to be more precise about the intellectual potential of premature babies, and more research on the subject is needed.

Postmaturity

It is now thought that postmaturity is a danger to the fetus, partly because of placental insufficiency.   The matter was reviewed by Lovell[52], who studied 106 postmature babies of 42 weeks' gestation or more.   He pointed out that when there is postmaturity there is a high incidence of fetal distress, of anoxia at birth and of abnormal neurological signs in the newborn period.   There was a significantly higher morbidity in the first year than in controls.   He thought that they were less socially mature than controls when they reached their first birthday.   It had long been recognised that fetal hypoxia increases pari passu with each postnatal week[6,17,18,23]: and that postmaturity ranks only second to prematurity as a cause of fetal morbidity and mortality, especially in the case of primiparae.   Alberman[3] found that 10 per cent of 159 cases of spastic diplegia had been the product of pregnancies lasting over 42 weeks.   Wagner[90] found that 28 per cent of 100 children with cerebral palsy had experienced a gestation period of 41 weeks or more.

The Effects of Irradiation in Utero

Miller[47] examined 33 children born by mothers at Hiroshima at the time of the explosion of the atomic bomb.   Fifteen were mentally retarded.   The incidence of mental deficiency was related to the distance from the hypocentre and to the gestational age at the time of the explosion.

Plummer[69] found that 7 of 11 infants born by mothers close to the hypocentre of the atomic explosion at Hiroshima were microcephalic idiots.   Yamazaki et al.[96] found that 4 of 16 infants similarly exposed at Nagasaki were mentally defective.

Courville and Edmondson[19,20] described a mentally defective child whose mother had been deliberately exposed to x-rays in an attempt to terminate pregnancy.   At autopsy the child's brain was found to be abnormal.   They referred to more than 60 cases in which mental deficiency was thought to have resulted from irradiation in utero.   They wrote that the clinical picture is a constant one, namely microcephaly with severe mental deficiency often associated with microphthalmos.

Maternal irradiation may lead to chromosomal abnormalities, including trisomies.[89]

Uterine Anomalies

Hydramnios, apart from its well-known association with obstructive lesions of the fetal alimentary tract, is associated with a somewhat higher incidence of achondroplasia, meningocele and mental deficiency. At the Jessop Hospital at Sheffield, it was found that of 287 births associated with hydramnios, 43 per cent of the babies were stillborn or died in the newborn period. Congenital abnormalities were present in 41 per cent of the infants.[73]

An abnormal situation of the placenta (e.g. placenta praevia) and retroversion of the uterus are associated with a higher than average incidence of prematurity and fetal anomalies.

Bleeding during pregnancy is associated with a higher than average incidence of cerebral palsy, mongolism and prematurity.

The administration of anticoagulants during pregnancy carries with it the risk of cerebral haemorrhage in the fetus.

Infections During Pregnancy

The principal infections in pregnancy known to affect the fetus and his subsequent postnatal development are rubella in the first trimester, the cytomegalovirus, toxoplasmosis and syphilis. The rubella virus affects the development of the infant by causing mental subnormality, encephalitis, deafness and other abnormalities. The cytomegalovirus causes mental deficiency and choroidoretinitis. Toxoplasmosis causes mental deficiency, choroidoretinitis and hydrocephalus.

The Effect of Drugs Taken in Pregnancy

The thalidomide disaster focused attention on the possible effect of drugs taken in the early weeks of pregnancy. The effect which thalidomide had on the child's intelligence is so far uncertain. It would be difficult to assess the development of a limbless infant, yet one has seen statements that 'thalidomide babies' are mentally normal. One paper purported to give the percentage of these babies who were mentally defective. As the figure given was considerably less than that of the population as a whole, the accuracy of the finding was questionable.

Other drugs taken by the mother may affect the child's development. Methotrexate may lead to deformities of the nervous system. Hypoglycaemic agents may have a damaging effect on the developing brain of the fetus. Drugs which increase a baby's jaundice, especially if he is prematurely born, may damage his brain; they include promethazine, sparine and large doses of Vitamin K. The occurrence of several cases of cerebral palsy on the shores of the Inland Sea in Japan was traced to the eating of fish contaminated by mercury which was discharged from a factory into the sea.[61]

Maternal Stress

Many efforts have been made to relate psychological stress in pregnancy to psychological abnormalities in the infant and child. Those interested should read Joffe's[47] critical review of the experimental work on animals and of published work on human beings. Joffe discussed in detail the difficulties in setting up suitable experiments and in interpreting work already done.

Stress in the pregnant animal has an adverse effect on the fetus. Thompson engendered strong anxiety in rats by exposing them to the fear of electric shocks at the sound of a buzzer; they were able to escape through a door. The rats were then mated and became pregnant, and were then exposed to the same fear, but the door was blocked so that they could not escape. Their offspring showed striking differences from controls when examined at 30 to 40 days and 130 to 140 days. Their responses were more slow, and in various ways they showed more 'emotionality' all through their adult life.

Keeley[48] subjected pregnant albino mice to stress by overcrowding. When their litters encountered unfamiliar stimuli they were less active than controls, they were slower to respond and their reaction times were longer. The differences persisted at 30 and 100 days of age. These experiments appeared to indicate that prenatal stress had an effect on the performance in later life.

Stott[84] reviewed the literature concerning the possible effect of stressful experiences in pregnancy on the human fetus. He considered that there is good evidence that psychological stress during pregnancy, such as that in wartime, is associated with an increased incidence of anomalies in the fetus. He quoted Klebanov as finding that when women gave birth to children within a year or so of release from concentration camps, the incidence of mongols and of malformations in the children was four or five times greater than normal. Drillien and Wilkinson[31] provided confirmation of Stott's work. They studied the events during the pregnancies which had resulted in the birth of 227 mentally defective children, of whom a third were mongols. There was a significantly higher incidence of severe emotional stress in the pregnancy of mothers giving birth to mongols than there was in the mothers of non-mongoloid defectives. This difference applied particularly when the mother was over forty.

Gunther[42] studied stress in pregnancy as a possible cause of premature labour, investigating 20 married mothers with no apparent physical cause for prematurity and 20 controls. Mothers with many psychosomatic symptoms and domestic crises were more likely to have infants of low birth weight.

Taft and Goldfarb[85] carried out a retrospective study of 29 schizophrenic children of school age, 39 siblings of schizophrenic children, and 34 public school children. There was a greater incidence of prenatal and perinatal complications in the case of the schizophrenic children, especially in boys. The complications included advanced maternal age, hyperemesis, antepartum haemorrhage, eclampsia and hypertension. Dodge[24] showed that there is an association between stress in pregnancy and the development of congenital pyloric stenosis.

Multiple Pregnancy

There is evidence that multiple pregnancy is associated with a higher incidence of mental retardation and of cerebral palsy than single pregnancies. The reasons are probably complex and interwoven. They include prematurity, abnormal delivery, hypoglycaemia in the second twin and placental abnormalities or insufficiency. There is a high perinatal mortality in a cotwin of a twin who has cerebral palsy, suggesting that there had been an antenatal factor acting on both twins. The smaller of twins is liable to suffer from hypoglycaemia in the newborn period, and so to suffer brain damage if it is severe and inadequately treated. Yet an American study of 75 twin sets[37a], in which white and coloured twins were investigated separately, revealed no difference in the performance of identical twins of dissimilar birth weight when assessed on the Bayley mental and motor examination at 8 months, and the Stanford-Binet scale at 4 years. The zygosity was determined on the basis of 37 major and minor blood group antigens or on histological examination of divided membranes in monochorionic placentas.

In a study of prematurity and multiple pregnancy in relation to mental retardation and cerebral palsy, we found[46] that of 729 mentally retarded children without cerebral palsy, 20·9 per cent were born prematurely and the incidence of twins was 3·8 per cent. In 651 children with cerebral palsy, the incidence of prematurity was 35·9 per cent, and that of twins was 8·4 per cent. By statistical analysis it was shown that the high incidence of twins in cerebral palsy was not related to the high incidence of prematurity, but that the high incidence of twins in the other group may be due to the factor of prematurity. Zazzo's book[97] on the personality and development of twins should be read by those interested in the subject. He pointed out that a genetic influence is not proved by the fact that there is greater concordance in monozygotic twins than in dizygotic ones. Monozygotic twins may be treated by parents as more alike than dizygotic twins, and monozygotic twins tend to be more firmly attached to each other and therefore to develop similar attitudes. Twins score on the average 5 points less than singletons[60]—and this is not due to differences in social class, family size or home conditions. Postnatal factors must be important, for if co-twins are stillborn or die in infancy, the mean I.Q. of the surviving twin is unlikely to be lower than that of a singleton.

Monozygotic twins tend to be smaller at birth, more prematurely born, to have a higher perinatal mortality and to be more delicate than dizygotic twins. They are more unsociable, introverted and timid than dizygotic twins (or singletons). The average age of mothers of dizygotic twins is higher than that of mothers of monozygotic twins. All these factors have an obvious bearing on development and indicate the complexity of the problem of the effect of nature and nurture on a child's personality and performance.

Abnormalities of Pregnancy and Birth

A series of papers from the Johns Hopkins Hospital[52,53,65,75] has related complications of pregnancy and delivery, such as toxaemia, antepartum haemorrhage, placenta praevia and breech presentation, to the subsequent findings of epilepsy, mental deficiency, cerebral palsy, overactivity, reading disorders and tics in the child. For controls the authors took the next registered birth, matched by race, place of birth and maternal age. They postulated 'a continuum of reproductive casualty', implying that whereas in the severest cases the result of these prenatal conditions is an abortion or stillbirth, in less severe ones there is organic disease, such as cerebral palsy, epilepsy or mental deficiency; while in the milder cases there are merely behaviour disorders and tics. Prechtl, working at Groningen, Holland[70,71,72], carried out a unique follow-up study of full term babies into school age, comparing their later performance with various features of the newborn period. They found that undue excitability in the newborn period was apt to be followed by hyperactivity, short attention span and learning difficulties in later years.

The antecedents of cerebral palsy are similar to those of mental retardation, and both conditions are frequently present in the same child. I have summarised elsewhere[45] the known antecedents of cerebral palsy. The most important single factor is prematurity: about one third of all children with cerebral palsy were low birth weight babies. Cerebral palsy is slightly more common in males, there is a genetic factor, it is more common in multiple pregnancies, there is a higher than average incidence of previous miscarriages and stillbirths, of antepartum haemorrhage and toxaemia, and of abnormal labour associated with anoxia rather than mechanical trauma.

Neonatal Asphyxia

The literature on the prognosis of neonatal asphyxia is extensive and mostly difficult to evaluate. A critical discussion by Graham and her colleagues[41] should be read by all interested in the problem. They emphasised the need for more research, with the use of more accurate definition of the degree, duration and clinical features of asphyxia.

There has been a considerable amount of experimental work into the problem of asphyxia. Windle and Becker[93] asphyxiated guinea pigs by clamping the uterine vessels of the mother or the umbilical cord of the fetus. All the piglets showed neurological signs and symptoms, including tremors, paralysis, spasticity, somnolence, and increased errors in the maze test. Two-thirds showed pathological changes in the nervous system, such as necrosis, oedema, chromatolysis and petechiae. Glial proliferation began at 5 days. In older specimens there was loss of nerve cells, atrophy of the brain and destruction of the pyramidal cells in the cortex.

In other papers Windle[94,95] described experiments on pregnant full term guinea pigs delivered by Caesarian section. Some animals were subjected to asphyxia by occlusion of the placental circulation, while others were delivered normally as controls. Those animals in whom circulation was occluded for 8 minutes or more showed clinical and pathological changes similar to those described above.

Pathological evidence of the effect of anoxia has been provided by many workers, and in particular by Courville[19,20]. The lesions described by him included focal necrosis and scarring in the cerebral cortex, widespread diffuse or nodular cortical atrophy, focal or diffuse alterations in the corpus striatum, areas of cortical and subcortical softening incident to arterial occlusion, and demyelination and cyst formation.

That asphyxia in later life can produce neurological sequelae is well known. Nielson and Courville[64] told the story of a boy who was throttled by a sailor and who 6 months later developed athetosis. Plum et al.[68] followed 5 patients who had suffered severe anoxia as a result of carbon monoxide poisoning, anaesthesia or cardiac arrest. Autopsy examination was carried out in two. The predominant damage was cerebral hemisphere demyelination without significant neuronal damage. Deterioration tended to occur after the patients were discharged and they had resumed activity. The symptoms were irritability, apathy, confusion, clumsiness and extrapyramidal rigidity.

Experimental work in the newborn baby included that of Apgar et al.[5] They set out to determine whether there was a relationship between the fetal blood oxygen saturation at birth and the subsequent intellectual development. Gesell tests were used in the younger children and Stanford Binet tests in the older ones. They could find no correlation. Thirty-three pre-school children who at birth had an Apgar score of 5 or less were compared with matched controls at 30 months. No difference was found.[79]

An infant may appear to make a complete recovery after anoxia and other adverse perinatal conditions, such as abnormal hypotonia and decreased movements, while in later years he may prove to have neurological sequelae. Prechtl[70] of Gröningen has described what he terms the choreiform syndrome in school children who at birth had suffered anoxia, and had seemed to develop normally thereafter. The features included distractibility, poor performance at school, reading difficulties, clumsiness, poor concentration, and labile emotional behaviour, fluctuating between timidity and aggressive outbursts.   They had twitchings of the extremities, head and tongue, unlike true chorea, but nevertheless characteristic.

Ernhart et al.[33] who had previously carried out valuable studies on the sequelae of perinatal asphyxia, examined 355 children at the age of 3 years, in order to determine whether those who had anoxia at birth were different from those whose condition at birth was satisfactory. One hundred and sixteen children constituted the anoxic group; 159 children were normal at birth, being full term, with an uneventful prenatal and neonatal course and an easy delivery.   In addition there was a complicated group of 80 children who had mixed difficulties such as prematurity, haemolytic disease, skull fracture and intracranial haemorrhage.   The definition of anoxia was satisfactory. The follow-up examinations were carried out without knowledge of the newborn classification.   The follow-up assessment consisted of a battery of psychological tests and a neurological examination.   The only significant psychological differences concerned the 'cognitive' or 'intellectual' functions.   There was a greater impairment in conceptional ability than in vocabulary skill in the anoxic children. In addition the I.Q. score was slightly less in the anoxic children than in the normal controls.   There were more abnormal neurological findings in the anoxic group than in the controls.   They commented that perinatal events contribute to the crippling of human capacity. The authors discussed the possibility that there may have been genetic factors which were associated with both the perinatal complications and the inferiority found at 3 years.   This was a carefully planned and controlled study, contributing useful information to our knowledge of the sequelae of perinatal asphyxia.

In an extensive Chicago study[10] children were selected from over 40,000 births on account of severe anoxia at birth.   They were compared with their sibling controls and others who had been delivered spontaneously.   The ages at follow-up ranged from 3 to 19 years. It was a retrospective study.   The incidence of feeblemindedness (as shown by intelligence tests) was 20 per cent in the anoxic group and 2·5 per cent in the controls.   E.E.G. abnormalities were found in 36 per cent of the anoxic group but in none of the control group. A battery of psychological tests, such as the Bender-Gestalt, figure completion and other tests, showed no other differences.   The authors made the point that only isolated children in the anoxic group were abnormal; there were no material differences between the group a whole.   Many of the anoxic children were of superior intelligence.

A valuable long term study was carried out at Aberdeen[37] where legitimate full term singletons with moderate or severe asphyxia at birth were followed up at the age of 7½ to 11½ by a full battery of psychological tests.   Very few showed either intellectual or neurological defects. The difficulty in interpreting these studies is partly due to the uncertainty as to what caused the anoxia. The cause, such as a prolapsed umbilical cord, is not often obvious. When there is no obvious cause, one fears that there may be an underlying brain defect; and one feels that chronic anoxia in utero, due, for instance, to placental insufficiency, is more likely to damage the fetal brain than an acute episode such as a prolapsed cord. In general the prognosis of babies who had severe anoxia at birth is surprisingly good: but only a prolonged follow-up will reveal how many of these children prove to be 'clumsy' or to have visuo-spatial difficulties at school age.

Neonatal Convulsions

The prognosis of neonatal convulsions depends on the cause. The most important causes are hypoglycaemia, hypocalcaemia and cerebral oedema or haemorrhage. Other causes include hyponatraemia, hypernatraemia, hypomagnesaemia, tetanus, meningitis and other infections, galactosaemia, fructosaemia, leucine sensitivity and other metabolic causes. Many of these causes are themselves of prenatal origin. For instance, it has been suggested that neonatal hypoglycaemia may result from a prenatal brain defect. Hence a satisfactory statement of the relationship between neonatal convulsions and subsequent development could only follow the fullest laboratory investigation followed by follow-up examination over a period of several years.

Rose and Lambroso[76] followed 137 children who had convulsions in the newborn period, for an average of 3·8 years. The following were their findings:

	Number	Normal	Died	Abnormal
Hypocalcaemia	28	23	3	2
Birth injury	20	13	3	4
Infections	13	4	5	4
Cerebral malformations	11	—	7	4
Anoxia	10	1	2	7
Postmaturity	8	1	2	5
Hypoglycaemia	7	4	—	3
Pre-eclamptic toxaemia	5	4	—	1
Miscellaneous	9	1	5	3
	38	23	4	11
Total (some listed twice)	149	74	31	44

Birth Injury

I have always disliked the terms 'brain damage' and 'birth injury'— unless the latter refers to Erb's palsy or a fractured humerus or other externally obvious result of trauma during delivery. Psychologists who use the term 'brain damage' may include the effect of noxious factors during pregnancy, such as maternal rubella, but parents inevitably interpret the words as indicating damage during birth.

Some psychologists refer to a child as being 'brain injured' or having suffered 'brain damage' or 'birth injury' if he is overactive, clumsy, impulsive, concentrates badly, is excessively talkative, and shows a discrepancy between verbal and performance tests.   These children are apt to be called 'bad mannered', 'badly brought up', 'spoilt' or 'odd'.

I object to the words for the following reasons.   (1) They distress the parents.   If a tragedy should befall any of us, it would be better if we were to feel that it was entirely unavoidable, than that we should feel that if more care had been taken by us or someone else, it could have been avoided.   It must be particularly distressing for a mother who has nurtured her fetus in utero for nine months to be told that her baby's brain has been damaged during delivery.   (2) The words brain damage and birth injury inevitably imply that the obstetrician, family doctor or midwife was to blame for the tragedy.   This is unfortunate, because parents are likely to try to find something which they or others have done to cause the child's handicap.   (3) The diagnosis is usually wrong.   It would be extremely difficult to prove to a scientific audience that the diagnosis of brain damage at birth is correct if the child survives.   How could one prove that a child's mental subnormality, cerebral palsy, overactivity or failure to concentrate was due to birth injury?   If one suspects a cerebral haemorrhage at birth it is commonly unwise to perform a lumbar puncture.   If one did perform one, one would find it difficult to prove that blood in the C.S.F. was not due to trauma by the needle.   One must remember that xanthochromia, a high C.S.F. protein or a cell count of 15 to 30 or more is normal in the newborn.   One cannot say how many children survive a cerebral haemorrhage.   If a child is prematurely born or has a breech delivery or is asphyxiated at birth, or has convulsions in the newborn period, and is subsequently found to be mentally defective, spastic or overactive, it would be unscientific and illogical to say that his symptoms are due to the prematurity, breech delivery or asphyxia.   One should look behind these prenatal or perinatal factors to their causes—the cause of the prematurity, breech delivery or asphyxia.   When a baby is born alive but severely asphyxiated and cannot be resuscitated, there is nearly always a major underlying brain defect.   Amongst prematurely born babies there is an eight times greater incidence of congenital anomalies than in the normal population.   Amongst mentally defective children there is a six times greater incidence of congenital anomalies; and amongst breech deliveries there is a high incidence of small for dates babies or congenital anomalies.   It was found in Sheffield that amongst babies with spina bifida, there is a five times greater incidence of breech delivery than in the normal population.   We also know that subnormal children fre-

frequently show obvious indications of prenatal factors, such as a single palmar crease, a malformed ear or dental enamel defects.

One knows that the child who has a readlly difficult delivery is not the one who subsequently proves to be spastic or mentally defective. Amiel-Tison[4] studied 41 babies which had a particularly traumatic delivery; none of them when followed up had cerebral palsy. She concluded that babies who survive obstetrical trauma are most unlikely to have sequelae, and that prenatal anomalies are responsible for the greater part of severe definitive encephalopathies.

Barker[8] investigated 607 subnormal children from a population of 73,687 single births, and concluded that 'recognised abnormalities of pregnancy and delivery seemed to play little part in determining subnormality'. McKeown and Record[60] could find little relationship of intelligence to abnormalities of pregnancy, such as toxaemia or difficulties in labour. They wrote that the most convincing evidence that prenatal influences have little effect on measured intellect is the observation that twins separated from their co-twin at or soon after birth have scores which are little lower than those of single births, in spite of their retarded fetal growth, short period of gestation and increased risks during birth.

When a child is older it is illogical to say that because he is overactive or concentrates badly, therefore he has suffered brain damage. There is no psychological test which proves brain damage. I have seen many children who were said to have suffered brain damage and in whom it seemed obvious that there were other likely causes for their difficulties. I was asked to see a seriously overactive but intelligent boy who had been seen by two psychologists, both of whom said that the boy had suffered brain damage. It was obvious at a glance that the boy merely took after his mother, and on questioning she said that she was exactly the same at his age. Troublesome overactivity is frequently a familial trait. Reger[74] wrote that all 43 symptoms said to be features of the brain damaged child occur in normal children—some of the symptoms in almost all children. He wrote that 'most of what is assumed to be known about the brain injured child is folk-lore'. "The fact that many children are distractible and hyperactive is no reason to assume that the concept of the brain injured child is useful and worth retaining. There is no justification whatsoever to continue to call children 'brain injured' if there is no reason to assume that these children have injuries to the brain". He added that the only way the diagnosis can be made with certainty is at autopsy. He wrote that 'the flippant way the label of brain injury is tagged on to children by people who frankly, do not know what they are talking about, is hardly likely to further the cause of the profession'. Birch[11] wrote about the fallacies of the diagnosis of birth injury.

I have referred elsewhere to the problems which the handicapped child has to face—the overprotection and the lack of environmental stimulation. This, with the delayed maturation sometimes seen in these children, may account for at least some of their features. The term 'minimal cerebral dysfunction', used in a symposium sponsored by the Spastics Society[9] is preferable to the expression 'brain injury', in that it does not imply that the cause of the difficulty is known and understood. In a comprehensive symposium[26] of 396 pages with 772 references, various experts discussed the concept of 'minimal brain dysfunction'. Leon Eisenberg wrote that it is a condition in which there is 'no evidence of brain pathology'. Masland expressed a similar view, writing that it is not a disease, but merely a term applied to a group of individuals with certain characteristics in common.

Kinsbourne wrote that 'the diagnosis of minimal brain dysfunction is based on findings that are abnormal only with reference to the child's age. If the child were younger, the findings would be regarded as normal. They indicate a relative delay in some aspect of neurological maturation as a result of slowed evolution of cerebral control after relevant activity.'

Nevertheless I do not wish to imply that the child may not suffer brain damage at birth. Prolapse of the cord may cause severe anoxia, and delay in treating it may damage the brain. A child may have a cerebral haemorrhage at birth and recover—but we do not know how many do, or what the sequelae are. A precipitate delivery is dangerous. But the diagnosis of brain damage at birth in a child who survives is almost always unjustifiable and probably wrong.

Conclusions

The study of the effect of prenatal and perinatal factors on subsequent development is beset with difficulties. Retrospective studies are rarely satisfactory, depending as they do on the memory of mothers or the accuracy of notes which were kept without any particular planned investigation in mind, so that essential data are missing. Prospective studies are difficult because of the number of years involved. Many prospective studies are unsatisfactory because the children have been followed up for a mere one or two years, while if the study is to be meaningful they should continue at least into early school age, when testing is more satisfactory, and differential testing is possible (e.g. for difficulties of spatial appreciation or learning disorders). Another major difficulty of prospective studies is the loss of subjects from the investigation. If only half of the subjects are followed, the investigator will have a trying time if he is to convince his audience and readers that those followed up were in all ways the same as those lost to the study.

A major difficulty lies in proving that when correlations between postnatal development and prenatal factors are found, the prenatal factors are causative and not themselves the result of other factors. A difficult pregnancy may affect the child's postnatal management and the mother's attitude to her child. Difficulties in pregnancy may themselves be related to the mother's genotype. An abnormality in the fetus may itself affect the pregnancy; for instance, fetal bulbar palsy or oesophageal atresia may cause hydramnios which then causes difficulties in labour or has other effects on the fetus. In studying the effect of maternal stress on the fetus one cannot exclude the possibility that personality and developmental features in the child together with the mother's psychological problems in pregnancy are not both genetic. Premature labour is associated with complications of pregnancy which are themselves due to environmental, genetic or other factors. Smallness of the fetus in relation to the duration of gestation may be due to placental insufficiency, and the cause of that is often unknown; and lightness for dates is commonly related to such factors as antepartum bleeding, prolonged rupture of the membranes, multiple births, pyeloncphritis, toxaemia, infections in pregnancy, previous relative infertility and recurrent abortions, illegitimacy, diabetes, smoking in pregnancy, malnutrition and other conditions.[92] It is easy to ascribe postnatal abnormalities in the child to any of a wide variety of prenatal or natal factors, without realising how hopelessly interwoven the various factors are. It is common to hear it said that a child's handicaps are obviously due to birth injury, because there was a breech delivery, when in fact the breech delivery was due to the child being small for dates, and this was due to placental insufficiency, with toxaemia, malnutrition and adverse socioeconomic factors in the background but highly relevant. In one study it was shown that half the infants suffering a birth hazard also suffered hazards in utero.[74] We know that postmaturity is a risk to the fetus; but the causes of postmaturity are obscure and may be relevant to subsequent handicaps.

Summary

A wide variety of prenatal and perinatal factors are related to the child's subsequent development; but it is only rarely possible to relate a child's difficulties to one of those factors, such as birth injury or asphyxia at birth, because one must look behind those factors to the conditions which caused them. Almost all prenatal factors are closely interwoven with other factors, including genetic ones.

REFERENCES

1. ADER, R. (1971). In Stoclinga, G. B. A., van der Werff ten Bosch, J. J. *Normal and abnormal development of brain and behaviour.* Leyden. Leyden University Press.
2. ADLAND, B. P. F., DOBBING, J. (1971). Vulnerability of developing brain: development of four enzymes in the brains of normal and undernourished rats. *Brain Research,* **28**, 97.
3. ALBERMAN, E. (1963). Birth weight and length of gestation in cerebral palsy. *Develop. Med. Child Neurol.* **5**, 388.

4. AMIEL-TISON, C. (1969). Cerebral damage in full term newborn. Aetiological factors, neonatal status and long term follow-up. *Biolog. Neonat.*, **14**, 234.
5. APGAR, V., GIRDANY, B. R., McINTOSH, R. TAYLOR, H. C. (1955) Neonatal Anoxia. A Study of the Relation of Oxygenation at Birth to Intellectual Development. *Pediatrics*, **15**, 653.
6. BAIRD, D. (1957). Foetal Post-Maturity. *Brit. Med. J.* **1**, 1061.
7. BAIRD, D. (1959) The contribution of Obstetrical Factors to Serious Physical and Mental Handicap in Children. *J. Obst. and Gyn.* B. E., **66**, 743.
8. BARKER, D. J. P. (1966). Low intelligence and obstetric complications. *Brit. J. Prev. and Soc. Med.*, **20**, 15.
9. BAX, M., MACKEITH, R. (1962). Minimal Cerebral Dysfunction. *Little Club Clinics in Developmental Medicine*. No. 10. London: Heinemann.
10. BENARON, H. B. W., BOSHES, B., TUCKER, B. E., COHEN, J., ANDREWS, J. P., FROMM, E., YACORZYNSKI, G. K. (1960) Effect of Anoxia during Labour and Immediately after Birth on the Subsequent Development of the Child. *Amer. J. Obstet. Gynec.*, **80**, 1129.
11. BIRCH, H. G. (1964) *Brain Damage in Children. The Biological and Social Aspects.* Baltimore. Williams Wilkins.
12. BRITISH MEDICAL JOURNAL ANNOTATION (1964) The Drugged Sperm, **1**, 1063.
13. CAMP, D. V. (1964) Psychological Evaluation of Children Who Had Neonatal Hyperbilirubinemia. *Amer. J. ment. Def.*, **68**, 803.
14. CHASE, N. S., BUTTERFIELD, L. J., WELCH, N. N., DABIÈRE, C. S., VASAN, N. S. (1972) Alteration in human brain biochemistry following intrauterine growth retardation. *Pediatrics*. **50**, 403.
15. CHURCHILL, J. A., NEFF, J. W., CALDWELL, D. F. (1966) Birth Weight and Intelligence. *Obstet. and Gynec.*, **28**, 425.
16. CHURCHILL, J. A., MASLAND, R. L., NAYLOR, A. A., ASHWORTH, M. R. (1974) The Etiology of Cerebral Palsy in Preterm Infants. *Develop. Med. Child Neurol.* **16**, 143.
17. CLIFFORD, S. H. (1954) Postmaturity—with placental dysfunction. *J. Pediatrics*. **44**, 1.
18. CLIFFORD, S. H. (1957) Pediatric aspects of the placental dysfunction syndrome in Postmaturity. *J. Am. Med. Ass.* **165**, 1663.
19. COURVILLE, C. B. (1952) Ultimate Residual Lesions of Antenatal and Neonatal Asphyxia. Their Relation to Certain Degenerative Diseases of the Brain Appearing in Early Life. *Amer. J. Dis. Child.*, **84**, 64.
20. COURVILLE, C. B., EDMONDSON, H. A. (1958) Mental Deficiency from Intrauterine Exposure to Irradiation. *Bull. Los Angeles neurol. Soc.*, **23**, 11.
21. DANN, M., LEVINE, S. Z., NEW, E. V. (1964) A Long Term Follow-up Study of Small Premature Infants. *Pediatrics*, **33**, 945.
22. DAVISON, A. N. (1972) Mental retardation and the biochemistry of the developing brain. *Proc. Roy. Soc. Med.* **65**, 583.
23. DAWKINS, M. J. R., MARTIN, J. D., SPECTOR, W. G. (1961) Intrapartum Asphyxia. *J. Obst. Gynec. Brit.* **68**, 604.
24. DAY, R., HAINES, M. S. (1954) Intelligence Quotients of Children Recovered from Erythroblastosis Foetalis Since the Introduction of Exchange Transfusion. *Pediatrics*, **13**, 333.
25. DAY, R. L. (1967) Factors Influencing Offspring. *Am. J. Dis. Child.*, **113**, 179.
26. DE LA CRUZ, F. F., FOX, B. H., ROBERTS, R. H. (1973) Minimal brain dysfunction. *Annals of New York Academy of Science*. **205**, pp. 1–396.
27. DODGE, J. A. (1973) Pyloric Stenosis. *Irish J. Med Science*. **142**, 6.
28. DOUGLAS, J. W. B. (1960) Premature Children at Primary Schools. *Brit. med. J.*, **1**, 1008.
29. DRILLIEN, C. M. (1972) Aetiology and outcome in low birth-weight infants. *Develop. Med. Child Neurol.* **14**, 563.
30. DRILLIEN, C. M. (1963) *The Growth and Development of the Prematurely Born Infant.* Edinburgh: Livingstone.

31. DRILLIEN, C. M., WILKINSON, E. M. (1964) Emotional Stress and Mongoloid Births. *Develop. Med. child Neurol.*, **6**, 140.
32. EID, E. E. (1970). Studies on the subsequent growth of children who had retardation or acceleration of growth in early life. *Ph.D. Thesis*, The University of Sheffield.
33. ERNHART, C. B., GRAHAM, F. K., THURSTON, D. (1960) *Arch. Neurol. (Chic)*, **2**, 504.
34. FITZHARDINGE, P. M., RAMSAY, M. (1973) The improving outlook for the small prematurely born infants. *Develop. Med. Child Neurol.* **15**, 447.
35. FITZHARDINGE, P. M., STEVEN, A. M. (1972) The small for dates infant. Neurological and intellectual sequelae. *Pediatrics.* **50**, 50.
35a. FRANCIS-WILLIAMS J. Davies P. A. (1974) Very low birth weight and later intelligence. *Develop. Med. Child Neurol.* **16**. 709.
36. FRASER, F. C. (1958) Genetic Counselling in Some Common Pediatric Diseases. *Pediat. Clin. N. Amer.*, May, p. 475.
37. FRASER, M. S., WILKS, J. (1959) The Residual Effects of Neonatal Asphyxia. *J. Obstet. Gynaec. (Brit. Emp.)*, **66**, 748.
37a. FUJIKURA, T. FROEHLICH, L. A. (1974) Mental and motor development in monozygotic co-twins with dissimilar birth-weight. *Pediatrics* **53**, 884.
38. GALTON, F. (1869) *Hereditary Genius. An Inquiry into Its Law and Consequences.* London: Macmillan.
39. GERRARD, J. (1952) Kernicterus. *Brain*, **75**, 526.
40. GERVER, J. M., DAY, R. (1950) Intelligence Quotient of Children Who Have Recovered from Erythroblastosis Foetalis. *J. Pediat.*, **36**, 342.
41. GRAHAM, F. K., CALDWELL, B. M., ERNHART, C. B., PENNOYER, M. M., HARTMANN, A. F. (1957) Anoxia as a Significant Perinatal Experience. *J. Pediat.*, **50**, 556.
42. GUNTHER, L. M. (1963) Psychopathology and Stress in the Life Experience of Mothers of Premature Infants. *Amer. J. Obstet. Gynaec.*, **86**, 333.
43. HEIMER, C. B., CUTLER, R. FREEDMAN, A. M. (1964) Neurological Sequelae of Premature Birth. *Amer. J. Dis. Child.*, **108**, 122.
44. HONZIK, M. P. (1957) Developmental Studies of Parent Child Resemblance in Intelligence. *Child Develpm.*, **28**, 215.
45. ILLINGWORTH, R. S. (1958) *Recent Advances in Cerebral Palsy.* London: Churchill.
46. ILLINGWORTH, R. S., WOODS, G. (1960) The Incidence of Twins in Cerebral Palsy and Mental Retardation. *Arch. Dis. Childh.*, **35**, 333.
47. JOFFE, J. M. (1969). Prenatal Determinants of Behaviour. Oxford: Pergamon.
48. KEELEY, K. (1962) Prenatal Influence on Behaviour of Offspring of Crowded Mice. *Science*, **135**, 44.
49. KNOBLOCH, H., PASAMANICK, B. (1958) Seasonal Variations in the Births of the Mentally Deficient. *Amer. J. publ. Hlth.*, **48**, 1201.
50. LANMAN, J. T. (1968) Delays During Reproduction and Their Effects on the Embryo and Foetus. *New Engl. J. Med.*, **278**, 993.
51. LANDER, E., FORSSMAN, H., AKESSON, H. O. (1964) Season of Birth and Mental Deficiency. *Acta genet. (Basel)*, **14**, 265.
52. LILIENFELD, A. M., PASAMANICK, B. (1954) Association of Maternal and Fetal Factors with the Development of Epilepsy. *J. Amer. med. Ass.*, **155**, 719.
53. LILIENFELD, A. M., PASAMANICK, B. (1955) The Association of Maternal and Fetal Factors with the Development of Cerebral Palsy and Epilepsy. *Amer. J. Obstet. Gynec.*, **70**, 93.
54. LORBER, J. (1965) The Family History of Spina Bifida Cystica. *Pediatrics* **35**, 589.
55. LOVELL, K. E. (1973) The effect of postmaturity on the developing child. *Med. J. Australia.* **1**, 13.
56. LUBCHENCO, L. O., DELIVORIA-Papadopoulos, M., BUTTERFIELD, L. J., FRENCH, J. H., METCALF, D., HIX, I. E., DANICK, J., DODDS, J., DOWNS, M., FREELAND, E. (1972). Long term follow-up studies of prematurely born infants. *J. Pediat.* **80**, 501.

57. LUBCHENCO, L. O., DELIVORIA-PAPADOPOULOS, M., SEARLS, D. (1972) Long term follow-up studies of prematurely born infants. *J. Pediat.* **80**, 509.
58. LYNN, R. (1959) Environmental Conditions Affecting Intelligence. *Educ. Res.*, **1**, 49.
59. MCDONALD, A. (1967) Children of Very Low Birth Weight. MEIU Research Monograph No. 1. London. Spastics Society and Heinemann.
60. MCKEOWN, T. RECORD, R. G. (1971). Early environmental influences on the development of intelligence. *British Medical Bulletin*, **27**, 48.
61. MILLER, R. M. (1967) Prenatal Origins of Mental Retardation : Epidemiological Approach. *J. Pediat.*, **71**, 454.
62. MILLER, R.W. (1956) Delayed Effects Occurring within the First Decade after Exposure of Young Individuals to the Hiroshima Atomic Bomb. *Pediatrics*, **18**, 1.
63. NEWCOMBE, H. B., TAVENDALE, O. C. (1965) Effect of Father's Age on the Risk of Child Handicap or Death. *Am. J. Human Genetics*, **17**, 163.
64. NIELSEN, J. M., COURVILLE, C. B. (1951) Asphyxia. *Neurology*, **1**, 48.
65. PASAMANICK, B. LILIENFELD, A. M. (1955) Association of Maternal and Fetal Factors with Development of Mental Deficiency. *J. Amer. med. Ass.*, **159**, 155.
66. PASAMANICK, B., KNOBLOCH, H. (1958) Seasonal Variation in Complications of Pregnancy. *Obstet. and Gynec.*, **12**, 110.
67. PENROSE, L. S. (1962) Paternal Age in Mongolism. *Lancet*, **1**, 1101.
68. PLUM, F., POSNER, J. B., HAIN, R. F. (1962) Delayed Neurological Deterioration after Anoxia. *Arch. intern. Med.*, **110**, 18.
69. PLUMMER, G. (1952) Anomalies Occurring in Children Exposed in Utero to the Atomic Bomb in Hiroshima. *Pediatrics*, **10**, 687.
70. PRECHTL, H. F. R., STEMMER, C. J. (1962) The Choreiform Syndrome in Children. *Develop. Med. Child Neurol.*, **4**, 119.
71. PRECHTL, H. (1963) in Foss. *Determinants of Infant Behaviour*. London. Methuen.
72. PRECHTL, H., BEINTEMA, D. (1964). The Neurological Examination of the Full term Newborn Infant. *Little Club Clinics in Developmental Medicine*. No. 12. London : Heinemann.
73. RAHIMTULLA, K. A. (1961) Hydramnios in Relation to Foetal Mortality. *Arch. Dis. Childh.*, **36**, 418.
74. REGER, R. (1965) *School Psychology*. Springfield. Charles Thomas.
75. ROGERS, M. E., LILIENFELD, A. M. PASAMANICK, B. (1955) Prenatal and Para-natal Factors in the Development of Childhood Behaviour Disorders. *Acta. psychiat. scand.* Suppl., 102.
76. ROSE, A. L. LOMBROSO, C. T. (1970) Neonatal Seizure States. *Pediatrics* **45**, 404.
77. RUBIN, R. A., ROSENBLATT, C. BALOW, B. (1973) Psychological and Educational Sequelae of Prematurity. *Pediatrics*. **52**, 352.
78. RUSSELL, C. S., TAYLOR, R. (1978) Smoking in Pregnancy. *Brit. J. Prev. Soc. Med.*, **22**, 119.
79. SHIPE, D., VANDENBERG, S.,WILLIAMS, R. D. B. (1968). Neonatal Apgar ratings as related to intelligence and behaviour in preschool children. *Child Development*, **39**, 860.
80. SKODAK, M. (1938) Children of Feeble-Minded Mothers. *Child Develpm.*, **9**, 303.
81. SKODAK, M., SKEELS, H. M. (1949) A Final Follow-up Study of 100 Adopted Children. *J. genet. Psychol.*, **75**, 85.
82. SPECTOR, R. (1964) Abnormal Spermatozoa and Perinatal Disease. *Develop. Med. child Neurol.*, **6**, 523.
83. STEWART, R. R.,WALKER,W., SAVAGE, R. D. (1970). A developmental study of cognitive and personality characteristics associated with haemolytic disease of the newborn. *Develop. Med. Child Neurol.*, **12**, 16.
84. STOTT, D. H. (1962) Abnormal Mothering as a Cause of Mental Abnormality. *J.ChildPsychol.* **3**, 79.

85. TAFT, L. T., GOLDFARB,W. (1964) *Develop. Med. child Neurol.*, **6**, 32.
86. TAKKUNEN, R. L., FRISK, M., HOLMSTROM, G. (1965) Follow-up Examination of 110 Small Prematures at the Age of 6–7 years. *Acta Paediat. scand.* Suppl. 159, p. 70.
87. TERMAN, L. M., ODEN, M. H. (1947) *The Gifted Child Grows Up.* Stanford: Stanford Univ. Press.
88. THOMPSON,W. R. (1957) Influence of Prenatal Maternal Anxiety on Emotionality in Young Rats. *Science*, **125**, 698.
89. UCHIDA, I. A., HOLUNGA, R., LAWLER, C. (1968). Maternal Radiation and Chromosomal Aberrations. *Lancet*, **2**, 1045.
90. WAGNER, M. G., ARNDT, R. (1968) Postmaturity as an etiological factor in 124 cases of neurologically handicapped children. *Clinics in Developmental Medicine* No. 27, p. 89.
91. WIENER, G., RIDER, R. V., OPPEL,W. C., HARPER, P. A. (1968) Prematures. Correlates of Low Birth Weight. Psychological Status at Eight to Ten Years of Age. *Ped. Research*, **2**, 110.
92. WILSON, M. G., PARMELEE, A. H., HUGGINS, M. H. (1963). Prenatal history of infants with birth weight of 1500 grammes or less. *J. Pediatrics*, **63**, 1140.
93. WINDLE, W. F., BECKER, R. F. (1943) Asphyxia Neonatorum. An Experimental Study in the Guinea-pig. *Amer. J. Obstet. Gynec.*, **45**, 183.
94. WINDLE, W. F. (1944) Structural and Functional Alterations in the Brain Following Neonatal Asphyxia. *Psychosom. med.*, **6**, 155.
95. WINDLE, W. F. (1958) *Neurological and Psychological Deficits of Asphyxia Neonatorum.* Springfield: Charles Thomas.
96. YAMAZAKI, J. N., WRIGHT, S. W., WRIGHT, P. M. (1954) Outcome of Pregnancy in Women exposed to the Atomic Bomb in Nagasaki, *Amer. J. Dis. Child.*, **87**, 448.
97. ZAZZO, R. (1960) *Les Jumeaux, le Couple et la Personne.* Paris. Presse Universitaires de France.

CHAPTER 4

ENVIRONMENTAL FACTORS AND DEVELOPMENT

The Importance of Environment

Not many now would agree with the extreme view of the behaviourist school of some decades ago, exemplified by Watson's comment[61] which ran as follows: 'Give me a dozen healthy infants, well formed, and my own specified world to bring them up in, and I'll guarantee to take any at random and train him to become any type of specialist I might select—doctor, lawyer, artist, merchant, chief, and yes, even beggar-man and thief, regardless of his talents, peculiarities, tendencies, abilities, vocations and race of his ancestors. There is no such thing as an inheritance of capacity, talent, temperament, mental constitution and characteristics'.

The environment, particularly at home and at school, has a profound effect on a child's intellectual development and on his personality. To some extent his intelligence and personality are interwoven; but in the section to follow I shall discuss the effect of environment on the intellectual development only, mentioning the effect on personality when it has a more direct bearing on his intellectual development.

Experimental Work

Ethology, the study of the behaviour of animals, has much of relevance to the behaviour of the child. Those interested should read the books by Rheingold,[47] Cooke,[15] Hinde,[31] Foss,[29] Glaser and Eisenberg[30] and others. Numerous experiments with rats, cats, dogs, goats, sheep and monkeys showed that separation of the animal from the mother at birth had a profound effect on the animal's development often for the rest of its life, even though it was returned to the mother within a matter of hours or days. The mother animal was likely to reject its young when returned to her, even though the separation had lasted only a matter of hours. Rats handled daily between birth and weaning are more active than those which have not been handled[20]. Newborn lambs may die if left without stimulation for as little as an hour. When animals such as goats or sheep are not allowed to lick their young at birth, they reject them even though the young are returned to their mothers in a few hours: but as little as five or ten minutes of contact with licking prevents this rejection.

There are increasingly sophisticated methods of studying the effect of environment on animals. Rats kept in a lively and active environment for 30 days[48] showed distinct changes in brain anatomy and chemistry as compared with animals kept in a dull non-stimulating environment. The cerebral cortex was thicker and weighed more; there were more glial cells, there was more synaptic contact, and more neuronal volume: there was greater acetylcholine and cholinesterase activity and an increased ratio of RNA and DNA.

Puppies kept in a kennel for the first seven weeks are not as affectionate as those kept in a more happy environment.[59]

Denenberg went further, and showed that one can determine the animal's personality by appropriate manipulation of the environment: one can make a rat emotional, aggressive, poor when exposed to stress inefficient in sex, bad at learning, and almost psychotic in behaviour[20].

Psychologists adopt many ways of regulating an animal's environment in order to determine the effect of environmental factors on behaviour. Denenberg[21] wrote as follows:

"We can take an animal and, within broad limits, we can specify the 'personality' of that animal as well as some of its behavioral capabilities by the appropriate manipulation of experiences in early life. For example, one can take a newborn rat and raise it under certain conditions so that in adulthood it will be highly emotional, relatively inefficient in learning, and less capable of withstanding environmental stresses and thus more likely to die from such stresses. On the other hand, we can also produce rats, through appropriate experiences in early life, which are non-emotional, highly curious and investigatory, efficient learning, and which are less prone to psychological upset when exposed to mildly stressful situations. Other research has shown that we can create animals which are more intelligent in the sense of being better able to solve problems to get to a goal. Turning to a different realm of behaviour, one can restrict the early experience of rhesus monkeys so that, when adults, they act in a bizarre psychotic-like manner, show almost a complete absence of appropriate sexual behavior (this is true both for the male and for the female) and, in the few instances where the females have become pregnant, they exhibit a profound lack of appropriate maternal behaviour."

Concept of the Sensitive Period

There is abundant evidence that in many animals there is a particular period of their development at which learning in response to the appropriate stimuli is easier than at other times. This is termed the sensitive period. Sometimes a stage of development comes beyond which learning is impossible: this is the so-called critical period. There are many examples of this in the books by Harriet Rheingold[47] entitled 'Maternal Behavior in Animals'. With a colleague,[32] I have reviewed the literature concerning the sensitive period and adduced evidence that there is a sensitive period for learning in human beings. For instnce, if a baby is not given solid foods when he can chew (usually at six or seven months) it becomes increasingly difficult to get him to take solids later. Red squirrels, if not given nuts to crack by a certain age, never acquire the skill of cracking them later. If chimpanzees are not given bananas to peel within a certain age they can never learn to remove the skin.

If a child's congenital cataract is not removed by a certain age, the child will not be able to see.   If a squint is not corrected in time, the child will become blind in the affected eye.   If a cleft palate is not operated on by the age of two or three, it becomes increasingly difficult to obtain normal speech.   The longer congenital deafness remains undiagnosed, the more difficult it becomes to teach the child to speak.   Whereas young children may learn to speak a foreign language fluently with a good accent, adults settling in a country may never learn to speak the language of that country fluently, however intelligent they are.

There is much interest amongst educationalists in the application of the concept of the sensitive or critical period to the development of the preschool child.   Maria Montessori[55] was one of the first to recognise the importance of these periods in the teaching of children. She found that children are more receptive for learning involving the sensory system, such as the learning of colour, shape, sound and texture, at the age of $2\frac{1}{2}$ years to 6 years than in later years.   It may be that the nursery school improves the performance of children from poor homes where the necessary stimulation at home is lacking.

Difficulties in spatial appreciation are common among black Africans.   Diagrams confuse Bantus, and they often find it difficult to understand pictures in which near objects (e.g. a mouse) appear to be larger than more distant objects (e.g. an elephant). Biesheuvel[4a,4b], who has carried out extensive studies on the learning difficulties of black Africans, ascribed these and similar problems to lack of early stimuli at the time of the sensitive period.   He wrote"The evidence suggests that for various functions there are critical maturational periods, during which physical well-being, mental stimulation, environmental interactions, have their optimum effect, and during which deployment of potentialities can be permanently affected, either positively or negatively."

Bayley[3] and others have shown that there is no difference in the test scores of negro and white infants in the first 15 to 18 months of their life.   Deutsch and others[22] showed that after this age there is an increasing gap between the performance of the whites and negroes, so that in early school life the mean I.Q. score of negro children is significantly less than that of white children.   Schaefer, in Denenberg's book,[21] wrote that the need for early education is suggested by studies that find that schools do not increase the low levels of intellectual functioning that disadvantaged children acquire prior to school entrance.

Baughman and Dahlstrom,[2] in a study of negro and white children in the Southern States of North America, wrote that 'the need to establish comprehensive preschool programs for children from culturally disadvantaged families has been demonstrated in many studies and in many settings.   As matters stand now, great numbers of these children are psychologically handicapped when they enter the first grade: they are prepared neither for normal first grade work nor for competition with their peers who have come out of more favourable home circumstances.'

Early Learning

In our book 'Lessons from Childhood'[34] we described many examples of children destined for fame who were given intensive teaching in the pre-school years and who displayed remarkable precocity in learning in later years. Well documented examples were those of John Stuart Mill, Karl Witte, Lord Kelvin and Blaise Pascal. Kellmer Pringle[46] showed that children starting at school early (4 years 6 months to 4 years 11 months) were considerably better at reading and arithmetic than late starters (5·0 years to 5 years 6 months). Elsewhere[45] she wrote that during the first five years of life, 'children learn more than during any other comparable period of time thereafter. What is more important, they learn how to learn, and whether learning is a pleasurable challenge or a disagreeable effort to be resisted as far as possible. Evidence is accumulating to show that early failure to stimulate a child's desire to learn may result in a permanent impairment of learning ability or intelligence. Learning to learn does not mean beginning to teach reading or arithmetic at the earliest possible time. It is far more basic and subtle and includes motivating the child to find pleasure in learning to develop his ability to pay attention to others, to engage in purposeful activity'.

Bloom[6] suggested that the whole pattern of learning is established before the child starts school. 'We are inclined to believe', he wrote, 'that this is the most important growing period for academic achievement'. He remarked that it is much easier to learn something new than it is to stamp out one set of learned behaviour and replace it by a new set. He wrote that the environment in the first years of life was vital for the child's subsequent learning, and laid down the pattern for the future. He suggested that failure to develop a good learning pattern in these years is likely to lead to continued failure later. He pointed out that the easiest time for a child to learn is when he is developmentally ready to learn, when he has no undesirable patterns to eliminate before he can learn new ones.

It may be that the child's progress in certain subjects at school and later may be related to the age at which he was first taught them. If he is taught too soon he will find it difficult and may develop such a dislike for them that he never learns them well: and if he is taught them too late, after he has lost interest in them, he may find it difficult to learn them later.

Wolff and Feinbloom[64] uttered a word of warning about efforts to teach a child in his first two years, rightly deprecating an atmosphere of urgency. They wrote that, 'there is no evidence at present to support the assertion that biologically fixed critical periods control the sequence of cognitive development, no evidence that scientifically designed toys are in any way superior to the usual household items available to most infants, no evidence that systematic application of such toys accelerates intellectual development, and no persuasive evidence that acceleration of specific skills during the motor phase of development, even if possible, has any lasting effects on intellectual competence.'

It is true that we do not know for certain how to help children to achieve their best. We do not know at what age positive steps should be taken to this end. We do not know what these steps should be— what toys to supply, neither do we know how successful those steps will be.

The problem is not just one of when teaching should begin and what should be taught. The problem is that of identifying factors which affect the child's development. Douglas[25] pointed to one of the factors in his follow-up study of 5,000 children born in the first week of March 1946. He showed how children in lower social classes are apt to be sent to schools where the standard of work is lower than that of schools to which children of the middle or upper classes are sent. Those in lower social classes tend to be placed in a lower stream than those of the middle classes and less is expected of them, so that they achieve less than others of the same level of intelligence. In addition, less is expected of children in poor homes, and they receive less stimulation at home— and so achieve less.

Nutrition and Development

Malnutrition is the commonest disease in the world. Part of the tragedy of malnutrition lies in the damage which it can inflict on the developing brain. There is evidence from Mexico, South Africa, the United States and Britain[12,56] that malnutrition in infancy has a harmful effect on subsequent mental development if the malnutrition is not corrected in the early weeks of infancy.

Winick in America and Dobbing in England[23,24,62,63] have shown that malnutrition reduces the number and size of cells in the brain together with the lipid, nucleic acid, enzyme and protein content. Winick studied the DNA content of the brain because it determines the total number of cells present; the amount of DNA in each cell is fixed, and an increase in DNA reflects that aspect of tissue growth which is due mainly to cell division; a reduced head circumference accurately reflects these changes. Undernutrition of the rat and pig in the early days caused permanent reduction in the weight of the brain. Even a brief period of postnatal fasting in newborn rabbits reduced the RNA, DNA, protein and cholesterol content of the brain.[49]. Winick investigated 10 normal brains from well nourished Chilean children who died accidentally with the brains of nine infants who died of severe malnutrition during the first year of life.

The latter were smaller in weight, protein content, RNA, DNA content and the number of cells. Delicardie and colleagues[19] compared infants who at 15 days weighed less than their birth weight with infants matched for birth weight, length and gestational age. The former continued to be smaller throughout their first year, lagging behind in length and head circumference. Eid[27] following children up to school age, made similar observations.

In South Africa grossly malnourished Cape coloured infants after correction of their malnutrition fared less well mentally and had a smaller head circumference than controls matched for age and sex. Cravioto[16,17] found that recovery from malnutrition is accompanied by mental improvement except in children who had severe malnutrition before the age of six months. He remarked that the human brain is growing at its most rapid rate in the early weeks (gaining 1–2 mg per minute in the perinatal period), and that damage at the period of maximum growth may be irremediable. Birch and colleagues[5] estimated the WISC score of 37 children who had been treated for kwashiorkor at the age of 6 to 30 months, and compared it with that of unaffected siblings. The mean score of the index cases was 68·5, compared with 81·5 in the case of the siblings. Compared with the controls, twice as many of the index cases had an I.Q. of below 70; four of the index cases and 10 of the controls had an I.Q. of 90 or more. One effect of malnutrition is apathy, which in turn affects the mother child interaction, so that the mother responds less to her baby and the baby receives less stimulation from the mother.[17] Studies all over the world have shown that severe growth retardation in the first year retards later mental development, and the longer the duration of the growth retardation, the greater is the effect on mental development.[16]

Even severe malnutrition arising from untreated congenital pyloric stenosis may be reflected by reduced visuomotor coordination and auditory memory in later years.[38] These findings on the effect of postnatal malnutrition should be considered in conjunction with the effect of intrauterine malnutrition described in the previous chapter. Chase and Martin[13] compared 19 children at a mean age of three and a half years of age who had suffered from malnutrition in the first year of life with controls of similar sex, race, social background and birth weight. The mean DQ of the controls was 99·4 and that of the test children was 82·1; but all those rehabilitated before the age of four months had a DQ above 80, but only in 10 admitted after four months was there a DQ over 80.

Practice and Development

An essential factor in development is the maturation of the nervous system.

Swaddling is still practised in many parts of the world, including

Russia, Iraq and Corfu.   Studies have shown that on release from swaddling at the end of the first year, babies in a matter of hours develop motor skills comparable with those of children who have been free to move their limbs.   Though practice had been denied them, maturation of the nervous system had progressed, so that no subsequent retardation occurred.   Futile efforts have been made to cause children to walk early by giving them special motor practice. The efforts failed because children cannot walk until there is the appropriate degree of maturation of the nervous system, particularly myelination.   Similar futile efforts have been made to teach children early sphincter control.

Emotional Deprivation

Emotional deprivation retards children physically and mentally. Bowlby[7] in his famous monograph summarised the world literature on the subject.

Children need love throughout their childhood and subsequently, but deprivation of love in their first three years may have a particularly profound effect.   It retards them in their development and in their physical growth.[51]   Children brought up in an institution are likely to be retarded in sitting, walking, sphincter control and in speech. In later childhood they are apt to display aggressiveness, selfishness, excessive thumbsucking or other body manipulations and defective verbal reasoning.   Motor behaviour is relatively less retarded than verbal, adaptive and other aspects of development.

I can never forget a visit to a home for illegitimate children in a foreign city.   In an upstairs room there were 20 to 30 children, aged 12 months to 3 years, sitting on the floor with no toys and no furniture apart from their cots, which had solid wood sides.   The children were not talking or crying or playing: they were sitting immobile.   The most startling feature was an open window reaching down to the level of the floor, with no bar or any other obstacle to prevent children falling out.   When we exclaimed in astonishment, we were told that no children had ever fallen out.   Seeing their immobility, we felt that they probably never would.

A later publication[8] reassessed Bowlby's monograph.   It was concluded that progressive retardation may be arrested or reversed if there is no further emotional deprivation after the first two years; but that prolonged and severe deprivation beginning early in the first year and continuing for as long as three years may lead to severe permanent effects, including the inability to give or receive affection in adult life.   Language impairment, abstract thought and capacity for strong and lasting interpersonal attachments were less likely to be reversed than other effects.

The book by Pavenstedt entitled 'The Drifters', a study of slum children, gives a valuable insight into the effect of a bad home.   It described the superior motor coordination of these children, combined with a lack of caution and self protective measures, resulting in frequent accidents, from which, however, they fail to learn. Pain is rarely expressed. The children tend to avoid difficult tasks instead of trying. In their relationship to others they are need-oriented, distrustful and shallow, constantly fearing aggression, retaliation and blame. They have no interest in books or stories, they are unable to take part in back and forth conversation, and their language development is poor, with a limited vocabulary.

A bad home is a major cause of backwardness in children. Cyril Burt[9] in his study of backward children, found that far fewer lived in better neighbourhoods of London, Hampstead, Lewisham and Dulwich, than in the poorer neighbourhoods, Lambeth, Hoxton and Poplar. He suggested that the factors are impairment of health and general knowledge by poverty; inadequate sleep and overcrowding; employment out of school hours; domestic duties; absence of room for play; poor intellectual atmosphere at home and absence of books; non attendance at school—serious non attendance being three times commoner amongst the backward than among controls; and too slow or too quick promotion at school. Jahoda and Warren[36] quoted work to the effect that there is no difference between the I.Q. of negro children in America and white children in the pre-school period; but that thereafter the negro children become separated from the white ones by an ever increasing gap. The mean I.Q. of negro school children is 85. It was postulated that this was due to the differences in the quality of the home, and socio-economic factors.

An educational study[65] found that 'it is becoming clear that the educational handicaps of the deprived child derive not so much from the physical factors of poverty, dirt and squalor, as from the intellectual impoverishment of the home, and from the parents' attitudes towards education, towards school and towards teachers.' Parents of disadvantaged children do not expect their children to succeed; they instil an attitude of hopelessness and expectancy of failure. Many studies have indicated the lack of intelligent conversation between child and parent in these homes. Children are not questioned, and their questions are not answered—so that the children stop asking them. Parents in these homes tend to be punitive, critical and constantly derogatory towards their children.

Children react differently to emotional deprivation. There may be genetic or constitutional factors which govern a child's response to his environment. Other factors are the quality of the parent child relationship before the deprivation occurred, the age at which it occurred, the length of separation, the experiences during the period of separation, the completeness of the separation, and the attitude of the parents when the child is returned to them.

It is a mistake to suppose that emotional deprivation is confined to institutions.   Some parents are afraid of loving their children, and so are afraid of picking the baby up when he cries.   Some mothers are unwilling to give up their work to look after their young children, and deprive them of their love just when they most need it.   There are mothers who turn a deaf ear to the 12 months old baby who is left crying all day in a pram outside with nothing but a brick wall to see.   Koupernik of Paris coined the phrase 'intrafamilial hospitalism' for this condition.

In recent years determined efforts have been made to reduce the risk of psychological trauma in young children, especially in those who have to be separated from their mothers in the first three years. Many authorities now avoid placing illegitimate infants in institutions, but place them in foster homes within 2 or 3 weeks of birth.   In view of early placement in foster homes it seems likely that psychological trauma from emotional deprivation, such as that described by Bowlby, is now much more rare than it used to be.

Many children have to be admitted to hospital in the first three years, but with the greater consciousness of the possibility of psychological trauma to such children, paediatricians and others have done a great deal to reduce or prevent emotional disturbance by such steps as the encouragement of daily visiting by the parents, admitting mothers with their children, and the adoption of a more humane approach to the sick child.

The mode of action of emotional deprivation is uncertain.   Some of the retardation of deprived children can be explained by lack of opportunity: the baby who is ready to sit or walk may miss the help which he needs.   No one has time to talk to him much, to play with him and towards the end of the first year to read to him—so that the development of speech is delayed.   When normally he would acquire control of the bladder, no one gives him the opportunity to use a suitable receptacle, so that sphincter control is delayed.   Emotional deprivation, in addition to damaging mental development, may also cause growth retardation: the mechanism of this is not fully understood.

Other Retarding Factors

Mental development may be held up by other factors, such as fatigue, chronic ill health, delay in starting school, prolonged or repeated absences from school, moves from one school to another, separation from a teacher liked by the child, dislike or fear of a teacher and by poor teaching.   They can be retarded by the side effects of drugs, particularly those used in the treatment of epilepsy.

Desirable Qualities in the Home

I have tried to summarise those qualities of the home which enable a pre-school child to achieve his best.[33]

Qualities suggested were:

Love and security; the constant avoidance of nagging, criticism, belittling, derogation, favouritism. Avoidance of prolonged separation from the parents.

Acceptance of the child, however meagre his performance; praise for effort rather than achievement.

Firm loving discipline, with a minimum of punishment. The teaching of behaviour acceptable to others. Inculcation of thoughtfulness for others, unselfishness, good moral values: avoidance of cheating; giving him a chance to practice his new skills, to develop any special interest which he shows.

Encouragement to try to find out, to explore, to be curious; but is unwise to allow him to fail. Success breeds success, and failure may lead to failure and refusal to try.

Encouragement, praise and reward rather than discouragement.

Encouragement of independence, and avoidance of over-protection. Calculated risks as distinct from thoughtlessness and carelessness.

Tolerance and understanding of the developing mind of the child, of his normal negativeness and aggressiveness.

Setting a good example—not only in behaviour, but in reading, television programmes, efforts to find out the causes of things.

Ambition for the child, but not over-ambition (expecting more of him than his endowment will permit). Expectation of success, of good behaviour.

Instillation of a sensible attitude to illness, without exaggeration of symptoms.

Instillation of a sensible attitude to sex.

Instillation of a tolerant attitude to others. Avoidance of criticism of others in his presence; instead teaching him to look for the good in people. Tolerance of nonconformity.

Provision of suitable play material—which will help him to use his hands, to think, to use his imagination, to construct, to determine how things work (e.g. interlocking bricks, pencils, crayons and paper, bead threading, picture dominoes, jigsaws, constructional toys such as bildit—but not mechanical toys).

Provision of suitable material which will help him to obtain the answer to questions which he has raised. Letting him develop his own play rather than telling him what to do. Encouragement of self initiated learning without providing all the ideas.

Encouragement of accuracy, thoroughness, self confidence, initiative, leadership.

Allowing him to make mistakes and learn from them.

Teaching him to argue, to ask for the reason why, to ask questions, to think round a subject, to question what the parent says, what the radio says, to seek evidence. To evaluate, determine what causes what, to seek similarities and dissimilarities.

Teaching persistence, creativity. It is thought that creativity is implanted in the home.

Giving opportunity to enlarge his vocabulary. Accuracy and clarity of speech.

Reading to the child (e.g. from 12 months onwards).

Providing experiences outside the home—visiting the countryside, seeing natural phenomena, visiting museums, factories.

Vernon[60] would add

Linguistic stimulation: teaching clarity of concepts, intelligent conversation with the child.

Demanding but democratic family environment, emphasising self-control and responsibility.

Tolerance of nonconformity.

Regular and prolonged schooling, emphasising discovery rather than rote learning.

If parents are to bring the best out of their children, they should begin in their child's first days to give him all the love which he wants: to talk to him, play with him and let him see the activities of the home. One cannot expect a child who is kept lying in a pram all day with nothing but a brick wall to see in his first year or so to be as advanced as a baby whose mother plays with him, gives him play material, talks to him, and towards the end of the first year reads to him.

I have discussed elsewhere the provision of suitable play material at different ages.[35]   It may be that the American 'operation head-start' designed to prevent the usual retardation experienced by children in poor homes, has proved disappointing because it enrolled children too late, when they were too old.

Environment and the Handicapped Child

The environment is important not only to the normal child, but to the handicapped child.

There is abundant scope for research into the effect of environment in handicapped children.   In one way or another the environment of the child with any but the mildest handicap is almost bound to be different from that of normal children.   He is apt to be over-protected at home, so that his physical or sensory handicap is augmented by lack of practice and opportunity to learn.   He may be the subject of favouritism or rejection.   He may be the target of unkind criticisms or comments made by neighbours in his presence.   He may be deprived of normal tactile and manipulative experience with toys and other materials.   He may be isolated from his fellows and lack their companionship.   His activities outside school hours are restricted. He has to be treated differently from normal children owing to his dependence on others. He may have to be separated from his parents at an early age in order that he can be trained in a residential school suitable for his handicap, and the problem of emotional deprivation is added to the physical defect. Bender[7] remarked that 'children can tolerate a certain amount of inflammation and structural damage to the brain if they have the emotional support they need and are not isolated and deprived'.

Parmelee et al.[43] emphasised the importance of distinguishing retardation in the blind child resulting from emotional deprivation and absence of opportunity and experience, from true mental retardation with a low I.Q. They wrote that 'the greatest evil that can befall a blind child is to be judged mentally retarded early in life and thereby be deprived of any opportunities for intellectual development. Almost as serious for both the blind child and his parents is the failure to recognise a child with serious mental impairment early enough to spare both the torments of trying to achieve impossible goals'.

A particularly valuable paper,[28] drew attention to the pseudo-retardation which may arise in blind children as a result of deprivation of the normal sensory and motor stimuli. Delay in giving solid foods may cause difficulty in chewing and eating: toilet training is apt to be delayed: they may be deprived of the opportunity to learn to dress themselves when developmentally ready to learn: they may lack the normal sensory stimuli because they are not given suitable toys: they may be stopped from placing objects in the mouth: the parents are liable to read to them less, so that their speech is retarded. They rightly emphasised that many blind children are classified as retarded or autistic, when the intelligence is not low, but they have merely lacked the necessary stimuli when they were developmentally ready to learn various new skills.

Much interest has been shown in recent years in the emotional problems of the mentally handicapped child. It is generally agreed that the mentally defective child is further retarded by being placed early in an institution. An interesting study by Kirk[37] showed how mentally retarded children can improve considerably with suitable education in the preschool period or later, and how they can deteriorate as a result of emotional deprivation. He conducted a 5 year study of the effect of preschool teaching of mentally retarded children. Thirty of 43 children (70 per cent.) receiving preschool education showed an improvement of their intellectual status. He concluded that: 'It would appear that, although the upper limits of development for an individual are genetically or organically determined, the functional level or rate of development may be accelerated or depressed within the limits set by the organism. Somatopsychological factors and the cultural milieu (including schooling) are capable of influencing the functional level within these limits.'

Schlanger[50] studied the speech of 21 matched pairs of mentally retarded children, one group being brought up in an institution, another group being looked after at home. The speech of those brought up in the institution was much inferior to that of the other group.

It follows that as the environment is of such importance in the handicapped child, it must always be borne in mind in assessing his intellectual potential. It is easy to underestimate such a child's ability, because due attention has not been paid to the retarding effect of his environment. One might add that it is also possible to make too much allowance for his environmental difficulties.

The aim should always be to assess the mentally or physically handicapped child's maximum potential and to help him to achieve it. When one first sees a handicapped child one must remember that owing to adverse environmental factors he may be functioning at an unnecessarily low level.

Intelligence and family size

Terman showed many years ago that the first born of a family tends to be more intelligent than subsequent children, but there are many exceptions to this. Environmental factors may be relevant, for later born children are likely to have less time devoted to them and their mothers are older. It is said that the eldest, youngest and only children tend to be more intelligent than intermediate ones. In two child families the mean I.Q. of the children is higher when there is a larger interval between births.

In a study of 2868 Aberdeen school children tested at 7, 9, 11 and 12 years[42] there was an inverse relationship between family size and test score.

In a study of 184 American students from multiple child families, it was found that the larger and more closely spaced the family, the lower was the tested intelligence of the children.[18] The size of family in relation to social class and other factors must be relevant in these findings.

Estimation of the Part Played by Environment

It has not proved to be a profitable exercise to try to determine how much of what we term intelligence is the product of nature and how much is the product of nurture or environment. The environment can greatly lower or raise the I.Q. score, and some feel that a really bad home can cause mental subnormality. Clarke,[14] discussing environmental factors in mental deficiency, concluded on the basis of measured recovery being equivalent to the degree of organic psychological damage, that cruelty and neglect may retard intellectual development by at least 16 points. In twin studies he calculated that the environment might have an even bigger effect on the I.Q.

Stott[57] estimated that the I.Q. score of maladjusted children may increase by 20 to 30 points when their anxiety is allayed.

Attempts to determine the relative parts played by environment and heredity on intelligence have been based on two groups of children. One group consisted of children of identical heredity (identical twins) brought up in different environments, and the other of children of different heredity brought up in the same environment (foster children). Foster children tended to have a higher I.Q. score than their parents—perhaps due to the fact that their foster parents wanted children and loved them.[10,52,53,54]

The follow up studies of Knobloch and Pasamanick[39] cast considerable light on the problem. They studied the development of white and negro children and found that whereas motor development remained comparable in the two groups, those aspects of development most subject to social influences showed considerable differences with increasing age. The adaptive behaviour quotient rose from 105·4 to 110·9 for the white children and fell from 104·5 to 97·4 for the negroes. Language ability likewise improved in the white children and decreased in the negroes. There were corresponding changes in the overall I.Q. scores.[39] Drillien[26] made similar observations in the premature babies which she followed up at Edinburgh. The difference in performance between the babies in different social classes increased with increasing age.

Barbara Tizard[58], interested in Jensen's theory that in the United States genetic factors explain much of the I.Q. differences between coloured and white races, studied the progress of children of different races in the identical environment of nurseries for illegitimate children. In one study of 39 children aged 24 to 59 months,—2 white, 22 West African or African and 24 mixed, in the nursery for at least six months, 70 per cent of them admitted before the first birthday and 86 per cent before the second, the mean test scores for non-verbal intelligence, language and comprehension were very similar, slightly favouring the coloured children. In another study of 64 children aged 53 months admitted by 4 months and staying in the nursery for at least 2 years, 36 were white, 9 black and 19 mixed: 24 were still in the institution, 24 were adopted into white families at the mean age of 37 months, and 15 were restored to their mothers. The occupations of the fathers were equated. The mean I.Q. scores of the racial group were similar, but those of the adopted children were the highest.

Newman et al.[41] in a study of 19 pairs of monozygotic twins separated in early life and brought up in different environments, found an extreme range of variation of intelligence of 24 per cent. Burt[11] traced 40 pairs of identical twins in London schools. The correlation between the education attainment of the twins who have been reared apart was only 0·62, as compared with 0·89 for twins brought up together. On the other hand, the correlations between the assessments for intelligence was as high as 0·88—almost identical with that of twins brought up together.   There was therefore a high correlation between scores for identical twins even when reared apart.

McKeown and Record[40] found that the mean I.Q. of twins reared together is 5 points less than that of twins separated at birth—and concluded that this was due to the retarding influence of one twin on the other.   But I think that there is another and better explanation: parents of twins reared together have less time to talk to their twins, to play with them and read to them, than have parents of a singleton or one twin when he is separated from his cotwin.

In conclusion, the extent to which environment can advance or retard intellectual development is uncertain.   The general opinion, based mostly on studies of identical twins reared apart, seems to be that not more than 20 to 40 per cent. of an intelligence test score is likely to be the product of environment, the rest being the product of heredity.   A more exact estimate cannot be given.   There are difficulties in the two main methods of study—those of twins brought up in different environments, and of children brought up in foster homes.   When identical twins are reared apart, one feels that some degree of selection of the environment is almost bound to occur, and that the environment selected is likely to be similar for each sibling. In the case of foster home studies, the main difficulty is the selection of the foster home and the attempt to match the infant's supposed mental qualities with those of foster parents.   There are difficulties in the equating of the environment of monozygotic twins:[1] the twins are apt to be managed differently by their parents: they may have different appetites and different illnesses: they may differ in personality and in physical growth—all factors which may affect their mental development.

Summary

The environment—the home, the neighbourhood, the school— has a profound effect on the child's development.

The concept of the sensitive or critical period described by ethologists may be applied to the developing child.   Evidence is adduced to the effect that the child should be enabled to learn when he is first ready to learn.

The role of nutrition in the early years, of love and security, of the opportunity to practice and to develop independence, are all emphasised.

The qualities of a bad home and of a good home are discussed. I have listed some of the ways of helping a child to achieve his best.

The effect of environment on the handicapped child is discussed.

In conclusion, a child's I.Q. can be considerably raised or lowered by his environment.   Genetic factors contribute a major part to the child's intelligence and ability; but the effects of nature and nurture are so intimately and intricately intermingled, that efforts to separate the effects of one from the effects of the other are doomed to failure, and are an unprofitable occupation.

REFERENCES

1. ALLEN, M. G., POLLIN, W., HOFFER, A. C. (1972) Parental, Birth and Infancy Factors in Infant Twin Development, In Chess, S., Thomas, S. *Annual Progress in Child Psychiatry and Development.* New York, Brunner Mazel.
2. BAUGHMAN, E. E., DAHLSTROM, W. G. (1968) Negro and white children. A psychological study in the rural South. New York: Academic Press.
3. BAYLEY, N. (1965) Comparisons of mental and motor test scores for ages 1–15 months by sex, birth order, race, geographical location, and education of parents. *Child Development*, **36**, 379.
4. BENDER, L. (1958) Emerging Patterns in Child Psychiatry. *Bull. N.Y. Acad. Med.*, **34**, 794.
4a. BIESHEUVEL, S. (1963) Symposium on current problems in the behavioural sciences in South Africa. South African J. of Science, p. 375.
4b. BIESHEUVEL, S. (1972) An examination of Jensen's Theory concerning Educability, hereditability and population differences. *Psychologica Africana* **14**. 87.
5. BIRCH, H. G., PINEIRO, C., ALCADE, E., TOCA, T., CRAVIOTO, J. (1971) Relational of Kwashiorkor in early childhood and intelligence at school age. *Pediatric Research* **5**, 579.
6. BLOOM, B. S. (1964) *Stability and Change in Human Characteristics* New York: Wiley.
7. BOWLEY, J. (1951) Maternal Care and Mental Health. *Bull. Wld. Hlth. Org.*, **3**, 357.
8. BOWLBY, J., AINSWORTH, M., BOSTON, M., ROSENBLUTH, D. (1956) Effects of Mother—Child Separation: Follow-up Study. *Brit. J. med. Psychol.*, **29**, 211.
9. BURT, C. (1950) *The Backward Child.* London: Univ of London Press.
10. BURT, C. (1955) The Evidence for the Concept of Intelligence. *Brit. J. educ. Psychol.*, **25**, 158.
11. BURT, C. (1959) General Ability and Special Aptitudes. *Educ. Res.*, **1**, 3.
12. CABAK, V., NAJDANVIC, R. (1965) Effect of undernutrition in early life on physical and mental development. *Arch. Dis. Childh.*, **40**, 532.
13. CHASE, H. P., MARTIN, H. P. (1970) Undernutrition and Child Development. *New Engl., J. Med.*, **282**, 933.
14. CLARKE, A. M., CLARKE, A. D. B. (1958) *Mental Deficiency. The Changing Outlook.* London: Methuen.
15. COOKE, R. (1968) *The Biological Basis of Pediatric Practice.* New York: McGraw Hill.
16. CRAVIOTO, J., DELICARDIE, E. R., (1970). Mental performance in school age children. *Amer. J. Dis. Child.* **120**, 404.
17. CRAVIOTO, J., ROBLES, B. (1965) Evolution of adaptive and motor behavior during rehabilitation from kwashiorkor. *Amer. J. Orthopsychiat.* **35**, 449.
18. DANDES, H. M., DOW, E., (1969) Relation of intelligence to family size and density. *Child Development.* **40**, 641.
19. DELICARDIE, E. R., VEGA, L., BIRCH, H. G., CRAVIOTO, J. (1971). The effect of weight loss from birth to fifteen days on growth and development in the first year. *Biology of the neonate*, **17**, 249.
20. DENNENBERG, V. H., (1969) *Experimental programmes of life histories in the rat.* In Ambrose A. Stimulation in early infancy. London. Academic Press.
21. DENENBERG, V. H. (1970) Education of the infant and young child. New York: Academic Press.

22. DEUTSCH M., KATZ I. JENSEN, A. R. (1967) Social class, race and psychological development. New York: Holt, Rinehart and Winston.
23. DOBBING, J. (1970) Undernutrition and the developing brain. *Amer. J. Dis. Child.*, **120**, 411.
24. DOBBING, J. (1970). The kinetics of growth. *Lancet*, **2**, 1358.
25. DOUGLAS, J.W. B. (1964). *The Home and the School*. London: Macgibbon & Kee.
26. DRILLIEN, C. M. (1961) Longitudinal Study of Growth and Development of Prematurely and Maturely Born Children. Mental Development 2–5 Years. *Arch. Dis. Childh.*, **36**, 233.
27. EID, E. E. (1971) A follow-up study of physical growth following failure to thrive in the first year of life. *Acta Paediat. Scand.*, **60**, 39.
28. ELONEN, A. S., ZWARENSTEYN, S. B. (1964) Appraisal of Developmental Lag in Certain Blind Children. *J. Pediat.*, **65**, 599.
29. FOSS, B. M. *Determinants of Infant Behaviour*. Vol. 1 (1961), Vol. 2 (1963), Vol. 3 (1965), Vol. 4 (1969). London: Methuen.
30. GLASER, K., EISENBERG, L. (1956) Emotional Deprivation. *Pediatrics*, **18**, 626.
31. HINDE, R. A. (1966) *Animal behaviour*. New York: McGraw Hill.
32. ILLINGWORTH, R. S., Lister, J. (1964) The Critical or Sensitive Period, with Special Reference to Certain Feeding Problems in Infants and Children. *J. Pediat.*, **65**, 839.
33. ILLINGWORTH, R. S. (1968) How to help a child to achieve his best. *J. Pediat.*, **73**, 61.
34. ILLINGWORTH, R. S., ILLINGWORTH, C. M. (1966) *Lessons from childhood*. Edinburgh: Livingstone.
35. ILLINGWORTH, R. S. (1975) The Normal Child. 6th Edn. London: Churchill.
36. JAHODA, M., WARREN, N. (1968) Intelligence, nature and nurture. *New Scientist*, **39**, 188.
37. KIRK, S. A. (1958) *Early Education of the Mentally Retarded*. Urbana: Univ. of Illinois Press.
38. KLEIN, P. S., FORBES, G. B., NADER, P. R. (1974) Effects of starvation in infancy on subsequent learning abilities. *Pediatric Research*. **8**, 344.
39. KNOBLOCH, H., PASAMANICK, B. (1962) Mental Subnormality. *New Engl. J. med.*, **266**, 1092.
40. MCKEOWN, T., RECORD, R. G. (1971) Early environmental influences on the development of intelligence. *British Medical Bulletin*, **27**, 48.
41. NEWMAN, H. H., FREEMAN, F. N., HOLZINGER, K. J. (1937) *Twins. A Study of Heredity and Environment*. Chicago Univ. Press., quoted by Slater, E. T. O. (1938). *J. Neurol. Psychiat.*, **1**, 239.
42. NISBET, J. D., ENTWISTLE, N. J. (1967) Intelligence and family size. *Brit. J. Educ. Psychol.* **37**, 188.
43. PARMELEE, A. H., FISKE, C. E., WRIGHT, R. H. (1959) The Development of Ten Children with Blindness as a Result of Retrolental Fibroplasia. *Amer. J. Dis. Child.*, **98**, 198.
44. PAVENSTEDT, E. (1967) *The Drifters*. Children of disorganised lower class families. London: Churchill.
45. PRINGLE, KELLMER, M. L. (1967) Speech, learning and child health. *Proc. Roy. Soc. Med.*, **60**, 885.
46. PRINGLE, KELLMER, M. L., BUTLER, N. R., DAVIES, R. (1966) 11,000 *Seven year olds*. London: Langham.
47. RHEINGOLD, H. L. (1963). *Maternal Behavior in Animals*. New York: Wiley.
48. ROSENZWEIGH, M. R., BENNETT, E. L., DIAMOND, M. C. (1972) *Scientific American*. **226**, 22.
49. SCHAIN, R. J., WATANABE, K., HAREL, S. (1973) Effects of brief postnatal fasting on brain development of rabbits. *Pediatrics*. **51**, 240.
50. SCHLANGER, B. B. (1954) Environmental Influences in the Verbal Output of Mentally Retarded Children. *J. Speech Dis.*, **19**, 339.

51. SILVER, H. K., FINKELSTEIN, M. (1967). Deprivation dwarfism. *J. Pediat.*, **70**, 317.
52. SKEELS, H. M. (1936) Mental Development of Children in Foster Homes. *J. genet. Psychol.*, **49**, 91.
53. SKODAK, M., SKEELS, H. M. (1949) A Final Follow-up Study of One Hundred Adopted Children. *J. genet. Psychol.*, **75**, 85.
54. SKODAK, M. (1950) Mental Growth of Adopted Children in the Same Family. *J. genet. Psychol.*, **77**, 3.
55. STANDING, E. M. (1957) *Maria Montessori*. London: Hollis and Carter.
56. STOTCH, M. B., SMYTHE, P. M. (1967) The effect of undernutrition during infancy on subsequent brain growth and intellectual development. *South African Med. J.*, **41**, 1027.
57. STOTT, D. H. (1959) Infantile Illness and Subsequent Mental and Emotional Development. *J. genet. Psychol.*, **94**, 233.
58. TIZARD, B. (1974) I.Q. and Race. *Nature*, **247**, 316.
59. VAUGHAN, V. C., (1966) New Insights in Social Behaviour. *J. Amer. Med. Ass.* **198**, 45.
60. VERNON, P. E. (1969) *Intelligence and Cultural Environment*. London: Methuen.
61. Watson, J. B. (1931) *Behaviourism*. London: Kegan Paul.
62. WINICK, M. (1972) Nutrition and Development. New York. Wiley.
63. WINICK, M. ROSSO, P. (1969) Head circumference and cellular growth of the brain in normal and marasmic children. *J. Pediat.*, **74**, 774.
64. WOLFF, P. H., FEINBLOOM, R. I. (1969) Critical periods and cognitive development in the first two years. *Pediatrics*, **44**, 999.
65. WORKING PARTY FOR SCHOOLS COUNCIL NO. 27 (1970) Cross'd with adversity. The education of socially disadvantaged children in secondary schools. London: Evans and Methuen International.
66. WORLD HEALTH ORGANISATION. (1962) Definition of Maternal Care. A Reassessment of its Affects. Public Health Papers No. 14. Geneva.

CHAPTER 5

REFLEXES AND REACTIONS
OF THE NEWBORN

While a vast amount has been written about the development of the infant and young child, the neurological examination of the newborn baby has been relatively neglected. The subject was barely mentioned by Arnold Gesell, whose developmental studies began with the child at 4 to 6 weeks of age. We owe our knowledge of the neurological and developmental examination of the newborn baby to a small body of workers, which includes especially Albrecht Peiper, André Thomas, Madame Saint Anne Dargassies and Heinz Prechtl. Their writings have been used extensively in the preparation of this section. Minkowski and Dargassies[21] have given me permission to quote their work at length.

Reflexes and Reactions in the Newborn Period

Some 70 or more primitive reflexes have been described in the newborn period, but the value of many of them for developmental diagnosis has not been established. Taft and Cohen,[34] in an outline of the clinical examination of the newborn infant, listed 48 reflexes. Such reflexes may repay further study and because their status for the establishment of diagnosis and prognosis is as yet uncertain I felt that some of them should be described in some detail here.

Much ingenuity has been used in attempting to describe new reflexes, holding, for instance, the baby's nose, applying curtain clamps, and even applying itching powder. Dennis[12] reviewed many of these responses. The use of eponyms has lead to confusion.

Oral Reflexes

Sucking and swallowing reflexes are present in full term babies and all but the smallest premature baby. Their absence in a full term baby would suggest a developmental defect. The sucking reflex is tested by introducing a finger or teat into the mouth, when vigorous sucking will occur.

The 'rooting' or 'search' reflex is present in normal full term babies. When the baby's cheek contacts the mother's breast or other part, he 'roots' for milk. It enables him to find the nipple without his being directed to it. When the corner of the mouth is lightly touched, the bottom lip is lowered on the same side, and the tongue moved toward the point of stimulation. When the examiner's finger slides away from that point, the head turns to follow it. When the centre of the upper lip is stimulated, the lip elevates, baring the gums, and the tongue moves towards the place stimulated. If the finger slides along the oronasal groove, the head extends. When the centre of the bottom lip is stroked, the lip is lowered and the tongue is directed to the site of stimulation. If the finger moves towards the chin, the mandible is lowered and the head flexes. The above reflexes are termed 'the cardinal points reflexes' of the French writers. We have found that these reflexes are difficult to elicit except when the child is near his feed time. They presumably correspond to the mouthing reflex described by Gesell.

Eye Reflexes

BLINK REFLEXES. Various stimuli will provoke blinking, even if the child is asleep, or tensing of the eyelids if the eyes are closed. For example, a sharp noise elicits the cochleo-palpebral reflex; a bright light elicits the visuo-palpebral or 'dazzle' reflex, in which there is blinking or closure of the eyes and a painful touch elicits the cutaneo-palpebral reflex. The naso-palpebral reflex consists of blinking in response to tapping the bridge of the nose. Peiper's optic reflex consists of opisthotonos when a bright light shines on the eyes. The ciliary reflex is blinking on stroking the eyelashes. McCarthy's reflex is homolateral blinking on tapping the supraorbital area. In abnormal babies the reflex is produced by stimulation at a distance from the supraorbital region—e.g. over the vertex of the skull. If it is difficult to elicit the reflex because the eyes are closed, stimulation of the circumoral region may cause the baby to open the eyes, so that the test can be more easily performed. The corneal reflex consists of blinking when the cornea is touched. The satisfactory demonstration of these reflexes shows that the stimulus, whether sound, light or touch, has been received, that cerebral depression is unlikely, and that the appropriate muscles can contract in response.

THE DOLLS EYE RESPONSE. This is so named because there is a delay in the movement of the eyes after the head has been turned. If the head is turned slowly to the right or left, the eyes do not normally move with the head. The reflex is always present in the first ten days, disappearing thereafter as fixation develops. It would be asymmetrical in abducens paralysis. The reflex may persist beyond the first few days in abnormal babies.

RESPONSE TO ROTATION. The subject of rotational nystagmus in neonates was discussed by Peiper,[28] and Paine[25] showed its value in clinical work. The examiner holds the baby facing him and tilted forwards at about 30°. He then spins round two or three times. During rotation the eyes deviate in the direction of the movement; on stopping they deviate in the reverse direction and coarse nystagmus occurs. This test depends on vestibular function, but it is particularly useful for demonstrating ocular palsies, as was shown by Benson.[3]

PUPIL REFLEXES. The pupil reacts to light, but in the premature baby and some full term babies the duration of exposure to the light

may have to be prolonged to elicit the reflex.   The light used should
not be bright, for a bright light will cause closure of the eyes.   Thomas
remarked about the remarkable integration of reflexes which enables
a newborn baby to turn his head towards the source of light.
The photic sneeze reflex[1] consists of a sneeze when a bright light is
shone into the eyes.

RESISTANCE TO PASSIVE OPENING OF THE EYES.   This is present
from birth.

André Thomas wrote that the baby only begins to respond to the
rapid approach of objects to the eyes after 7 or 8 weeks or later.

Special Senses (see also Chapter 13)

The newborn baby can taste, smell and hear.   A sudden loud
noise causes blinking of the eyes, the startle reflex or a change in the
respiration rate.

A sugar-coated finger in the mouth produces sucking and licking
of the lips.   The finger is followed when it is withdrawn.

A salt-coated finger causes a grimace, with little or no sucking
movement.   The finger is forced back with the tongue towards the
lip, along with irregular head movements.   The finger is not
followed.

The olfactory sense of the neonate has been studied by several
writers, with variable results.[29]   Infants grimace when an unpleasant odour is passed under their noses, and it would be surprising if the olfactory function were not developed in the neonate, for it
is derived from the primitive brain.

Moro Reflex

Much of what has been written about the Moro reflex since its
original description by Moro in 1918 was reviewed by Mitchell.[22]
It occurs spontaneously perhaps as a result of some movement in
29·4 per cent of newborn infants.[38]

The reflex can be elicited in two ways.   The baby is placed supine
and the back of the head is supported on the palm of the hand an inch
or so above the table.   Rapid release of the head initiates the reflex.
The alternative method is to hold the hands and gently raise the baby
a little way off the table (Fig. 1).   Rapid release of the hands causes the
sudden movement of the cervical region which initiates the reflex.
A sharp bang on the table will produce the reflex, but this method is
not as satisfactory as the previous two methods.

The reflex consists of abduction and extension of the arms.   The
hands open, but the fingers often remain curved.   This is shown well
in Fig. 3.   This phase is followed by adduction of the arms as if an
embrace.   André Thomas has termed it 'The arms of the Cross
reflex'.   The reflex is also accompanied by crying, extension of the
trunk and head with movement of the legs (the nature of which

depends upon their original position).   The Moro reflex is present
in premature babies, except the very small ones, but the arms tend to
fall backwards on to the table during the adduction phase because the
anti-gravity muscles are much weaker than in the full term baby.
After a month or two the hand of the full term baby does not open as
fully as that of the newborn child.
    The Moro reflex has been assessed in various ways.   McGraw's[18a]
classification is based upon the maturity of the reflex, Stirnimann's[33]
upon the type of the reflex, and Gordon's[15] upon the intensity.   For
clinical work we have found it useful to classify the reflex in the
following way:

(a) Increased.   The reflex is elicited easily, the movements are
    exaggerated and a tremor of the hands may occur.

(b) Decreased, due to hypertonus.   The full movement of the
    arms is prevented by the increased muscle tone.   Three grades
    of severity are seen.   The mildest is failure to open the hands at
    the height of the reflex, next is incomplete movement of the
    arms, and most severe is the inability to elicit the reflex because
    the arms are so tightly flexed.

(c) Decreased, due to hypotonus.   In cases with muscle weakness,
    for example severe hypotonia, it is difficult to obtain the reflex.

(d) Decreased, due to cerebral damage or sedation of the mother.

(e) Asymmetrical.   This type of response is usually seen with a
    peripheral injury, such as Erb's palsy or fracture of the clavicle
    or humerus, and in spastic hemiplegia.   The response may be
    asymmetrical as a result of inhibition on one side if the hand is
    clenched or holding an object.   It follows that when one is
    eliciting the response the infant's head should be in the midline
    and the hands should be open.   It may not occur if the child is
    crying.   It may be unobtainable in hypotonic or hypertonic
    babies, in severely shocked or otherwise abnormal infants, or in
    babies who are asleep or heavily sedated by barbiturates.   In
    hypertonic babies abduction is limited and the hands may
    remain closed.

    The reflex may be difficult to obtain in premature babies, but it is
always present when they are awake and otherwise normal.
    The Moro response is a vestibular reflex.   It disappears by about 3
or 4 months of age.

The Startle Reflex

    This is often confused with the Moro reflex.   In the startle reflex,
obtained by a sudden loud noise or by tapping the sternum, the elbow
is flexed (not extended, as in the Moro reflex), and the hand remains
closed.[26]   Based on observations of 12 normal newborn infants, it
was said that in the Moro reflex there are more outward and inward

arm movements than in the startle reflex, and they are more simultaneous and more symmetrical in distance of movement.[2]

The Grasp Reflex

This was termed by André Thomas the 'Tonic reflex of the finger flexors'. It consists of two parts, the grasp reflex, and the response to traction. The grasp reflex is elicited by introducing a finger or other suitable object into the palm from the ulnar side. When the palm is stimulated the fingers flex and grip the object. The head should be in the midline during this test. If it is not, it will be found that the grasp reflex is more easily elicited on the side to which the occiput is directed. The dorsum of the hand should not be touched during the test because this excites the opposite reflex and the hand opens. This is one of the best examples of the conflict between reflexes, a phenomenon which is discussed in the writings of André Thomas and his colleagues.[35]

Once the grasp reflex is obtained the finger can be drawn gently upwards. As this is done in the full term baby the grip is reinforced and there is a progressive tensing of the muscles from the wrist to the shoulder, until the baby hangs from the finger momentarily. The record for this feat appears to be a grasping strength of 2·2 kg. as measured by a dynamometer. It is facilitated by the initiation of sucking movements. In the premature baby the arm can be drawn upwards, but when traction is applied the grip opens and there is much less tensing of the arm muscles.

A similar response can be demonstrated by gently stroking the sole of the foot behind the toes. With patience the grasping response of both the hands and the feet can be obtained, so that the baby is made to hang suspended like an oppossum supported by his hands and feet.

The grasp reflex is much weaker by the age of 2 months and has disappeared in most normal babies by the age of 3 months. The grasp reflex is strongest at term.

The grasp reflex is assessed partly with regard to intensity, partly with regard to symmetry, and partly with regard to persistence after it should have disappeared. An exceptionally strong grasp reflex may be found in the spastic form of cerebral palsy and in kernicterus. It may be asymmetrical in hemiplegia and in cases of cerebral damage. It should have disappeared in 2 or 3 months and persistence may indicate the spastic form of cerebral palsy.

Foot Reflexes

The grasp reflex of the foot is mentioned above. The withdrawal reflex consists of a brisk flexion of the limb and occurs in response to a noxious stimulus such as a pin prick applied to the sole of the foot. It is commonly unobtainable in children with a meningomyelocele. It may be absent or weak in a baby born as a breech with extended legs.

The crossed extension reflex is obtained by holding one leg extended at the knee and applying firm pressure to or stroking the sole of the foot on the same side.   The free leg flexes, adducts and then extends, giving the impression of attempting to push away the stimulating agent.   It is not normally obtained after the first month.   It may be obtained in the premature baby, but the adduction component of the reflex does not appear until the thirty-seventh week of gestation.

André Thomas suggested that the plantar response is best obtained by holding the foot perpendicular to the ground and stimulating the anterior part of the first interosseous space.   Asymmetry of response was regarded as of particular importance.   He found that the typical Babinski response with fanning of the toes, as seen in the older child, is rarely seen when the outer side of the sole of the foot is stimulated. Stimulation of the sole of the foot does, however, cause movement of the ipsilateral limb away from the stimulus and movement of the contralateral limb towards it.   Vajnorsky et al.[36] described a similar reflex.   Passive dorsiflexion of the big toe causes flexion of the other toes.   Ninety-eight per cent of 632 mature, healthy infants showed this reflex in the early months.   It disappeared by the age of 8 months.

Wilkinson and Brain[8] found that in infants up to 8 days of age, the plantar response is almost always extensor.   But Hogan and Milligan[16] tested the plantar response in 100 newborn babies, and taking the first movement of the great toe as the important one, found that in 93 the response was flexor on both sides, in three it was flexor on one side and extensor on the other, and in four it was bilateral extensor.

In disease of the pyramidal tracts (Ch. 17) in older infants and children the extensor plantar response may be obtained over a wide area—by stroking the tibia (Oppenheim's sign), squeezing the gastrocnemius (Gordon's sign), flexing the hip against resistance, and often by stimulating the skin of the abdomen, thorax or even the neck.

The interpretation of the plantar response in young infants may be difficult.   One may sometimes obtain a false extensor response merely by holding the leg up (flexing the hip).   One may obtain a false flexor response by carrying the stimulus across the side of the foot, thus introducing the plantar grasp reflex, instead of confining the stimulus to the distal half of the outside of the foot.

I have examined the plantar response in many hundreds of babies in the well baby clinic at about six weeks of age, and find it almost invariably to be flexor unless the child has cerebral palsy of the spastic type.

Hip Reflexes

When one leg is flexed at the hip the other leg flexes.   If strong pressure is applied to the femoral nerve in the inguinal canal the contralateral and less often the homolateral leg extends.   A flexion reflex in response to strong inguinal pressure has been described as a sign of meningitis.

Placing and Walking Reflexes

The placing or limb placement reaction[39,40] is elicited by bringing the anterior aspect of the tibia or ulna against the edge of a table.   The child lifts the leg up to step onto the table, or elevates the arm to place the hand on the table.   The reflex is constantly present at birth in full term babies weighing over 1,800 g., and after the first twenty-four hours in premature babies weighing over 1,700 g.

The walking or stepping reflex is obtained by holding the baby upright over a table, so that the sole of the foot presses against the table.   This initiates reciprocal flexion and extension of the legs, simulating walking.   Owing to the action of the adductor muscles, one leg often gets caught behind the other.   This must not be confused with adductor spasm.   A walking reflex can be demonstrated in premature babies, but they differ from full term babies in walking on their toes.   The walking reflex disappears in normal children by the age of 5 or 6 weeks, but can be demonstrated for several more weeks if the baby's head is extended when his foot is flat on the couch.[20]

Heel Reflex

Percussion of the heel or pressure on the sole of the foot causes extension of the limb.

Leg Straightening Reflex (A Righting Reflex)

When the sole of the foot is pressed on to the couch, the legs and body straighten.   This presumably corresponds to the 'positive and negative supporting reactions' described by Bobath and Bobath.[4] They described the positive reaction as consisting of simultaneous contraction of extensors and flexors of the leg when the ball of the foot makes contact with the floor.   The negative reaction occurs when the muscles relax as the foot is raised.   The Bobaths also described the crossed extension reflex, which enables one leg to support the weight of the body when the other leg is lifted.

The Magnet Reflex

When the child is supine the examiner's finger is pushed against the sole of the foot, and the knee and hip flex, and as the finger is withdrawn, the foot follows the finger.

Trunk Incurvation (Galant's reflex)

When the child is held in ventral suspension or is placed in the prone position, stimulation of the back lateral to the spine, or of the lumbar

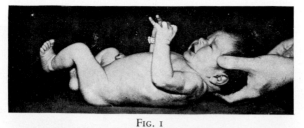

FIG. 1

Moro reflex, position for eliciting the reflex.

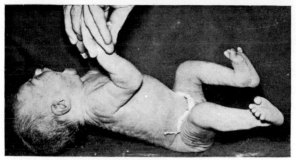

FIG. 2

Moro reflex, alternative position for eliciting the reflex.

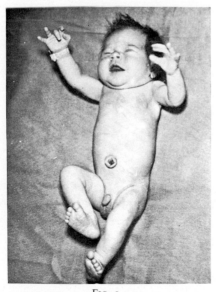

FIG. 3

Moro reflex, at height of abduction phase.

facing page 86

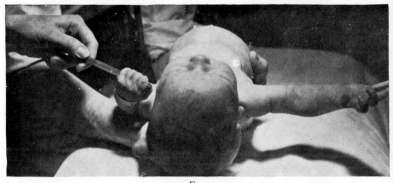

FIG. 4

Inhibition of Moro response in left hand because it is holding object.

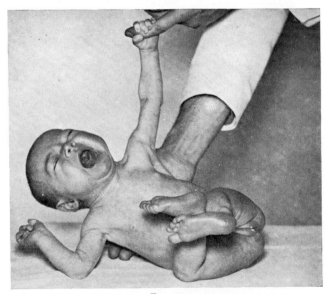

FIG. 5

Grasp reflex.

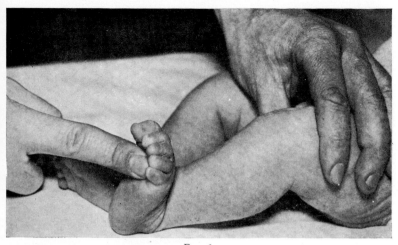

FIG. 6
Plantar grasp reflex.

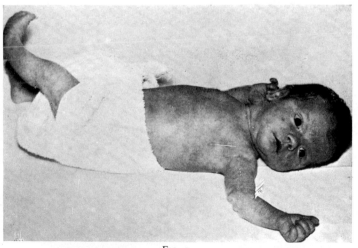

FIG. 7
The asymmetrical tonic neck reflex.

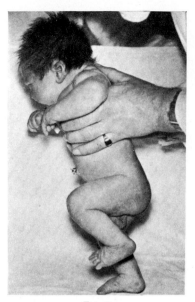

FIG. 8
The walking reflex.

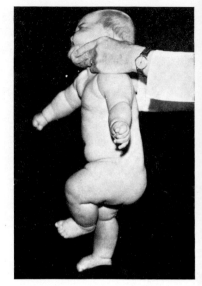

FIG. 9
Walking reflex in five month old baby,
seen when the neck was extended.

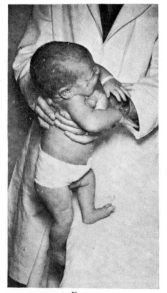

FIG. 10
Placing reaction of lower limbs.
When the front of the leg touches
the edge of the table, the baby
steps over the edge.

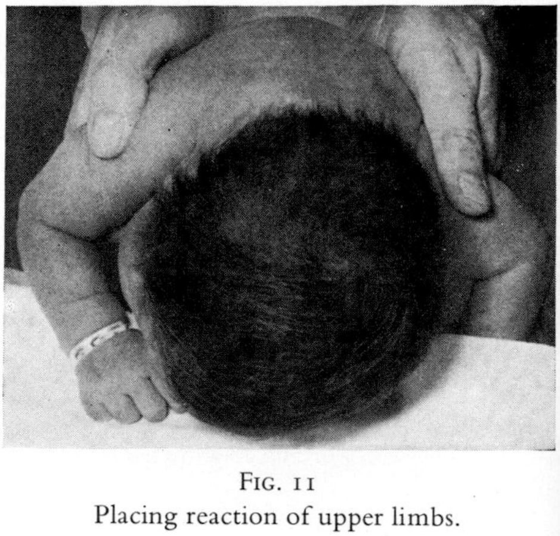

FIG. 11
Placing reaction of upper limbs.

FIG. 12
Galant's reflex (trunk incurvation).

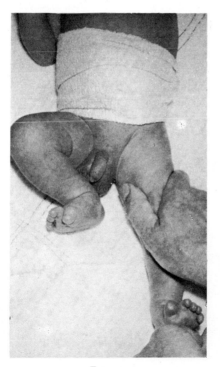

FIG. 13
Crossed extension reflex. First phase;
flexion of contralateral leg.

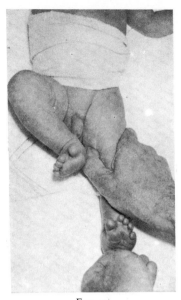

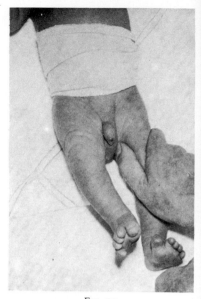

FIG. 14
Crossed extension reflex.
Second stage—Adduction.

FIG. 15
Crossed extension reflex.
Third stage—Extension.

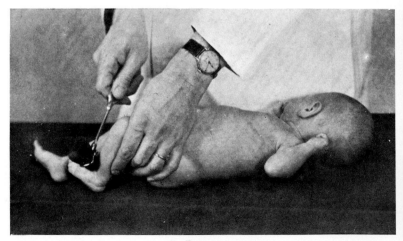

FIG. 16
Method of testing knee jerk. One begins by tapping over the dorsum of the
ankle and works up to the patellar tendon. The heel must be resting on the
couch, with the leg relaxed.

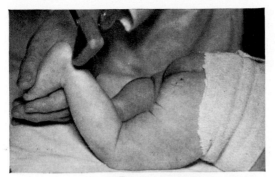

Fig. 17

Method of testing ankle jerk.

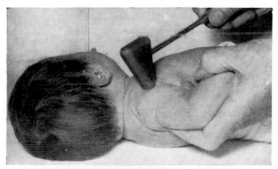

Fig. 18

Method of testing for biceps jerk—beginning over shoulder.

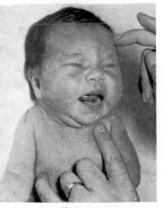

Fig. 19

Method of testing for McCarthy's reflex. (Baby crying, and therefore the response is not shown.)

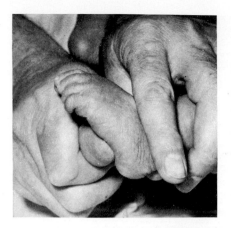

FIG. 20

Plantar response — incorrect method. Stimulation across sole of foot has elicited the grasp reflex.

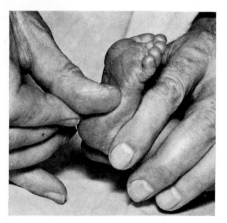

FIG. 21

Plantar response — correct method of eliciting it; stimulation of distal half of outside of foot.

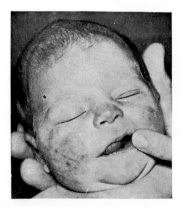

FIG. 22

Cardinal points reflex.

region, causes flexion of the trunk towards the side of the stimulus (Fig. 12).

The Perez Reflex

All newborn babies show this. When the child is in the prone or ventral suspension, pressure is applied upwards along the spine from the sacrum towards the head. The infant flexes the arms and legs, extends the neck and cries.

When the glutei are pricked on the outer side of the buttocks, the trunk flexes to the side stimulated.

Redressment Du Tronc

This is another reflex derived from the French workers. The baby is held with his back to the examiner. Firm stimulation of the soles of the feet causes extension at the hips and elevation of the trunk. The reflex appears at about 35 weeks' gestation, but extension of the spine does not begin until about 37 weeks.

The Tonic Neck Reflexes

These are asymmetrical and symmetrical. The asymmetrical one is the better known, and is seen at intervals in young babies in the first two months. When the child is in the supine position and not crying, he may be seen to lie with the head turned to one side with the arm extended to the same side. The contralateral knee is often flexed. In normal babies passive rotation of the head causes some increase of tone of the upper limb on the side to which the rotation occurs, but one rarely sees full extension of the limb. The reflex normally disappears by the age of 2 or 3 months. In severe cerebral palsy the reflex persists and may increase. One may see obvious extension of the arm when the head is passively rotated. These reflexes are important in determining the posture of the neonate.

The reflex is more marked in spastic babies, and persists longer than in normal babies. The reflex is partly responsible for preventing the child rolling from prone to supine or vice versa in the early weeks. According to Bobath[4,5] the reflex prevents the spastic child from moving the arms forward and from bringing his hands together in the midline or bringing his hands to his mouth. It impairs hand eye co-ordination, preventing him from holding his head in the midline. The symmetrical tonic neck reflex is evoked by flexion or extension of the neck.

On raising the head of a kneeling child, extensor tone increases in the arms, and flexor tone in the legs. If the reflex is strong, the child extends the arms and flexes the legs. Flexing the neck has the opposite effect. The influence of this reflex is seen in normal children when they raise the head and shoulders in the prone: it helps them to support themselves on the arms and to get on to hands and knees. The reflex disappears when they learn to crawl, a movement which demands independence of movement of the limbs from the position of the head. In cerebral palsy the reflex is usually overactive.   The child can only extend his arms in kneeling when the head is raised: the legs are then fixed in flexion.   As long as the head is raised the child is unable to extend his legs.   If the head is lowered, the arms flex, the legs extend and the child falls on his face, so that he is unable to crawl.

Tonic Labyrinthine Reflexes

These reflexes affect all four limbs and interact closely with the tonic neck reflexes.   Their action in normal children is uncertain, but in children with cerebral palsy they cause marked changes in muscle tone.   Their effect is most clearly seen on the head, shoulders, arms and trunk. While lying supine, the head of the child with cerebral palsy is pulled backwards and passive flexion may be strongly resisted.   In the prone position, flexion of the head, neck and spine occurs and passive raising of the head is resisted.

When the normal child of 4 months or more is in the prone position and the chin is passively raised, there is a protective extension of the arms, with the use of the hands for support.   In the child with cerebral palsy, the response depends on the relative predominance of the tonic labyrinth and symmetrical tonic neck reflexes.   If the former predominate, the child draws the arms up in flexion and remains in mid-air suspended by his head.   He cannot support his body weight on his arms.   He falls on his face when placed into the kneeling posture.   He cannot get on to his hands and knees and cannot raise his head and extend the spine.

If the symmetrical tonic neck reflex predominates, there is tonic extension of the arms with flexion of the legs.   If the head is flexed passively, the arms flex, the hips extend and the child falls on his face. He cannot crawl, because the legs show strong flexor spasticity as long as the head is raised.

RIGHTING REFLEXES

These make their appearance in a definite chronological order and are responsible for certain basic motor activities.   They enable the child to roll from prone to supine and supine to prone.   They help him to get on to his hands and knees and to sit up.   They are responsible for the ability to restore the normal position of the head in space and to maintain the normal postural relationship of the head, trunk and limbs during all activities.   The reflexes include: (a) Neck righting reflex.   This is present at birth and is strongest at the age of 3 months.   Turning of the head to one side is followed by movement of the body as a whole; (b) Labyrinth righting reflex acting on the head.   This is present at 2 months of age, and strongest at 10 months. It enables the child to lift the head up in the prone position (when 1 to

2 months old) and later when in the supine position; (c) The body
righting reflex, acting on the body. This appears at 7 to 12 months.
It modifies the neck righting reflex and plays an important rôle in the
child's early attempts to sit and stand. In severe cases of cerebral palsy the righting reflexes are absent.
The child cannot turn to one side, as the neck righting reflex is inhib-
ited by the tonic labyrinth reflex. The child cannot raise the head
in the supine or prone position. The child has great difficulty in
turning over and sitting up. In severe cases of cerebral palsy it will
be found that when the examiner attempts to flex the child's head,
holding the back of the head, there is strong resistance to flexion: the
head will extend and the whole back may arch.

THE LANDAU REFLEX

When the child is held in ventral suspension, the head, spine and
legs extend: when the head is depressed, the hip, knees and elbows
flex. According to Mitchell[23] the reaction is normally present
from the age of three months, is present in most infants in the second
six months, and becomes increasingly difficult to evoke after the age
of one year. Absence of the reflex over the age of three months is
seen in cases of motor weakness, cerebral palsy and mental deficiency.
He regarded the reflex as a combined effect of labyrinthine, neck and
visual reactions.

In many cases of cerebral palsy, the Landau reflex is absent, as the
child cannot lift the head in this position, owing to the inhibition of
the labyrinth righting reflex acting on the head by the tonic labyrinth
reflex. With the head flexed, the child has too much flexor activity
and is unable to extend the trunk and legs.

The Parachute Reaction

This appears at six to nine months and persists throughout life.
The reflex is elicited by holding the child in ventral suspension and
suddenly lowering him towards the couch. The arms extend as if
to protect him from falling. In children with cerebral palsy the
reflex is absent or incomplete owing to the strong flexor tone in this
position. In a child with hemiplegia the reflex would be normal on
the unaffected side.

The propping reactions are similar: from about five to seven
months, when the child in the sitting position is tilted to one side or
backwards, the arms extend to the appropriate position as if to protect
him from falling.

Tendon Reflexes

André Thomas paid surprisingly little attention to the knee jerks
and other tendon jerks, and did not regard them as being important.
I disagree with this attitude, because I consider that they provide

information of considerable value in developmental assessment. When the knee jerk is elicited in a newborn infant, there is commonly an associated adduction of the opposite leg. When the knee jerk is not obtained, the adduction of the opposite leg may occur alone. The jerks may be absent in a severely shocked child or in a child who has a brain defect. They are exaggerated in the spastic form of cerebral palsy. The most useful tendon jerks and the easiest to test are the biceps, supinator jerks and knee jerks. They are likely to be exaggerated in the spastic form of cerebral palsy. In diseases of the pyramidal tracts the area over which the tendon jerks are obtained is greatly increased— just as in older children the area over which the plantar response is obtained is increased. Consequently one begins to test for the biceps jerk over the shoulder, and tap at intervals until the biceps tendon is reached. One begins to test for the knee jerk by tapping over the dorsum of the foot. One taps at intervals up the leg until the patellar tendon is reached. A brisk response over the shoulder may be the only indication that there is involvement of the upper limbs in a child previously thought to have a spastic paraplegia: a brisk response over the dorsum of the foot raises the suspicion of the spastic form of cerebral palsy. Asymmetry of muscle tone or of tendon jerks is likely to denote neurological damage, though it will not necessarily be permanent. The response must be interpreted in association with the findings. One should determine how long a reflex remains abnormal. Apparent variations from the normal may be only temporary and must not be taken to indicate permanent neurological disease.

Ankle Clonus

Ankle clonus is elicited by flexion and abduction of the hip, flexion of the knee, and then rapid but gentle dorsiflexion of the ankle to elicit the stretch reflex. The test should be carried out only when one feels that the limb is relaxed and the child is not resisting. Ankle clonus is an indication that the muscle tone is more marked than usual, but it by no means necessarily signifies disease, even if the clonus is fairly well sustained. The finding of unusually brisk tendon jerks and ankle clonus is merely an indication that the child should be re-examined in a month or two. It is true that the older the child with ankle clonus in the early weeks, the more likely it is to be significant. The diagnosis of cerebral palsy or other abnormality must never be made on the finding of single signs (such as unusually brisk tendon jerks with or without ankle clonus), but only on a combination of signs (see Chapter 17).

Superficial Reflexes

Harlem and Lönnum[15a] have shown that the abdominal reflexes can always be obtained in the newborn baby. They studied two hundred full term infants, allowing the child to suck a pacifier if desired, and using a blunt needle as the stimulant. If the baby was crying they waited for him to quieten. They found that the reflex was reduced if there was abdominal distension. In that case they retested after the distension had disappeared. The reflex was difficult to obtain if the skin were dry, and in that case they oiled the skin.

In addition to the usual contraction of the abdominal muscles, as seen in adults, there is commonly a curving of the trunk to the affected side, with a tendency to contraction of the muscles on the opposite side. The response is more extensive than in adults, and the zone over which the reflex is obtained is wider. During or immediately after the response there is commonly flexion of the homolateral leg or of both legs. The reflex was not obtained in babies with serious cerebral lesions.

The Palmomental and Similar Reflexes

Babkin described a reflex consisting of opening of the mouth when the infant's palm is pressed. When the thenar or hypothenar eminences are stroked, there may be contraction of the chin muscles and uplifting of the leg. When the child is asleep in the supine position, and the neck is touched, the hand strokes it while the head rotates. If the right ear is touched, the left hand strokes the neck. If the nose is tickled, both hands reach for the face. The reflex is usually present in the first three years, but may persist longer in mentally retarded children.[17]

Head Thrust Responses

The baby is held in the sitting position, with the body leaning slightly backwards. A hand placed against the back of the head thrusts the head forwards. The head opposes the movement.

When the baby is held in the sitting position, slightly leaning to one side, the head is flexed to that side. When the head is pushed to the other side, there is strong resistance by the lateral flexor muscles.

Thomas remarked that this response is marked even in premature babies, though there is a notable head wobble when the body is passively moved. There is a less marked response when the head is thrust backwards when the child is held sitting with the body flexed. The reaction to thrust increases as the child matures and the head wobble decreases.

The Jaw Jerk

Tapping the chin causes elevation of the mandible.

Other Reflexes

When the baby is held under the armpits and shaken, the head wobbles in all directions, but the limbs do not move.   The opposite occurs in the older child.

Stimulation in the temporal region causes rotation of the head to the opposite side.

Vollmer[37] described a reflex consisting of a vigorous cry, flexion of extremities, lordosis of the spine and elevation of the head, when the infant, held in ventral suspension, is firmly stroked down the spine. It is said to be present in the first months and it disappears by the age of three months.   This corresponds to the Perez reflex (p. 87).

André Thomas described a reflex in the hand.   Stimulation of the ulnar border of the closed hand causes extension of the digits, beginning with the little finger.

Rubbing the ear causes rotation of the head to the opposite side.

Kratschmer's reflex consists of respiratory arrest when the baby experiences a bad smell.

Infants exhibit a protective skin reflex after about ten days.   They scratch the skin if there is an itch.   Peiper remarked that a child is seriously ill if he cannot keep flies off the face.

Other Reactions

Psychologists are perhaps somewhat belatedly finding that the human newborn infant is a fascinating creature to study and that there is much that we do not know about him and about the development of his mind.   They are using several sophisticated methods of studying his responses.[9,11]   For instance the newborn turns his eyes to sound and can be seen to localise smell by turning away from an unpleasant one.   In one study when a mother spoke through a glass screen, the baby could see her but only hear her by means of two stereo speakers: the balance on the stereo system could be adjusted so that the sound could appear to come from straight ahead or from other positions.   The baby was seen to be contented if the sound appeared to come from straight ahead, but if the mother's voice and mouth, as seen by the baby, did not coincide, the baby was disturbed.[6,7]   The infant therefore shows auditory localisation, auditory-visual co-ordination, and expectation that the sound comes from the mouth.

The newborn baby can adjust to distance: if an object is moved towards his face he pulls his head back in defence.   This was shown not to be due to movement of air, because he shows the same response to a visual object on the screen.

It has long been known that conditioning can be developed during the first week.   A three day old infant can learn to turn his head to one side to obtain a reward when a bell sounds and to the opposite side when a buzzer sounds.   A three week old baby may imitate tongue protrusion, mouth or finger movement, indicating that he has some body image.

A newborn baby will look at black and white patterns longer than an equally bright but non-patterned gray patch; he will look at a black on white drawing of a face longer than three black dots on white.[10] Habituation occurs, for when he sees the pattern repeatedly he turns away to look at a new one. Psychologists have studied the amount of time infants spend on looking at patterns or objects at a fixed distance from the eyes. It has been noted that as early as two weeks of age infants watch their mother's face longer than a stranger's face. Infants respond to patterned (square wave) tones and to the human voice more than to pure (sine wave) tones: habituation occurs, and they then show renewed response if the tone or frequency changes.

McCall[18] discussed the study of habituation and dishabituation in infants. A stimulus is repeatedly presented, and a progressive decline in attention indicates habituation. When a new stimulus is applied, dishabituation is indicated by an increment in attention. McCall analysed this phenomenon; he noted that the child has to remember, and it is not merely a matter of fatigue; the speed at which habituation occurs increases with the maturity of the baby: it is slower in the case of infants of the uneducated class, or of infants with a low Apgar score. He suggested that habituation and the response to differing stimuli reflect cognitive processes, the processing of perceptional information, the acquisition of memory engrams and the retrieval of such memories to evaluate new stimuli. The rate of habituation at 3 months was said to correlate with Binet tests at three and a half years.

Various electronic devices are being used to monitor an infant's behaviour, meaning the physical activity, the response to different sounds and objects seen. Devices are used to study infant–mother interaction and synchrony[19]—with particular regard to the infant watching his mother as she talks to him, later smiling and later still vocalising in response to her overtures.

On reading the fascinating studies being carried out by psychologists, one feels, perhaps wrongly, that they tend to disregard the wide differences in the maturity of babies in the newborn period—even if they are born at term. Newborn babies are going to grow up to have widely differing levels of intelligence: to some extent these differences are reflected in their early responses. For instance, I cannot believe that a mentally defective baby would smile at his mother in response to her overtures when he is four or five days old, but I have seen this in the case of babies who later proved to be mentally superior. On hundreds of occasions one has seen babies who only began to smile at a later than usual age, and who almost invariably turned out to be mentally subnormal. To a considerable extent some of these early responses depend on the maturation of the nervous system. These differences are apparently not taken into consideration by psychologists studying the newborn; and sophisticated tests such as they are new developing may well turn out to be good indicators of future potential.

In 1928 Aldrich conditioned a response to pain in the form of pin scratch on the sole of the foot in association with the sound of a dinner gong: the babies were three months old. Morgan and Morgan[24] puffed air into the face of babies and obtained a wink: five seconds later they watched to see if a further wink occurred in anticipation— and a further puff was given. Forty two babies were tested: all but one responded by 65 days of age, but the response could not be established in any before 54 days. Rendle-Short[30], experimenting with conditioning stimulated by a puff of air, found that the younger the baby, the more difficult it was to establish a conditioned response:' in early infancy 100 to 300 paired stimuli might be needed, while at 12 months two or three were sufficient. The subject was reviewed by Gollin[14] with references to previous work.

Summary

There are numerous reflex responses in the newborn. They are of considerable neurological interest. The value of many of these for clinical assessment is as yet in doubt.

For practical purposes the reflexes which provide important information for developmental diagnosis are mainly the following:
The moro reflex.
The grasp reflex.
The asymmetrical tonic neck reflex.
The biceps and knee jerks and the plantar response.
Absence of the sucking and swallowing reflex except in the small premature baby suggests a neurological defect.

In the management of cerebral palsy other reflexes are important. They include the tonic neck and labyrinthine reflexes.

REFERENCES

1. ANDERSON, R. B., ROSENBLITH, J. F. (1968) Photic Sneeze Reflex in the Human Newborn. *Develop. Psychobiology*, **1**, 65.
2. BENCH, J., COLLYER, T., LANGFORD, C., TOMS, R. (1972). A comparison between the neonatal sound-evoked startle response and the head-drop (Moro) reflex. *Develop. Med. Child Neurol.* **14**, 308.
3. BENSON, P. F. (1962) Transient Unilateral External Rectus Muscle Palsy in newborn Infants. *Brit. med. J.*, **1**, 1054.
4. BOBATH, K., BOBATH, B. (1955) Tonic Reflexes and Righting Reflexes in the diagnosis and Assessment of Cerebral Palsy. *Cerebr. Palsy Bull.*, **16**, No. 5.
5. BOBATH, K., BOBATH, B. (1956) The diagnosis of Cerebral Palsy in Infancy. *Arch. Dis. Childh.*, **31**, 408.
6. BOWER, T. (1974). Competent newborns. *New Scientist* **61**, 672.
7. BOWER T. (1974) Development of Infant Behaviour. *British Medical Bulletin.* **30**, 175.
8. BRAIN, R., WILKINSON, M. (1959) Observations on the Extensor Plantar Reflex and its Relationship to the Functions of the Pyramidal Tract. *Brain*, **82**, 297.
9. BRYANT P., (1974) Infants' Inferences. *New Scientist.* **62**, 68.
10. CARPENTER, G. (1974) Mother's face and the newborn. *New Scientist.* **61**, 742.

11. Costello, A. (1974) Are Mothers Stimulating? *New Scientist*, **62**, 316.
12. Dennis, W. (1934) A Description and Classification of the Responses of the Newborn Infant. *Psychol. Bull.*, **31**, 5.
13. Dubowitz, V. (1965) Asymmetrical Moro Response in Neurologically Normal Infants. *Develop. Med. child. Neurol.*, **7**, 244.
14. Gollin, E. S. (1967) Research trends in infant learning. In Hellmuth, J. *Exceptional Infant*. Seattle. Special Child Publications.
15. Gordon, M. B. (1929) The Moro Embrace Reflex in Infancy: its Incidence and Significance. *Amer. J. Dis. Child.*, **38**, 26.
15a Harlem, O. K., Lönnum, A. (1957) A Clinical Study of the Abdominal Skin Reflexes in Newborn Infants. *Arch. Dis. Childh.*, **32**, 127.
16. Hogan, G. R., Milligan, J. E. (1971) The plantar reflex of the newborn. *New Engl. J. Med.*, **285**, 502.
17. Little, T. M., Masotti, R. E. (1974) The palmo-mental reflex in normal and mentally retarded subjects. *Develop. Med. Child Neurol.* **16**, 59.
18. McCall, R. B. (1971) Behavioural and other measurements in the neonate. *Proc. Roy. Soc. Med.* **64**, 465.
18a. McGraw, M. B. (1937). The Moro Reflex. *Amer. J. Dis. Child.*, **54**, 240.
19. Macfarlane, A. (1974). If a smile is so important. *New Scientist.* **62**, 164.
20. MacKeith, R. C. (1965) The Placing Response and Primary Walking. *Guy's Hosp. Gaz.*, **79**, 394.
21. Minkowski, A., Saint-anne Dargassies, S. (1956) Le Retentissement de l'Anoxie Foetale sur le Systeme Nerveux Central. *Rev. franc. Etud. clin. biol.*, **1**, 531.
22. Mitchell, R. G. (1960) The Moro Reflex. *Cerebr. Palsy Bull.*, **2**, 135.
23. Mitchell, R. G. (1962) The Landau Reaction. *Develop. Med. Child Neurol.*, **4**, 65.
24. Morgan, J. J. B., Morgan, S. S. (1944). Infant learning as a developmental index. *J. Genet. Psychol.* **66**, 281.
25. Paine, R. S. (1960) Neurologic Examination of Infants and Children. *Pediat. Clin. N. Amer.*, **7**, 471.
26. Parmelee, A. H. (1964) Critical Evaluation of the Moro Reflex. *Pediatrics*, **33**, 773.
27. Peiper, A. (1949) *Die Eigenart der Kindichen Hirntatigkeit*. Leipzig: Thieme.
28. Peiper, A. (1963) *Cerebral Function in Infancy and Childhood*. London. Pitman.
29. Pratt, K. C. (1954) *Manual of Child Psychology*. Ed. L. Carmichael. 2nd ed. Chap. 4. London: Chapman & Hall.
30. Rendle-Short, J. (1961). The Puff test. *Arch. Dis. Childh.* **36**, 50.
31. Saint-anne Dargassies. (1954) Methode d'Examen Neurologique du Nouveau-né. *Etud. néo-natal*, **3**, 101.
32. Schaffer, R. (1974). Behavioural Synchrony in infancy. *New Scientist.* **62**, 16.
33. Stirnimann, F. (1943) Ueber den Moroschen Umklammerungs-Reflex beim Neugenborenen. *Ann. Paediat. (Buseg)*, **160**, 1.
34. Taft, L. T., Cohen, H. J. (1967) Neonatal and infant reflexology in Hellmuth, J. Exceptional Infant, Vol. 1. Seattle: Special Child Publications.
35. Thomas, A., Chesni, Y., Saint-anne Dargassies. (1960) The Neurological Examination of the Infant. *Little Club Clin. develop. Med.*, **1**.
36. Vajnorsky, J., Brachfeld, K., Strakova, M. (1958) A Contribution to the Reflexes of the Newborn Period. *Cs. Pediat.*, **13**, 277.
37. Vollmer, H. (1948) A New Reflex in Young Infants. *Amer. J. Dis. Child.*, **95**, 481.
38. Willemse, J. (1961) *De Motoriek van de Pasgeborene in de Eerste Levensuren*. Utrecht: Bisleveld.
39. Zapella, M. (1963) Placing Reaction in Newborn. *Develop. Med. child. Neurol.*, **5**, 497.
40. Zapella, M., Foley, J., Cookson, M. (1964) The Placing and Supporting Reactions in Children with Mental Retardation. *J. ment. Defic. Res.*, **8**, 1.

CHAPTER 6

THE ASSESSMENT OF MATURITY

In the past, the term 'premature baby' was taken to include all babies who at birth weighed 5½ lbs or less at birth (2500 g), irrespective of the duration of gestation. This definition is no longer acceptable, because of the obvious fact that many babies weigh less than 2500 g at birth though born at term. Others, though born before term, are smaller than the average for the duration of gestation. It is usual now to refer to those born before 37 weeks of gestation as 'pre-term' babies, and to those weighing 2500 g or less as 'low birth-weight' babies. Low birth weight in relation to the duration of gestation may be due to malnutrition, abnormalities of the placenta, hereditary or other factors. The behaviour of the 'small for dates' baby is different at birth from the truly premature baby of the same birth weight, and because the prognosis with regard to subsequent mental and physical development is different, it is of importance to recognise the distinguishing physical and neurological features.

A baby may be 'small for dates' and also born prematurely. For instance, a baby of 36 weeks gestation may weigh only 3 lbs. 8 ozs. (1590 g). The average weight at birth in relation to the duration of gestation in England and Wales is as follows:

28 weeks	..	2 lbs 4 ozs	..	1023 g
32 weeks	..	3 lbs 8 ozs	..	1590 g
36 weeks	..	5 lbs 3 ozs	..	2358 g
40 weeks	..	7 lbs 8 ozs	..	3410 g

I am told that in Finland the mean weights are considerably higher than in England and Wales.

The distinction between the 'small for dates' and 'premature' baby is of more than academic interest. A mother's dates may not be accurate, and it is useful to be able to check her dates by an objective examination. It may be important for assessment for adoption or for medicolegal reasons to be able to assess a baby's development. If one carries out an examination at 17 weeks, and one does not know whether the 1590 g baby was 8 weeks premature or born at term, one cannot assess his development. One does not know whether to compare him with an average 17 week old baby, or with a baby of 17 − 8 i.e. 9 week old infant. For the knowledge of this subject we are indebted to the French workers[17] [18]. The following are the main differences between a premature baby and a full term one (see Table 3, for summary). Wherever possible I have included illustrations of the points described, but have not referred to the figure numbers in the text.

1. *The premature baby sleeps for the most part of the day and night.*

The full term baby may also sleep for a large part of the twenty-four hours, but not as much as the average premature baby.

2. *The Cry.* The premature baby cries infrequently; the cry is feeble and not prolonged. The cry of the full term baby is more prolonged and vigorous.

3. *Movements.* The premature baby shows faster, wilder and more bizarre movements of the limbs, with writhing of the trunk. The full term baby shows more frequent movements, which are more co-ordinated than those of the premature baby. The 28 to 32 week premature infant does not move one limb at a time, movement being generalised; the full term baby commonly moves one limb.

4. *Feeding Behaviour.* The premature baby cannot be relied upon to demand feeds, while the normal full term baby can. The premature baby may be unable to suck or swallow. He is liable to regurgitate and to inhale feeds, with resultant cyanotic attacks when being fed. Mouthing reflexes are difficult to elicit in the infant born before about 34 weeks of gestation: they are easily obtained in the full term baby.

5. *Muscle Tone.* The muscle tone of the premature baby is less than that of the full term infant. Muscle tone increases first in the legs (by about seven and a half months of gestation) and later in the arms.

6. *Posture.* In the prone position the premature baby characteristically lies flat on the couch, with the pelvis low and the knees at the side of the abdomen, the hips being acutely flexed. The full term baby lies with the pelvis high and the knees drawn up under the abdomen.

In the supine position the twenty-eight week premature baby lies with the lower limbs extended and the hips abducted, so that the limbs are flat on the couch, in a 'froglike' attitude. The upper limbs lie in a similar position. The thirty-two week premature baby lies with the arms extended, but with the lower limbs flexed at the knee and abducted at the hip. The thirty-six week premature lies less froglike, mainly flexed. The full term infant lies with the limbs strongly flexed. The head in the twenty-eight to thirty-two week infant is turned to one side. The full term baby tends to keep the head aligned with the trunk.

7. *Head Rotation.* In the twenty-eight week premature baby the head can be rotated so far that the chin is well beyond the acromion: in the full term baby the chin can rotate only as far as the acromion.

8. *The Scarf Sign.* This depends on the deltoids, teres major and rhomboids. During the test the baby should be comfortable, in the supine position, with the head central. The hand is led across the chest to the opposite side of the neck. The hand of the twenty-eight week premature baby reaches well past the acromion: that of the full term baby does not go beyond the acromion. In the poster-

ior scarf sign, which depends on the pectoralis major and latissimus dorsi, the hand is led behind the neck to the opposite side. There is a similar difference in the range achieved in the premature and full term baby.

9. *The Moro Reflex.* This is present in premature babies, except the very small ones, but the arms tend to fall backwards on to the table during the adduction phase because the antigravity muscles are weaker than in the full term baby.

10. *Wrist Flexion.* Flexion of the wrist of the 28 week premature baby is incomplete, so that a 'window' is formed between the hand and the forearm; that of the full term baby is complete, so that the hand is in contact with the forearm.

11. *The Grasp Reflex.* This is difficult to obtain in the twenty-eight week premature baby. There is no flexion of the elbow or contraction of muscles at the shoulder. In the full term baby the elbow and shoulder take an active part in the response.

The grasp reflex is at its strongest at forty weeks.

12. '*Redressement du Tronc*'—so called by the French writers—. When the infant is held with his back to one the young premature baby cannot extend the trunk. At thirty-five weeks' gestation the back begins to extend: at thirty-seven weeks the back extends and the child extends the neck, as in the case of the full term infant.

13. *Crossed Extension Reflex.* (Chapter 5). The reflex is incomplete in the young premature baby. In the case of the twenty-eight week premature baby there is flexion of the opposite leg without extension or adduction. In the case of a thirty-two week baby some extension occurs after flexion: in the thirty-six week baby slight adduction follows the extension.

14. *Knee Extension.* When the hip is flexed so that the thigh is in contact with the side of the abdomen, the knee of the young premature baby can be fully extended. As maturity increases from twenty-eight weeks' gestation, less and less extension is obtained. In the full term baby extension is incomplete by about 20°.

15. *Dorsiflexion of the foot.* In the twenty-eight week premature baby, dorsiflexion is incomplete, so that there is a fairly wide gap between the foot and the foreleg. In the full term baby the foot is brought into contact with the front of the leg.

16. *The Grasp Reflex in the Foot.* This is much weaker in the premature baby than in the full term one.

17. *The Walking Reflex.* This is very feeble in the twenty-eight week premature baby, but it is easily elicited in the thirty-six week baby and the full term one. The thirty-two week premature baby usually walks on the toes, whereas the full term baby walks with the foot flat on the couch.

18. *Ventral Suspension.* Held in ventral suspension, the young premature baby hangs limply, with no extension of the spine or neck,

and with no flexion of the elbows, hips or knees.   The full term baby has a straighter back, holds the head up a little, and flexes the elbows and knees and slightly extends the hips.

One of the French workers, Claudine Amiel-Tison,[1] has written a brief clear account of her method of assessing the maturity of the baby, basing the method largely on the assessment of tone.

Robinson[16] carried out 219 neurological examinations on 62 infants having a gestation period varying from 25 to 42 weeks.   He found that the five most useful tests of gestational age were the reactions of the pupil to light, consistently absent under 29 weeks and present after 31 weeks, the glabellar tap reflex, which is absent before 32 weeks and present after 34 weeks, the traction test for head lag, which is positive after 33 weeks, the neck righting reflex, which causes the trunk to rotate when the examiner rotates the head, present by 34–37 weeks, and the turning of the head to light, by 32 to 36 weeks.

Farr[10] used 10 signs in her attempt to estimate the gestational age; they were the degree of motor activity, reaction of the pupil to light, rate of sucking, closure of the mouth when sucking, stripping action of the tongue, passive resistance, forearm recoil, plantar grasp, the pitch and the intensity of the cry.   We found that the reaction of the pupil to light is a difficult sign to elicit in the newborn baby.

Experience has shown that there is a significant degree of variation in the age at which these neurological signs appear.   In consequence it seems reasonable to advocate that an assessment should never be made on the basis of single signs, but on a combination of signs.   For instance, if ten signs are tested for, the mean maturational age for the total of the ten should be calculated.

Parkin[14] reviewed the various methods of assessing the maturity, including the date of the last menstrual period, quickening, the size of the uterus, vaginal cytology, the examination of the amniotic fluid for cells, sodium, creatinine and bilirubin: x-ray for ossification centres; ultrasonic fetal cephalometry, measurement of the head circumference, the length of the child, the chest circumference and the skin folds.   He studied the amount of vernix, the texture of a fold of abdominal skin, the colour of the skin, oedema, lanugo, the length and texture of the nails, the firmness of the ears, breast size, the localisation of the testes, prominence of the labia minora, the hardness of the skull, and the creases on the soles of the feet.   He found that if the skin was pink, the gestational age was unlikely to be less than 36 weeks; if pale, 40 weeks.   If all the vernix was off, it was unlikely to be less than 39 weeks; if there were areas of baldness—no less than 37 weeks; if the testes were fully descended—not less than 36 weeks: if the breast is palpable, not less than 34 weeks. The most useful signs were the skin colour and texture, the breast size and the firmness of the ears, in combination.

tests and eliminated tests which were difficult to elicit. They found that it was often difficult to observe the pupillary reflex, because the baby is apt to close his eyes: and they find that the neck Dubowitz and his colleagues at Sheffield[5,6,12,13] have refined the righting reflex was sometimes unsatisfactory. The glabellar tap reflex was present in all infants over 30 weeks gestation, and so was of little value. They showed, as did Finnström[11] that a combination of physical and neurological features gave the highest degree of accuracy. Moosa and Dubowitz[12,13], also working at Sheffield, showed that the motor nerve conduction velocity gave an accurate estimate of gestational age; and that it gave a good guide as to gestational age even six months after birth. It has been said that the maturation of visual evoked responses is valuable for distinguishing the premature baby from the small-for-dates infant. They gave a score of 0 to 4 to various items, as shown in figure 51 and table 3.

SOME NOTES ON TECHNIQUES OF ASSESSMENT OF NEUROLOGIC CRITERIA

POSTURE: Observed with infant quiet and in supine position.   Score 0: Arms and legs extended; 1: beginning of flexion of hips and knees, arms extended; 2: stronger flexion of legs, arms extended; 3: arms slightly flexed, legs flexed and abducted; 4: full flexion of arms and legs.

SQUARE WINDOW: The hand is flexed on the forearm between the thumb and index finger of the examiner (Fig. 3).   Enough pressure is applied to get as full a flexion as possible, and the angle between the hypothenar eminence and the ventral aspect of the forearm is measured and graded according to diagram.   (Care is taken not to rotate the infant's wrist while doing this manoeuvre.)

ANKLE DORSIFLEXION: The foot is dorsiflexed onto the anterior aspect of the leg, with the examiner's thumb on the sole of the foot and other fingers behind the leg (Fig. 4).   Enough pressure is applied to get as full flexion as possible, and the angle between the dorsum of the foot and the anterior aspect of the leg is measured.

ARM RECOIL: With the infant in the supine position the forearms are first flexed for 5 seconds, then fully extended by pulling on the hands, and then released.   The sign is fully positive if the arms return briskly to full flexion (Score 2).   If the arms return to incomplete flexion or the response is sluggish it is graded as Score 1.   If they remain extended or are only followed by random movements the score is 0.

LEG RECOIL: With the infant supine, the hips and knees are fully flexed for 5 seconds, then extended by traction on the feet, and released.   A maximal response is one of full flexion of the hips and knees (Score 2).   A partial flexion scores 1, and minimal or no movement scores 0.

POPLITEAL ANGLE: With the infant supine and his pelvis flat on the examining couch, the thigh is held in the knee-chest position by the examiner's left index finger and thumb supporting the knee.   The leg is then extended by gentle pressure from the examiner's right index finger behind the ankle and the popliteal angle is measured.

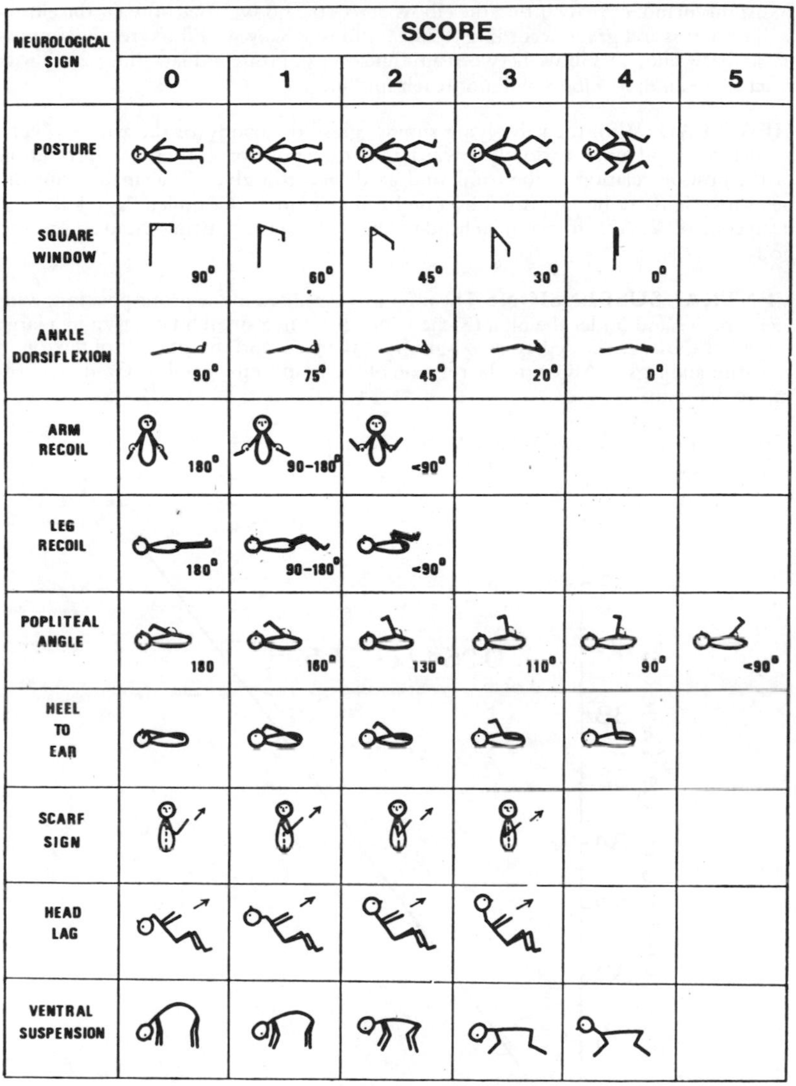

FIG 51

HEEL TO EAR MANOEUVRE: With the baby supine, draw the baby's foot as near to the head as it will go without forcing it. Observe the distance between the foot and the head as well as the degree of extension at the knee. Grade according to diagram. Note that the knee is left free and may draw down alongside the abdomen.

SCARF SIGN: With the baby supine, take the infant's hand and try to put it around the neck and as far posteriorly as possible around the opposite shoulder.

Assist this manoeuvre by lifting the elbow across the body.   See how far the elbow will go across and grade according to illustrations.   Score 0: Elbow reaches opposite axillary line; 1: Elbow between midline and opposite axillary line; 2: Elbow reaches midline; 3: Elbow will not reach midline.

HEAD LAG: With the baby lying supine, grasp the hands (or the arms if a very small infant) and pull him slowly towards the sitting position.   Observe the position of the head in relation to the trunk and grade accordingly.   In a small infant the head may initially be supported by one hand.   Score 0: Complete lag; 1: Partial head control; 2: Able to maintain head in line with body; 3: Brings head anterior to body.

VENTRAL SUSPENSION: The infant is suspended in the prone position, with examiner's hand under the infant's chest (one hand in a small infant, two in a large infant).   Observe the degree of extension of the back and the amount of flexion of the arms and legs.   Also note the relation of the head to the trunk.   Grade according to diagrams.

If score differs on the two sides, take the mean.

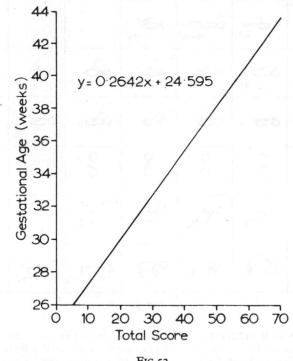

$$y = 0.2642x + 24.595$$

FIG 52

Their scoring system has proved to be a reliable technique.   The paediatric residents at the Jessop Hospital for Women at Sheffield carry out the assessment as a routine on all babies born in the hospital,

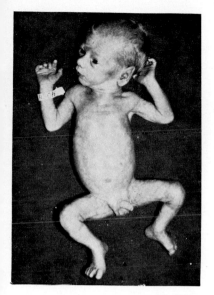

FIG. 23
Premature baby, supine.

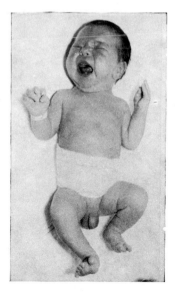

FIG. 24
Full term baby, supine, flexed
position.

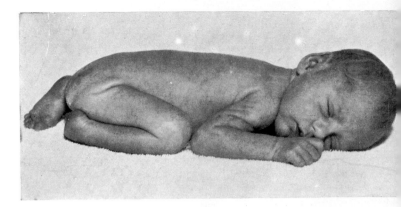

FIG. 25
For comparison with Fig. 26.
Prone position in premature baby. (At 9 weeks before term.)
Hips abducted, but flexed; pelvis less high than in full term baby.

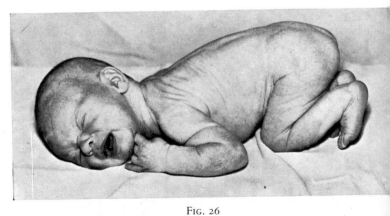

FIG. 26
Prone position, full term baby. (Above 0-2 weeks of age.)
Pelvis high, knees drawn up under abdomen.

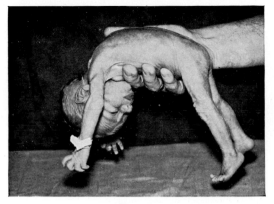

FIG. 27
Premature baby, ventral suspension.

FIG. 28
Full term baby, ventral suspension.

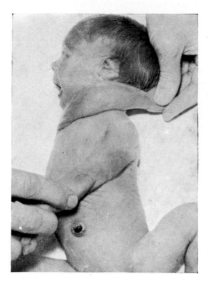

FIG. 29
Scarf sign. Premature baby. Note
position of elbow and hand.

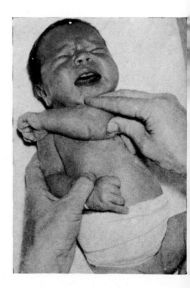

FIG. 30
Scarf sign. Full term baby. Note
position of elbow and hand.

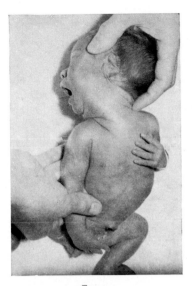

FIG. 31
Premature baby. Head rotation.
Chin beyond tip of shoulder.

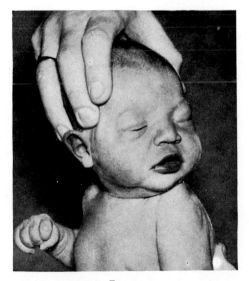

FIG. 32
Range of head rotation. Full term baby.
Chin on acromion.

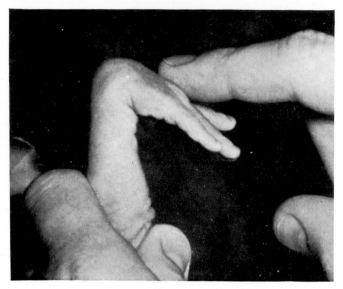

FIG. 33
Window sign, premature baby.

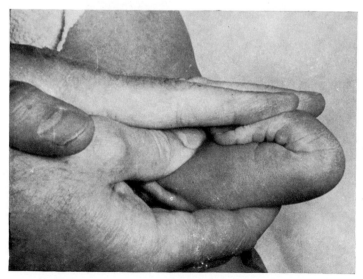

FIG. 34
Window sign, full term baby.

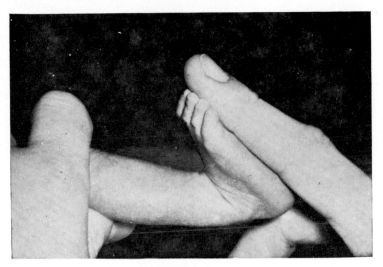

FIG. 35
Dorsiflexion of foot; premature baby.

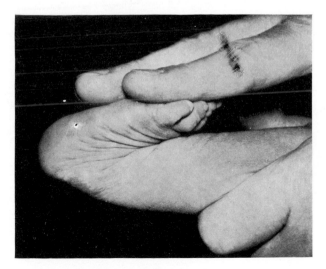

FIG. 36
Dorsiflexion of foot; full term baby.

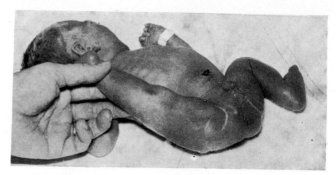

Fig. 37
Premature baby, hip flexed, full knee extension.

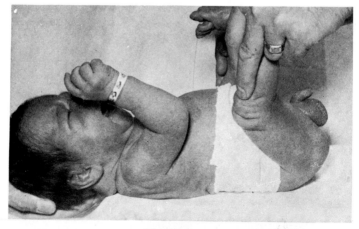

Fig. 38
Full term baby, hip flexed, limited knee extension.

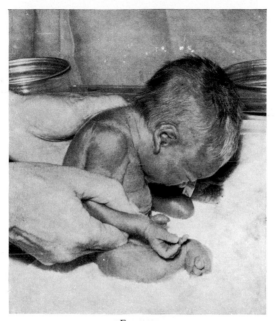

FIG. 39

Premature baby, sitting position.

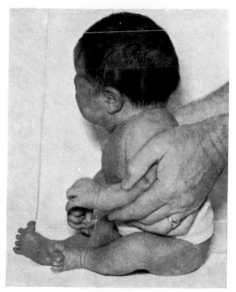

FIG. 40

Full term baby, sitting position.

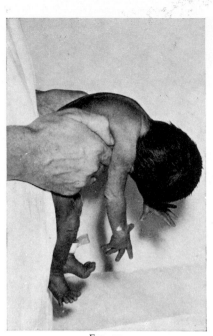

FIG. 41

Redressement du Tronc, premature baby. Unable
to straighten back.

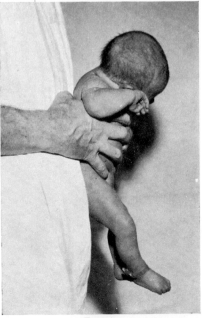

FIG. 42

Redressement du Tronc, full term baby. Straightens back.

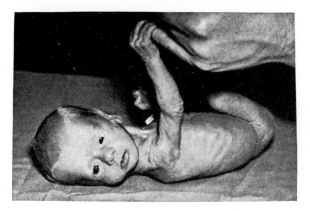

FIG. 43
Grasp reflex, premature baby.

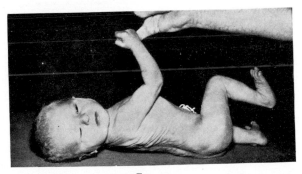

FIG. 44
Grasp reflex, full term baby.

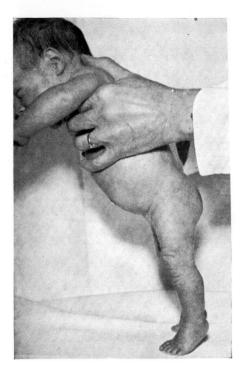

FIG. 45
Premature baby, 30 weeks
gestation, birth weight 3 lbs. 3 oz.
(1443g) 9 weeks after birth.
Standing on toes.

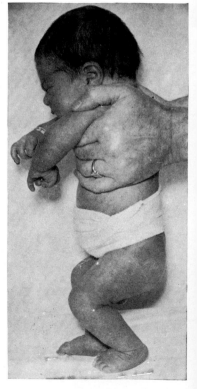

FIG. 46
Full term baby, sole of foot flat on
couch.

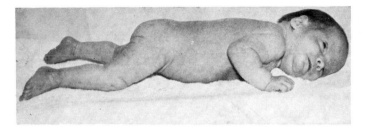

FIG. 47

Prone. Same baby as Figure 45. Compare full term, Figure 26, and
premature baby, Figure 25, and 6 weeks' baby, Figure 72.

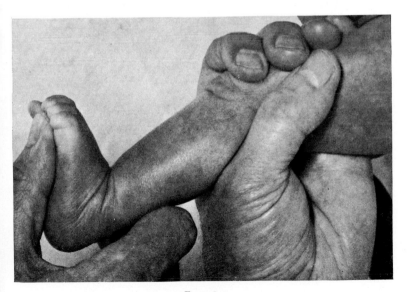

FIG. 48

Same baby as Figure 45.
Dorsiflexion of foot. Compare full term baby, Figure 36.

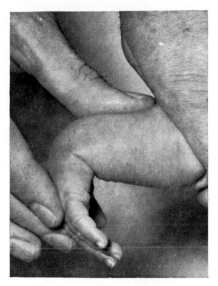

FIG. 49
Flexion of wrist. Same baby as Figure 45.
Compare full term baby, Figure 34.

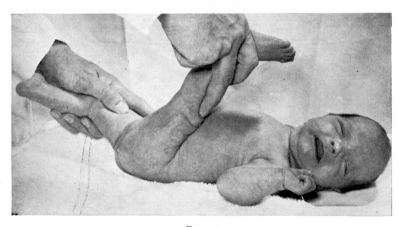

FIG. 50
Hip flexed, extension of knee. Same baby as Figure 45. Compare full term
baby, Figure 38.

TABLE 3

Scoring system for external criteria

External sign	Score*				
	0	1	2	3	4
Edema	Obvious edema of hands and feet; pitting over tibia	No obvious edema of hands and feet; pitting over tibia	No edema		
Skin texture	Very thin, gelatinous	Thin and smooth	Smooth; medium; thickness. Rash or superficial peeling	Slight thickening. Superficial cracking and peeling especially of hands and feet	Thick and parchment-like; superficial or deep cracking
Skin color	Dark red	Uniformly pink	Pale pink; variable over body	Pale; only pink over ears, lips, palms, or soles	
Skin opacity (trunk)	Numerous veins and venules clearly seen, especially over abdomen	Veins and tributaries seen	A few large vessels clearly seen over abdomen	A few large vessels seen indistinctly over abdomen	No blood vessels seen
Lanugo (over back)	No lanugo	Abundant; long and thick over whole back	Hair thinning especially over lower back	Small amount of lanugo and bald areas	At least $\frac{1}{2}$ of back devoid of lanugo
Plantar creases	No skin creases	Faint red marks over anterior half of sole	Definite red marks over anterior $\frac{1}{2}$; indentations over anterior $\frac{1}{3}$	Indentations over anterior $\frac{1}{3}$	Definite deep indentations over anterior $\frac{1}{3}$
Nipple formation	Nipple barely visible; no areola	Nipple well defined; areola smooth and flat, diameter 0.75 cm.	Areola stippled, edge not raised, diameter 0.75 cm.	Areola stippled, edge raised, diameter 0.75 cm.	
Breast size	No breast tissue palpable	Breast tissue on one or both sides, 0.5 cm. diameter	Breast tissue both sides; one or both 0.5-1.0 cm.	Breast tissue both sides; one or both 1 cm.	
Ear form	Pinna flat and shapeless, little or no incurving of edge	Incurving of part of edge of pinna	Partial incurving whole of upper pinna	Well-defined incurving whole of upper pinna	
Ear firmness	Pinna soft, easily folded, no recoil	Pinna soft, easily folded, slow recoil	Cartilage to edge of pinna, but soft in places, ready recoil	Pinna firm, cartilage to edge; instant recoil	
Genitals Male	Neither testis in scrotum	At least one testis high in scrotum	At least one testis right down		
Female (with hips $\frac{1}{2}$ abducted)	Labia majora widely separated, labia minora protruding	Labia majora almost cover labia minora	Labia majora completely cover labia minora		

From DUBOWITZ, LILLY M. S., DUBOWITZ, VICTOR, and GOLDBERG, Cissie. 1970 Clinical assessment of gestational age in the newborn infant. J. Pediat., 77, 1–10, adapted from Farr and associates. Develop. Med. Child Neurol., 8, 507, 1966.

totalling about 3000 per year, and they find that the whole procedure occupies about 10 minutes. The test gives 95 per cent confidence limits of 2·0 weeks.

Other Distinguishing Features

Schulte *et al.* in Germany[19] and Dubowitz in Sheffield[5] simultaneously announced that there was a close correlation between motor nerve conduction velocity for ulnar and tibial nerves and the conceptional age. Small for dates infants had significantly higher conduction velocity values than preterm infants of comparable weight.

Engel and colleagues[8,9] used photic and acoustic evoked responses in the electroencephalogram for the estimation of maturity. Photic latency was found to be inversely related to conceptional age. It was interesting to note that full term girls responded faster to light than full term boys. Several other attempts have been made to assess maturity by electroencephalographic means.[4 15]

Bishop and Corson[3] estimated conceptional age by cytological examination of the amniotic fluid. They wrote that the cells of the amniotic fluid are primarily composed of desquamated fetal cells, squamous and sebaceous. The percentage of lipid containing cells reflects the progressive development of sebaceous glands with increasing gestational age. After a study of 350 specimens, it was found that when the count was less than two per cent, 85 per cent were premature; when the count was over 20 per cent, all were over 36 weeks gestation.

Several workers have studied the maturity of enzyme systems and of other biochemical features for the estimation of maturity. It is said[2] that the proportion of albumin and gamma globulin in the umbilical vein is less in premature babies than in full term ones.

The Prematurely Born Baby who has reached Term

When the prematurely born baby has reached term (e.g. a baby born at thirty weeks gestation, ten weeks after birth), there are certain differences from the full term baby. (Figures 45 to 50).

1. Held in the walking position, he tends to walk on his toes, while the full term baby walks with the foot flat on the couch. In the walking reflex, the rhythm of the stepping movements is less regular than that of a full term infant.

2. Muscle tone is less than in the full term baby.

3. Dorsiflexion of the foot and flexion of the wrist is less than in the full term infant, but extension of the knee with the hip flexed is more complete.

4. He tends to be more active than the full term infant.

5. In the prone position he kicks out more, holds the head up better, and tends to be more active than the full term baby. He lies flat,

like a six week old full term baby. In the supine position the premature baby shows more varied and ample movement than the full term one.

Summary

For many reasons it is important to be able to assess the maturity or duration of gestation of the new born baby. The maturity can be assessed with considerable accuracy by a combination of neurological signs, but not by single signs; by a combination of physical features, but not by single features; and by the motor nerve conduction velocity. Other methods are still experimental.

REFERENCES

1. AMIEL-TISON, C. (1968). Neurological Evaluation of the Maturity of Newborn Infants. *Arch. Dis. Childh.*, **43**, 89.
2. BAZSO, J., ASZTALOS, M. KASSAI, L. (1966) Excerpta Med. Monogr. p. 585. Proc. of Symposium in Prague.
3. BISHOP, E. H., CORSON, S. (1968) Estimation of Fetal Maturity by Cytological Examination of Amniotic Fluid. *Am. J. Obst. Gyn.*, **102**, 654.
4. DREYFUS-BRISAC, C., MINKOWSKI, A. (1967) Electroencephalographic Maturation and low Birth Weight. To be published.
5. DUBOWITZ, V. (1968) Nerve Conduction Velocity—An Index of Neurological Maturity of the Newborn Infant. *Develop. Med. Child Neurol.*, **10**, 741.
6. DUBOWITZ, L. M. S., DUBOWITZ, V., GOLDBERG, C. (1970) Clinical assessment of gestational age in the newborn infant. *J. Pediatrics*, **77**, 1.
7. DUBOWITZ, L. M. S. (1972) Assessment of gestational age in the newborn infant. M.D. Thesis, University of Sheffield.
8. ENGEL, R., CROWELL, D., NISHIJIMA, S. (1969) Visual and Auditory Response Latencies in Neonates. Festschrift in honour of C. C. de Silva. Colombo: Kularatne.
9. ENGEL, R., BENSON, R. C. (1968) Estimate of Conceptional Age by Evoked Response Activity. *Biol. Neonat.*, **12**, 201.
10. FARR, V. (1968). Estimation of Gestational Age by Neurological Assessment in First Week of Life. *Arch. Dis. Childh.*, **43**, 353.
11. FINNSTRÖM, O. (1972) Studies on maturity in newborn infants. *Acta Paediat. Scand.* **61**, 24, 33.
12. MOOSA, A., DUBOWITZ, V. (1971) Postnatal maturation of peripheral nerves in preterm and full-term infants. *J. Pediat.*, **79**, 915.
13. MOOSA, A., DUBOWITZ, V. (1972) Assessment of gestational age in newborn infants: nerve conduction velocity versus maturity score. *Develop. Med. Child Neurol.* **14**, 290.
14. PARKIN, J. M. (1969) The assessment of gestational age. M.D. Thesis. University of Newcastle upon Tyne.
15. PARMELEE, A. H., SCHULTE, F. J., AKIYAMA, Y., WENNER, W. H., SCHULTZ, M. A., STERN, E. (1968) Maturation of E.E.G. Activity During Sleep in Premature Infants. *Electroenceph. Clin. Neurophysiol.*, **24**, 319.
16. ROBINSON, R. J. (1966) Assessment of Gestational Age by Neurological Examination. *Arch. Dis. Childh.*, **41**, 437.
17. SAINT-ANNE DARGASSIES (1955) La Maturation Neurologique des Prématurés. *Etudes Neonatales*, **4**, 71.
18. SAINT-ANNE DARGASSIES (1962) Le Nouveau-Né à Terme. Aspect Neurologique. *Biol. Neonat. (Basel)*, **4**, 174.

19. SCHULTE, F. J., MICHAELIS, R., LINKE, I., NOLTE, R. (1968) Nerve Conduction in Newborns. *Pediatrics*, **42**, 17.
20. WATANABE, K., IWASE, K., HARA, K. (1972) Maturation of visual evoked responses in low birth weight infants. *Develop. Med. Child Neurol.* **14**, 425.

CHAPTER 7

ASSESSMENT OF THE NEWBORN BABY

The Value of the Neurological Examination

Hardly a day passes in a large Obstetrical Unit without a child being born who gives some anxiety with regard to his immediate survival, and if he survives, with regard to the ultimate developmental prognosis. Toxaemia, hypertension, antepartum haemmorrhage, prematurity, fetal anoxia and difficult labours remain regrettably common, and all of them predispose to fetal abnormalities. Cyanotic attacks and convulsions are frequently seen in the newborn baby, and both these conditions are associated with a higher incidence of abnormality than that found in normal infants. Craig found a strong correlation between cerebral irritability in the newborn period and abnormalities in later months. Prechtl and his co-workers in Groningen,[7,18,19] found an important correlation between neonatal hyperexcitability (with overactivity, exaggerated Moro reflex, and a low frequency high amplitude tremor of the lower limb), and the development of the choreiform syndrome in later years. This syndrome, as mentioned in Chapter 4, includes overactivity, learning difficulties, short attention span, negativism, and jerky movements of the limbs, tongue and eyes.

The neurological examination is important for the study of the effect of trauma and anoxia on the baby[9,18] and this may have a bearing on future obstetrical management.

The Assessment at Birth

Apgar described a method of evaluating the infant at birth (Table 4). The score is established 60 seconds after birth, and at 4 or 5 minutes.

The lower the score the greater is the mortality and later neurological morbidity.

We have found it useful to make serial Apgar scores. At the Jessop Hospital, Sheffield, we studied 85 babies with an Apgar score of 4 or less at one minute, and rescored them at minute intervals for 15 minutes after birth. In most babies the score began to rise in a minute or two and gradually reached normal. In 11 babies, all born by Caesarian section, the score fell in the first few minutes and then rose. 40 per cent of the 85 babies had a score of 4 or less at 5 minutes and 15 per cent at 10 minutes. The longer the score remained low, the worse was the prognosis. We suggest that in asphyxiated babies it is useful to assess the Apgar score at least at one minute, three minutes and 10 minutes.

Graham et al.[9,10,11] have described a more complex method of evaluating the newborn baby. They have attempted to distinguish

TABLE 4
Evaluation of the Newborn Infant One Minute after Birth*
(APGAR)

Score	Heart Rate	Respiratory Effort	Reflex Irritability	Muscle Tone	Colour
2	100–140	Normal cry	Normal	Good	Pink
1	100	Irregular and shallow	Moderately depressed	Fair	Fair
0	No beat obtained	Apnoea for more than 60 sec.	Absent	Flaccid	Cyanotic

*Each type of observation scored as indicated. Total scores: 8–10, good; 3–7, fair; 0–2, poor condition.

normal from 'traumatised' babies by assessing the pain threshold, the maturation scale, eye fixation, irritability and muscle tone. The pain threshold was measured by the strength of electric shock necessary to elicit a specified response (movement of the stimulated foot or leg). The maturation scale consisted of the assessment of the strength of the grasp reflex, the persistence and vigour of movements, the pushing out of the feet and kicking movements, the auditory reaction, the response to irritation by cotton or paper over the nose, and the head posture in the prone. The visual reactions consisted of uncoordinated eye movements, fixation, pursuit, and the ease of elicitation, the direction and distance through which the eyes move in response to a stimulus. The irritability was assessed by the sensitivity to stimuli which cause crying, the tone of the cry, and the ease with which the child is quietened. The muscle tone was assessed by the amount of spontaneous movement of limbs in the relaxed state, the frequency of trembling and the degree of head lag when the child was pulled to the sitting position. They carried out the tests on 265 infants without perinatal complications, and compared them with 81 infants suffering from anoxia, neonatal birth injury or diseases or infections associated with brain damage. The scores were significantly different in the 2 groups. Previous attempts by the authors to correlate blood oxygen levels with the effects of delivery had failed, because it was found that the oxygen levels were too transitory and changeable.

Desmond et al.[6] found that prolonged pulsation of the umbilical artery after birth was associated with fetal distress, and carried with it a high mortality. This can presumably be explained by the fact that anoxia causes relaxation of the umbilical artery, as opposed to constriction.

Brazelton[4] described a complex series of obser ations in the examination of the newborn, including observation of the child when asleep and awake, his alertness, eye following, response to sound, irritability, social interest in the examiner, passive movement of the arms, habituation, vigour, tremulousness and consolability, with response to 15 primitive reflexes—the examination taking 25–35 minutes. In a later paper he amplified this,[5] describing a 20 to 30 minute examination involving 30 different tests and manoeuvres. He suggested that in order one should observe the infant for two minutes, to assess the state of consciousness, depth of sleep, alertness if awake: apply a flashlight 3 to 10 times through closed lids, use the rattle and bell, test 5 times with light pin-prick, test for ankle clonus, the plantar grasp reflex, the plantar response, passive movement and tone, auditory and visual orientation, the palmar grasp, the response to pulling him from the supine to the sitting position, the standing and walking position, the limb placement reflex, Galant's reflex, ventral suspension and prone position, the glabellar tap reflex, response to spinning, defence response (cloth over face), tonic neck, startle and Moro reflexes, the lability of skin colour, and other elicited responses.

For research purposes such an extensive examination may be of value: but for practical purposes in a large obstetrical unit such a long examination is impossible, except in the case of selected babies. Although Brazelton has described the examination and the suggested tests in detail, he did not in his paper state the reason for selecting those tests. I am unable myself to determine the developmental significance of many of his tests, e.g. that for the Galant reflex. For practical purposes, as distinct from research, it is necessary to focus down on those tests which matter because they give specific developmental or neurological information.

The Neurological Examination

The aim of the examination is the detection of abnormality of the nervous system due to maldevelopment, injury or infection; the assessment of the maturity of the nervous system; and the estimation of the child's developmental potential.

The examination is preceded by a careful history. In this case the history concerns those factors which may affect the integrity and development of the nervous system. They include genetic factors, infection, drugs taken during pregnancy and the obstetrical history.

Before the examination one must determine other factors which affect the condition of the baby. These include the time of the last feed, the nature of drugs given in the preceding 24 hours, and any symptoms which suggest an abnormality, particularly convulsions, vomiting, cyanotic attacks, irritability or drowsiness.

Conduct of the Examination

The conduct of the examination must be standardised because many of the signs are influenced by both internal and external factors.[20]   If only one examination is carried out this should be delayed until the third day or later because the signs are particularly variable earlier than this.   One examination is insufficient, however, and Mdme. Saint Anne Dargassies wrote that one looks for criteria of normality in the first 5 days, for criteria of maturity between 6 and 9 days, and for criteria of progression of development from 10 to 15 days.[21]

About two hours after the last feed the baby is usually sufficiently alert to be responsive to the tests and yet is not too fretful.   He should be placed on a table sufficiently large to allow rolling from side to side without any risk of falling.   The room should be warm and reasonably draught free.   There should be a good diffuse light.   It is often advantageous to carry out the examination in front of the mother, who gains confidence from seeing her baby handled, and any points which arise can then be discussed at once.

For the purposes of research, or for the evaluation of minor signs, the standard practice must be adhered to, but in the busy daily care of the newborn this may not be possible, and the examiner must select the most useful parts of the examination, concentrate upon the babies at risk, and develop experience to avoid drawing conclusions from signs influenced by external factors.

The examination is carried out in the following sequence: observation; estimation of alertness; estimation of muscle tone; elicitation of special reflexes; examination of cranial nerves and special senses; and the performance of special tests.

Observation

Careful observation amply repays the time spent upon it.   The examiner must train his powers of observation to be aware of the many significant signs which can be seen from the moment the baby is first approached and not just when he is placed on the examination table.

The following features in particular must be noted.

The Posture

The normal full term baby lies on his side with arms and legs flexed.   Placed on his back he rolls to one side or the other.   Placed prone the head is turned to one side so that his breathing is unrestricted.   His limbs are flexed and the pelvis is raised from the couch with the knees drawn high up under the abdomen.   When he is supported in ventral suspension gravity is stronger than the extensor tone, and the head, arms and legs hang downwards, usually with some flexion of the elbow and knee and some extension of the hip.   In contrast, when held in dorsal suspension the stronger flexor tone counteracts the effects of gravity and the baby lies in a position of incomplete extension.

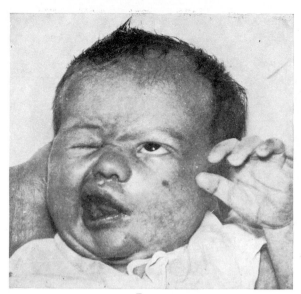

FIG. 53
Facial palsy.

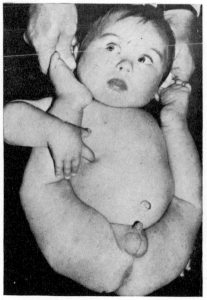

FIG. 54
Mongol, showing marked hypotonia.

facing page 110

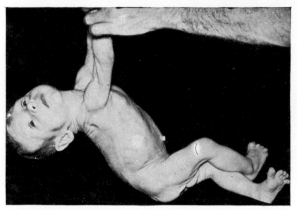

FIG. 55

Defective child with severe head lag, age 8 weeks.

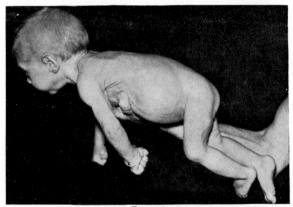

FIG. 56

Same child, with deceptive excessive extensor tone, giving
impression of good head control in ventral suspension.

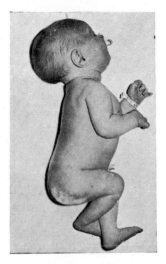

FIG. 57
Face presentation. Characteristic position, resembling opisthotonos, but muscle tone
normal. Age 4 weeks.

LIMBS IN NEWBORN INFANTS

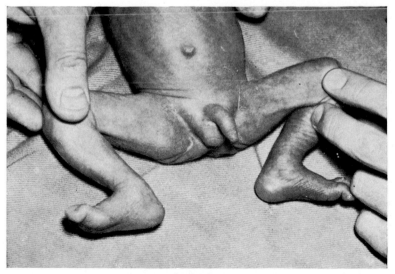

FIG. 58
Abduction of hip.

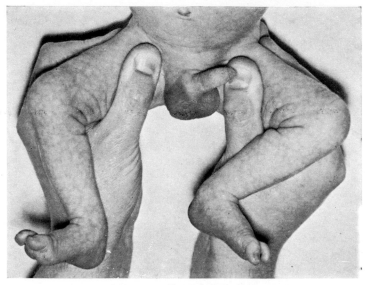

FIG. 59

Method of testing for subluxation of hips (Stage 1). The baby lies
on his back with the hips and knees flexed and the middle finger of
each hand is placed over each great trochanter.

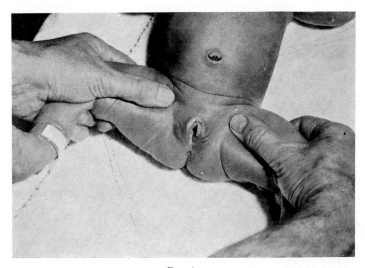

FIG. 60

The thumb of each hand is applied to the inner side of the thigh
opposite the lesser trochanter.

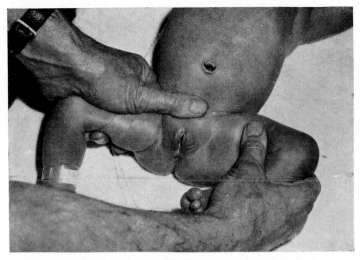

FIG. 61

In a doubtful case the pelvis may be steadied between a thumb over the pubis and fingers under the sacrum while the hip is tested with the other hand.

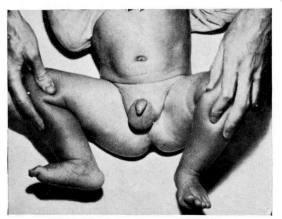

FIG. 62

Subluxated left hip, showing limited abduction.

When the baby is placed in the supine position, and the arm is extended and then released, the arm returns to the flexed position. If the arm is flexed and then released, it extends. When held inverted by the ankles, the hips and knees are flexed; the arms are flexed and adducted across the chest. Full extension of the legs would suggest increased muscle tone. The frog-like appearance of the younger premature infant in the supine position would suggest hypotonia. It must be remembered that if the infant were born as a breech with extended legs, the infant is likely to keep the legs fully extended in the newborn period.

Opisthotonos is usually abnormal: but after a face presentation the head is commonly arched back, so that the baby gives the appearance of opisthotonos. Muscle tone, however, would be normal, whereas in true opisthotonos one would expect to find hypertonia.

It is important to note asymmetry of posture. This may result from asymmetry of muscle tone (as in spastic hemiplegia), or from fracture of the clavicle or humerus, or from a brachial plexus injury.

The Cry

A good nurse unfailingly recognises the high-pitched cry of an abnormal baby. The paediatrician readily recognises the hoarse cry of a cretin, or the 'cri du chat' of the rare chromosome abnormality. The cry may be absent altogether, or excessive and continuous. The former would be abnormal and the latter may be so.

The Movements

Movements are spontaneous or provoked. Spontaneous movements include tremors, twitchings and sudden shock-like movements without any apparent stimulus. The Moro and startle reflexes are examples pf provoked movement. It is particularly important to note symmetry or asymmetry of movement.

Prechtl[18] described the hyperexcitable child as showing low frequency, high amplitude tremors, exaggerated reflexes, and a low threshold Moro reflex. There may be a marked startle reflex on gently tapping the sternum. The McCarthy reflex is obtained by tapping the skull some distance from the supraorbital region. Some such babies are hyperkinetic and cry excessively. He described the apathetic baby as having a high threshold for stimulation of reflexes, some responses being absent altogether. Such infants move less than normal babies, show a decreased resistance to passive movement, and are difficult to arouse. Twitching and rapid rhythmical movements are usually abnormal, though occasional tremors of the chin are normal. Dijkstra[7] paid attention to the occurrence of a limb tremor of low frequency (about five per second).

Wakefulness and Sleep

Abnormal babies commonly sleep for excessively long periods.

Other Features

A thumb across the palm in a clenched hand is usually abnormal.

It is useful to note the respiratory movements, because irregularity of respiration and apnoeic periods (cyanotic attacks) are often associated with cerebral damage.

The face repays careful study. The baby with kernicterus has a wide-eyed, anxious expression, and the baby with hydrocephalus has a prominent forehead, bulging fontanelle, distension of the scalp veins, and a down turning of the eyes so that a complete superior rim of sclera can be seen, giving a 'setting sun' sign.   There may be a roving inco-ordinated movement of the eyes.   Facial palsy should be noted.

Other features which are noticed during the observation period include the presence of congenital malformations, the colour, the presence of skin pigmentation and of naevi.

Estimation of Alertness

It is so important to correlate the findings of the neurological examination with the general condition of the baby that we find that the next most useful step in the examination is to make an assessment of the alertness of the baby.

The following are useful criteria for assessing this.

(*a*)   General appearance and facial expression.

(*b*)   Spontaneous activity.

(*c*)   Respiration.

(*d*)   The response to noxious stimuli, for example, pinching the lobe of the ear to cause the head to turn away, and pricking the sole of the foot to cause withdrawal.

(*e*)   Elicitation of oral reflexes.

(*f*)   Observation of feeding.

Items (*e*) and (*f*) are considered further.   The seeking and obtaining of the nipple, and the whole process of feeding, is a complex mechanism which repays observation.   Early feeding difficulties are frequently encountered with mentally retarded children.   It is interesting that Turoskaya suggested that this is because the oral reflexes in these cases do not acquire their purposeful character which normally occurs about the second day of life.   The ease of elicitation of the oral reflexes is a good test of the alertness of the baby.   Persistent absence of the reflexes is abnormal and carries a poor prognosis.

Ingram[14] considered that individual feeding reflexes give relatively little information about the state of maturation of the infant's nervous system.   There are great variations in the ease with which the reflexes can be elicited, not only between one baby and another, and between one time and another, but with regard to the age at which the reflexes disappear.

Estimation of Muscle Tone

Muscle tone is difficult to define.   It is that condition of the muscle, determined by physical, chemical, and nervous influences, which, although it is not an active contraction, determines the body posture, the range of movement at joints, and the feel of the muscle.[12]   Tone is examined in the following way.

(a) Observation of posture.   Posture is determined by the distribution of muscle tone, and already in observing the baby an impression will have been made as to whether flexor or extensor tone predominates.

(b) Consistency of the muscles.   The muscles are gently squeezed between the finger and thumb, and the resistance is graded as normal, increased or decreased.   If the consistency of the baby's muscle is always compared to the consistency of one's own muscle in the first interosseus space between the thumb and index finger, it is soon possible to use this as a standard for fairly accurate subjective judgments.

(c) Extimation of the range of movement.   This is reduced in hypertonia and increased in hypotonia.   Several of the manoeuvres used for assessing maturity are really methods of assessing muscle tone, which is less in a premature baby than in a full term one.

The range of movement should be estimated in the neck—by rotating the head, flexing it and extending it, and bending it sideways. When the child is held in the sitting position, the child should be able to raise the head a little; when he is half pulled to the sitting position, he should be able to raise it momentarily.   The range in the shoulder muscles should be determined by eliciting the anterior and posterior scarf signs.   The range in the elbows, wrists, hips, knees and ankles should be estimated in the usual way.   In estimating the range of movement in the hip, it is advisable to use a constant method, e.g. flexing the hips to a right angle before abducting them.   Normally the knees in a newborn infant should touch or almost touch the examination table.   Abduction of the hip is restricted in hypertonia (and almost always in the spastic form of cerebral palsy), congenital subluxation of the hip, and occasionally in older children due to contracture of the adductor muscles.

It was stated that extension of the knees with the hips fully flexed is complete in premature babies, but not in full term ones, unless they were born as breech with extended legs.

Flexion of the knee in the prone position with the hip extended gives an indication of the tone of the quadriceps muscle.

Reduced dorsiflexion of the foot is almost invariable in the spastic form of cerebral palsy, and is therefore a most important sign to elicit.

The tone of the trunk muscles is estimated by flexing the hip on the thorax and by bending it sideways.   It is also estimated by holding the baby in the supine position with one's hand under the back.   In ventral suspension, excessive muscle tone may give the wrong impression of unusually good 'head control' (Fig. 56).   The tone of the trunk muscles is also determined in the 'redressement du tronc' test (Ch. 6).

(d) Hypertonic infants show excessive resistance to passive movement: but one can readily be misled by the baby's voluntary resistance to movement.

(e) The recoil.   The arms are extended and then suddenly released. There should be a brisk flexion at the elbow.   In hypotonic or apathetic babies there may be no response at all.

(f) 'Flapping' the limb—the French 'Passivité'.   The distal part of the limb is shaken in order to produce rapid 'flapping' of the hand or foot.   The arm is held below the elbow and the leg below the knee, and the limb is then vigorously and rapidly shaken.   This test presumably measures the excitability and strength of the stretch reflexes, because normally the muscles tense and quickly arrest the flapping movements after a few beats.   It is easy to detect hypotonia or hypertonia by this test.

A corresponding test is used in the older baby for testing head control.   When he has been pulled to the sitting position, the body is wobbled from side to side in order to assess the degree of lateral movement of the head.   By the age of six months this should be minimal. At four months the lateral movement is considerable.

(g) The tendon jerks and ankle clonus (Ch. 5).   The briskness of the tendon reflexes and the area over which the reflex can be obtained give an indirect idea of the muscle tone in spastic children.   A well-sustained ankle clonus is a good confirmatory sign of suspected spasticity—though the sign is by no means always significant, for it may disappear a few weeks after birth.

Whatever the method used, it is essential to note the symmetry of the muscle tone.   Asymmetry is more important than increased but symmetrically increased tone.

Hypotonia is important because it has a vital bearing on the assessment of motor development.   For a full review of the causes of hypotonia the reader is referred to the papers by Dubowitz.[8]

Hypotonia involving the lower limbs alone may be due to a meningomyelocele or diastematomyelia.   It follows that the back of the child must be examined with these two conditions in mind. One also routinely examines the whole of the midline of the back for a congenital dermal sinus.   A sinus in the cervical, dorsal or lumbar region, sometimes revealed by a tuft of hair or patch of pigmentation, may pass right through to the subarachnoid space, and cause recurrent meningitis or other neurological signs.   There is a rare form of cerebral palsy in which in the early weeks there is hypotonia with signs of mental subnormality.

There are considerable variations in muscle tone in normal children. It must not be assumed that because muscle tone is greater than usual, organic disease is necessarily present.

The Hips

Up to the age of about two, the routine examination of any child includes examination of the hips, in order to exclude congenital dislocation. This is not strictly part of the developmental examination, but estimation of the range of abduction of the hips is part of the routine examination, and if the range is restricted, one has to distinguish the two commonest causes—hypertonia and dislocation.

Certain factors increase the risk that the child will have a dislocated hip. These are as follows:–

Family history of dislocated hip.
Geographical factors. (Dislocation is particularly common in Northern Italy.)
Breech delivery.
Severe hypotonia—as in meningomyelocele.
Severe spasticity.
Bilateral talipes in a girl.
Arthrogryposis.

Many articles have been written about the diagnosis of congenital dislocation of the hip in the newborn infant.

I feel confused by the description of the tests given in most of these papers, largely because of the use of the words backwards, forwards, upwards, and downwards. Hence I asked my orthopaedic colleague, J. Sharrard, F.R.C.S. to describe the principal tests in simple words which I could readily understand. Below is his wording:–

"1. *Ortolani's Test.* The child is laid on his back with the hips flexed to a right angle and the knees flexed. Starting with the knees together the hips are slowly abducted and if one is dislocated, somewhere in the 90 degrees arc of abduction the head of the femur slips back into the acetabulum with a visible and palpable click. This test can be done at any age but a click may not be produced in many babies particularly in the newborn period.

2. *Barlow's Test—Part 1.* The baby is laid on his back. The hips are flexed to a right angle and the knees are fully flexed. The middle finger of each hand is placed over the greater trochanter and the thumb of each hand is applied to the inner side of the thigh close to but not quite in the groin. The hips are carried into abduction. With the hips in about 70 degrees of abduction the middle finger of each hand in turn exerts pressure away from the examining couch as if to push the trochanter towards the symphysis pubis. In a normal

child no movement occurs.   If the hip is dislocated, the greater trochanter and the head of the femur with it can be felt to move in the direction in which the pressure has been applied.

3. *Part 2.*   With the hips in the same position as described in the last paragraph, the thumb, which is applied over the upper and inner part of the thigh, exerts pressure towards the examination couch.   In a normal child no movement occurs.   In a child with a dislocatable hip the head of the femur can be felt to slip out and to come back immediately the pressure is released".

After 4 or 5 weeks, the best single sign of subluxation or dislocation of the hip is limited abduction, with the hips flexed to a right angle.

The main causes of limited abduction of the hip are as follows:–

Normal variation.   The hips of some normal babies abduct further than those of others.   In part this is due to differences in muscle tone, but it also depends on the ligaments of the hip.

Increased muscle tone (in the adductors).   As always, it is impossible to draw the line between the normal and the abnormal. Increased muscle tone is the most common reason for unusually limited abduction of the hip in babies seen in a well baby clinic. I have on numerous occasions seen children with a spastic hemiplegia who were suspected of having a subluxated hip because of the limited abduction.

Pathological hypertonia (cerebral palsy, usually of the spastic type).

Subluxation of the hip.

Coxa Vara.

A variety of hip diseases.

Ligamentous abnormalities, as in Trisomy E.

Muscle contracture—mainly in hypotonic babies and children who lie constantly in one position.

Examination of the Cranial Nerves

NERVES 2, 3, 4 and 6.   The study of ocular movements in babies is extremely difficult.   Gross faults can usually be recognised, using in particular the response to rotation (Ch. 7), and the doll's eye response.   The reaction to light and the blink responses are tested. Ophthalmoscopic examination of the eye is a necessary part of the examination in a child suspected of being abnormal.

André Thomas used the following test for vision.[1]   The child is held vertically, facing the dark part of the room.   He is then turned on his body axis to make him face the lighted part of the room.   The head and eyes turn more quickly to this part of the room.   The eye which is nearer to the window opens wider.   Finally the head and eyes are raised towards the sky.   The child is rotated further so that he turns away from the source of light.   His head and eyes do not follow the rest of the body as long as the light is perceptible.   They return to their original position as soon as the light gives way to darkness.

Paine[17] used another rotation test. The baby is held facing the examiner, who rotates two or three times (Fig. 152). The baby opens his eyes. The eyes deviate in the direction of movement as long as the rotation continues, and rotatory nystagmus in the opposite direction occurs when the movement stops. The responses are incomplete if there is weakness of the ocular muscles or defective vision. Vision can also be tested by the use of a revolving drum on which stripes have been painted; the presence of nystagmus indicates that vision is present.

A good description of the methods used to test 7 day old babies was given by Boston workers.[3] One to two hours after a feed the infants were tested by a bright red two inch diameter ball suspended by a rubber band 6–10 inches from the face. The ball was moved slowly in different directions. One examiner handled the baby while two examiners observed the degree of horizontal and vertical deviation of the eyes, the duration of responsiveness and the associated head movements. Opticokinetic responses to a special moving drum were also recorded. The capacity to fix, follow and alert to the visual stimulus provided good evidence of an intact visual apparatus.

Newborn infants tend to keep the eyes closed when one tries to examine them, and any attempt to retract the eyelids makes the baby close the eyes all the more tightly. Babies may be induced to open the eyes by inducing sucking, or by swinging them round in one's hands.

Abnormalities which one may note in the neurological examination include fixation of the pupils, conjugate deviation of the eyes, slow lateral movements, or marked strabismus. Nystagmus (lateral, vertical or rotatory) is abnormal if it is sustained. The so-called 'setting sun sign', so commonly seen in the presence of hydrocephalus, may be normal.

NERVE 5
The cardinal points reflex depends on the sensory tracts of this nerve.

NERVE 7
Facial weakness is detected when the baby is crying, feeding, or being tested for various facial and oral reflexes.

NERVE 8
Newborn babies respond to a loud sound by a startle reaction, a facial grimace, blinking, gross motor movements, quieting if crying, or crying if quiet, opening the eyes if they are closed, inhibiting their sucking responses, or by a catch in the respirations. There may be a

change in the heart rate, as demonstrated by the cardiotachometer, and changes in the E.E.G.

NERVES 9, 10 and 12

A clue to lesions of these nerves will be obtained by noting abnormalities of the palate and tongue movements, the gag reflex and swallowing, and the cry.

NERVE 11

The strength of the sternomastoids and trapezii is usually apparent on inspection, and on rotation of the head.

Small-for-dates Babies

The behaviour of 22 full term newborn babies who were small in relation to the duration of gestation was compared by German workers[16] with that of 25 full term babies who were of normal birth weight.   The examinations were carried out between the third and seventh day.   The following differences were found:

(i) The Moro reflex.   In phase 1, normal birth weight infants showed only short extension and abduction of the arms, followed by marked flexion and adduction; in the small for dates babies, the Moro reflex was often characterised by more extension and abduction of the arms, not always followed by flexion and adduction.

(ii) The asymmetrical tonic neck reflex was weak or absent in the normal birth weight infants, but sustained and marked in the other group.

(iii) Windmill movements of the arms were weak or absent in the normal birth weight infants, but frequent in the small for dates babies.

(iv) The normal birth weight infants stood on the lateral part of the sole of the foot and showed a more marked walking reflex, while the small for dates infants had a weaker or absent walking reflex, and stood predominantly on the full sole.

The Interpretation

The greater one's experience of developmental assessment, the more difficult it appears to become.   This applies especially to the assessment in the newborn period.

The main difficulty is that abnormal neurological signs detected in the newborn period or in the early weeks may completely or almost completely disappear.   For instance, the range of muscle tone varies widely in normal babies.   All that one can say is that the further away from the average a child is in any feature, the less likely is he to be normal.   Excessive tone may be a temporary phenomenon, and so may hypotonia, unless it is severe.   One pays more attention to asymmetry of tone, but even marked degrees of asymmetry of tone, suggestive of a spastic hemiplegia, may disappear in a few weeks. Exaggerated knee jerks and even a well sustained ankle clonus by no means signifies a permanent physical defect. One pays more attention to a combination of abnormal signs than to a single one. I would pay no attention to exaggerated tendon jerks in an otherwise normal baby. I would regard a well sustained ankle clonus merely as an indication for examination at a later date, and I certainly would not even hint to the mother that there might be an abnormality. If, however, a baby in addition to displaying a well sustained ankle clonus had a small head circumference in relation to his weight, or showed delayed motor development, or had not begun to smile at his mother by six weeks (if full term), then I would certainly suspect an abnormality. I would also be influenced by a history of important 'risk factors'. For instance, if a baby showed exaggerated muscle tone, and had suffered hypoglycaemic convulsions, or had been a small premature baby, or was one of twins, I would be more suspicious that the child was abnormal. On the other hand, one must remember that babies who suffered severe anoxia at birth are likely to be normal in later months and years.

Amongst many impressive examples of recovery after displaying grossly abnormal signs in the newborn period are the following :–

(a) A baby with suprabulbar palsy whose mother had had hydramnios. He had signs of spastic quadriplegia, with well sustained ankle clonus, exaggerated tendon jerks, excessive muscle tone and tightly clenched hands. He had to be sucked out every 10 to 15 minutes for the first few weeks. By 12 weeks the sign of spasticity had largely disappeared. By 6 months the only residual sign was a slightly abnormal hand approach to an object. At 10 years he was normal, though there was a trivial tremor in the hands within normal limits. His progress at a normal school was average. In a paper on dysphagia I have described other examples of the complete disappearance of dysphagia due to bulbar palsy or inco-ordination of the swallowing mechanism.

(b) A child with typical signs of spastic hemiplegia in the first three months, one arm being notably stiff and relatively immobile. At the age of 12 years the only residual sign was a unilateral extensor plantar response, with no symptoms.

(c) Unilateral hypertonia in the early weeks. At school age no sign or symptom apart from slight general clumsiness.

As already stated, one can never be quite sure that when abnormal signs have disappeared a few weeks after birth, fine tests of manual, motor or spatial dexterity will not in later years reveal some degree of abnormality.

If the child had neonatal convulsions, the outlook depends in large part on the cause of the convulsions. If they were due to hypoglycaemia, there is much more likely to be residual abnormality than if they were due to hypocalcaemia. Hypoglycaemia may itself be a manifestation of an underlying brain defect. Severe hyperbilirubinaemia should now no longer occur; but if it does, the child is at grave risk of being abnormal later.

Signs which are particularly liable to be followed by a permanent disability include the following:–

A shrill or high pitched cry.

A head circumference which is unusually small or large in relation to the size of the baby, when there is no relevant familial factor.

Excessive drowsiness or apathy.

Opisthotonos.

Excessive irritability.

Absence of the Moro reflex, oral reflexes or blink reflexes.

The Minimum Examination

It is not always possible to carry out a full examination, either because the condition of the baby will not permit this, or because there is a shortage of time.

The following is the minimum examination of the newborn baby from the neurological or developmental aspect:

assessment of maturity
observation of the cry
observation of the face—for facial palsy, facies of disease
eyes—for cataract, opacity due to retinoblastoma etc., nystagmus
movements—for quality, quantity, symmetry
posture—for excessive extension, as in spasticity
palpation of the anterior fontanelle and cranial sutures
estimation of muscle tone
Moro and grasp reflexes
measurement of the head circumference
examination of hips
knee jerks, ankle clonus
examination of back for congenital dermal sinus
if possible rough test for hearing
screening for phenyketonuria

If there is doubt as to whether there is hydrocephalus, the skull should be transilluminated.

REFERENCES

1. ANDRÉ-THOMAS, CHESNI, Y., SAINT-ANNE DARGASSIES (1960) The Neurological Examination of the Infant. *Little Club Clinics in Developmental Medicine.* No. 1. London. National Spastics Society.
2. APGAR, V., HOLADAY, D. A., JAMES, L. S.,WEISBROT, I. M., BERRIEN, C. (1958) Evaluation of the Newborn Infant—Second Report. *J. Amer. med. Ass.*, **168**, 1985.

3. BRAZELTON, T. B., SCHOLL, M. L., ROBEY, J. S. (1966) Visual Responses in the the Newborn. *Pediatrics*, **37**, 284.

4. BRAZELTON, T. B., FREEDMAN, D. G., (1971), in Stoelinga, G. B. A., and J. J. VAN DER WERFF TEN BOSCH. Normal and abnormal development of brain and behaviour. Leiden University Press.

5. BRAZELTON, T. B. (1974). Neonatal behavioural assessment scale. Clinics in Developmental Medicine. No. 50. London. Heinemann.

6. DESMOND, M. M., KAY, J. L., MEGARITY, A. L. (1959) The Phases of Transitional Distress Occurring in Neonates in Association with Prolonged Postnatal Umbilical Cord Pulsations. *J. Pediat.*, **55**, 131.

7. DIJKSTRA, J. (1960) *De Prognostische Cetekenis van Neurologische le Afwijkingen by Pasgeboren Kinderen Thesis*. Groningen.

8. DUBOWITZ, V. (1969) *The Floppy Infant. Clinics in Developmental Medicine*. London: Heinemann.

9. GRAHAM, F. K., MATARAZZO, R. G., CALDWELL, B. M. (1956) Behavioural Differences between Normal and Traumatized Newborns. *Psychol. Monogr.* **70**, Nos. 427, 428.

10. GRAHAM, F. K. (1956) Behavioural Difference between Normal and Traumatized Newborns. *Psychol. Monogr.*, **70**, 1, 17.

11. GRAHAM, F. K., PENNOYER, M. M., CALDWELL, B. M., GREENMAN, M., HARTMANN, A. F. (1957) Relation between Clinical Status and Behaviour Test Performance in a Newborn. Group with Histories suggesting Anoxia. *J. Pediat.*, **50**, 177, 556.

12. HOLT, K. S. (1963) The Measurement of Msucle Tone and Posture. Little Club Clinics in Developmental Medicine, No. 8. London: Heinemann.

13. ILLINGWORTH, R. S. (1969) Sucking and Swallowing Problems in Infancy: The Diagnostic Problem of Dysphagia. *Arch. Dis. Childh.* **44**, 655.

14. INGRAM, T. T. S. (1962) Clinical Significance of the Infantile Feeding Reflexes. *Develop. med. Child. Neurol.*, **4**, 159.

15. LINDON, R. L. (1961) Risk Register. *Cerebr. Palsy Bull.*, **3**, 481.

16. MICHAELIS, R., SCHULTE, F. J., NOLTE, R. (1970) Motor behaviour of small for gestational age newborn infants. *J. Pediatrics*, **76**, 208.

17. PAINE, R. S. (1960) Neurological Examination of Infants and Children. *Ped. Clin. N. Am.*, **7**, 471.

18. PRECHTL, H. F. R. (1961) *Little Club Clin. develop. med.*, No. 2.

19. PRECHTL, H. F. R. (1961) In Foss, B. M. *Determinants of Infant Behaviour*. London: Methuen.

20. RICHARDS, T.W. (1936) The Importance of Hunger in the Bodily Activity of the Neonate. *Psychol. Bull.*, **33**, 817.

21. SAINT-ANNE DARGASSIES (1962) Le Nouveau-né à Terme. *Aspect neurol. Biol. neo-natal.*, **4**, 174.

22. SHARRARD, J.W. J. (1969) Personal Communication.

23. TUROSKAYA, A. (1957) Nature of Sucking Movement in Babies. *Akad. Ped. Nauk. R.S.F.S.R.*, **2**, 105.

CHAPTER 8
THE HEAD CIRCUMFERENCE

The measurement of the maximum head circumference is an essential part of the examination of a baby.   The growth of the head depends on the growth of the cranial contents.   If the brain does not grow normally to its full extent, the head will be small, and so an unusually small head circumference is a pointer to mental subnormality.   On the other hand an obstruction in the cerebrospinal fluid pathways will increase the volume of the cranial contents, and an unusually large head circumference may be the first pointer to hydrocephalus.   There have been several studies of the relationship of head size in infancy to subsequent intelligence.[6]

Table 5 shows the mean head circumference in the first three years as found by Westrop and Barber[8] and Table 6 our own figures in relation to the child's weight.

TABLE 5
Mean Head Circumference
(Westrop and Barber)

Age	Boys Mean			Girls Mean		
	Inches	Cm		Inches	Cm	
1 month	14·7	37·3	1·54	14·3	36·5	1·41
3 months	16·1	40·7	1·43	15·6	39·8	1·39
6 months	17·2	43·6	1·45	16·7	42·5	1·42
9 months	18·0	45·7	1·40	17·6	44·6	1·41
1 year	18·4	46·8	1·40	17·9	45·6	1·30
1½ years	18·9	47·9	1·40	18·5	47·0	1·32
2 years	19·4	49·1	1·47	18·8	48·0	1·35
3 years	19·8	50·4	1·35	19·6	49·5	1·45

The head circumference must be related to the size of the baby.   A large baby is likely to have a larger head than a small baby, and a small baby a smaller head than a large baby.   It is surprising that so many papers on the relation between head size and intelligence fail to take the size of the baby into account: unless they do so the studies are meaningless.   In a study of 1,000 babies at the Jessop Hospital, Sheffield, seen at birth, 6 weeks, 6 months and 10 months, we related the head circumference to the weight.

We set out to determine which was the best measurement to which to relate the head circumference.   We related the head circumference to the weight, chest circumference, supine length and crown rump

TABLE 6
Sheffield figures
for head circumference and weight.

	Males (Total approximately 360)				Females (Total approximately 310)			
	Head Circumference		Weight		Head Circumference		Weight	
	Inches	Cm.	lbs and ozs	Grammes	Inches	Cm.	lbs and ozs	Grammes
Birth	13·7	34·8	7·5	3180	13·8	35·0	7·5	3180
6 weeks	15·3	38·9	10·13	4860	14·9	37·8	10·0	4500
6 months	17·5	44·4	18·12	8520	17·0	43·2	17·7	7840
10 months	18·4	46·7	22·2	10,460	17·9	45·5	20·1	9380

length at birth, 6 weeks, three months and six months, in 50 boys and 56 girls. We found that the head circumference was highly correlated with the body weight and that it also correlated well with the chest circumference.

If one is in doubt about the significance of the head circumference, one should plot the figure on a centile chart, and if possible make serial measurements. One them plots the weight on the weight chart. The placings of the head circumference and the weight should approximate to each other, though familial factors may play a part: for instance, there may be a familial tendency for its members to have an unusually small head size.★ Figure 63 shows the chart of a normal child with a small head: serial measurements indicate that the head is growing normally.

Figure 64 shows the measurements of a child with microcephaly: the growth of the head size is defective.

Figure 65 shows the development of hydrocephalus.

But Figure 66 shows a normal increase of head size in association with a rapid increase in body weight: this would have been shown better by a simultaneous weight chart.

Figures 67 and 68 show that although the head circumference may be exactly average, it must be related to the weight, for if the weight is excessive, the child may have microcephaly, while if a child's weight is below average he may have hydrocephalus.

The examination of the head includes not only the measurement of head circumference. One automatically palpates the anterior fontanelle and the degree of separation of the sutures.

One also assesses the shape, remembering, however, that some degree of asymmetry is common and normal. Severe degrees, due to craniostenosis, hypertelorism and other conditions, are another

★In the case of a very fat baby, the position on the weight and head charts may not correspond, the position being lower on the head chart.

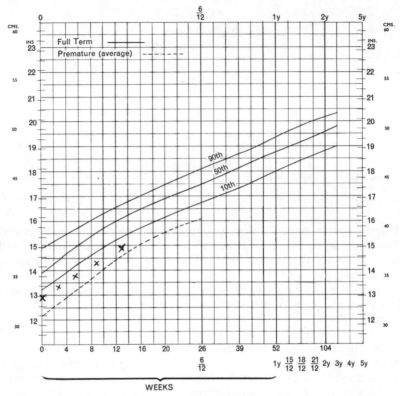

FIG. 63.   Normal small child with small head.

matter.   Although the maximum circumference is of great importance, it is not the only feature which matters.   One pays more
attention to the shape of the head.   The head of a microcephalic
child tapers off towards the vertex, and there is often a sloping forehead.   Some children have what can only be called a badly-shaped
head—the sort of head which one knows from experience is likely to
be associated with poor mental development.   This includes in
particular the flat occiput.

A skull may be broad in the lateral direction, and narrow from
back to front.   In such a case the maximum circumference is greater
than one would guess.   I suspect that a head of this shape is more
likely than others to be associated with mental deficiency.

Children with fairly severe or severe mental deficiency usually
have microcephaly if the defect dates from birth or before birth.
When a child develops normally for the first few months, and then
develops mental deficiency as a result of some postnatal factor, the
appearance of the head depends on the age of onset of the mental
deficiency.   The brain reaches half the adult size by the age of 9

months and three-quarters by the age of 2 years. If severe mental deficiency develops any time in the first year, the head is likely to be small. If it develops after that, the head size is likely to remain normal. This is an interesting differential feature between mental deficiency of early onset and that of later onset.

It must be remembered that an unusually small head circumference by no means necessarily signifies mental deficiency. It may be a genetic trait. An open fontanelle in an older infant with a small head (e.g., in an infant of 9 to 12 months of age) is a useful indication that the child has not true microcephaly. Microcephaly must also be distinguished from craniostenosis by palpation and X-ray study of the sutures. A large head may be a familial feature. We wrote in our book 'Lessons from Childhood',[4] which concerns the childhood of famous men and women, that Napoleon, Thackeray and Swinburne had notably large heads. The latter had the largest hat at Eton, and was said to resemble a pumpkin balanced upon a forked radish.

A large head may be due to hydrocephalus, hydranencephaly, subdural effusion, a cerebral tumour or megalencephaly (a large

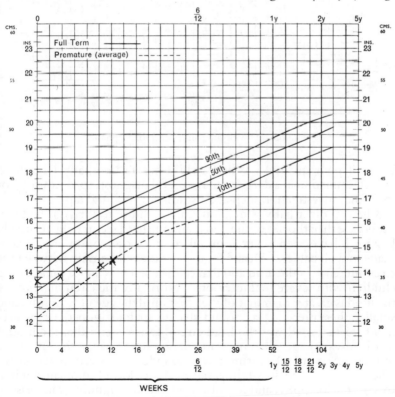

FIG. 64. Developing signs of microcephaly.

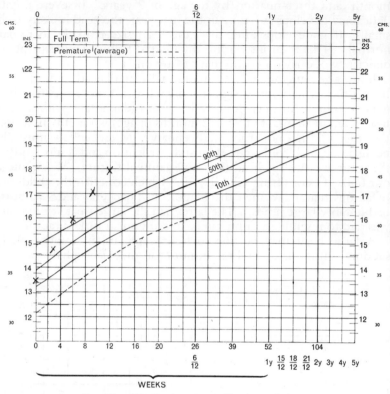

FIG. 65. Developing signs of hydrocephalus.

brain of poor quality). When a child has an unusually large head transillumination in a dark room is a useful diagnostic procedure prior to further investigation such as air studies or subdural taps.

When an older baby is malnourished ('failure to thrive') the brain suffers less than the rest of the body, and the head seems to be relatively large. I have seen several mistaken diagnoses of hydrocephalus made in such babies. Dean[2] found that the relationship between the circumference of the head and that of the chest was useful for assessing children with severe malnutrition. Normally the circumference of the head is greater than that of the chest until the age of 6 months, and smaller thereafter. Dean found that in malnutrition the measurement least affected was the head circumference, and that the head is nearly always larger than usual in relation to the size of the infant as a whole. A word of warning was sounded by Swedish workers.[7] They examined the size of the cerebral ventricles of Ethiopian children by encephalography, and found a moderate but significant increase in ventricular size in those suffering from Kwashiorkor, but not other

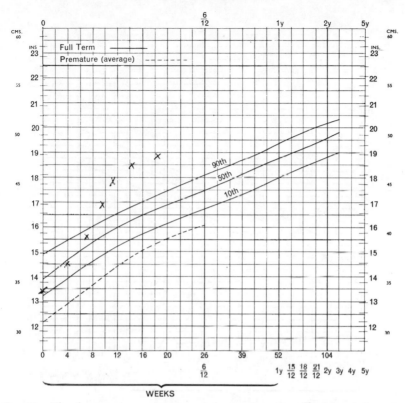

FIG. 66.   The chart at one stage suggested the development of hydrocephalus.   In fact the rapid increase in the size of the head coincided with a rapid spurt in the growth of the baby as a whole.

forms of marasmus.   The head circumference in these children would be deceptive.

The prematurely born baby has a relatively large head, and I have seen incorrect diagnoses of hydrocephalus made in such babies.   The average skull circumference in premature babies given by Crosse (1957), is shown in Table 7.

TABLE 7

Head circumference of premature babies

Duration of Gestation	Inches	Cm.
28	11	25
32	11·5	29
36	12·8	32
40	14·0	35

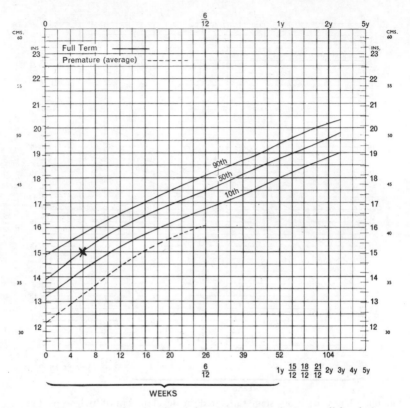

FIG. 67.   Head circumference chart, showing apparently 'normal' head circumference.   In fact the child was a microcephalic.   See Fig. 68.

Summary

The measurement of the maximum circumference of the head is an
essential part of the examination of an infant.   It gives an invaluable
pointer to mental subnormality, hydrocephalus and other
abnormalities.

The head circumference must be related to the baby's weight.

The following are the causes of a head being unusually small:

Normal variation
    Small baby
    Familial feature
    Mental subnormality
    Craniostenosis

The following are the causes of a head being unusually large:

Normal variation
    Large baby
    Familial feature

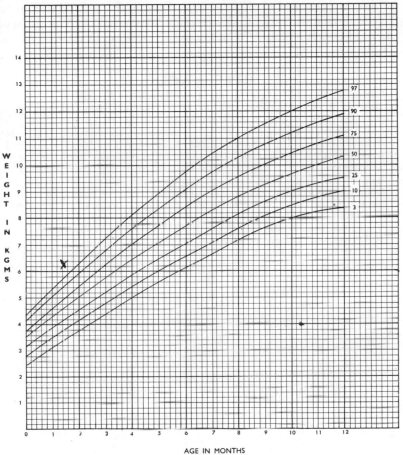

AGE IN MONTHS

Percentile figures taken from Tarmer & Whitehouse chart.

FIG. 68. Weight chart, same child as Fig. 67. Child well above average weight. Head circumference small in relation to weight.

Hydrocephalus
Megalencephaly
Hydranencephaly
Cerebral tumour
Subdural effusion

The head is relatively large in premature babies and in older infants suffering from malnutrition.

When assessing a baby's development, if one finds that the head is unduly small in relation to his weight, even though in all other aspects of development he is up to the average, one should be wary of passing him as normal: one should see him again at a suitable interval, reassess his development and again plot his head circumference and weight on the centile charts in order to determine whether the centile position of the head circumference is maintaining its position in relation to the centile lines.

REFERENCES

1. CROSSE, V. M. (1957) The Premature Baby. London: Churchill.
2. DEAN, R. F. A. (1965) Effects of malnutrition, especially of slight degree, on the growth of young children. Courrier de Centre de l'enfance, 15, 73.
3. ILLINGWORTH, R. S., EID, E. E. (1971) The head circumference in infants and other measurements to which it may be related. Acta Paediat. Scand., 60, 333.
4. ILLINGWORTH, R. S., ILLINGWORTH, C. M. (1966) Lessons from Childhood: some aspects of the early life of unusual men and women. Edinburgh: Livingstone.
5. ILLINGWORTH, R. S., LUTZ, W. (1965) Measurement of the infant's head circumference and its significance. Arch. Dis. Childh., 40, 672.
6. NELSON, K. B., DEUTSCHBERGER, J. (1970) Head size at one year as a predictor of four-year I.Q. Develop. Med. Child. Neurol., 12, 487.
7. VAHLQUIST, B., ENGSNER, G. SJÖGREN, I. (1971) Malnutrition and size of cerebral ventricles. Acta. Paed. Scand., 60, 533.
8. WESTROP, C. K., BARBER, C. R. (1956) Growth of the skull in young children. J. Neurol Psychiat., 19, 52.

CHAPTER 9

NORMAL DEVELOPMENT

THE PRINCIPLES OF DEVELOPMENT

These may be summarised as follows:

1. Development is a continuous process from conception to maturity. This means that development occurs in utero, and birth is merely an event in the course of development, though it signals the beginning of extraneous environmental factors.

2. The sequence of development is the same in all children, but the rate of development varies from child to child. For example, a child has to learn to sit before he can learn to walk, but the age at which children learn to sit and to walk varies considerably.

There is a sequence of development within each developmental field, but the development in one field does not necessarily run parallel with that in another. For instance, though the stages in the development in grasping and in locomotion (sitting and walking) are clearly delineated, development in one field may be more rapid than in another. A child with cerebral palsy involving the lower limbs only will be late in learning to walk, but if his intelligence is normal the development of manipulation will be average. I have termed this lack of parallelism between different fields of development 'Dissociation'.[13]

3. Development is intimately related to the maturation of the nervous system. For instance, no amount of practice can cause a child to walk until his nervous system is ready for it.

4. Generalised mass activity is replaced by specific individual responses. For instance, whereas the young infant wildly moves his trunk, arms and legs, and pants with excitement when he sees something interesting which he wants, the older infant merely smiles and reaches for it.

5. Development is in the cephalocaudal direction. The first step towards walking is the development of head control—of strength in the neck muscles. The infant can do much with his hands before he can walk. He can crawl, pulling himself forward with his hands, before he can creep, using hands and knees.

6. Certain primitive reflexes, such as the grasp reflex and walking reflex, have to be lost before the corresponding voluntary movement is acquired.

THE SEQUENCE OF DEVELOPMENT

In the section to follow I shall outline the sequence of development in locomotion, manipulation and other fields, basing it almost entirely on the work of Arnold Gesell. In all cases the figures given are average ones. Most children acquire the skills a little earlier or later than the dates given. They refer to full term babies: for prematurely born babies an appropriate addition must be made to the ages mentioned.

In order to avoid overlapping and confusion I have combined a description of the normal course of development with the results of developmental tests. The equipment needed for these tests and the method of testing will be discussed in Chapter 13.

The Development of Locomotion

Every child goes through an orderly sequence of development, from the development of head control, to the stage of mature walking, running and skipping. The development of locomotion can be observed when the infant is held in ventral suspension, when he is placed in the prone position and when he is pulled to the sitting position. Subsequently it is seen in the sitting and upright posture.

VENTRAL SUSPENSION. When the newborn baby is held off the couch in the prone position with the hand under the abdomen, there is an almost complete lack of head control. By 6 weeks he reaches an important and easily determined milestone, when he momentarily holds the head in the same plane as the rest of the body. By 8 weeks he can maintain this position, and by 12 weeks he can maintain the head well beyond the plane of the rest of the body. After this age the position of ventral suspension is not used for assessing head control in normal babies.

The position of the limbs of the young infant is important. By 4 weeks the elbows are largely flexed and there is some extension of the hips with flexion of the knees.

Summary

Newborn	Head hangs completely down.
4 weeks	Head momentarily lifted up. Elbows flexed. Some extension of hips and flexion of knees.
6 weeks	Head held momentarily in same plane as rest of body.
8 weeks	Head maintained in same plane as rest of body: momentarily lifted beyond this.
12 weeks	Head maintained well beyond plane of rest of body.

PRONE. The newborn baby lies with his head turned to one side, the pelvis high and the knees drawn up under the abdomen. As he matures the pelvis becomes lower and the hip and knees extend. By 4 weeks he can momentarily lift the chin off the couch. By 12 weeks he holds the chin and shoulders off the couch with the legs fully extended. Soon he lifts the front part of his chest off the couch, so that the plane of the face is at 90 degrees to it, bearing his weight on the forearms. By 24 weeks he keeps the chest and upper part of the abdomen off the couch, maintaining his weight on the hands with extended elbows. He rolls from prone to supine, and a month later from supine to prone. He shows the 'frog' position, with the legs abducted, the soles of the feet coming together. By 28 weeks he can bear the weight on one hand. He can usually crawl by 9 months, though the first stage is accidental progression backwards. He pulls himself forward with the hands, the legs trailing behind. A month later he creeps on hands and knees with the abdomen off the couch. Later he intermittently places one foot flat on the couch, and finally may creep like a bear on hands and feet, the last stage before walking.

Summary

Newborn	Head to one side, pelvis high, knees under abdomen.
6 weeks	Knees only intermittently under abdomen. Intermittent kicking out. Chin intermittently off couch.
8 weeks	Head mostly in midline. Lifts chin off couch so that plane of face is at angle of 45 degrees to couch.
12 weeks	Pelvis flat on couch. Plane of face reaches angle of 45 to 90 degrees to couch.
16 weeks	Chest off couch. Plane of face at angle of 90 degrees to couch. 'Swimming'—limbs stretched out in full extension, whole weight on abdomen.
20 weeks	Weight on forearms.
24 weeks	Weight on hands with extended arms. Chest and upper part of abdomen off couch. Rolls, prone to supine.
28 weeks	May bear weight on one hand.
36 weeks	Progress backwards in attempt to crawl.
40 weeks	Crawls on abdomen.
44 weeks	Creeps, hands and knees.
48 weeks	Creeps, sole of foot intermittently on floor.
52 weeks	Walks like bear.
15 months	Creeps up stairs. Kneels without support.

SITTING. When the newborn baby is pulled to the sitting position there is complete head lag. When half pulled up he will raise his head. When in the sitting position the back is uniformly rounded: he may lift the chin up momentarily. The head lag decreases with maturation, so that by 12 weeks it is only slight and by 20 weeks there is no lag at all. A month later he lifts the head off the couch when he is about to be pulled up, and at 28 weeks he raises it spontaneously and repeatedly. Meanwhile the back is straightening, so that by 24 weeks he can sit propped up in his pram with trunk erect. A month later he sits on the floor with his arms forward for support, and at 28 weeks without support for a few seconds. He learns to sit more and more steadily so that by 40 to 44 weeks he is really steady and can perform various movements such as righting himself. By 15 months he can seat himself in a chair.

Summary

Newborn	Pulled to sit—complete head lag.
4 weeks	Held sitting—rounded back. Momentarily lifts the head up. Pulled to sit—almost complete head lag.
12 weeks	Head mostly held up when supported sitting, but it tends to bob forward.
16 weeks	Only slight head lag in beginning of movement when pulled to sitting position. In sitting position—head wobble when body is swayed. Back curved only in lumbar region.
20 weeks	No head lag when pulled up. No head wobble when body swayed by examiner. Back straight.
24 weeks	Sits supported in pram or high chair. Lifts head off couch when about to be pulled up.
28 weeks	Sits on floor with hands forward for support.
32 weeks	Sits momentarily on floor without support.
36 weeks	Sits steadily on floor for 10 minutes. Leans forward (but not sideways) and recovers balance.
40 weeks	Can go over into prone and change from prone to sitting. Can pull self to sitting position.
48 weeks	Can twist round to pick up object.
15–18 mnths.	Seats self in chair.

STANDING AND WALKING.   The walking reflex disappears by the age of 2 to 3 weeks except when the neck is extended.   At 8 weeks the baby holds his head up momentarily when held in the standing position.   In the early weeks the baby sags at the hip and knee, but by 24 weeks he can bear almost all his weight if his mother has given him a chance.   At 36 weeks he stands holding on to furniture and can pull himself up to the standing position, but cannot let himself down. At 44 weeks he is seen to lift one foot off the ground, and at 48 weeks he walks, holding on to the furniture.   He walks without help at 13 months, with a broad base and steps of unequal direction and length, usually with the shoulder abducted and elbows flexed.   At 15 months he creeps upstairs and can get into the standing position without help. At 18 months he can get up and down stairs without help, and pulls a doll or wheeled toy along the ground.   At 2 years he can pick an object up without falling, can run and walk backward.   He goes up and down stairs with 2 feet per step.   At 3 he can stand for a few seconds on one leg.   He goes up stairs one foot per step, and down stairs 2 feet per step.   He can ride a tricycle.   At 4 he goes down stairs one foot per step and can skip on one foot.   At 5 he can skip on both feet.

Summary

Newborn	Walking reflex (first 2–3 weeks)—elicited for several more weeks when the neck is extended.
8 weeks	Held in standing position, able to hold head up more than momentarily.

24 weeks	Bears almost all weight.
28 weeks	Held standing, bounces with pleasure.
36 weeks	Stands holding on to furniture. Pulls self to stand.
44 weeks	Standing, lifts foot.
48 weeks	Walks holding on to furniture. Walks 2 hands held.
52 weeks	Walks, one hand held.
13 months	Walks, no help.
15 months	Creeps up stairs. Gets into standing position without help. Kneels without support. Cannot go round corners or stop suddenly.
18 months	Can get up and down stairs without help. Pulls wheeled toy. Seats self on chair. Beginning to jump (both feet).
2 years	Up and down stairs alone, 2 feet per step. Walks backward in imitation. Picks up object from floor without falling. Runs. Kicks ball without overbalancing.
2½ years	Jumps with both feet. Can walk on tiptoes.
3 years	Jumps off bottom step. Goes up stairs, one foot per step; down, 2 feet per step. Stands on one foot for seconds. Rides tricycle.
4 years	Goes down stairs, one foot per step. Skips on one foot.
5 years	Skips on both feet.

Other Forms of Progression

Before babies learn to walk they may learn to move from place to place by a variety of methods.

1. They may become proficient at getting about by rolling.

2. They may lie in the supine position and elevate the buttocks and entire lower part of the body from the ground, progressing by a series of bumps on the buttocks.

3. They may hitch or shuffle—getting about on one hand and one buttock, or on both hands and both buttocks.   It is said that this method of progression may be familial.[22]   It often continues for about 7 months.

4. They may crawl backwards.

Other methods are also adopted.

Postures when Child is held in Inverted Position

McGraw[17] studied the postures in 77 children when held in the inverted position by the ankles.   She described four phases.

1. The newborn or flexor phase, in which the knees and hips usually flex; the arms are flexed and adducted across the chest.   After 4 to 6 weeks there are fleeting extensor movements in the neck.

2. The extensor phase, mostly between 4 and 6 months.   There is full extension of the whole vertebral column.   The arms are extended and abducted.   There is less flexion of the knee and hip.

3. The righting phase.   After a few more months there is flexion of

his hands come together as he plays, and he pulls his dress.   He tries
posture.
4. The relaxed or mature phase.   The arms hang loosely down.
There is no pronounced flexion or extension of the spine or hips.
These patterns of posture are referred to again in the chapter on
cerebral palsy.

Manipulation

The primitive grasp reflex of the first 2 or 3 months disappears
before the voluntary grasp begins.   At 4 weeks the hands are still
predominantly closed, but by 12 weeks they are mostly open.   One
can see at this stage that the baby looks at an object as if he would like
to grasp it.   He will hold an object placed in the hand.   At 16 weeks
the hips, neck and spine, with a deliberate effort to regain the upright
to reach for an object, but over-shoots the mark.   At 20 weeks he
can grasp an object voluntarily.   He plays with his toes.   Thereafter
his grasp has to go through several stages from the ulnar grasp—with
the cube in the palm of the hand on the ulnar side, to the radial grasp
and then to the finger-thumb grasp in the last 3 months of the first
year.   In the first 6 months the cube is grasped in the palm of the hand
on the ulnar side: from 24 to 32 weeks it is held against the thenar
eminence at the base of the thumb.   From 32 to 40 weeks the index
finger usually with the help of the ring and little finger presses the
cube against the lower part of the thumb; and between 40 and 60
weeks the cube is grasped between the volar pads of the finger
tip and the distal volar pad of the thumb.   The rapidity with which he
drops the cube is a good index of the maturity of the grasp.   If he
repeatedly drops it in a matter of seconds the grasp is unlikely to be a
mature one.   At first he is ataxic and overshoots the mark, but soon
he is able to reach for an object with precision.   At 6 months he
transfers objects from hand to hand, and as he can now chew, he can
feed himself with a biscuit.   He plays with his toes in the supine
position.   He loves to play with paper.   Everything goes to the
mouth.   It is not till 40 weeks that he can pick up a small object of the
size of a currant, bringing finger and thumb together.   He goes for
objects with his index finger.   He can now deliberately let go of
objects, but true casting—deliberately throwing bricks on to the floor,
one after the other—usually reaches its height between 12 and 13
months.   Before that he learns to hand a toy to the parent, at first
refusing to let it go, but later releasing it.   He spends long periods at
44 weeks and onwards putting objects in and out of a basket.   He
stops taking things to his mouth by about a year.   By 13 months he
can build a tower of 2 one-inch cubes, but he cannot build a tower of
10 until 3 years of age.   By 15 months he can pick up a cup, drink
from it and put it down without much spilling.   At 18 months he
turns 2 or 3 pages of a book at a time, but turns them over singly by the

age of 2 years. By 2 years he can put his socks on, by 2½ he can thread beads, and by 3 he can fasten buttons, dressing and undressing himself. He can draw and paint.

Summary

Newborn	For first 2 or 3 months—grasp reflex.
4 weeks	Hands predominantly closed.
8 weeks	Hands often open. Only slight grasp reflex.
12 weeks	No grasp reflex. Plays with rattle placed in hand for several seconds. Pulls at his dress. Hands mostly open. Looks as if he would like to grasp object.
16 weeks	Hands come together as he plays. Pulls dress over face in play. Tries to reach object but overshoots. Plays with rattle placed in hand for prolonged period and shakes it.
20 weeks	Able to grasp object voluntarily. Ataxia, asynergia, dysmetria. Plays with toes. Objects to mouth. Bidextrous approach to objects.
24 weeks	Holds bottle. Grasps his feet. Palmar grasp of cubes. Drops one when another is given.
28 weeks	Transfers object from hand to hand. Unidextrous approach. Feeds self with biscuit. Bangs objects on table. Retains one cube when second is offered.
36–40 wks.	Finger-thumb apposition; can pick up currant between finger and thumb.
40 weeks	Index finger approach. Release beginning. Offers toy to examiner. Will not release it.
44 weeks	Puts one object after another into basket.
48 weeks	Gives toy to examiner.
1 year	Mouthing nearly stopped.
12–15 months	Casting objects on to the floor.
15 months	Builds tower of 2 or 3 one inch cubes Holds 2 cubes in one hand
18 months	Tower of 3 to 4 cubes.
2 years	Tower of 6 to 7 cubes. Turns door knob. Unscrews lids. Puts on shoes, socks, pants.
2½ years	Holds pencil in hand instead of fist. Begins to draw.
3 years	Tower of 9 to 10 cubes. Dresses and undresses fully. Manages buttons except back ones. Drawing—copies a circle.

For other tests after 1 year—see Chapter 13.

The Use of the Eyes and Ears.

The reflex responses of the eye of the newborn baby have been described elsewhere (p. 81). The baby blinks at birth in response to sound, movement or touching the cornea, but not on the approach of an object. When he is a few weeks older he displays a protective response to an object moving towards him.

The pupil responds to light after about the 29th week of gestation, and the baby begins to turn his head to diffuse light at about the 32nd or 36th week. The 26–30 week premature baby dislikes a bright light.

At birth he can barely fix with his eyes, but he can follow a moving object, such as a dangling ring, with difficulty in a range of about 45° when it is held 8 to 10 inches away. By 4 weeks he can follow in a range of 90° and by three months within a range of 180°. There is little convergence before 6 weeks of age. By three months he can fixate well on near objects. By 3 or 4 weeks he watches his mother intently as she speaks to him, fixating on her face, and by 4 to 6 weeks he begins to smile at her as she speaks to him. He will also smile at a face sized card with two eye dots—and still more at one with six dots. By three months or so he fixes his eyes well on his feeding bottle, and by four months he can fix his eyes on a half inch brick ('grasping with his eyes'). The newborn baby cannot integrate head and eye movements well; the eyes lag behind if his head is passively rotated to one side (doll's eye reflex). The response disappears by two or three months.

The eyes of the newborn baby tend to move independently. Binocular vision begins at six weeks and is fairly well established by four months. To achieve binocular vision the visual fields must overlap so that corresponding parts of each retina have a common visual direction and form similar images. As binocular vision matures the infant learns by trial and error to associate the visual fields and fusion becomes established. After six months lack of conjugate movements, strabismus, means that treatment is required.

From 12–24 weeks he characteristically watches his hand (hand regard) as he lies on his back; but 'hand regard' can also occur in blind children, and so it is really a developmental pattern not requiring visual stimulation.[9]

At five months he excites when his feed is being prepared, and at 6 months he adjusts his position to see objects—bending back or crouching to see what he is interested in. He cannot follow rapidly moving objects until he is nearly a year old.

According to Brown[5] the following is the visual acuity to be expected in the first five years:–

Age	4 months	6 months	1 year	18 months	2 years	5 years
Acuity	3/60	4/60	6/60	6/24	6/12	6/6

Mary Sheridan tested 100 five to seven year old school children with the stycar method at 20 feet: she found that a visual acuity of 6/9 should be regarded as sub-optimal.

There have been several studies relating to the ability of the fetus to hear in utero.[21] Different tones were produced by a Jackson audio-frequency oscillator and amplified. Fetal heart sounds were picked up by a Bush microphone attached to the maternal abdomen, a gap of air space being maintained between the sound-producing apparatus and the mother's abdomen. Each stimulus was preceded by a warning. The sudden fetal movements and acceleration of the fetal heart indicated that the fetus could hear. The responses of the newborn baby to sound were discussed on pages 83 and 92.

At three or four months of age the baby begins to turn his head towards the source of sound.

Murphy[19,20] described the sequence of development of sound localisation, making a sound approximately 18 inches from the ear. These are as follows:

1. The infant turns the head to the side at which the sound is heard (3 months).
2. The infant turns the head towards the sound and the eyes look in the same direction. (3 to 4 months).
3. He turns the head to one side and then downwards, if the sound is made below the ear. (5 to 6 months).
4. He turns the head to one side and then upwards, when the sound is made above the level of the ear. (About 6 months). i.e. downward localisation occurs before upward localisation.
5. He turns the head in a curving arc towards the sound source. (About 6 to 8 months).
6. The head is turned diagonally and directly towards the sound. (About 8 to 10 months).

He may imitate sounds by 6 months, and by 7 months he may respond to his name. By the age of 9 to 12 months he knows the meaning of several words, including the names of members of his family.

By the first year the ability to localise a sound source is almost as good in the older child and adult. From about 9 months the baby learns to control and adjust his responses to sounds. He may delay his response or inhibit it altogether. He may listen to hear the sound again and not attempt to localise it. This represents a further step towards understanding and controlling his environment.

Summary

(i) Vision

4 weeks	Watches mother intently when she speaks to him. Opens and closes mouth. Bobs head up and down. Follows dangling object when brought to midline, less than 90 degrees.
6 weeks	Smiles. Follows moving person. Supine—follows moving object from side to midline (90 degrees).

8 weeks   Fixation, convergence, focusing.

12 weeks   Hand regard.

              Follows moving toy from side to side (180 degrees).

20 weeks   Smiles at mirror image.

              No more hand regard after 24 weeks.

28 weeks   Pats image of self in mirror.

              Adjusts position to see objects.

40 weeks   Looks round corner for object.

(ii) Hearing

First two months   When sound made quietens if crying, cries if quiet, startle reflex, blink.

3 months   Turns head to sound made on level with ear.

6 months   Turns to sound below ear. Imitates sound.

7 months   Turns head to sound above ear.

12 months   Turns to own name.

General Understanding

The first sign of understanding can be seen any time from 1 to 4 weeks of age, when he begins to watch his mother when she speaks to him. He quiets, opens and closes his mouth and bobs his head up and down. By 6 weeks he begins to smile and 2 weeks later to vocalise. By the second or third month he may imitate his mother's mouth movement or tongue protrusion. Trevarthen[26] pointed out that to do so he must have a model of his mother's face in his brain, and this model must be mapped on to the motor apparatus of his own face. At 12 weeks he shows considerable interest in his surroundings, watching the movements of people in the room. He may refuse to be left outside alone, preferring the activity of the kitchen. He excites when a toy is presented to him. He recognises his mother and turns his head to sound. He may turn his head away when his nose is being cleaned by cotton wool. Between 12 and 16 weeks he anticipates when his bottle or the breast is offered, by opening his mouth when he sees it approach. At 20 weeks he smiles at his mirror image and shortly after looks to see where a dropped toy has gone to. At 24 weeks when lying down he stretches his arms out when he sees that his mother is going to lift him up. He smiles and vocalises at his mirror image. At 6 months he imitates acts such as tongue protrusion or a cough. He may try to establish contact by coughing. He enjoys peep-bo games. At 32 weeks he reacts to the cotton wool swab by grasping his mother's hand and pushing it away. He tries persistently to reach objects too far away. He responds to 'No.'

At 40 weeks he may pull his mother's clothes to attract her attention. He imitates 'patacake' and 'byè-bye'. He repeats a performance laughed at. At 44 weeks he helps to dress by holding his arm out for a coat, his foot out for a shoe or transferring an object from one hand to another so that a hand can go through a sleeve. At 48 weeks he begins to anticipate movements in nursery rhymes. He begins to show interest in books and understanding of words. At 11 to 12 months he may laugh when his mother puts an unusual object on her head. At 1 year he may understand a phrase such as 'where is your shoe?'

After the first birthday he shows his understanding in innumerable different ways. His increasing understanding is shown by his comprehension of what is said to him, by the execution of simple requests, by his increasing interest in toys and books, by his developing speech. His play becomes more and more complex and imaginative. He begins to appreciate form and colour and by $2\frac{1}{2}$ years he can tackle simple jig-saws.

The main test objects used for observing his developing understanding are the pencil and paper, the picture book, the picture card with pictures of common objects and formboards or cut-out forms.

Summary

4 weeks	Watches mother intently as she speaks to him.
6 weeks	Smiles.
8 weeks	Smiles and vocalises.
12 weeks	Much interest in surroundings.
	Excites when toy presented.
	Recognises mother.
	Turns head away when nose cleaned.
	Squeals of pleasure.
	'Talks' a great deal when spoken to.
16 weeks	Anticipates and excites when feed prepared.
	Shows interest in strange room. Laughs aloud.
20 weeks	Smiles at mirror image.
24 weeks	Displeasure at removal of toy.
	Holds arms out to be picked up. Likes and dislikes.
	Smiles and vocalises at mirror image.
	When he drops cube he looks to see where it has gone to.
	Excites on hearing steps.
	Beginning of imitation. Laughs when head is hidden in towel.
28 weeks	Expectation in response to repetition of stimulus.
	Imitates acts and noises.
	Tries to attract attention by cough.
	Enjoys peep-bo games.
	Responds to name.
	Keeps lips closed when offered food which he does not want.
32 weeks	Reacts to cotton wool swab by grasping his mother's hand and pushing it away.
	Reaches persistently for toys out of reach.
	Responds to 'No'.
	Imitates sounds.
36 weeks	Compares 2 cubes by bringing them together.
	Puts arms in front of face to avoid having it washed.
40 weeks	Pulls clothes of mother to attract attention.
	Waves bye-bye. Patcake.
	Repeats performance laughed at.

Looks round corner for object.
Responds to words, e.g. 'Where is daddy?'
Holds object to examiner but will not release it.
44 weeks   Drops object deliberately, to be picked up.
Helps to dress.
48 weeks   Rolls ball to examiner.
Will give toy to examiner.
Anticipates body movements when nursery rhyme being said.
Interest in picture book.
Plays peep-bo, covering face.
Plays game 'up, down'.
Shakes head for 'No'.

For tests of general understanding after 1 year—see Chapter 13.

Pleasure and Displeasure

All babies express displeasure before they learn to show pleasure.
The first sign of pleasure shown by the baby is the quieting in the first few days when picked up.   During his feeds he shows his pleasure by the splaying of his toes and by their alternate flexion and extension. The smile at 6 weeks when he is spoken to is followed in 1 or 2 weeks by vocalising.   At 3 months he squeals with delight.   He then shows his pleasure by a massive response—the trunk, arms and legs move, and he pants with excitement.   At 16 weeks he laughs aloud.   He plays with the rattle placed in his hand.   He smiles when pulled up to the sitting position.

After 5 or 6 months he takes pleasure in newly acquired skills—sitting, standing, walking and feeding himself.   He enjoys games from 6 months and by 9 months likes to be read to and enjoys nursery rhymes.   He is ticklish by 4 or 5 months and soon responds by a laugh when he sees a finger approaching to tickle him.   He enjoys games and company more and more as he gets older.

Feeding and Dressing

The young baby cannot usually approximate his lips tightly round the areola of the breast or the teat of the bottle, so that milk leaks out at the corners of the mouth, he swallows air and so has 'wind'.   As he matures he gets less wind because of the complete approximation of his lips to the sucking surface.

In the first 4 months or so the baby's tongue tends to push food out if food is placed on the front of the tongue.   Food, therefore, should be placed well back.   Babies can approximate their lips to the rim of a cup by 4 or 5 months and cup-feeding at this time is likely to be quicker than bottle feeding.

The next milestone of importance is the beginning of chewing at 6 months, together with the ability to get hold of objects, enabling a child to feed himself with a biscuit.   He likes to hold his bottle.

At any time after 6 months the baby may begin to hold his spoon, and some babies can feed themselves fully with the spoon by 9 or 10 months, though the average age for this is about 15 months. In the early days of self feeding the fingers go into the food, and much is spilt, accidentally or deliberately.

When he is first allowed to use a cup, he lets it go when he has had what he wants. If he is given a chance to learn, however, he should be able to manage the cup fully by 15 months of age. Children can manage a knife and fork by the age of $2\frac{1}{2}$ to 3 years.

The age at which children learn to dress themselves varies greatly. Much depends on how much chance the mother gives the child to dress himself. A child of average intelligence can dress himself fully by the age of 3, provided that he is advised as to back and front, and as to the appropriate shoe for the foot. He will also need help with difficult buttons. He should be able to tie his shoelaces by 4 or 5 years, and so to be fully independent.

Summary

24 weeks	Drinks from cup when it is held to lips.
6 months	Chews. Eats biscuit.
15 months	Manages cup, picking it up, putting it down without much spilling.
	Rotates spoon near mouth.
	Feeds self fully, no help.
	Takes off shoes.
18 months	Takes off gloves, shoes, socks, unzips.
	No more rotation of spoon.
2 years	Puts on and takes off shoes, socks, pants.
3 years	Dress self fully apart from buttons behind.
	May put shoes on to wrong feet. Unbuttons front and side buttons.
5 years	Can tie shoe lace.

Opening of Mouth When the Nose is Obstructed

The young baby does not usually open his mouth spontaneously when his nose is obstructed until he is about four or five months old. This is of importance under various circumstances. For instance, the infant with choanal atresia gasps for breath and becomes cyanosed until he opens his mouth to cry or until an airway is inserted.

Speech

There have been several extensive studies on the speech of infants. A good simple review of the subject was provided by Lillywhite[16] and Sheridan.[23] The latter described the stages of preverbal and verbal communication. They are smiling, nestling, clinging, vigorous welcoming, frowning, resistive stiffening or pushing away, formless emotionally charged vocalisations, pulling the mother in his direction, pointing or taking the mother's hand and placing it near the object which he desires. Laughter, screaming and temper tantrums are other methods of communication.

Speech begins with the vocalisations of the 5 to 6 weeks old infant. Some infants vocalise sooner than this. The sounds are mostly vowels but some consonants may be heard. By 12 to 16 weeks the baby characteristically has long 'conversations' with his mother. Towards the latter end of this period he begins to use consonants m, k, g, p, and b. He laughs, gurgles and coos. By 20 weeks he says 'Ah goo' and makes syllables like 'Ba', 'da', and 'ka' at 28 weeks. When crying he makes sounds like 'mum'. There is much vocal play at this time, with razzing and more intonation. A nasal tone may be heard and tongue-lip activity develops. At 32 weeks he combines syllables, like 'da-da', but does not say a word with meaning until he is 44 to 48 weeks old. At 32 weeks he adds d, t, and w. At 8 months, he makes noises to attract attention. At 10 months he comprehends 'no' and obeys orders. The average child can say 2 or 3 words with meaning by 1 year.

In the early weeks of speech he frequently omits the first or last part of a word—saying 'g' for 'dog'. Between 15 and 18 months the child jargons, speaking in an unintelligible but expressive language of his own, with modulations, phrasings and dramatic inflections but with only an occasional intelligible word. He may repeat phrases such as 'Oh dear', but the average child begins to join words together spontaneously by 21 to 24 months. Substitution of letters may occur with lisping as a result of protruding the tongue between the teeth when saying 's'. By the age of 3 he is talking incessantly, but some substitution of letters and repetition of syllables is usual rather than the exception.

Karelitz and Rosenfeld[14] described a fascinating study of infants' vocalisations. They took 1,300 recordings of the vocalisations of normal and 'brain damaged' infants in their first two years. They described the cry of the young infant as short, staccato and repetitive. It builds up in a crescendo as the stimulus is applied. As he develops, the duration of the individual cry increases, and eventually becomes polysyllabic. The pitch becomes more varied and the inflections become more plaintive and meaningful at about six months of age. Later syllables (mumum) and real words and subsequently phrases can be heard as part of the cry.

Summary

5–6 weeks	Vocalises.
12 weeks	Squeals of pleasure.
	'Talks' when spoken to.
16 weeks	Laughs aloud.
20 weeks	Razzing, 'Ah-goo'.
28 weeks	Syllables 'ba', 'da', 'ka'. Four or more different sounds.
32 weeks	Combines syllables—'da-da', 'ba-ba'.
48 weeks	One word with meaning.
	Imitates sounds.

1 year	2 or 3 words with meaning.
	Imitates animals.
15 months	Jargon
18 months	Jargon, but many intelligible words.
21–24 mnths	2 or 3 words joined together (not in imitation).
	Repeats things said.
	Uses 'I', 'me', 'you'.
2–3 years	Lisping and some 'stuttering' common.
3 years	Normal speech.

Sphincter Control

In the newborn period, micturition is a reflex act. It can be stimulated by handling the baby and other non-specific measures. Babies usually empty the bowel or bladder immediately after a meal. They can be conditioned at any age (e.g. at a month or so) to empty the bladder when placed on the pottie, the bladder emptying when the buttocks come into contact with the rim of the pottie. Voluntary control does not begin until 15–18 months of age when the baby first tells his mother that he has wet his pants. He then tells her just before he passes urine, but too late, and a little later he tells her in time. By about 16 to 18 months he may say 'No' if asked whether he wants to pass urine. There is great urgency at this time, so that as soon as he wants to pass urine he must be offered the pottie immediately, or it will be too late. As he matures the urgency disappears—though in enuresis of the primary type diurnal urgency may continue for some years. By the age of two to two and a half years he can pull his pants down and climb on to the lavatory seat unaided. He is apt to forget to go to the lavatory when occupied with some new toy or play, but later can remember to look after his needs.

Most children are reasonably dry by day at 18 months. By two, 50 per cent are dry at night: by three, 75 per cent, and by 5 some 90 per cent are dry. This means that about one in ten at the age of five will still be wetting the bed at least occasionally.

Bowel control is usually acquired before control of the bladder.

Summary

15 months	Tells the mother that he wants to use the pottie.
	Indicates wet pants.
18 months	Dry by day, occasional accidents.
2 years	Dry by night if lifted out in evening.
2½ years	Attends to own toilet needs without help, except for wiping.

Handedness

Amongst famous people who were left handed were Holbein, Durer, Landseer, Ravel, Johann Sebastian Bach, Rev. Charles Dodgson (Lewis Caroll) and Thomas Carlyle.

Left-handedness is not just the opposite of right handedness. Those with right-handedness are usually consistent in the use of the right hand, but most left-handed persons are inconsistent in the use of the left hand.

The question of whether handedness is predominantly environmental or genetic in origin has not been decided. The subject has been reviewed by Zangwill[29,30] Clark,[7] Barsley[4] and others.

Bakwin[3] wrote that archaeological studies of implements show that hand preference among aboriginal men was about equally divided, and that during the Bronze Age there was a shift to right-handedness. He stated that the incidence of left-handedness in female adults is 3·8 per cent., as compared with 6·6 per cent in male adults. Morley[18] found that between 6 and 7 per cent of the Newcastle-on-Tyne children in her survey were left-handed. The incidence in uniovular twins is three times greater than that in the normal population. There is more left-handedness amongst manual workers than amongst the middle and upper classes, and more amongst those of low intelligence. Whereas the incidence of left-handedness in British school children is about five per cent, that in special schools is 12 per cent. According to Eames[8] the incidence is higher in children who were prematurely born than in those who were born at term.

Watson[28] wrote that 'handedness is not an instinct. It is socially conditioned'. Gesell and Ames[10] regarded handedness as developmental in origin. Hildreth[11] wrote that: 'Achieving handedness is essentially a learning process, involving habit formation, spontaneous reactions, postural adjustment, expression of choice, and responding in social situations'. He thought that the question of whether handedness is hereditary or environmentally conditioned has never been satisfactorily determined. Ausubel[2] remarked that 85 per cent are predominantly right-handed by the end of the second year, but by the age of 6, 93 per cent are right-handed. He regarded handedness as partly genetic and partly due to deliberate training measures and the cumulative impact of innumerable environmental cues. He added that cerebral dominance might be a consequence rather than a cause of handedness.

Clark[7] wrote as follows: 'The position may be summed up by saying that genetic studies have revealed that the development of handedness preference has a hereditary basis, in other words, that one's chances of being left-handed are greater if there are instances of left-handedness in the family. Few would deny, however, that factors other than genetic help to determine whether any particular individual will be right- or left-handed, the actual society in which he lives and its attitude to left-handedness. Other environmental factors, temperamental differences, and so on, all these play a part in determining whether latent left-handedness will be cultivated or suppressed. These factors will probably have their greatest effect on the intermediate, assuming left-handedness to be a quantitative trait'. It is certainly one's experience that a high proportion of left-handed children have a left-handed parent, but that is not conclusive proof of a genetic factor.

Readers are referred to the comprehensive account of the genetic and neurological aspects of handedness written by Annette.[1] While the cause of handedness is uncertain, the relationship to certain aspects of development is also undecided. It seems to be agreed by many that the training of a left-handed child to use the right hand does not in itself cause stuttering. It is felt that it is the way in which the child is taught which matters. If the training is a source of stress, stuttering may result. In this connection it should be remembered that in some cultures left-handedness is regarded as a stigma on the child, and this in itself might lead indirectly to insecurity and so to behaviour problems or stuttering. Zangwill[29,30] wrote that, 'Handedness and speech are in some way related. It is striking how often a degree of backwardness in reading, poor spelling, occasional clumsiness, or defects in spatial judgement, are linked with atypical or inconsistent laterality or sometimes with frank left-handedness. The combination of right handedness and left hemisphere dominance seems to offer the best guarantee of normal language development, and of the scholastic accompaniment based on it.'

There seems to be some association between handedness and intelligence. Karlin and Strazzulla[15] discussed the literature concerning this, and indicated that there is a high incidence of left handedness in mental defectives. Burt[6] found that left-handedness is half as common again in backward children as it is in the normal population, and twice as common among mental defectives as it is in others. This finding might be in some way due to delayed maturation in some mentally defective children, or to the fact that if there is ambidexterity, it is more difficult to train a retarded child to use one hand more than the other, or that less effort would be made to teach him to use the right hand in preference to the left.

Clark[7] concluded that there was no significant difference in the writing of left- and right-handed children. Elsewhere, however, she wrote that there is some truth in the suggestion that left-handers are bad writers. She wrote that 'it is a generalisation with only a certain amount of truth in it'. She felt that they suffer from more fatigue when subjected to prolonged periods of writing than those using the right hand. She wrote that 'there is an intimate connection between the development of speech and dominant handedness. There may be a connection between retarded speech and lack of dominance'. The role of crossed laterality was thought to be uncertain.

Hillman[12] wrote that 'all the evidence contained in the investigation of 1,847 children points to the fact that there is no connection between reading failures and handedness, eyedness or crossed laterality, or the lack of hemispherical dominance which may be associated with those characteristics.   The papers show that the incidence of backwardness, normality and advanced reading is approximately the same in all the various groups of laterality characteristics'.

Spitzer et al.[25] investigated the incidence of mixed dominance in 103 children with reading disabilities, and 288 controls.   There was no difference between the two groups.

Vernon[27] in her book on reading difficulties, summed up her views as follows: 'The relationship to reading disabilities of incomplete lateralisation and cerebral dominance is extremely obscure.   It may, perhaps, be concluded that left-handedness need not in itself be a handicap to reading.   But inevitably writing is harder for the left-handed child; and this may both make it more difficult for him to acquire an understanding of the correct order of letters in the word, but also set up a general dislike of linguistic pursuits, and anxiety over their performance.   It is doubtful whether sightedness is of great importance: and lack of dominance of one visual cortical area over the other is still of doubtful significance.   But ambidexterity and mixed handedness can only be associated with incomplete dominance of the major over the minor hemisphere, and this in turn produces general immaturity in motor and or linguistic functions, or in certain of these functions in particular'.

'In some cases of reading disability incomplete lateralisation may be an important factor, especially when it is congenital.   But it is doubtful whether this in itself is sufficient to cause permanent inability to read, unless reinforced by some additional factor'.

In conclusion, there are many problems of handedness which remain unsolved.   Handedness is partly genetic and partly environmental in origin.   The role of handedness in reading and writing difficulties has been exaggerated in the past, and it is probable that handedness is of little importance in these problems.   Left-handedness is more common in mentally defective children, but the reason for this is not obvious.

The Development of Handedness

Gesell and Ames[10] suggested that the first indication of handedness may be the direction of the asymmetrical tonic-neck reflex.   In 19 children followed from infancy to 10 years, the direction of the tonic-neck reflex was predictive of handedness in 14.   In 4 children left-handedness was correctly foretold in infancy by a persistently left tonic neck reflex.

There are shifts from side to side in the first year.   At 18 months a period of bilaterality is often found, followed by a definite use of the dominant hand at the age of 2 years.   Often however, dominance is not fully established for 3 or 4 years later.

Development by Age

In the following section I have put together the main features of development at different ages. I have combined with these milestones a variety of simple developmental tests, mainly culled from Gesell.

THE AVERAGE LEVEL OF DEVELOPMENT AT DIFFERENT AGES

4 Weeks

GROSS MOTOR

Ventral suspension—(held in prone position with hand under abdomen), head held up momentarily. Elbows flexed, hips partly extended, knees flexed.

Prone—pelvis high, knees drawn up largely under abdomen. Intermittent partial extension of hip and knee. Momentarily lifts chin off couch. Head predominantly to one side.

Pulled to sit—almost complete head lag.

Held in sitting position—back uniformly rounded. May hold head up momentarily.

Supine—asymmetrical tonic neck reflex seen when at rest.

Held standing—flops at knees and hips. May be residual walking reflex when sole of foot is pressed on flat surface.

HANDS

Hands predominantly closed.

Grasp reflex.

GENERAL UNDERSTANDING

Watches mother's face when she talks to him and he is not crying. Opens and closes mouth. Bobs head up and down.

VISION

In supine—regards dangling object (e.g. ring on string) when brought into line of vision (3 feet from the eyes), but not otherwise when in midline. Follows it less than 90 degrees.

SOUND

Quiets when bell is rung.

6 Weeks

GROSS MOTOR

Ventral suspension—head held up momentarily in same plane as rest of body. Some extension of hips and flexion of knees. Flexion of elbows.

Prone—pelvis high, but knees no longer under abdomen. Much intermittent extension of hips. Chin raised intermittently off couch. Head turned to one side.

Pulled to sit—head lag considerable but not complete.
Held in sitting position—intermittently holds head up.
Held standing—no walking reflex.   Head sags forward.   May
hold head up momentarily.
Supine—tonic neck reflex at rest intermittently seen.

HANDS
Often open.   Grasp reflex may be lost.

GENERAL UNDERSTANDING
Smiles at mother in response to overtures.

VISION
Eyes fixate on objects, and follow moving persons.
In supine—looks at object held in midline, following it as it
moves from the side to midline.   (90 degrees).

8 Weeks
GROSS MOTOR
Ventral suspension—can maintain head in same plane as rest of
body.
Prone—head mostly in midline.   Intermittently lifts chin off
couch so that plane of face is at angle of 45 degrees to couch.
Pull so sit—less head lag.
Held in sitting position—less rounding of back.   Head is held
up but recurrently bobs forward.
Supine—head chiefly to side.   Asymmetrical tonic neck reflex
seen intermittently at rest.
Held in standing position—able to hold head up more than
momentarily.

HANDS
Frequently open.   Only slight grasp reflex.

VOCALISATION
Smiles and vocalises when talked to.

VISION
Fixation, convergence and focusing.   Follows moving person.
In supine—follows dangling toy from side to point beyond
midline.

12 Weeks
GROSS MOTOR
Ventral suspension—head held up for prolonged period beyond
plane of rest of body.
Prone—pelvis flat on couch.   Holds chin and shoulders off
couch for prolonged period so that plane of face is at angle

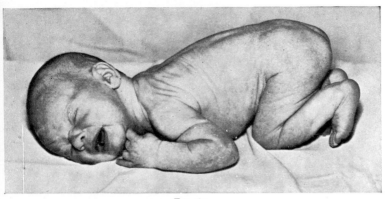

FIG. 69
About 0–2 weeks of age.
Pelvis high, knees drawn up under abdomen.

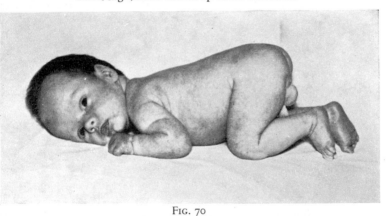

FIG. 70
About 3 or 4 weeks of age.
Pelvis high, but knees not under abdomen.

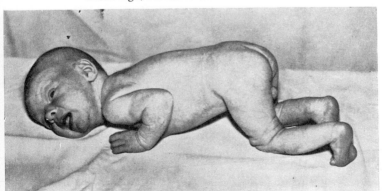

FIG. 71.—About 4 to 6 weeks of age. Pelvis still rather high.
Intermittent extension of hips.

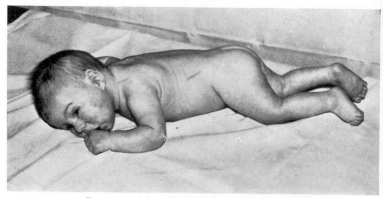

FIG. 72.—6-8 weeks. Pelvis flat. Hips extended.

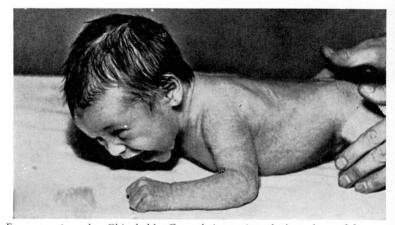

FIG. 73.—6 weeks. Chin held off couch intermittently but plane of face not as much as angle of 45° to couch.

FIG. 74
10 to 12 weeks.
Plane of face almost
reaches angle of 45°
to couch.

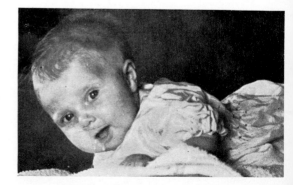

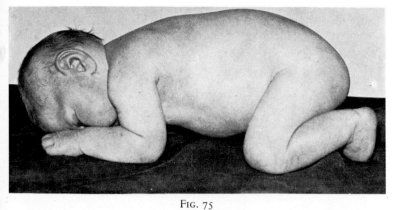

FIG. 75

Microcephalic mentally defective child, aged 9 weeks, showing prone position similar to that of newborn boy.

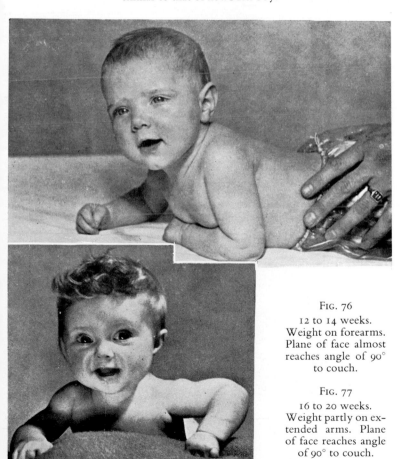

FIG. 76

12 to 14 weeks. Weight on forearms. Plane of face almost reaches angle of 90° to couch.

FIG. 77

16 to 20 weeks. Weight partly on extended arms. Plane of face reaches angle of 90° to couch.

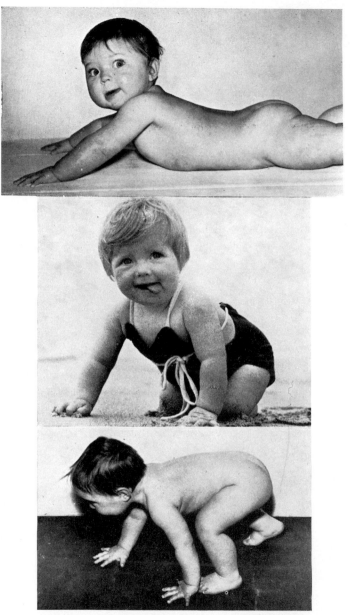

FIG. 78.—24 weeks. Weight on hands, with extended arms.
FIG. 79.—44 weeks. Creep position.
FIG. 80.—25 weeks. Walking like a bear.

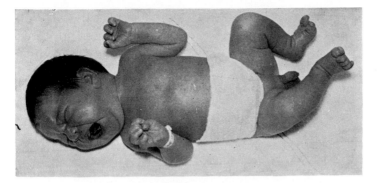

FIG. 81
Full term newborn baby, flexed position.

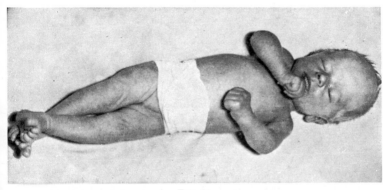

FIG. 82
Abnormal appearance of child aged 8 days. Hands very tightly closed.
The legs tend to cross and they are unusually extended. Knee jerks normal.
Cerebral haemorrhage. Severe convulsions age 3 days.

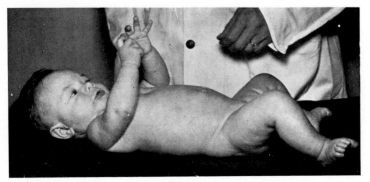

FIG. 83
11-20 weeks. Hand regard.

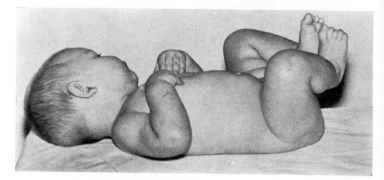

FIG. 84
12–16 weeks. Soles of feet come together.

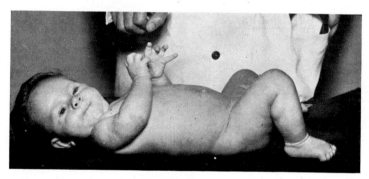

FIG. 85
16 weeks. Soles of feet on couch.

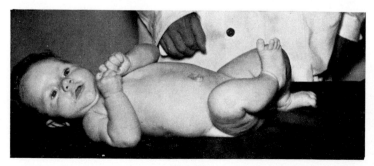

FIG. 86
16 weeks. Foot on opposite knee.

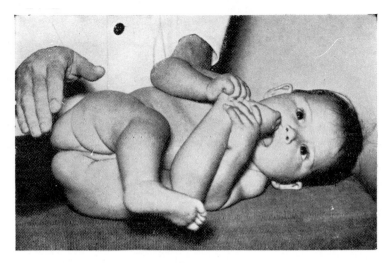

FIG. 87
20 weeks. Feet to mouth.

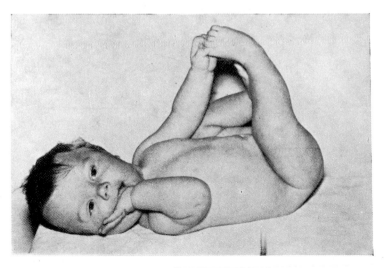

FIG. 88
20 weeks. Plays with feet.

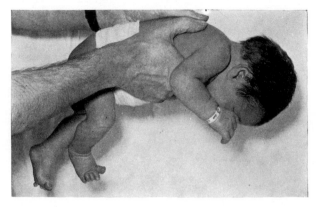

Fig. 89

Full term newborn baby, ventral suspension. Note flexion of elbows and knees, with some extension of hips.

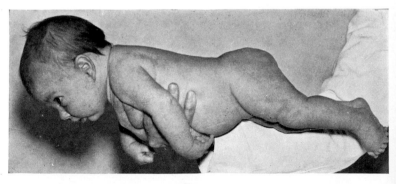

Fig. 90

Six weeks old baby, head held in same plane as rest of body.

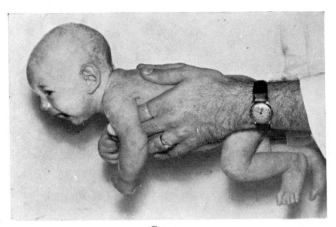

FIG. 91
Normal posture at 8 weeks.
Head held up well beyond plane of rest of body.

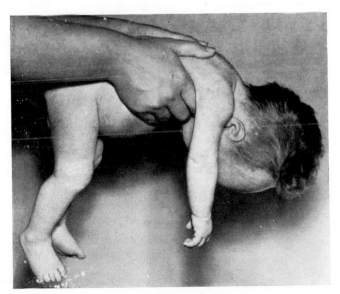

FIG. 92
Abnormal posture. Child of 6 weeks.
Head hangs down too much. Arms and legs extended. No
extension of hips.
(Child with cerebral palsy.)

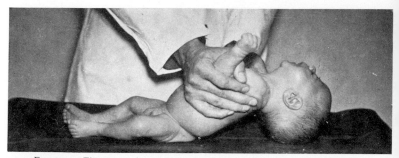

FIG. 93.—First 4 weeks or so. Complete head lag when being pulled to the sitting position.

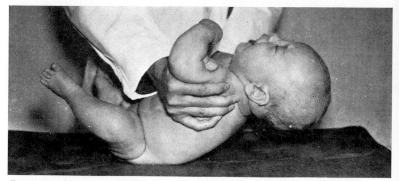

FIG. 94.—About 2 months. Considerable head lag when he is pulled to the sitting position, but lag not complete.

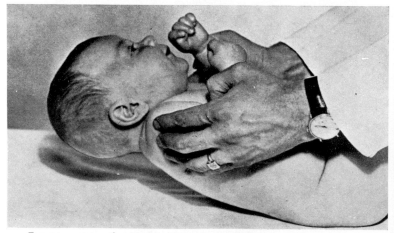

FIG. 95.—4 months. No head lag when pulled to the sitting position.

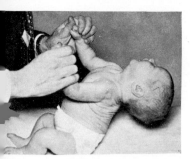

FIG. 96

Newborn baby, half pulled to
sitting position: head lag.

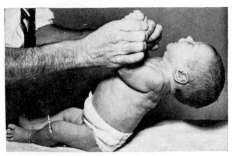

FIG. 97

Same, seconds later, lifting
head up slightly.

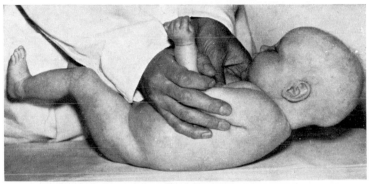

FIG. 98

5 months. Lifts head from supine when about to be pulled up.

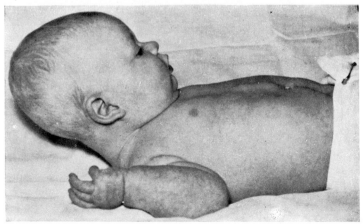

FIG. 99

6 months. Head lifted up spontaneously from supine position.

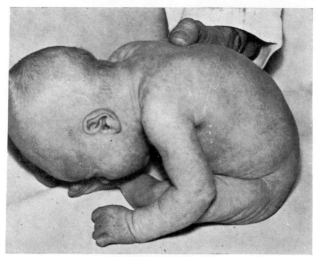

FIG. 100
First 4 weeks or so.
Completely rounded back.

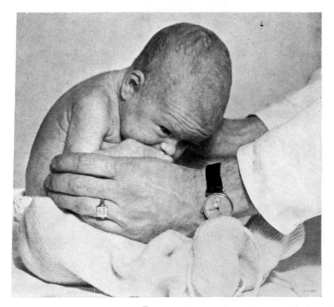

FIG. 101
4 to 6 weeks.
Rounded back. Head help up intermittently.

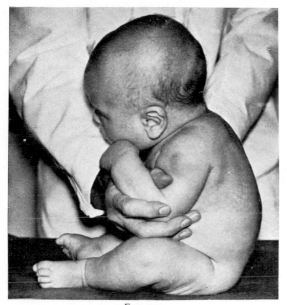

FIG. 102
8 weeks.
Back still rounded. Now raising head well.

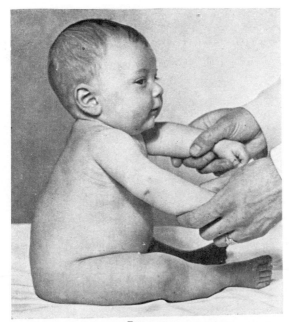

FIG. 103
16 weeks.
Back much straighter.

FIG. 104
26 weeks. Sitting with the hands
forward for support.

FIG. 105
7 months onwards. Sitting without support.

FIG. 106
11 months. Pivoting—turning
round to pick up a toy without
overbalancing.

FIG. 104

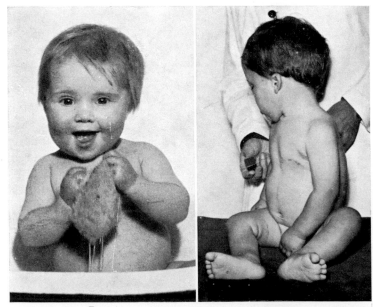

FIG. 105   FIG. 106

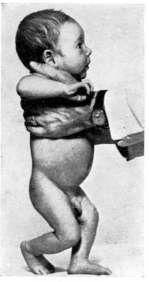

FIG. 107
About 12 weeks.
Bearing much weight.

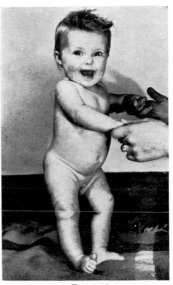

FIG. 108
24 weeks.
Bearing almost all weight.

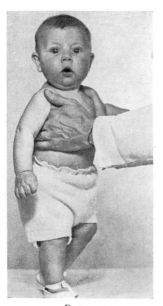

FIG. 109
28 weeks.
Bears full weight.

FIG. 110
48 weeks.
Can stand holding on to furniture
and can walk holding on to it.
('Cruises'.)

FIG. 111
48 weeks.
Walks, 2 hands held.

FIG. 112
52 weeks.
Walks, 1 hand held.

FIG. 113
13 months.
Walks, no help. Arms abducted,
elbows flexed, broad base. Steps
of varying length and direction.

FIG. 114
15 months.
Kneels without support.

of 45 degrees to 90 degrees from couch, weight borne on forearms.

Pulled to sit—only slight head lag.

Held in sitting position—head mostly held up, but still bobs forward.

Supine—no more asymmetrical tonic neck reflex.

HANDS

No grasp reflex.

Hands loosely open.

When rattle is placed in hand, holds it for a minute or more.

Looks as if he would like to grasp object, but cannot without it being placed in hand.

VOCALISATION

Squeals of pleasure.

'Talks' a great deal when spoken to.

VISION

Supine—characteristically watches movements of his own hands. ('Hand regard').

Follows dangling toy from side to side.   (180 degrees).

Promptly looks at object in midline.

HEARING

Turns head to sound.

16 Weeks

GROSS MOTOR

Prone—head and chest off couch so that plane of face is at angle of 90 degrees to couch.

'Swimming'—limbs stretched out in full extension.

Pull to sit—only slight head lag in beginning of movement.

Held in sitting position—head held up constantly.

Child looks actively around.

Head wobbles when examiner suddenly sways child, indicating that head control is incomplete.

Back now curved only in lumbar region.

Supine—head in midline.

HANDS

Hands come together as he plays.   Hand regard still present.

Pulls dress over face in play.

Tries to reach object with hands but overshoots it.

Plays with rattle placed in hand for long period and shakes it, but cannot pick it up if he drops it.

GENERAL UNDERSTANDING
Excites when food prepared, toys seen, showing massive reaction involving all 4 limbs and respirations.
Shows pleasure when pulled to sitting position. Likes to be propped up.

VOCALISATION
Laughs aloud.

VISION
Supine—immediate regard of dangling object.

20 Weeks
GROSS MOTOR
Prone—weight on forearms.
Pull to sit—no head lag.
Held in sitting position—no head wobble when body swayed by examiner.
Back straight.
Supine—feet to mouth.
Held in standing position—bears most of weight.

HANDS
Able to grasp objects voluntarily.
Plays with toes.   Crumples paper.
Splashes in bath.   Objects taken to mouth.

CUBE
Grasps; bidextrous approach; takes it to mouth.

VOCALISATIONS
Razzing; 'Ah-goo'.

GENERAL UNDERSTANDING
Smiles at mirror image.
Pats bottle.

24 Weeks
GROSS MOTOR
Prone—weight on hands, not forearms; chest and upper part of abdomen off couch.
When about to be pulled to sit, lifts head off couch.
Sits supported in high chair.
Held in standing position—almost full weight on legs.
Rolls prone to supine.
No more hand regard.

HANDS
    Holds bottle.
    Grasps his feet.

CUBE
    Palmar grasp of cube.
    Drops one cube when another is given.

FEEDING
    Drinks from cup when it is held to lips.

GENERAL UNDERSTANDING
    When he drops a toy he looks to see where it has gone to and tries
        to recover it.
    May excite on hearing steps.
    Mirror—smiles and vocalises at mirror image.
    Stretches arms out to be taken.
    Shows likes and dislikes.
    May show fear of strangers and be 'coy'.
    Displeasure at removal of toy.

PLAY
    Laughs when head is hidden in towel.

IMITATION
    Imitates cough or protrusion of tongue.

28 Weeks

GROSS MOTOR
    Prone—bears weight on one hand.
    Sits with hands on couch for support.
    Rolls from supine to prone.
    Supine—spontaneously lifts head off couch.
    Held standing—bounces with pleasure.

HANDS
    Feeds self with biscuit.
    Likes to play with paper.
    Unidextrous approach.

CUBES
    Bangs cube on table.
    Transfers it from hand to hand.
    If he has one cube in hand he retains it when second is offered.

FEEDING
    Chews.
    Keeps lips closed when he is offered more food than he wants.

GENERAL UNDERSTANDING
    Imitates simple acts.
    Pats image of self in mirror.
    Responds to name.
    Tries to establish contact with person by cough or other method.
    Expectation in response to repetition of stimulus.

SPEECH
    Syllables—ba, da, ka.

32 Weeks

GROSS MOTOR
    Sits momentarily on floor without support.
    Adjusts posture to reach object, e.g. leans forward to reach.
    Readily bears whole weight on legs when supported. May
        stand holding on.

GENERAL UNDERSTANDING
    Reaches persistently for toys out of reach.
    Responds to 'No'.
    Looks for dropped toy.

IMITATION
    Imitates sounds.

SPEECH
    Combines syllables—da-da; ba-ba.

36 Weeks

GROSS MOTOR
    Prone—in trying to crawl progresses backwards.
    May progress by rolling.
    Sits steadily on floor for 10 minutes.
    Leans forward and recovers balance but cannot lean over side-
        ways.
    Stands, holding on to furniture. Pulls self to stand.

HANDS
    Can pick up object of size of currant between tip of finger and
        thumb.

CUBES
    Compares two cubes by bringing them together.

GENERAL UNDERSTANDING
    Puts arms in front of face to prevent mother washing his face.

40 Weeks

GROSS MOTOR

Prone—crawl position, on abdomen.
Crawls by pulling self forward with hands.
Sitting—can go over into prone, or change from prone to sitting.
Can pull self to sitting position.
Sits steadily with little risk of overbalancing.
Standing—can stand holding on to furniture. Collapses with a
bump.

HANDS

Goes for objects with index finger.

CUBES

Beginning to let go of objects (release).

GENERAL UNDERSTANDING

Looks round corner for object.
Responds to words, e.g. 'Where is daddy?'
Pulls clothes of another to attract attention. Holds object to
examiner but will not release it.
Repeats performance laughed at.

IMITATION

Waves bye-bye. Plays patacake.

44 Weeks

GROSS MOTOR

Prone—creeps, abdomen off couch.
Standing—lifts foot.

CUBES

Beginning to put objects in and out of containers.

DRESSING

Holds arm out for sleeve or foot out for shoe.

GENERAL UNDERSTANDING

Will not give object to examiner: holds it but will not release it.
Drops objects deliberately so that they will be picked up.

48 Weeks

GROSS MOTOR

Prone—when creeping, sole of foot may be flat on couch.
Sitting—pivots, twisting round to pick up object.
Walks, holding on to furniture.
Walks, 2 hands held.

GENERAL UNDERSTANDING
    Rolls ball to examiner.
    Will now give toy to examiner, releasing it.
    Anticipates body movements when nursery rhyme being said.
    Shows interest in picture book.
    Shakes head for 'No'.

PLAY
    Plays peep-bo, covering face.
    Plays game—'Up, down'.

SPEECH
    One word with meaning.

1 Year*

GROSS MOTOR
    Prone—walks on hands and feet like a bear.
    Walks, 1 hand held.
    May shuffle on buttock and hand.

HANDS
    Mouthing virtually stopped.
    Beginning to throw objects to floor.

GENERAL UNDERSTANDING
    May understand meaning of phrases, 'Where is your shoe?'
    May kiss on request.
    Apt to be shy.

SPEECH
    Two or three words with meaning.
    Knows meaning of more words.

SLOBBERING
    Virtually stopped.

15 Months*

GROSS MOTOR
    Creeps up stairs.   Kneels without support.
    Walks without help (from 13 months).
    Can get into standing position without support.
    Falls by collapse.
    Cannot go round corners or stop suddenly.

HANDS
    Constantly throwing objects on to floor.

    *For details and method of examination, see Chapter 13.

CUBES
Builds tower of 2.
Holds 2 cubes in one hand.

BALL
Cannot throw without falling.

DRESSING
Likes to take off shoes.

FEEDING
Feeds self, picking up cup, drinking, putting it down.
Manages spoon but rotates it near mouth.
Feeds self fully, no help.

PENCIL
Imitates scribble or scribbles spontaneously.

GENERAL UNDERSTANDING
Asks for objects by pointing.
May kiss pictures of animal.
Beginning to imitate mother in domestic duties—sweeping,
cleaning.

SPHINCTER CONTROL
Begins to tell mother that he wants to use pottie.
Indicates wet pants.

SPEECH
Jargoning.
Several intelligible words.

SIMPLE FORMBOARD
Inserts round block without being shown.

18 Months★

GROSS MOTOR
Gets up and down stairs, holding rail, without help.
Walks up stairs, one hand held.
Walks, pulling toy or carrying doll.
Seats self on chair.
Beginning to jump (both feet).

CUBES
Tower of 3 or 4.

BALL
Throws ball without fall.

★For details and method of examination, see Chapter 13.

DRESSING
   Takes off gloves, socks, unzips.

FEEDING
   Manages spoon well without rotation.

PENCIL
   Spontaneous scribble.
   Makes stroke imitatively.

GENERAL UNDERSTANDING
   'Domestic mimicry'.   Copies mother in dusting, washing,
      cleaning.

PARTS OF BODY
   Points to 2 or 3 (nose, eye, hair, etc.).

SIMPLE ORDERS[1]
   Two.

COMMON OBJECTS[2]
   One.

PICTURE CARD[3]
   Points to one ('Where is the . . .?')

BOOK
   Turns pages, 2 or 3 at a time.
   Points to picture of car or dog.
   Shows sustained interest.

SPHINCTER CONTROL
   Dry by day; occasional accident.

SPEECH
   Jargon.   Many intelligible words.

SIMPLE FORMBOARD
   Piles 3 blocks.

2 Years★

GROSS MOTOR
   Goes up and down stairs alone, 2 feet per step.   Walks backward
      in imitation (from 21 months).
   Picks up object without falling.
   Runs.   Kicks ball without overbalancing.

[1]Take ball to mother, put it on chair, bring it to me, put it on table.
[2]Penny, shoe, pencil, knife, ball.
[3]Picture card.   See Figure 130.
★For details and method of examination, see Chapter 13.

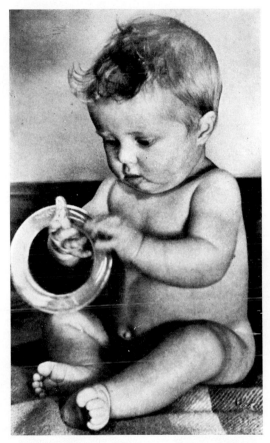

FIG. 115
Manipulation. 6 months. Transfers objects.

facing page 158

Fig. 116.—6 months. Immature palmar grasp of cube.
Fig. 117.—8 months. Grasp, intermediate stage.
Fig. 118.—1 year. Mature grasp of cube.

Fig. 118

Fig. 116

Fig. 117

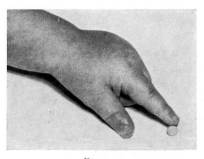

FIG. 119
40 weeks. Index finger approach to
object.

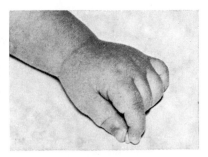

FIG. 120
40 weeks. Finger–thumb apposition,
enabling child to pick up pellet.

FIG. 121
40 weeks. Pokes clapper of bell
with index finger.

FIG. 122
10 month old child feeding himself.
Note the immature grasp.

FIG. 123

4 weeks old baby, showing the baby's intent regard of his mother as she speaks to him. Note his open mouth.

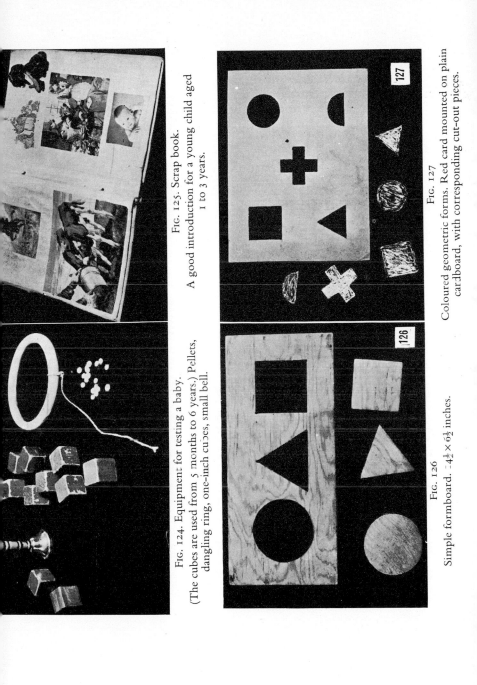

Fig. 124. Equipment for testing a baby.
(The cubes are used from 5 months to 6 years.) Pellets, dangling ring, one-inch cubes, small bell.

Fig. 125. Scrap book.
A good introduction for a young child aged 1 to 3 years.

Fig. 126
Simple formboard. $4\frac{1}{2} \times 6\frac{1}{2}$ inches.

Fig. 127
Coloured geometric forms. Red card mounted on plain cardboard, with corresponding cut-out pieces.

HANDS
Turns door knob, unscrews lid.
Washes and dries hands.

CUBES
Tower of 6 or 7.   (5 or 6 at 21 months).
Imitates train of cubes, without adding chimney.

BALL
Kicks.

DRESSING
Puts on shoes, socks, pants.
Takes off shoes and socks.

PENCIL
Imitates vertical and circular stroke.

GENERAL UNDERSTANDING
Pulls people to show them toys (from 21 months).

PARTS OF BODY
Points to 4.

SIMPLE ORDERS[1]
Obeys 4 (3 at 21 months).

COMMON OBJECTS[2]
Names 3 to 5

PICTURE CARD[3]
Points to 5 ('Where is the . . .?')
Names 3 ('What is this?')

BOOK
Turns pages singly.

SPHINCTER CONTROL
Dry at night if lifted out in evening.

SPEECH
Asks for drink, toilet, food.
Repeats things said (from 21 months).
Uses 'I', 'me', 'you'.
Joins 2 or 3 words in sentences (from 21–24 months), other than
in imitation.
Talks incessantly.

[1]Take ball to mother, put it on chair, bring it to me, put it on table.
[2]Penny, shoe, pencils, knife, ball.
[3]Picture card.   See Figure 130.

SIMPLE FORMBOARD
Places all. (Places 2 or 3 at 21 months). When formboard is rotated, places 3 in correctly, after 4 errors.

PLAY
Wraps up doll. Puts it to bed.
Parallel play. Watches others play and plays near them, but not with them.

$2\frac{1}{2}$ Years*

GROSS MOTOR
Jumps with both feet.
Walks on tiptoes when asked.

CUBES
Tower of 8.
Imitates train, adding chimney.

PENCIL
Holds pencil in hand instead of fist.
Imitates vertical and horizontal stroke.
Two or more strokes for cross.

GENERAL UNDERSTANDING
Helps to put things away.
Begins to notice sex differences.
Knows full name.
Knows sex.

COMMON OBJECTS
Names 5.

PICTURE CARDS
Points to 7: ('Where is the . . .?')
Names 5: ('What is this . . .?').

DIGITS
Repeats 2 in 1 of 3 trials (e.g. say 'Eight five').

COLOURED FORMS
Places 1.

SPHINCTER CONTROL
Attends to toilet need without help, except for wiping.
Climbs on to lavatory seat.

COLOUR SENSE
Names one colour.

*For details and method of examination, see Chapter 13.

SIMPLE FORMBOARD
Inserts all three, adapting after errors.

3 Years*

GROSS MOTOR
Jumps off bottom step.
Goes up stairs, one foot per step, and down stairs, two feet per step.
Stands on one foot for seconds.
Rides tricycle.

HANDS
Can help to set table, not dropping china.

CUBES
Tower of 9.
Imitates building of bridge.

DRESSING
Dresses and undresses fully if helped with buttons and advised about correct shoe.
Unbuttons front and side buttons.

PENCILS
Copies circle (from a card).
Imitates cross.
Draws a man on request.

GENERAL UNDERSTANDING
Knows some nursery rhymes.
May count up to 10.

PICTURE CARD
Names 8: ('What is this?').

DIGITS
Repeats 3: (1 of 3 trials).

COLOURED FORMS
Places 3.

UNCOLOURED GEOMETRIC FORMS
Places 4.

PREPOSITIONS[1].
Obeys 2.

[1]Put the ball under the chair, at the side of the chair, behind the chair, on the chair.

*For details and method of examination, see Chapter 13.

COLOUR
    Names 1.

SIMPLE FORMBOARD
    Adapts, no error, or immediate correction.

GESELL 'INCOMPLETE MAN'.
    Adds 1–2 parts.

SPEECH
    Constantly asking questions.   Uses pronoun.

PLAY
    Dresses and undresses doll; speaks to it.
    Now joins in play.

$3\frac{1}{2}$ Years*
CUBES.   Copies bridge.

PICTURE CARD.   Names 10.

DIGITS.   Repeats 3: (2 of 3 trials).

PREPOSITIONS.   Obeys 3.

UNCOLOURED GEOMETRIC FORMS.   Places 6.

GODDARD FORMBOARD.   56 seconds (best of 3 trials).

PLAY.   Imaginary companion.

4 Years*
GROSS MOTOR
    Goes down stairs, one foot per step.
    Skips on one foot.

HANDS
    Can button clothes fully.

CUBES
    Imitates gate.

PENCIL
    Copies cross.

GENERAL UNDERSTANDING
    Questioning at its height.   Says which is the larger of 2 lines.
    Tells tall stories.

    *For details and method of examination, see Chapter 13.

DIGITS
   3 (3 of 3 trials).

COLOURED FORMS
   Places all.
UNCOLOURED FORMS
   Places 8.

PREPOSITIONS
   Obeys 4.

SPHINCTER CONTROL
   Attends to own toilet needs.

GODDARD FORMBOARD
   46 seconds: (best of 3 trials).

GOODENOUGH TEST
   4.

GESELL 'INCOMPLETE MAN'.
   Adds 3 parts.

PLAY
   Imaginative play with doll (e.g. being a nurse).

4½ Years*

CUBES.   Copies gate.

PENCIL.   Copies square.

DIGITS.   4: (1 of 3 trials).

UNCOLOURED GEOMETRIC FORMS.   Places 9.

GODDARD FORMBOARD.   40 seconds: (best of 3 trials).

GOODENOUGH TEST.   6.

GESELL 'INCOMPLETE MAN'.
   Adds 6 parts.

5 Years*

GROSS MOTOR
   Skips on both feet.

CUBES
   Cannot make steps.

*For details and method of examination, see Chapter 13.

DRESSING
Can tie shoelaces.

PENCIL
Copies triangle.

GENERAL UNDERSTANDING
Gives age.
Distinguishes morning from afternoon
Compares 2 weights.

UNCOLOURED GEOMETRIC FORMS
All.

DIGITS
Repeats 4: (2 of 3 trials).

GODDARD FORMBOARD
35 seconds: (best of 3 trials).

GOODENOUGH TEST
8.

GESELL 'INCOMPLETE MAN'
Adds 6–7 parts.

COLOURS
Names 4.

PREPOSITION (triple order).
Put this on the chair, open the door, then give me that book'.

6 Years*
PENCIL
Copies diamond.

DIGITS
Repeats 5.

GENERAL UNDERSTANDING
Knows number of fingers.   Names weekdays.
Knows right from left.
Counts 13 pennies, not in a row.   Names 4 coins.

GODDARD FORMBOARD
27 seconds: (best of 3 trials).

*For details and method of examination, see Chapter 13.

GOODENOUGH TEST
12.

GESELL 'INCOMPLETE MAN'
Adds 7 parts.

Essential Milestones

Many milestones of development may be important, but the following are the essential milestones which anyone responsible for assessing babies needs to know:

Birth	Prone—pelvis high, knees under abdomen.
	Ventral suspension—elbows flex, hips partly extended.
4–6 weeks	Smiles at mother.
6 weeks	Prone—pelvis flat.
12–16 weeks	Turns head to sound.
	Holds object placed in hand.
12–20 weeks	Hand regard.
20 weeks	Goes for objects and gets them, without their being placed in the hand.
26 weeks	Transfers objects, one hand to another.
	Chews.
	Sits, hands forward for support.
	Supine—lifts head up spontaneously.
	Feeds self with biscuit.
9–10 months	Index finger approach.
	Finger thumb apposition.
	Creep.
	Patacake, byebye.
	Helps dress—holding arm out for coat, foot out for shoe, or transferring object from hand in order to insert hand in sleeve.
13 months	Casting (ceases by about 15 months).
	Walks, no help.
	2–3 single words.
15–18 months	Domestic mimicry.
15 months	Feeds self fully if given a chance, picking up a cup, drinking, putting it down without help.
	Casting stops. Mouthing stops.
18 months	Begins to tell mother about wetting.
21–24 months	Joins 2–3 words together spontaneously.
2 years	Mainly dry by day.
3 years	Mainly dry by night.
	Dresses self, except for buttons at back, if given a chance.
	Stands momentarily on one foot.

REFERENCES

1. ANNETTE, M. (1968) Aspects of human lateral asymmetry and its bearing on intellectual development in childhood hemiplegia. Report to the Spastics Society, London.
2. AUSUBEL, D. P. (1958) Theory and Problems of Child Development. New York: Grune and Stratton.
3. BAKWIN, H. (1950) Lateral Dominance. *J. Pediat.*, **36**, 385.
4. BARSLEY, M. (1966) The Left Handed Book. London: Souvenir Press.

5. BROWN, C. A. (1961) The Development of visual Capacity in the Infant and Young Child. *Cerebral Palsy Bulletin.*, **3**, 364.
6. BURT, C. (1950) The Backward Child. London: Univ. of London Press.
7. CLARK, M. M. (1957) Left Handedness. London: Univ. of London Press.
8. EAMES, T. H. (1957) Frequency of Cerebral Lateral Dominance Variations among School Children of Premature and Full Term Birth. *J. Pediat.* **51**, 300.
9. FREEDMAN, D. G. (1964) Smiling in Blind Infants and the Issue of innate VS acquired. *J. Child Psychol.*, **5**, 171.
10. GESELL, A., AMES, L. B. (1947) The Development of Handedness. *J. genet. Psychol.*, **70**, 155.
11. HILDRETH, G. (1949) The Development and Training of Hand Dominance. *J. genet. Psychol.* **75**, 199.
12. HILLMAN, H. H. (1956). Abstract in Child Developm. Abstr. (1957) 31, No. 401.
13. ILLINGWORTH, R. S. (1958) Dissociation as a Guide to Developmental Assessment. *Arch. Dis. Childh.*, **33**, 118.
14. KARELITZ, S., KARELITZ, R. E., ROSENFELD, L. S. (1960) In Bowman, P. W., Mautner, H. V. *Mental Retardation.* New York: Grune and Stratton.
15. KARLIN, I. W., STRAZZULLA, M. (1952) Speech and Language Problems of Mentally Defective Children. *J. Speech Dis.*, **17**, 286.
16. LILLYWHITE, H. (1958) Doctor's Manual of Speech Disorders. *J. Amer. med. Ass.*, **167**, 850.
17. McGRAW, M. B. (1940) Neuromuscular Mechanism of the Infant. *Amer. J. Dis. Child.*, **60**, 1031.
18. MORLEY, M. E. (1957) The Development and Disorders of Speech in Childhood. London: Livingstone.
19. MURPHY, K. P. (1964) Learning Problems of the Cerebrally Palsied. Study Group, Oxford. London. Spastics Society.
20. MURPHY, K. P. (1962) Ascertainment of Deafness in Children. Panorama, Dec. 3rd.
21. PEIPER, A. (1963) *Cerebral Function in Infancy and Childhood.* London: Pitman.
22. ROBSON, P. (1970) 'Shuffling, hitching, scooting or sliding—some observations in 30 otherwise normal children.' *Develop. Med. Child. Neurol.*, **12**, 608.
23. SHERIDAN, M. (1964) Disorders of Communication in Young Children. *Mth. Bull. Minist. Hlth Lab. Serv.*, **23**, 20.
24. SHERIDAN, M. (1974). What is normal vision at five to seven years? *Develop. Med. Child Neurol.* **16**, 189.
25. SPITZER, R. L., RABKIN, R., KROMER, Y. (1959) The Relationship between Mixed Dominance and Reading Disabilities. *J. Pediat.*,**54**, 76.
26. TRAVERTHEN, C. (1974). Conversations with a two-month old. *New Scientist*, **62**, 230.
27. VERNON, M. D. (1957) Backwardness in Reading. Cambridge: Cambridge University Press.
28. WATSON, J. B. (1931). Behaviourism. London: Kegan Paul.
29. ZANGWILL, O. (1960). Cerebral dominance and its relation to psychological problems. London: Oliver and Boyd.
30. ZANGWILL, O. L. (1968)ʼ. in DORFMAN, A. Language and language disorders. Child Care in Health and Disease. Chicago: Year Book Publishers.

CHAPTER 10

VARIATIONS IN INDIVIDUAL FIELDS OF DEVELOPMENT

'Whoever, said the old goat sheep, divided all living things into sheep and goats, was ignorant that we neutrals and nondescripts outnumber all the rest, and that your sheep and your goat are merely freak specimens of ourselves, chiefly remarkable for their rarity'.—R. L. Stevenson: *Fable of the Goat Sheep*.

In the study of the development of infants and children, it is essential to remember that all children are different. If they were all the same the study of development would be easy. As they are all different, and different in a wide variety of ways, the study is one of great difficulty. We can all say what the average level of development is for a child of a given age, but none can say what the normal is, for it is impossible to draw the dividing line between normal and abnormal. We can say that the further away from the average he is, the more likely he is to be abnormal.

There are several different patterns of development. They are as follows:

1. Average.
2. Average, becoming superior.
3. Advanced in certain fields.
4. Advanced in all fields.
5. Average or superior, deteriorating, or slowing down in development.
6. Retarded in all fields.
7. Retarded in all fields, becoming average or superior.
8. Retarded in some fields.
9. Lulls in development. A child may appear to make no progress in one field of development, such as speech, for several weeks, and then for no apparent reason he very rapidly advances in that field.

The truly average child, the child who is average in everything, is a rarity. Some appear to be merely average at first, but later prove to be mentally superior; it may be that the early developmental tests were not able to detect the signs of superiority, or else full maturation was delayed. Some are advanced or retarded in certain fields of development—often because of a familial trait, or, in the case of retardation, because of a physical factor (such as deafness in the case of delayed speech). The course of development of some children slows down, as in mongols, while in others tragic deterioration occurs because of severe emotional deprivation, poor education, degenerative diseases, psychosis, encephalitis or metabolic diseases. Retardation in all fields usually signifies mental subnormality, but can occasionally be merely a feature of delayed maturation.

In this chapter the variations in the various fields of development and the reasons for the variations will be discussed in detail.

Variations in Motor Activity

Infants and children vary enormously in the degree of motor activity. One knows that active wiry babies are liable to posset more than the fat placid, less active ones.

Variations in Gross Motor Development

There are considerable normal variations in the age of sitting, walking and other manifestations of gross motor development. In many children with delayed development there is no discoverable reason for the delay. In others there is a variety of factors, such as conditions affecting muscle tone or mental retardation. It is probable that an important factor which governs the age of sitting and walking is myelination of the appropriate part of the nervous system.

ADVANCED MOTOR DEVELOPMENT. Some children learn to sit and walk at an unusually early age. One often finds that there is a family history of similarly advanced motor development. Advanced motor development can be detected early, often as soon as the third or fourth week, and early sitting can be predicted by the sixth week with a good degree of accuracy. For the purpose of demonstrating this I took cinematograph records of infants with advanced motor development in the first 8 weeks, and showed the predictive value of the early tests by refilming the infants at later ages to show the unusually early development of sitting and walking.

Advanced motor development gives no indication of mental superiority. Precocious puberty is not associated with advanced motor development.

I saw a boy who was able to creep actively at $4\frac{1}{2}$ months (not crawl), and to pull himself readily to the standing position at $5\frac{1}{2}$ months. I expressed the opinion at that time that his I.Q. was not better than the average. At the age of 6 months he could walk holding on to furniture and at 8 months he could walk without support. At $4\frac{1}{2}$ years he could not dress himself fully, and could not draw anything or count. His I.Q. score at 5 years was 88. I saw another boy who could walk well without support at 8 months. His I.Q. score at the age of 6 years was 103.

Numerous studies have shown that the motor development of negro infants is commonly more advanced than that of white infants. The advancement does not extend to adaptive, fine motor, language or personal social development. Geber and Dean[13] claimed that newborn African children behaved like European children at 3 or 4 weeks of age: later they commonly sit unsupported at 3 or 4 months for a few seconds and for half an hour or more at 5 months.   At 7 months they could stand without support and walk alone at 9 months. It is not certain whether this advancement occurs in certain tribes and countries or in negro children as a whole.   The advanced motor development of Uganda infants was discussed by Mary Ainsworth.[2]   She suggested that the precocious development was in some way related to close infant-mother relationship, and that social and cultural factors were responsible.   Others have made similar suggestions.[54]   Yet in five longitudinal European studies, carried out in England, Belgium, France, Sweden and Switzerland, no social (or sex) differences were found in the age of walking.

Lateness in Gross Motor Development

The following are the usual factors related to delayed motor development.

1. *Familial Factors*.   The age at which children learn to walk is often a familial feature.   It probably depends on the familial rate of myelination of the spinal cord.

2. *Environmental Factors*.   Children who are brought up in an institution from early infancy are likely to be late in motor development, as in other fields.   This may be in part due to lack of practice. If mothers deliberately keep their infants off their legs to prevent them developing rickets, knock-knee or bow legs, they weaken the child's legs and may retard walking.

3. *Personality*.   The personality of the child has some bearing on the age of walking, in that children with little confidence and much caution, or children who lose confidence as a result of falls, may be delayed in learning to walk.   A child with extreme delay in learning to walk (4 years) had no mechanical difficulty and had a normal I.Q. She was able to walk with one finger held for a whole year before she eventually summoned up enough courage to walk alone.   When a child like this eventually walks without support, it is at once obvious that the gait is a mature one, indicating that he could have walked long before if his confidence had permitted.   Slippery shoes in a child of 12 months may be enough to cause falls and delay in walking.

4. *Mental Subnormality*.   Most mentally retarded children are late in learning to sit, but not all (Ch. 15).   Mongols are later in learning to walk than other mentally defective children of a comparable level of intelligence.   The reason for this may be hypotonia.

As a general guide, one can say that a child with an I.Q. of less than 20 may learn to walk, as long as he has no cerebral palsy: a child with an I.Q. of 20 to 40, in the absence of cerebral palsy, can certainly be expected to learn to walk.

5. *Abnormalities of Muscle Tone*.   If there is excessive muscle tone, as in cerebral palsy, walking will be delayed.   Some children with

cerebral palsy never walk.   It would not be profitable to analyse the average age at which children with different forms of cerebral palsy learn to sit or walk, because there is an additional vital factor, the intelligence, which has a profound effect on motor development.

In the case of the spastic form of cerebral palsy, the child with hemiplegia is likely to learn to walk sooner than the child with diplegia or quadriplegia, especially if his I.Q. is satisfactory.   I have seen an occasional hemiplegic child with a good I.Q. who learned to sit and walk at the usual age.   The child with diplegia with a normal I.Q. may not be late in sitting, but he will be considerably delayed in learning to walk.   I do not know what factors, other than the I.Q., decide the age at which a child with diplegia will be able to sit unsupported.   They may include the amount of spasm in the hamstrings and of the trunk muscles, the amount of extension thrust, and the presence and strength of the tonic neck reflex.   I have seen some children with severe diplegia who could sit at the usual age without support (7 months).

The usual story of diplegia with a good I.Q. is average or somewhat retarded sitting, with grossly delayed walking, but normal development in all other fields.   Below is an example.

Case Report.—This girl was born prematurely, weighing 2325 g.   She grasped a rattle voluntarily at 5 months, sat unsupported at 8 months and held and could manage a cup at 15 months.   Slight general backwardness with diplegia was then diagnosed.   She said single words at 20 months and put words together at 24 months.   She walked alone at 6½ years, when her I.Q. score was 85.

I have seen a child with a mild to moderate diplegia but with a normal I.Q. who was able to walk without help at 18 months.   The child with spastic quadriplegia is almost invariably retarded in both sitting and walking, and his I.Q. is usually lower than that of the child with hemiplegia or diplegia.

The child with athetosis is usually late in learning to sit and walk, but not always, provided that the I.Q. is normal.

The child with rigidity is virtually always severely mentally defective and may never walk.

The child with ataxia or tremor is usually late in learning to walk.

The child with hypotonia is late in learning to sit or walk, and if the condition is severe he will never learn to do either.   There are probably other related conditions.   The child with benign congenital hypotonia will learn to sit and walk very late.   I have seen several who were able to walk between the age of 4 and 6 years.

A child who develops hypotonia as a result of severe illness, rickets, or acrodynia, will be delayed in gross motor development, but as the underlying disease improves his motor development advances.

A child with meningomyelocele with involvement of the lower limbs will be unable to walk without a series of skilled orthopaedic procedures, including muscle transplants.

The following is an example of hypotonia, with a moderately low I.Q.

Case Report.—This girl was born at term, without asphyxia, but she was limp and caused anxiety.   The tendon jerks were normal.   At 5 months there was complete head lag.   At 13 months she showed mature transfer of objects, but the head control was that of a 10 week old baby.   She was retarded in other fields.   A diagnosis of benign congenital hypotonia with mental retardation was made.   She was able to join words together at 27 months and to walk unaided at 5 years, when the I.Q. was 59.

The usual story in cases of benign congenital hypotonia is that of defective gross motor development, with normal development in other fields—smiling, chewing and manipulation, with late sitting and walking.

Another child was referred to me at the age of 8 months for confirmation of the diagnosis of mental defectiveness.   The developmental history was not reliable.   The head control was that of a 4 months old baby, but he was interested in test objects.   His manipulative development was not less than that of an average 8 months old baby.   He rapidly transferred objects from hand to hand, and his grasp was a mature one.   He was seen to chew.   He was markedly hypotonic, and he showed the typical signs of pink disease.   He made an uninterrupted recovery, and on follow-up examination was normal in all respects.

6. *Neuromuscular Disease.*   In the case below the only complaint was lateness in walking.

Case Report.   Delayed walking due to Werdnig-Hoffmann's Disease
This girl was referred to me when she was 12 months' old because she was not nearly able to walk.   Her developmental history was average.   She had begun to smile at 5 weeks, to grasp objects voluntarily and to chew at 5 months, to imitate at 6 months, to wave bye-bye and to hold her arm out for clothes at 9 months, and to say several words with meaning by 11 months.   She was able to sit unsupported on the floor at 7 months, but the mother thought that she was not quite as steady when sitting 2 months ago as she was 3 months ago.

On examination she was an interested, alert girl with good concentration, vocalising well.   The manipulation was normal, and there was prompt finger-thumb apposition.   She was able to sit steadily, but she bore virtually no weight on the legs.   She was an obese girl, and there was slight hypotonia.   Knee jerks could not be obtained, but tendon jerks elsewhere were normal.   There was no congenital dermal sinus or other spinal abnormality.   The gluteal and thigh creases were asymmetrical, but the X-ray of the hips was normal.   No fibrillary twitching was seen, but the tentative diagnosis of Werdnig Hoffmann's disease was made.   She was observed for 5 months, during which time no change in her condition occurred.   It was then decided that further investigation should be carried out, and the electrical reactions, muscle biopsy and electro-myogram confirmed the diagnosis of Werdnig-Hoffmann's disease.   The cerebrospinal fluid was normal.
In this case the developmental examination revealed the neurological disease.

7. Children with the *Duchenne type of muscular dystrophy* are often late in motor development.   This may be due to the commonly associated slight mental subnormality and to reasons unknown.

8. *Shuffling*. The peculiar mode of progression known as shuffling or hitching on one hand and one buttock may delay the onset of walking. The child learns to progress rapidly in this way. The retardation caused is not severe.

9. *Blindness*. Blind children have to be taught to walk. In one study only two out of 12 children crawled before they learnt to walk. A blind child's motor development may be retarded because he is not given the same chance to learn to walk as normal children. His parents may be so afraid that he will hurt himself that they do not let him practise walking.

10. *Cause Unknown* If gross motor development is considerably delayed, there is usually a good cause for it, but this is by no means always the case. I have seen a dozen or more children with no physical or mental handicap, who were unable to walk without help until the second birthday or later. There was no discoverable cause for this in any of them. All were followed up and were shown to be normal children.

Case 1.—This boy was delivered normally at term. He began to smile at 6 weeks, to vocalise at 8 weeks, to grasp objects voluntarily at 5 months, to transfer them from hand to hand at 6 months and to chew at that age. He began to release objects and to play patacake at 11 months. On the other hand he could not sit without support till 19 months, or walk without help until 30 months. At the age of 5 years his I.Q. test score was 104 and there were no abnormal neurological signs.

Case 2.—A girl who was delivered normally at term could grasp objects voluntarily at 4 months, manage a cup of milk without help at 10 months, and was speaking in sentences at 12 months. She sat without support at 9 months, but could not walk without help till 4 years. Her I.Q. at 5 years was in the region of 125. There was no physical disability.

Others walked without help at 24 months (I.Q. average), 24 months (with advanced speech in long sentences); 25 months (I.Q. just average), and 30 months (I.Q. 108).

Delayed walking is *not* due to congenital dislocation of the hip. It is *not* due to obesity. Norval found that thin or tall babies tend to walk earlier than fat ones, but others thought that this was an old wives' tale. I saw a grossly obese child, weighing 25·4 kg at 15 months, who walked without help at 10 months.

OTHER VARIATIONS IN MOTOR DEVELOPMENT. One of my colleagues at Sheffield[17] has shown that the current tendency in the United States to place young babies in the prone position for sleep and play apparently led to an alteration of the developmental pattern in the prone and supine positions. Babies managed in this way seemed to be more advanced in the prone position than babies who are placed on their back for sleep and play. It was suggested that the relationship of posture to observed developmental variations might repay further study. Others could not confirm Holt's work on this subject.[37]

For reasons unknown some children omit the stage of creeping.

Crawling and Walking Before Sitting

Below is a bizarre example of unusual motor development.

Case Report.—This girl, aged 19 months when first seen (birth weight 1080 g) was referred because she could not sit, although she could crawl forwards and walk well with one hand held, or walk while holding on to furniture.

She had been able to go for objects and get them from 4 months. She had begun to say words with meaning at 9 months. She could pick up a cup, drink and put it down without help from one year, and she had begun to walk, holding on to furniture, at that date.

She was a bright, interested girl, talking and jargoning well. She was seen to walk well, holding on to the edge of the desk. When placed in the sitting position, although head control was full, the back was markedly rounded, but there was no spasm of the hamstrings. She repeatedly fell backwards. The grasp with each hand was normal. The knee jerks were normal and there was no ankle clonus. There was no shortening in either leg. Spinal muscles were normal and there was no evidence of vertebral or spinal anomalies.

The clinical diagnosis was either congenital shortening of the gluteus maximus or congenital shortening of the hamstrings.

Another child who was able to crawl before he was able to sit had suffered from emotional deprivation by being brought up in an institution. The explanation of the anomaly of development may have laid in the fact that he could crawl without help, but needed help to sit, and the staff had not time to give him that help.

Another child who showed this variation had congenital hypotonia.

Grasping and Manipulation

Voluntary grasping may begin as early as 3 months, but that is rare. It is unusual for a normal full term child not to be able to grasp objects by 6 months.

The subsequent development of manipulation depends not only on intelligence, but on the child's aptitudes—some showing early manipulative ability greater than others of comparable intelligence.

Smiling

The earliest age at which I have personally seen a child smile in response to social overture was 3 days. From that day onwards smiling became rapidly more frequent. He was a uniformly advanced baby, holding and playing with a rattle, for instance, for several minutes at $2\frac{1}{2}$ weeks, and following an object for 180 degrees at 3 weeks. He proved to have a high I.Q. in later years. Although it is difficult to date the first smile accurately, the sequence of relevant aspects of development indicated that in this case (and in two other examples seen by me) the dating was likely to be correct.

Söderling[96] analysed the age of the first smile in 400 normal full term infants. The following were the figures:

First smile	Percentage
Before 2 weeks	0
2–3 weeks	11
3–4 weeks	49
4–5 weeks	21
5–6 weeks	19

Few normal full term babies reach 8 weeks of age without having begun to smile.   There is little latitude in this direction for normal babies.   Nevertheless, I have seen an occasional full term baby who did not begin to smile until 8 to 10 weeks of age, without delay in other fields, and who subsequently turned out to be normal.

I had a child referred to me with a diagnosis of mental deficiency, because of the absence of smiling by the age of 1 year.   She was an example of the Möbius syndrome of congenital facial diplegia, with an I.Q. score of about 75.   A similar difficulty would arise with a baby suffering from myotonic dystrophy.   A baby with infantile autism is unresponsive towards his mother and would probably be late in beginning to smile.

It should be noted that mothers are apt to interpret any facial movement as a smile, and have the extraordinary idea that they smile when they suffer pain from wind.   Mothers commonly tickle the circumoral area of a baby to get him to smile, and the resultant reflex responses ("cardinal points reflex") may be wrongly interpreted as a smile.

Delayed Visual Maturation

Delayed visual maturation may cause serious doubts as to whether a child is blind or not.[22]   I described a boy first seen by me at the age of just under four months, because he did not appear to see.   He did not smile at his mother, or watch her face or focus his eyes.   He had begun to vocalise at seven weeks and to turn his head to sound at twelve weeks.   On examination he was developmentally up to the average in all respects.   On ophthalmoscopic examination (by me and by two ophthalmologists) no abnormality was found, and there was no nystagmus.   The provisional diagnosis of delayed visual maturation was made, and the parents were informed that there were good grounds for optimism, though because of the rarity of the condition it was impossible to be sure.

He showed signs of seeing at five months, and by six months he was following a light and beginning to follow a dangling ring.   He appeared to be normal in all respects at ten months.   At the age of five years he showed evidence of a better than average intelligence at an ordinary preparatory school.   He had a slight strabismus, for which glasses were worn, but the vision was normal.

I also saw a girl who apparently saw nothing for the first six months.

She had spasmus nutans.   No abnormality was found by an ophthalmologist.   She began to show signs of seeing at six months and by a year of age was normal.   At school age she showed a better than average intelligence, with normal vision.

It is not possible to say whether these children were genuinely unable to see, or whether they were unable to interpret what they saw (visual agnosia).

The Blind Child

If blindness develops shortly after birth the muscles round the eye—the orbicularis oculis, corrugator supercilii and frontalis muscles—are not involved in facial expression, remaining rigid and motionless. If the child becomes blind sometime after birth, the facial expression is normal.[42]

Blind children may show a variety of mannerisms,[53] such as eye-boring, pressing the finger into the eye—beginning in the first year and ending by the fifth or sixth year.   The child may show rapid symmetrical flapping of the hands, hyperextension or flexion of the head, twirling, massive to and fro body swaying, jumping backwards and forwards or facial grimacing.

The assessment of the development of a blind child is difficult; the tests used and the problems of assessment were discussed by the Bakwins.[3]   They wrote that over the age of three the Interim Hayes Bint Intelligence Test is favoured by many.   Apparent backwardness may be due to unsatisfactory tests, restricted past experiences, inadequate opportunities for learning or overprotection.   The mean I.Q. of blind children is less than that of the normal population (see Chapter 16).

It would be expected that blindness would retard smiling.[12]   Not only does he not receive the stimulus of seeing his mother's face, but he is 'at risk' of being mentally retarded—and therefore late in his milestones of development.

Blind children may show what Gesell termed 'hand regard'.   This 'hand regard', seen in normal infants from 12 to 24 weeks of age, is presumably a developmental phenomenon and not related to vision.

It must be remembered that under certain circumstances children may recover vision after complete blindness.   Lorber[30] has described this after prolonged blindness resulting from hydrocephalus and tuberculous or other pyogenic meningitis.

Delayed Auditory Maturation

Some children who are mentally normal appear to be deaf for some weeks or months, and subsequently respond normally to sound. Ingram[23] studied several examples of this.   He suggested that it may be the result of damage to the auditory nerve or its central connections before birth, and that recovery then follows.   He wrote that some infants with kernicterus do not begin to respond to sound until the age of 4 or 5 months. He considered that some children with brain damage appear to be deaf in the early weeks, but later are found to hear, though they may be later in distinguishing their parent's or sibling's voices, and late in learning to perceive or distinguish what is said. Others have difficulty in perceiving sounds and distinguishing them, and are late in acquiring speech. They are slow to react to sound, and slow to differentiate them or perceive their significance. He termed this developmental auditory imperception.

Sheridan[72] saw children who appeared to be deaf for some weeks after an attack of meningitis, and were then found to hear normally.

Chewing

There is little variation in the age at which normal infants learn to chew. They may begin as early as 5 months, but nearly all full term infants can chew by the age of 7 months. The age of chewing is delayed if a sufficiently mature baby is given thickened feeds only, with nothing solid to bite on.

Feeding and Dressing

The age at which children learn to feed and dress themselves depends not only on their intelligence and manipulative ability but on the opportunity to learn. The age at which they do it also depends on their personality and desire for independence.

Sphincter Control

There are great individual variations in the age at which sphincter control is acquired. It is difficult to say how soon control can be acquired, because it is not easy to distinguish the early conditioning from voluntary control. I doubt whether voluntary control begins before the age of 12 months.

Many children do not acquire control of the bladder for several years. Thorough investigation reveals no abnormality, though some would disagree with this. When one sees a child who has never had a dry night, and has long passed the usual age for acquiring control of the bladder, there is usually a family history of the same complaint. This is termed primary enuresis, and it is almost certainly due basically to delayed maturation of the nervous system. This cannot be the only factor, however, because primary enuresis is more common in the lower social classes than in the upper. The quality of home care is relevant. Many of these children retain the primitive urgency into school years. It is normal for an 18 to 24 month old child to have great urgency, so that he cannot wait to pass urine, but as he matures he loses this urgency; the child with primary enuresis commonly retains this urgency for several years.

The Newcastle team[35] found that a low social class, emotional deprivation, deficient physical care, social dependence, marital instability, parental crime and defective family supervision were strongly related to the incidence of enuresis. I agree with Miller's conclusion,[36] on the basis of the Newcastle work, that 'the social correlations were such that it is reasonable to think that most enuresis occurs in a child with a slow pattern of maturation when that child is in a family where he does not receive sufficient care to acquire proper conditioning. We doubt if the continuous type of enuresis is caused by major psychological difficulties at the onset, though we acknowledge that psychological difficulties can occur as an overlap'. 'Enuresis is not only a disturbance of development in an individual child, but also a reflection of family relationships and attitudes'.

Early conditioning has been discussed in Ch. 9. The sensitive or critical period for learning may be relevant: faulty training or the occurrence of psychological stress at the time when the child is first able to control the bladder may be of great importance. Laziness may be a factor when housing is poor and the only lavatory is out of doors.

When a child who has been dry at night begins to wet (secondary enuresis), the cause is almost always psychological, but may be due to the development of frequency of micturition or to polyuria, in either case particularly if he has only recently acquired control of the bladder. The cause usually lies in insecurity, separation from the parents, jealousy or other emotional trauma.

The acquisition of sphincter control can be delayed by over-enthusiastic 'training'—compelling the child to sit on the pottie when he is trying to get off, and punishment for failure to do what is expected of him, so that his normal negativism comes into play, and he may furthermore come to associate the pottie with unpleasantness, and become conditioned against it.

Organic causes of delayed sphincter control are of great importance. The development of frequency or polyuria, especially during the sensitive period of learning, may cause incontinence. Some blame a small bladder capacity for primary enuresis. Constant dribbling incontinence in a boy suggests urethral obstruction, and in a girl it suggests an ectopic ureter entering the vagina or urethra. In either sex the incontinence may be due to a meningomyelocele or other spinal abnormality. Occult spina bifida is always irrelevant. The surgical causes of enuresis were fully reviewed by Smith in Australia.[45]

The Newcastle workers found that least nine per cent at five were still wetting the bed habitually or frequently. This corresponds closely with White's figure[52] of 'nearly 10 per cent' for Croydon children.

In a study of 1129 enuretics[10a]—it was found that without the use of an electric buzzer the annual spontaneous cure rate was at age 5–9 years, 14 per cent, 10–14 years 16 per cent, 15–19 years 16 per cent. and that three per cent were still wetting over the age of twenty.

On the basis of the papers mentioned above, the review by Kolvin, MacKeith and Meadow[20] and my own experience, I support the view that urinary incontinence is related to numerous factors, many of them interacting: they include maturation of the nervous system, conditioning, the nature, quality and timing of training methods, the sensitive or critical period, the child's ego and personality and the personality of the mother, the mother's ignorance of normal development and variations in it, psychological stress, social factors, laziness, bladder capacity, polyuria and organic disease. I have discussed the problem in more detail elsewhere.[19]

Speech

The development of speech depends on a range of factors: genetic, auditory, environmental, intellectual and constitutional, one interacting with the other. As would be expected there are wide variations in speech development in children. On the one hand, normal children may begin to say words with meaning by the age of 8 months, and even make sentences spontaneously before the first birthday: on the other hand many children of superior intelligence may not begin to speak at all until the third or fourth birthday and have defective speech by the age of 5. Girls learn to speak earlier than boys.

Morley,[39] in her sample of 114 children from the Newcastle-on-Tyne 1,000 family survey, found that 73 per cent of the children were using words with meaning by the first birthday, with a range of 8 to 30 months, and 40 per cent had begun to join words together, other than in imitation, by the age of 18 months. The range for this was 10 to 44 months. Eighty-nine per cent had begun to join words by the age of 24 months. In 10 per cent speech was not intelligible at the age of 4 years. Seventeen per cent had defects of articulation of serious degree at 4 years, and 14 per cent at 5 years. All these children had an I.Q. within the normal range. These figures, though based on a small sample in one city, give a good idea of the variations in speech development in normal children. In the same survey[35] it was found that speech defects such as stammering were more common in social classes 4 and 5 and in homes with poor maternal care.

Gesell et al. wrote that a normal 2 year old may have a vocabulary of a few words or more than 2,000.

UNUSUALLY EARLY DEVELOPMENT OF SPEECH. There are several stories of unusually early speech. Some of these were described by Barlow. We discussed these in our book 'Lessons from Childhood' concerning the childhood of famous men and women.

Delay in the Development of Speech and Asphasia

GENERAL ANALYSIS OF CAUSES

In any analysis of speech problems it is difficult to determine how selected the cases were.   Only a limited number of children with delay in speech development are referred to a speech clinic.   Morley[39] analysed a series of 280 children referred to her speech clinic at Newcastle-on-Tyne, and gave the following figures:

Hearing defects — — — — — —	110
Developmental expressive aphasia — — —	72
Mental retardation — — — — —	71
Cerebral palsy — — — — — —	22
Psychogenic retardation — — — —	3
Developmental receptive aphasia (congenital auditory imperception) — — — —	2

Goodwin[14] analysed 454 cases of speech retardation in a mental centre.   Their average age was 50 months.   277 were boys and 177 were girls.   His figures were as follows:

	Percentage
Mental retardation alone. (I.Q. less than 70) — —	35·7
Brain damage — — — — — —	26·4
Functional — — — — — —	11·7
Hearing loss — — — — — —	4·8
Deferred — — — — — — —	21·4

If one includes the mentally retarded children with brain damage, the total percentage of children with mental retardation was 53.

Although I have not made a statistical analysis, I have no doubt that by far the commonest cause of delay in the development of speech as seen in an out-patient clinic is mental retardation.   Only a few of these are referred to the speech therapy department.   The next commonest cause is the familial factor: lateness of speech is a feature of family development.

Mental Retardation.   There is a strong relationship between intelligence and speech, and mental retardation has a profound effect on speech development.   Speech development is relatively more retarded in mentally backward children than other fields of development.   The retarded child takes less notice of what is said to him, has poor concentration, is late in imitation, and is backward in the expression and comprehension of words.   Though defective articulation occurs in these children, probably to a greater degree than in children of average intelligence, the main problem is delay in the onset of speech and in its use as a means of expression.   Common defects in older children include irrelevancy of ideas, echolalia (repetition of questions put instead of answering them), and perseveration—repeating phrases which have just been said.

It would be useful if one could predict the likelihood of speech development in severely retarded children.   We know that the vast majority of mongols learn to speak in time.   Karlin and Kennedy found that of 32 children with an I.Q. of less than 20, seen between the age of 7 and 38, 20 had complete mutism and 10 had a 'jabber with an occasional intelligent word'. Of 32 children with an I.Q. of 20 to 50, seen between the age of 5 and 26, 7 had mutism, and 24 had defective speech. Of 249 children with an I.Q. of 50 to 70, none had mutism.

One commonly hears the story in the case of a retarded child that he began to say single words clearly and then appeared to forget them, so that they were not heard again for many months.

Defects of Hearing.   If there is a severe defect of hearing, the child will not learn to speak until special methods of teaching him are used. If the defect is less severe, he may learn to make sounds such as b, f, w, which he can see made, but not the g, l, and r.   He substitutes for these, and is apt to say 'do' for go, 'yady' for lady, 'wed' for red.

When there is only high tone deafness, involving those tones used in human speech, i.e. between 512 and 2,048 double vibrations per second, the child is late in learning to talk, or more commonly his speech is defective through the omission of certain high-pitched sounds such as the 's' and 'f' which the child does not hear in the speech of others.   He tends to omit the final consonants in words. He does, however, respond to the low frequency whispers, clinks and clapping of hands commonly used as hearing tests.   He can hear the car passing and the door banging and the aeroplane, and will listen to the wireless, so that his parents and often the doctor do not consider the possibility of deafness.

If the defect of hearing develops after speech has been acquired, speech is not severely disturbed; but a relatively slight defect at an early stage of development will cause a serious defect of speech.

Delayed Maturation.   It is commonly thought that the development of speech depends on the maturation of the nervous system and probably on its myelination.   It follows that no amount of practice can make a child speak before his nervous system is ready for it, and that speech therapy has only a limited place in the treatment of the mentally retarded child who is late in learning to speak.

In all normal children the understanding of the spoken word long precedes the ability to articulate.   A patient of mine at the age of 15 months could only say 4 or 5 words with meaning, but he could readily point out 200 common objects in picture books, when asked, 'Where is the . . . ?' (drum, cup, soldier, etc.). I saw another child who at 2½ could say 4 or 5 words only.   His father and sister were late in speaking.   Three weeks later he was speaking freely in 5 word sentences.   Einstein gave his parents reason for anxiety about his mental development because of his retarded speech when he was 4. He lacked fluency of speech at 9.

Familial Factors.   When a child is notably late in learning to speak, and has normal hearing with a normal level of intelligence, and has no mechanical disability such as cerebral palsy, it is common to find that there is a family history of the same problem—particularly in the mother or father. The reason may lie in a familial delay in the maturation of the appropriate part of the nervous system.

Association with Dyslexia. Delay in speech development is commonly associated with later dyslexia and dysgraphia (see p. 190). This syndrome has been reviewed by Ingram[42], and those interested should read his papers in detail.

The Environment. It is customary to find in textbooks and papers the statement that over protection is an important cause of retardation of speech. It is supposed to retard speech by making speech unnecessary, everything being done for the child before he asks for it.[4] I have never seen evidence to this effect, neither have I seen a child in which there was anything to suggest that such 'over-protection' had any bearing on the child's development. If it were true, one would expect to find that speech would tend to be delayed more in the first child of a family, in whom overprotection is more likely to occur than in subsequent children. There is no such evidence, and in fact the reverse is the case, first born children tending to speak earlier than subsequent ones.

It is well known that language development is retarded in children who are brought up in an institution. It has been said that this retardation can be detected as early as the second month of life, by the variety and frequency of phonemes emitted. These children tend to be late in acquiring speech and subsequently in sentence formation. It must be exceptional for lack of stimulation to be so extreme in a private house that delay in speech development results. Carrel and Bangs[5a] wrote that 'lack of adequate stimulation as a cause for delayed language development requires only brief mention, although the notion that most speechless children do not talk because they don't have to, or because they are just lazy, is not only very common, but sometimes crops up where a more intelligent attitude might be expected'. Karlin[26] wrote that 'the concept that lack of stimulation will delay language development has been over-emphasised'.

Several workers have mentioned the relation of social class to speech development. In the upper social classes there is greater parent-child contact, there are better speech models in the home, and higher parental expectation regarding verbal accomplishment. In addition there is a higher mean level of intelligence. It is generally recognised that speech development occurs earlier in the upper social classes than the lower ones. Speech development and vocabulary are considerably retarded in slum children.

Eisenson[10] reviewed evidence that there was a tendency for parents of children with delayed speech to be unrealistic, rigid, perfectionist and overprotective. The home environment was said to be characterised by confusion and lack of organisation. There was a tendency for the mothers to be maladjusted and neurotic. He suggested that parental rejection which takes the form of continuous disapproval and criticism of speech as well as of other forms of behaviour may cause the child to stop efforts to talk. Solomon[47] compared the background of a group of children with functional defects of articulation with that of normal controls. He found significant differences in overall adjustment and sleeping behaviour in the two groups. Affected children had less good relationships with their parents and more sleep problems, and tended to be passive, to internalise their responses, to be submissive, timid and needing approval. It would certainly seem to be reasonable to suggest that severe rejection might cause at least partial mutism.

It is customary to say that delay in the acquisition of speech is due to jealousy. The new baby is blamed for a lot of things, but I have never seen any reason to blame him for this. It would indeed be difficult to prove that jealousy of a sibling has delayed speech, and I have never seen evidence to that effect.

Many workers ascribe delay in speech to 'laziness'. It is argued that the child does not speak because he cannot be bothered to do so. I have never seen an example of this. I have seen serious harm done by advice given to parents by a family doctor that the child should be made to express his needs, on the ground that his failure to speak is just 'laziness'. Really troublesome behaviour problems result from the consequent thwarting. In fact the reason why the children were not speaking was that they could not. I agree entirely with Morley that laziness is rarely if ever the cause of delayed speech development.

In any consideration of psychological problems in relation to speech development it must be borne in mind that speech problems, including delay in the onset of speech and indistinctness of speech or stuttering, may themselves cause psychological problems, insecurity and withdrawal from the fellowship of others. It is easy to ascribe the speech problems to the psychological difficulties, when in fact the psychological difficulties are due to the speech problem.

For a good review of speech delay, the reader should refer to the book by Renfrew and Murphy.[43]

Psychosis. (See p. 261).

Mutism may be a manifestation of schizophrenia. I have seen one example of mutism due to hysteria.

Speech Delay in Twins and Triplets. It has long been recognised that speech tends to develop later in twins. Day[7] made a special study of the subject, investigating the development of speech in 80 pairs of twins, and comparing their speech with that of singletons of the same age, sex and socioeconomic status. He analysed the length of speech response to toys, the results of Piaget functional tests, the grammatical construction of sentences and the use of words. The twins were retarded in language development in each of the 4 tests. They learned to talk on an average a month later than their older siblings.

The retardation increased with age. Twins of the upper social classes were superior in all tests to those of the lower classes. The twins were below average in intelligence tests, but the retardation in language was greater than that of the intelligence quotient. More than a fifth were left-handed.

The usual reason given for the delayed speech development in twins is exemplified by the statement of Jersild that 'the type of companionship which twins provide each other means that there is less reason for using language to communicate with others'. Morley[39] pointed out, however, that the speech defect is rarely the same in both twins; that speech disorders may occur in one twin and not the other; and that twins may each have a speech disorder but of dissimilar type and degree. It would seem, therefore, that other factors are involved. It is said that language retardation is greater in middle class twins than in those from the 'working' class. It is likely that the main cause is the fact that the mother of twins has not as much time to devote to the two children as she would have for a singleton: she reads to them less, and has less time to teach them the names of objects. Another cause may lie in the twin imitating the speech of his co-twin instead of that of an adult.

Russian psychologists have described an experiment on twins who were said (without satisfactory evidence) to be uniovular.[31] They had 5 older siblings, but their home environment was unsatisfactory. They were left to play with each other without toys. They never heard a book read, were never told stories and few spoke to them. Their mother and her brother were late in speaking. The twins were retarded in speech but the I.Q. was not tested. There were indications, however, that the I.Q. may have been low. There appeared to be an element of receptive aphasia, but the question of high tone deafness was not mentioned. The authors thought that the retardation in speech was due to the fact that they did not need to speak to anyone else but each other. The psychologists therefore separated them, placing them in different kindergartens, and one in addition was given speech therapy. In each case the speech underwent rapid improvement and they ascribed this to the separation of the twins. It was obvious, however, that other factors were involved—familial speech retardation, probably a low I.Q., some degree of receptive aphasia, and the absence of normal stimulation at home. The possibility that the children would have talked equally early if left as they were was not mentioned. Lulls in speech development, with subsequent rapid progress, are well known.

Lulls and Spurts. Many children go through phases in which the development of speech seems to come to a complete stop. Shirley pointed out that when one skill is being actively learned another skill tends to go into abeyance. The child seems to make no progress for some months, and then suddenly, for no apparent reason, he makes rapid headway.   These lulls cause considerable anxiety to parents.   I have seen one child who at 15 months was well below the average in speech, being able to say only 4 or 5 words, while at 18 months he was much better than the average, speaking in long sentences.   Another child at the age of 30 months was only able to say 4 or 5 single words. Three weeks later he was speaking well in 5-word sentences.   His father and sister had been late in learning to talk.

When a child is learning to speak, deterioration in the clarity of speech may occur when he has a respiratory infection, apart from the effect of nasal obstruction.

Lateral Dominance and Crossed Laterality.   The relationship of lateral dominance and crossed laterality to speech problems has been discussed elsewhere (Ch. 4).

Cleft Palate.   A cleft palate in itself causes only trivial retardation of speech development, though it causes indistinctness of speech if treatment is inadequate.   I have shown elsewhere, however, that the intelligence of children with cleft palate tends to be on the average somewhat less than that of other children.[18]   A low level of intelligence will affect speech development.   Lillywhite[29] suggested that a cleft palate may also cause some retardation because consonant sounds p, b, t, d, k, g needed by the child to establish his early vocabulary are the ones most disturbed by the open palate, with the result that some prelanguage activity is omitted.   It should be remembered that deafness commonly develops in children with cleft palate—usually, however, after speech has been acquired.

Other Defects.   A submucous cleft or adenoids cause nasal speech. Rhinolalia may follow adenoidectomy, possibly as a result of decreased postoperative movement of the palate.

Malocclusion affects speech, especially if there is micrognathia or 'an open bite'.

There is a difference of opinion as to whether '*tongue-tie*' affects speech or not.   It would seem that the opinion of American speech therapists is against it.   Some workers believe that the child with a short frenulum has difficulty in pronouncing the letters n, l, t, d, and th.   It is certain that tongue-tie does not cause delay in the onset of speech.

Speech in Cerebral Palsy.   Speech problems are common in cerebral palsy.   They include both delay in beginning to speak, receptive aphasia and dysarthria.   Dunsdon found speech defects in 70 per cent of her cases, and Floyer found a speech defect in 46 per cent of the Liverpool school age children.   The figure for the athetoid children was 88 per cent.

There are several causes for the speech problems of children with cerebral palsy.   They include a low level of intelligence, hearing difficulties, inco-ordination or spasticity of the muscles of speech and respiration, the effect of prematurity and of multiple pregnancy, cortical defects, psychological factors and perhaps laterality problems. Fifty per cent of children with cerebral palsy have an I.Q. of less than 70.[21] Defects of hearing are common, particularly in children with the athetoid form of cerebral palsy. Twenty per cent or more have a significant defect of hearing. Inco-ordination of the muscles of the tongue, larynx and thorax interferes with articulation, especially in di-athetoid children. Thirty per cent of all children with cerebral palsy were prematurely born and about 8 per cent were products of multiple pregnancy—both factors related to speech delay. Psychological factors are important, for children with cerebral palsy may well lack normal stimulation and the contact of others. In addition there are probably other factors related to the cortical defect in cerebral palsy. Many factors, therefore, may operate to cause delays and difficulties in speech in these children.

Speech is not delayed by tongue tie, it is not delayed by laziness, it is not delayed by 'Everything being done for him'. A child does not speak because he cannot speak.

Aphasia

It is almost always impossible to draw the line between normal and abnormal. There are great variations in the age at which speech develops in normal children, and it is not clear at what stage of delay in development in relation to the I.Q. one should use the word aphasia.

One must try to distinguish the receptive form of aphasia (e.g. congenital auditory imperception) from the expressive form. Whereas the child with receptive aphasia cannot understand written or spoken language, the child with expressive aphasia can understand, but cannot use meaningful language. Karlin[26] thought that many children showed a combination of both forms.

Receptive aphasia is more common in boys than in girls. The child can hear what is said, but cannot understand the spoken word. There have been numerous papers on this condition. The term 'congenital auditory imperception' was suggested by Worster-Drought,[55] in a valuable article on the subject. He wrote that the essential feature is a failure to understand spoken language when it is spoken in his hearing but out of his sight. There is a striking difference between the child's ability to comprehend spoken language heard from that which is seen. He added that in addition to failure to appreciate the significance of spoken words, there is also an inability to distinguish between less specialised sounds than those of spoken language. He therefore regarded 'congenital word deafness', a term used by others, as too limited. The child may cause confusion in diagnosis by repeating words said by another—but he fails to understand them. The condition may be familial. He advocated treatment as for deaf-mutism, with lip reading and the use of the kinaesthetic sense—the child feeling the shape of carved letters as they are spoken.   He suggested that the defect may lie in aplasia of the post-temporal cortex on both sides.

Stuttering.   Numerous famous men are said to have stuttered. They include Moses, Aristotle, Aesop, Demosthenes, Virgil, Charles I, Robert Boyle, Aneurin Bevan, Lewis Caroll, Somerset Maugham, Charles Lamb and Charles Darwin.   Hippocrates, Aristotle, Galen and Celsus discussed the causes of the problem.

In the section below the worts stutter and stammer are used as synonymous.

According to Jenks, Dieffenbach in Berlin was one of the first to attempt the cure of stuttering by dividing the lingual muscles.   He wrote that Mrs. Leigh and Dr. Yates of New York opened the New York institution for correcting impediments of speech in 1830.   The stammerer had to press the tip of the tongue as hard as he could against the upper teeth, had to draw a deep breath every 6 minutes, and was instructed to keep silent for 3 days, during which period the deep respirations and tongue pressure had to be continued without interruption.   For the night small rolls of linen were placed under the tongue in order to give the tongue the right direction during sleep. Other treatment included teaching the child to speak with pebbles in the mouth or with a cork between the teeth.

The onset of stuttering is usually between 2 and 4 years.   It rarely begins after 7.   About 1 to 2 per cent of the school population stutter. It is 3 times commoner in young boys than girls, but much more common in older boys than girls—indicating that girls are more likely to recover from it than boys.

Morley[39] estimated that less than 3 per 1,000 of the population has a persistent stammer.   There is no relationship between the incidence of stuttering and the intelligence quotient.

It is almost impossible to avoid over-simplification in writing a short section on stuttering.   It is a complex problem with many facets and several aspects which are little understood.   In the comments below I shall attempt to give what seem to me to be the most widely accepted views on the problem.

Many agree with Wendell Johnson[25] that a vital cause of stuttering is the diagnosis of stuttering.   By this it is meant that parents or relatives fail to realise that normal children between 2 and 4 years of age frequently repeat words and stumble over them, particularly when they are excited.   The parents, perhaps guided by a relative or neighbour, become alarmed about their child's speech and think that he is beginning to stutter.   They thereupon tell the child to repeat himself, to speak clearly and distinctly, to 'take a big breath before he speaks', thus making the child self-conscious and drawing his attention to his speech, so that true stuttering begins.   Johnson wrote that, 'We simply could not escape the fact that, to all appearances, most of the parents of the young stutterers were applying the label "stuttering" to the same types of speech behaviour that other parents were labelling "normal speech".' Johnson advised that parents should 'do absolutely nothing at any time, by word or deed or posture, or facial expression, that would serve to call his attention to his interruptions in speech". One is reminded of the centipede:

> 'The centipede was contented, quite
> Until the toad one day in spite
> Said, say, which foot comes after which?
> This so wrought upon her mind
> She lay distracted in a ditch,
> Considering which came after which'.

It is probable that several other factors are involved. These are:
(1) The familial factor. The significance of this is not understood. There is a possibility that imitation plays a part, or that a parent who stutters or has stuttered himself shows undue anxiety about his own child's speech and so causes him to stutter.
(2) Lateral dominance and crossed laterality. Though many have shown that there is a higher incidence of crossed laterality and ambidexterity in stutterers than there is in the normal population, its significance is not understood. It is commonly believed that stuttering which develops when a left-handed child is taught to use the right is due to tension created in trying to bring about the transfer of dominance, and that it is the method of teaching which is responsible rather than the fact of teaching him to use the opposite hand.
(3) Insecurity. Though insecurity may be a factor in causing stuttering, some psychological problems may be the result rather than the cause of the stuttering. Nevertheless, there is good evidence that insecurity is a factor, provided that it operates before speech is fully established.
(4) Constitutional factors. Berry compared the antecedents of 500 stutterers with those of 500 controls. He found that the stutterers were somewhat later in learning to walk than the controls. In the stuttering group there was more often retardation in the initiation of speech and the development of intelligible speech.
(5) The personality of the child. It may be that if the other factors operate as well, the more sensitive child by nature is more likely to stutter than the more placid child of even temperament.
It is perhaps unwise to describe stammering as 'a narcissistic neurosis—a pregenital conversion neurosis'.[4]

Indistinctness of Speech. In this section I have included dysarthria, dyslalia and nasal speech. Many children during the process of developing go through a stage of substituting consonants or other sounds (dyslalia), or of repeating certain sounds. They may omit consonants and make speech difficult to understand. The commonest form of dyslalia is the lisp, due usually to the protrusion of the tongue between the teeth on pronouncing an 's'. At the age of seven 13·5 per cent of children in a national sample were not fully intelligible:[41] this was twice as common in boys. Ten per cent were said by teachers to be difficult to understand: 10 to 13 per cent at the age of seven had some speech impairment.

The cause of dyslalia is obscure. Powers wrote that 'although the etiology of functional articulation disorders remains unestablished, it is at least clear that it is complex'. She felt that it was likely to be related to an unsatisfactory parent–child relationship, leading to intellectual and emotional immaturity.

I find it difficult to know how much parents should be blamed for their children's dyslalia. One sees many examples of dyslalia in which the family background appears to be entirely satisfactory, and there are certainly vast numbers of families in which the background is unsatisfactory in a wide variety of ways and in which no child has dyslalia. Dyslalia seems to be due to immaturity in speech formation, but the explanation of that immaturity is not clear. Apart from the lisp, dyslalia usually disappears without treatment as the child matures, and it is probable that speech therapy is irrelevant for dyslalia except for the lisp. Children usually learn to say g, d, k and t before r, l, w, y, th and fs.

In all cases of delayed or indistinct speech, the hearing should be tested.

Ingram[24], in an excellent discussion of the problems of delayed speaking and reading, regarded many of the common speech difficulties as being grades of severity of one problem, rather than as separate and distinct problems. His four grades are as follows:

Mild—dyslalia.

Moderate—retarded acquisition of language with dyslalia, but normal comprehension of speech.

Severe—both comprehension and expression of speech defective. Congenital word blindness.

Very Severe—true auditory imperception. Defect of comprehension together with a failure to perceive the significance of sounds.

Perceptual and Allied Problems in Cerebral Palsy and Other Children

Only a brief note can be included here concerning certain sensory defects, involving particularly spatial appreciation and body image. They occur notably in children with cerebral palsy, particularly those with a lesion in the right hemisphere, and especially in young children who have been deprived of experience in the handling of toys and other objects because of their physical handicap.

Perceptual difficulties are by no means confined to children with cerebral palsy.   They occur in normal children, perhaps as a result of genetic factors, or of delayed maturation, or of lack of the relevant experience in the early months.   In this connection there is interesting work concerning perceptual difficulties in Africans.[51]   Bantus, for instance, have difficulty in understanding pictures.   They cannot connect a drawing of a mechanical object with the object itself nor can they see 'depth' in a picture.

These problems may follow severe anoxia at birth.   Children at risk of these problems also include those who were small for dates or had neonatal hyperbilirubinaemia.[9]

The handicaps include particularly:

1. *Difficulty in Appreciating Space and Form*, so that an unduly poor score is achieved on formboards, and on pattern making and pattern copying, e.g. with bricks or with strips of cardboard.   Difficulty may be expected in the 'posting box' test.

2. *Defect of Body Image.*   The child finds it difficult to reproduce movements of the lips, tongue or other parts of the body.   His drawings of the human figure (as in the Goodenough 'draw-a-man' test) are poor.   If given the outline of a face and asked to insert cardboard models of the eyes, lips, nose, etc., he has difficulty in placing them in the appropriate position.

3. *Difficulty in Estimating Size, Depth, Distance, Time.*   The child may find it difficult to estimate depth in walking down stairs, to estimate size in sorting out objects of different sizes, to estimate distance in jumping from one line to another on the floor, to estimate time in beating a rhythm.   When older he may find it difficult to find his way round a page of print.

4. *Perseveration.*   He finds it difficult to change from one task to another.   When writing he may repeat the last letter.   When counting cubes he fails to stop counting at the last brick in a row.

5. *Concentration.*   Concentration tends to be unduly poor in relation to the I.Q.   There is undue distractibility.   There is a tendency for the child to be distracted by unimportant minutiae, such as the page number in a book, flaws in the paper, the teacher's dress.   He is unduly distracted by sound or movement in the environment.

6. *Hyperkinesis and other Uninhibited Behaviour.*

From the point of view of developmental assessment, the possibility of these sensory defects in children with cerebral palsy must be borne in mind in testing, for they may lead to an unduly low score and to an underestimate of the child's ability.   They also lead to an unduly poor performance in the nursery school and subsequent schools.

The subject was also reviewed by Albitreccia in France, Cruickshank,[6] and Abercrombie.[1]

Reading Disability (Dyslexia) and Specific Learning Disorders

Reading disability is more a problem in the child of school age than of the pre-school child; but it has its origin in pre-natal or other pre-school factors, and will therefore be discussed briefly here. Amongst many reviews of the subject are those of Hermann,[16] Keeney,[27] Natchez,[40] Vernon,[50] Ingram,[24] Mason,[34] Money[38] and Franklin.[11]

Dyslexia has been defined as a reading age two years or more below the mental age. It is commonly found in association with other handicaps under the general title 'Specific learning disorders'. Boder[5] wrote that the diagnosis must be made

(i) by exclusion—exclusion of mental deficiency, visual or auditory defects, emotional causes, dyslalia, emotional deprivation and poor teaching or

(ii) direct observation—of crosses laterality, right left disorientation, clumsiness, WISC and Bender visual motor gestalt, Goodenough test, reversals of letters and extraneous and omitted letters.

It is remarkable, if true, that dyslexia is ten times more common in Western Countries than in Japan (Makita, 1969). Makita wrote that theories which ascribe the etiology of reading disability to local cerebral abnormalities, to lateral conflict, or to emotional pressure may be valid for some instances, but the specificity of used language, the very object of reading behaviour, is the most contributing factor in the formation of reading disability. Reading disability is more of a philological than a neuro-psychiatric problem'. 'It is unthinkable that the Americans and the Europeans have ten times the population with maldevelopment or malformation of cerebral gyri than do the Japanese. It is hardly believable that the prevalence of hemispheral dominance conflict or split laterality is ten times less in the Japanese than in Westerners. It is equally absurd to suspect that children with emotional distress are ten times less frequent in Japan'. 'The impression I myself gathered in Europe was that the largest numbers of reading disabilities were from English speaking countries, next from German speaking countries and least from Latin speaking countries such as Italy or Spain.'

In our book about the childhood of famous men and women,[20] we noted the problem of dyslexia and allied learning disorders in several children destined for fame. They included Thomas Edison, Harvey Cushing, Yeats and many others. Dr. John Hunter, famous British physician, could not read till he was 17, despite all efforts to teach him, and this caused great distress to his family. Auguste Rodin, as a result of his difficulty in reading and writing, was described as 'the worst pupil in school'. His father said 'I have an idiot for a son', and his uncle said that 'he is ineducable'.[49] Spelling baffled him throughout his life. Others who had difficulty in spelling throughout their life included General Patton, Woodrow Wilson, William James, Paul Ehrlich, Hans Christian Andersen and Gertrude Bell.

The problem is commonly associated with delayed speech, difficulty in spelling and bad writing. The factors related to delayed reading are as follows:

1. A low level of intelligence.
2. Emotional factors. Insecurity in its broadest sense may be one of the causes of delayed reading. Features commonly found in the home background are tense, critical, punitive parents, and a variety of behaviour problems in the child. The reading disability is often merely a small part of a much wider emotional difficulty. The child may become so convinced that he cannot learn to read that he stops trying; he is expected to fail and he does.
3. Other environmental problems. Factors commonly found in the history of affected children include a poor home where there are no books and no suitable toys, where no-one reads to the child and where the vocabulary is poor. There is often a history of over-ambition, overanxiety and overprotection, of failure to encourage curiosity and learning, and of failure to appreciate the importance of education. Poor teaching, including unsuitable teaching methods, is commonly found. The problem is much more common in large families and in the lower social classes.

It is known that reading difficulties are more common in children who were prematurely born than in those born at term.

4. Visual, auditory and spatial difficulties. Visuospatial difficulties include the transposition of letters. There may be poor auditory discrimination of speech sounds, so that common sounds are forgotten, or failure to synthesize into their correct words letters sounded correctly individually (e.g. C-L-O-C-K pronounced 'COCK'). According to Mason[34] delayed reading, always includes one or more visuospatial difficulties, poorly established laterality, clumsiness or poor writing, but these disappear except in children with 'pure' dyslexia.

5. Genetic. When the above causes of delayed reading have been eliminated, there remains the 'specific' dyslexia, which is genetic in origin, though emotional problems may well be super-added. It is more common in boys than in girls. There is almost always a family history of the same complaint. Hermann[16] showed that if dyslexia occurs in one of uniovular twins, it occurs in the other too; the incidence in both of binovular twins is much less.

The problem is associated with easier than usual mirror reading, with reversal of letters (reading 'tub' for 'but'), with a tendency to read from right to left, and with ambidexterity or left handedness. A semi-colon may be interpreted as a question mark, an 'h' as 'y'. There is reversal of words, rotation of letters, confusion over letters of similar shape, a low reading speed and misreading of words.

Gesell wrote that reading difficulties may be anticipated by the

following features:–
  Scattering and inconsistency of the individual developmental
  examination.
  Inconsistency of results on successive examinations.
  Specific weakness in drawing tests.
  Specific weakness in number tests (e.g. 'give me three blocks').
  Strephosymbolia.   (Reversal of symbols).
  Family history of sinistrality.
  Family history of reading disability.
  Speech anomalies—delay in speech, dyslalia, stuttering.
  Immature or excitable personality.

More recently a variety of other tests have been tried in order to
predict reading failure.[8]   They include visual and auditory perceptual tests, language tests, including language comprehension, auditory
memory span, tests for fine manual control (fitting pegs into a peg
board, tying a knot, hand reference, pencil control, throwing, drawing a man), and the Bender Gestalt test.

Reading difficulty is a complex problem, due to a variety of causes,
which are often closely intermingled.   Expert psychological help is
required to unravel them, and without such help the diagnosis of
specific dyslexia should not be made.

Advanced reading ability may be a feature of an unusually high level
of intelligence, in a child with a good home where the parents have
read to him from an early age, shown him pictures, given him pre-
reading toys, such as picture matching, jigsaws, picture dominoes,
and cardboard or plastic shapes and forms; and where he is given the
opportunity to practice visuospatial development.

Multiple Factors Affecting Development

One often sees a combination of retarding factors which make a
developmental assessment extremely difficult.   I found it almost
impossible to determine the level of intelligence in an athetoid child
who was blind and deaf.   Retardation of walking in children with
cerebral palsy is usually due to at least two factors—the mechanical
disability due to the hypertonia and the mental retardation.   Institutional care and emotional deprivation is often a third factor.

The following case record illustrates the difficulty which multiple
factors cause in developmental assessment:

  Case Record.—This girl was referred at the age of 28 months on account of
lateness in walking.   She was born at term, weighing 3630 g.   The history of many
of the previous milestones could not be obtained.   It seemed that she had learnt to
sit at 16 months, to play patacake, to hold her arms out for clothes, and to wave
bye-bye at 22 months.   She was only saying one word with meaning.   She could
only just manage a cup, and she had no sphincter control.

On examination she was a bright girl, interested in her surroundings, with moderate concentration, and co-operated well in developmental tests, in which her performance lay between that of an 18 and 24 month old child. The D.Q. was about 60. She had a mild degree of spastic diplegia. She was a very long way off learning to walk. Her siblings, who were otherwise normal, had only begun to speak at 3 and 3½ years respectively.

In this case the spastic diplegia and mental retardation retarded the walking, and the mental retardation and probably the familial trait retarded the speech. One could not use the development of speech to assess the I.Q. because of the family history of late speech development.

Owing to the alertness and good concentration, I gave a guarded prognosis, saying that she would be educable, and that she might well fare better than appeared likely from her present level of development.

Summary and Conclusions

1. All children are different. They differ in the rate of development as a whole, and in the rate and pattern of development within each field.

2. Motor development may be advanced. In certain ethnic groups of negroes, children may show notable motor advancement. Gross motor development (sitting and walking) may be considerably delayed without any discoverable cause, some normal children being unable to walk until 2 to 4 years of age.

Known causes of delayed motor development are:

Familial factors.

Environmental factors; emotional deprivation, lack of opportunity to practice.

Personality—excessive timidity.

Mental subnormality.

Hypotonia or hypertonia; gross spinal defects.

Neuromuscular disorders.

Shuffling.

Blindness.

It is *not* due to congenital dislocation of the hip or to obesity.

3. There is much less variation in fine motor development (manipulation), except in association with mental retardation and cerebral palsy.

4. Delayed visual and auditory maturation may occur.

5. There is little variation in the age of chewing, except in association with mental retardation.

6. The age at which children learn to feed and dress themselves is affected by their intelligence, aptitudes, opportunities given to them to learn, and by mechanical difficulties.

7. Acquisition of sphincter control is delayed by:

Mental subnormality.

Familial factors.

Psychological factors: stress, laziness.
Overenthusiastic or neglectful training.
The ego and personality of the child; the personality of the mother.
Polyuria, frequency, organic disease.
8. Speech is delayed by:
Low intelligence.
Genetic factors.
Hearing defects.
Delayed maturation and familial factors.
Poor environment.
Twinning.
Psychoses.
Disturbance of lateral dominance.
Cerebral palsy.
Problems related to dyslexia and aphasia.

It is *not* delayed by tongue tie, by jealousy, or 'everything being done for him'.

The frequency of lulls in the development of speech is emphasised.

Stuttering is discussed briefly.   The main known factors are:

(a) Parental efforts to make the child speak distinctly, together with their failure to recognise that the child's apparently hesitant speech is normal.
(b) Familial factors.
(c) Problems of laterality.
(d) Insecurity.
(e) Constitutional factors.
(f) The personality of the child.

It is probable that stuttering only develops when there is a combination of these factors in operation during the early months of speech development.

Known causes of indistinctness of speech include cleft palate, submucous cleft, malocclusion, adenoids, cerebral palsy and possibly tongue-tie.

9. The ability to read is delayed by:
Low intelligence.
Emotional factors.
Environmental factors.
Delayed maturation.
Poor teaching.
Visual, auditory and spatial difficulties.
Genetic factors ('specific dyslexia') or specific learning disorders.

10. The frequency with which there is a combination of retarding factors is emphasised.

REFERENCES

1. ABERCROMBIE, M. L. J. (1964) Perceptual and Visuomotor Disorders in Cerebral Palsy. *Clinics in Developmental Medicine*. No. 11. London. Heinemann.
2. AINSWORTH, M. (1967) *Infancy in Uganda*. Baltimore: Johns Hopkins Press.
3. BAKWIN, H., BAKWIN, R. M. (1966) *Clinical Management of Behaviour Disorders in Children*. Philadelphia: Saunders.
4. BLOCH, E. G., GÖODSTEIN, L. D. (1960) Concepts of stammering. *J. Speech Hearing Disorders* **25**, 24.
5. BODER, E. (1971) Developmental Dyslexia: prevailing diagnostic concepts and a new diagnostic approach: in Myklebust, H. R. Progress in learning disabilities. New York. Grune and Stratton.
5a. CARRELL, J. A. BANGS, J. L. (1951) Disorders of Speech comprehension associated with Idiopathic Language Retardation. *Nervous Child* **9**, 64.
6. CRUICKSHANK,W. M., BICE, H. V.,WALLER, N. E. (1957) *Perception and Cerebral Palsy*. Syracuse Univ. Press.
7. DAY, E. J. (1932) Development of Language in Twins. *Child Develpm.*, **3**, 179. 299.
8. DE HIRSCH, K., JANSKY, J. J., LANGFORD, W. W. (1966) *Predicting Reading Failure*. New York: Harper and Row.
9. DENHOFF, E., HAINSWORTH, P. K., HAINSWORTH, M. S. (1972) The child at risk for learning disorders. *Clinical Pediatrics*. **11**, 164.
10. EISENSON, J. (1956) in Cruickshank, W. M., *Psychology of Exceptional Children and Youth*. London: Staples Press.
10a. FORSYTHE, W. I., REDMOND, A. (1974) Enuresis and spontaneous cure rate. *Arch Dis Childh.* **49**, 259.
11. FRANKLIN, A. W. (1962) *Word Blindness or Specific Developmental Dyslexia*. London: Pitman.
12. FREEDMAN, D. G. (1964) Smiling in Blind Infants and the Issue of Innate VS Acquired. *J. Child Psychol,*, **5**, 171.
13. GEBER, M., DEAN, R. !. A. (1964) Le Developpement Psychomoteur et Somatique des Jeunes Enfants Africains en Ouganda. *Courier*, **14**, 425.
14. GOODWIN, F. B. (1955) A Consideration of Etiologies in 454 Cases of Speech Retardation. *J. Speech Dis.*, **20**, 300.
15. GORDON, N. (1968) Visual Agnosia in Childhood. *Develop. Med. Child. Neurol.*, **10**, 377.
16. HERMANN, K. (1959) *Reading Disability*. Copenhagen: Munksgaard.
17. HOLT, K. S. (1960) Early Motor Development. Postural Induced Variations. *J. Pediat.*, **57**, 571.
18. ILLINGWORTH, R. S., BIRCH, L. B. (1956) The Intelligence of Children with Cleft Palate. *Arch. Dis. Childh.*, **31**, 300.
19. ILLINGWORTH, R. S. (1975) The Normal Child. London. Churchill Livingstone. 6th Edn.
20. ILLINGWORTH, R. S., ILLINGWORTH, C. M. (1966) *Lessons from Childhood*. Edinburgh: Livingstone.
21. ILLINGWORTH, R. S. (1958) *Recent Advances in Cerebral Palsy*. London: Churchill.
22. ILLINGWORTH, R. S. (1961) Delayed Visual Maturation. *Arch. Dis. Childh.*, **36**, 407.
23. INGRAM, T. T. S. (1960) Personal Communication.
24. INGRAM, T. T. S. (1963) Delayed Development of Speech with Special Reference to Dyslexia. *Proc. R. Soc. Med.*, **56**, 199.
25. JOHNSON, W. (1949) An Open Letter to the Mother of a Stuttering Child. *J. Speech Dis.*, **14**, 3.
26. KARLIN, I. W. (1954) Aphasias in Children. *Amer. J. Dis. Child.*, **8**,752.
27. KEENEY, A. H., KEENEY, V. D. (1968) *Dyslexia. Diagnosis and Treatment of Reading Disorders*. St. Louis: C. V. Mosby.
28. KOLVIN, I., MACKEITH, R. C., MEADOW, S. R. (1973) Bladder control and

enuresis. Clinics in Developmental Medicine. Nos. 48 and 49. London. Heinemann.
29. LILLYWHITE, H. (1958) Doctor's Manual of Speech Disorders. *J. Amer. med. Ass.*, **167**, 850.
30. LORBER, J. (1967). Recovery of vision after prolonged blindness in children with hydrocephalus or following pyogenic meningitis. *Clinical Pediatrics*, **6**, 699.
31. LURIA, A. R., YUDOVICH, I. (1959) *Speech and the Development of Mental Processes in the Child.* London: Staples.
32. McGREGOR, S. M., BACK, E. H. (1971) Gross Motor development in Jamaican infants. *Develop. Med. Child Neurol.* **13**, 79.
33. MAKITA, K. (1969) The rarity of reading disorders in Japanese children. In CHESS, S., THOMAS, A. Annual progress in Child Psychiatry and Child development. New York. Brunner Mazel.
34. MASON, A. W. (1967) Specific (Developmental) Dyslexia. *Develop. Med. Child. Neurol.*, **9**, 183.
35. MILLER, F. J. W., COURT, S. D. M., WALTON, W. S., KNOX, E. G. (1960) *Growing up in Newcastle-upon-Tyne.* London: Oxford University Press.
36. MILLER, F. J. W. (1966) Child Morbidity and Mortality in Newcastle Upon Tyne. *New Engl. J. Med.*, **275**, 683.
37. MODLIN, J., HAWKER, A., COSTELLO, A. J. (1973) An investigation into the effect of sleeping position on some aspects of early development. *Develop. Med. Child Neurol.* **15**, 287.
38. MONEY, J. (1962) *Reading Disability.* Baltimore: Johns Hopkins Press.
39. MORLEY, M. E. (1972) *The Development and Disorders of Speech in Childhood.* Edinburgh: Livingstone.
40. NATCHEZ, J. (1968) *Children with Reading Problems.* New York: Basic Books Inc.
41. PECKHAM, L. S. (1973). Speech disorders in a national sample of children aged seven years. *Brit. J. Disorders of Communication.* **8**, 2.
42. PEIPER, A. (1963) *Cerebral Function in Infancy and Childhood.* London Pitman.
43. RENFREW, C., MURPHY, K. (1964) The Child Who does not Talk. *Clinics in Developmental Medicine.* No. 13. London. Heinemann.
44. SHERIDAN, M. (1960) Personal Communication.
45. SMITH, E. D. (1967) Diagnosis and Management of the Child with Wetting. *Australian Paediat. J.*, **3**, 193.
46. SÖDERLING, B. (1959) The FirstSmile. *Acta Paediat, (Uppsala),* **48**, Suppl. 117. 78.
47. SOLOMON, A. L. (1961) Personality and Behaviour Patterns of Children with Functional Defects of Articulation. *Child Developm.*, **32**, 731.
48. SROUFE, L. A., WUNSCH, J. P. (1972) The development of laughter in the first year. *Child Development*, **43**, 1326.
49. THOMPSON, L. J. (1968) Language disabilities in men of eminence. Reprint No. 27. Connecticut: The Orton Society.
50. VERNON, M. D. (1957) *Backwardness in Reading.* Cambridge: Cambridge Univ. Press.
51. VERNON, P. E. (1969) *Intelligence and Cultural Environment.* London: Methuen.
52. WHITE, M. (1968). A Thousand Consecutive Cases of Enuresis. *Medical Officer,* **120**, 151.
53. WILLIAMS, C. E. in O'GORMAN, G. (1968) *Modern Trends in Mental Health and Subnormality.*
54. WILLIAMS, J. R., SCOTT, R. B. (1953) Growth and Development of Negro Infants. IV. Motor Development and its Relationship to Child Rearing Practices in Two Groups of Negro Infants. *Child Develop.*, **24**, 103.
55. WORSTER-DROUGHT, C. (1943) Congenital Auditory Imperception (Congenital Word Deafness and its Relation to Idioglossia and Allied Speech Defects). *Med. Press*, **110**, 411.

CHAPTER 11

VARIATIONS IN THE GENERAL PATTERN OF DEVELOPMENT

In this chapter I have described variations in the general pattern of development as distinct from variations in individual fields. The main factor related to development as a whole is the level of intelligence.

Variations in Intelligence

The lowest level of intelligence is so low that it is unscorable, and therefore there are no precise figures for the lowest levels. We have only limited information about I.Q. levels at the other extreme of the scale—at the very top.

Bakwin and Bakwin[1] gave the following range:

150 and over	—	—	—	—	—	0·1
130–149	—	—	—	—	—	1·0
120–129	—	—	—	—	—	5
110–119	—	—	—	—	—	14
100–109	—	—	—	—	—	30
90–99	—	—	—	—	—	30
80–89	—	—	—	—	—	14
70–79	—	—	—	—	—	5
Below 70	—	—	—	—	—	1

Michal Smith[7] gave the following figures for the upper end of the scale:

Over 180 —	—	—	—	—	1 in	1,000,000
Over 170 —	—	—	—	—	1 in	100,000
Over 160 —	—	—	—	—	1 in	10,000
Over 150 —	—	—	—	—	1 in	1,000
Over 140 —	—	—	—	—	1 in	170
Over 136 —	—	—	—	—	1 in	100
Over 125 —	—	—	—	—	1 in	17

Apart from variations in the level of intelligence, there are many important variations in the pattern of development. All those who are concerned with developmental diagnosis should read and re-read the book entitled *Biographies of Child Development*, by Arnold Gesell and his colleagues.[3] This is a collection of biographical sketches to show the wide range of variations seen in human development.

In the sections to follow I shall describe some of the important variations in development as a whole.

Mental Superiority

It has proved difficult to detect mental superiority in infancy. Gesell[2] discussed the early signs of superiority in some detail. He emphasised the fact that superior endowment is not always manifested by quickened tempo of development, but the signs are there for careful observation. He wrote that superiority 'manifests itself in dynamic excellence, in intensification and diversification of behaviour, rather than in conspicuous acceleration. The maturity level is less affected than the vividness and vitality of reaction. The young infant with superior promise is clinically distinguished not so much by an advance in developmental age, as by augmented alertness, perceptiveness and drive. The infant with superior equipment exploits his physical surroundings in a more varied manner, and is more sensitive and responsive to his social environment'. He added that consistent language acceleration before 2 years is one of the most frequent signs of superior intelligence, while general motor ability and neuromuscular maturity, as revealed by drawing and co-ordination tests, are not necessarily in advance.

Elsewhere Gesell and Amatruda wrote: 'The acceleration comes into clearer prominence in the second and third years, with the development of speech, comprehension and judgment. However, personal social adaption and attentional characteristics are usually excellent even in the early months. The scorable end products may not be far in advance, but the manner of performance is superior'. They added that the superior infant is emotionally sensitive to his environment, looks alertly, and displays an intelligent acceptance of novel situations. He establishes rapport. He gives anticipatory action to test situations. He shows initiative, independence and imitativeness. He gives a good performance even if sleepy. He is poised, self-contained, discriminating, mature. The total output of behaviour for a day is more abundant, more complex, more subtle than that of a mediocre child. They described twins with an I.Q. of 180 who talked in sentences at 11 months. Terman described a child who walked at 7 months, and knew the alphabet at 19 months. The I.Q. was 188.

Amongst many stories of prodigies, one of the best known is that of Christian Heineken, born in Lubeck. It is said that at 14 months he knew the whole Bible: at $2\frac{1}{2}$ he was conversant with history, geography, anatomy and 800 latin words, learning over 150 new ones weekly. He could read German and Latin, and spoke German, Latin and French fluently. When 3 years old he could add, subtract and multiply, and in his fourth year he learned 220 songs, 80 psalms, and 1,500 verses and sentences of Latin writers. He died at 4 years and 4 months. Many other stories of mental precocity in childhood have been described in our book 'Lessons from Childhood'.[6]

Hollingworth[4] wrote that nearly all superior children learned to read at about 3 years of age.   Most of the children with an I.Q. of over 150 walked or talked or walked and talked earlier than usual. They ranked average in music and drawing.   Stedman, in a discussion on the education of gifted children, found most of them friendly and co-operative, and not conceited, egotistical or vain.   Hollingworth[4] described 31 children with an I.Q. of over 180: 12 of them were children she had seen, and 19 were cases from the literature. They tended to read a great deal, to be tall and healthy and to have a powerful imagination.   Their problems included difficulty in 'learning to suffer fools gladly'; physical difficulties—their mental development having outstripped their physical development: a tendency to idleness: a tendency to be discouraged easily: and problems of immaturity.   It was difficult for them to find enough interests at school, to avoid being negativistic toward authority, and to avoid becoming lonely, because of reduced contacts with others of their own age.   One feels that Michal-Smith[7] went a little too far with regard to the difficulties of children with a superior level of intelligence when he included a chapter on 'Mentally Gifted Children' in his book entitled *Management of the Handicapped Child*.

Terman and Oden,[9] in their unique study of 1,528 Californian children with an I.Q. of 135 or more, who were followed up to an average age of 35, found that compared with controls they had tended to walk and talk earlier: they had a better physique and fewer illnesses: they had been less boastful and more honest, and they were more stable emotionally: and they tended to have earlier puberty.   They had a wide range of interest and they showed curiosity, sustained attention and creative ability.   Nearly half had learned to read before going to school.   (The age of starting school is later in America than that in England.)   Their greatest superiority was in reading, language usage, arithmetical reasoning and information in science, literature and the arts.   They were less good in arithmetical computation, spelling and factual information about history.   Their main interests were reading and collecting.   There was no difference from controls in play interests.   The early indications of superior intelligence most often noted by parents were quicker understanding, insatiable curiosity, extensive information, retentive memory, large vocabulary and unusual interest in number relations, atlases and encyclopedias.

When these children were followed up it was found that they suffered less insanity and alcoholism than the controls: the suicide rate and incidence of juvenile delinquency was less.   The marriage rate was higher and they tended to marry earlier.   They had fewer children than the controls.   They tended to choose a partner in marriage of higher intelligence than did the controls.   The divorce rate was lower.   Their income was greater.   Six per cent became minor clerical workers, policemen, firemen or semi-skilled craftsmen.

One became a truck driver. Six per cent became doctors. The mean I.Q. of the 384 offspring was 127·7 and the proportion of children with an I.Q. of 150 or more was 28 times that of the general population.

Uniformly Advanced Development

Subsequent high I.Q.

Below are two personally observed examples of uniformly advanced development, in which the early promise was fully maintained. The tests used were mainly those of Gesell.

Case 1:

1st day	listened when spoken to and looked intently.
3rd day	smiled in response to overture.
	Virtually no grasp reflex.
9th day	advanced head control. Very interested in surroundings. Extremely interested in other children.
18 days	turned head repeatedly to sound. Holding rattle placed in hand almost indefinitely. Vocalising.
8 weeks	Hand regard. 'Grasping with eyes' (Gesell).
11 weeks	smiling at self in mirror.
14 weeks	able to go for object and get it.
19 weeks	sitting on floor for seconds without support. Holds arms out to be pulled up. Laughs at peep-bo game. Rapid transfer of objects. Attention-seeking noises —e.g. cough.
23 weeks	chewing well. Feeding self with biscuits. Stands, holding on to furniture. Advanced vocalisation. Notably good concentration on toys.
29 weeks	progressing backwards in attempting to crawl.
35 weeks	laughs at familiar rhymes. Puts hands on feet and toes when hears 'This little pig went to market'. Bricks in and out of basket. Pulls self to stand. Casting. Crawling.
44 weeks	single words with meaning. Picks up doll on request.
48 weeks	standing and walking without support. Points to 2 objects in picture when asked, 'Where is the . . .?' 8 words with meaning.
13 months	knows numerous objects in books and 7 parts of body. Carries out numerous errands on request. Feeds self with imaginary fruit from pictures of fruit in books.
16 months	simple formboard—all 3 in without error. All pieces into Goddard formboard.

	Words together into sentences.
20 months	knows several rhymes.
	Answers questions intelligently, e.g. 'Where is your toothbrush?' Answer, 'Upstairs in the bathroom'.
	Spontaneously describes pictures shown to her.
	Counts 2 objects spontaneously.
	Speaking in 10 word sentences.
	Asks questions.
	Makes jokes—e.g. calling sibling a rogue and laughing.
24 months	'Reads' books in jargon, describing each page. Spontaneously changes name in a rhyme for sibling's name and laughs.
26 months	geometric forms—9 correct.
	Goddard formboard, 76 seconds.
	Repeats 4 digits, 2–3 trials.
	Prepositions—4.
33 months	Goddard formboard, 44 seconds.
	Goodenough 'draw a man' test = 51 months.
	Dressing self fully without help.
44 months	Goodenough 'draw a man' test = 78 months.
	Repeats 5 digits, 3–3 trials. (6 not tried).
	Goddard formboard, 30 seconds.
	Able to read school books.
47 months	holds imaginative conversations with doll in 2 voices— i.e. replying in a different voice.
49 months	qualifies statements by, 'It depends on whether...'
	Showed memory of 18 months' span.
	Reading simple books very easily.
62 months	Goodenough 'draw a man' test = 9 years.
	Repeats 7 digits easily.

Case 2:

3rd day	smile in response to social overture. Virtually no grasp reflex. Intent gaze when spoken to.
7th day	head well off couch in prone position.
3 weeks	followed moving object 180 degrees. Very good vocalisations.
9 weeks	'grasping with the eyes'.
	Advanced vocalisations, including 'Ah—goo'.
12 weeks	able to go for objects and get them. Ticklish.
14 weeks	smiles at mirror. Full weight on legs.
	Splashes in bath.
18 weeks	coughs to attract attention. Enjoys peep-bo game.
22 weeks	chews. Sitting without support on floor.
	Very good concentration.

24 weeks stands, holding on to furniture.
30 weeks laughs loud at 'This little piggie' game.
            Turns head to name.
            Pulls self to standing position.
            Matches cubes. Casting repeatedly.
35 weeks great determination and concentration. Plays game
            of spilling milk from cup and laughing loudly.
40 weeks hands a toy. Release.
            Patacake.
            Holds out foot for 'This little piggie' game.
44 weeks knows meaning of numerous words.
            Will creep for object on request.
            Feeding self fully, managing cup without help.
            Obeys commands—get up, sit down.
            Creeping up stairs.
12 months walks, no help. Moos or quacks when asked what
            cow, duck, says. Tries to take cardigan off on
            request.
13 months tower of 6 cubes. Spontaneously 'picks cherries off
            pictures' and pretends to eat them.
16 months carries out complicated commands, e.g. 'Go into the
            kitchen and put this into the toy cupboard'.
20 months recognises colours. Knows what page in book has
            certain nursery rhymes on it.
            Advanced sentences.
21 months Goddard formboard, 55 seconds.
            Geometric forms—all correct, immediately.
            Picture identification—all correct, immediately.
24 months asks 'Why?' when told to do things.
30 months repeats 5 digits easily, 3–3 trials.
            Asks 'What does this say?' when looking at books.
            Counts up to 25.
33 months dressing self fully without help.
36 months reading simple books readily.
39 months Goddard formboard, 20 seconds.
            Goodenough 'draw a man' test = 6 years. (The
            first man he had ever drawn).
            Cubes—made gate from model immediately, and
            made steps from 8 cubes.
50 months able to do 78 piece jigsaw rapidly.
60 months Goodenough 'draw a man' test = $7\frac{9}{12}$ years.
            Goddard formboard, 16 seconds (one attempt only).
            Repeats 4 digits backwards (i.e. say 8-4-3-6 back-
            wards).
            Subsequent performance confirmed the early pre-
            diction of a very high I.Q.

COMMENT

The above are two examples of consistently advanced development. They are by no means typical of all children with a high level of intelligence, in whom development in most fields appears to be merely average in the first few months, though certain features, such as unusually good concentration, interest in surroundings and social responsiveness, may be seen by the discerning eye.

Delayed Maturation (*'Slow starters'*)

In the previous chapter I described children who were unaccountably late in acquiring certain individual skills, such as sitting, walking, talking and sphincter control, and have ascribed these, for want of anything better, to delayed maturation of the appropriate part of the nervous system.

One occasionally sees children who were retarded in the first few weeks, not only in motor development, but in other fields as well, and who catch up to the 'normal' and are later shown to have an average level of intelligence without any mechanical or other disability. They can be termed 'slow starters'. One can only presume that it is due to widespread delay in maturation of the nervous system. These cases are rare but important because of the ease with which mental deficiency could be wrongly diagnosed. Below are brief illustrative case histories:

Case 1.—This girl had a full term normal delivery, and was well in the newborn period. At 13 weeks there was complete head lag when held in ventral suspension or when pulled to the sitting position. She did not follow with her eyes until 17 weeks or smile till 18 weeks. She appeared to 'waken up' at about 17 weeks and then made rapid headway. At 25 weeks her head control was equivalent to that of a 16 weeks' old baby. She was able to sit like an average baby at $7\frac{1}{2}$ months, to stand holding on at 10 months, to walk with one hand held and to say 10 words with meaning at 1 year. At the age of 5 years there was no mechanical disability and her I.Q. test score was 122.

Case 2.—This boy (birth weight, 3400 g) had a proved cerebral haemorrhage at birth, grade 3 asphyxia (using Flagg's classification), and severe neonatal convulsions. He was born at home and the facts about the duration of apnoea are uncertain. He was seen in an apnoeic state approximately half an hour after birth and was given oxygen. Three hours after birth he made one spontaneous respiration each 30 seconds, and $3\frac{1}{2}$ hours after birth he made one each 20 seconds. Oxygen was continued until respirations were properly established 5 hours after birth. Blood was withdrawn under high pressure by lumbar puncture.

In the early weeks he showed gross retardation in development. At 4 weeks of age, for instance, his motor development corresponded to that of an average newborn baby. At 27 weeks his motor development was that of a 4 months old baby. At 1 year he was standing and walking without support, saying several words with meaning, had no mechanical disability and was normal in all respects.

I have a cinematographic record of his progress from gross retardation to normality.

Case 3.—This girl had a normal full term delivery. There was no abnormality in the neonatal period.

She was able to grasp objects voluntarily at 6 months, but could not sit without support till 1 year or walk without help until 3 years.   She was saying words with meaning at 1 year.   She could not manage buttons until the age of 6 years.   The diagnosis made was that of minimal birth injury, as described by Gesell, because there were minimal but non-specific neurological signs.

Her subsequent progress was good, but it was interesting to note that although she could run fast, ride a bicycle, play hockey and take a full part in sport, she had an unusual tendency to stumble in Physical Education classes, her hand movements were slow, and she could only type 50 words per minute.   She was top of her class at a technical school and passed her General Certificate of Education at 17.

Case 4.—This girl (birth weight, 3685 g) had a proved cerebral haemorrhage on full term delivery, repeated lumbar punctures having to be performed on account of severe vomiting due to increased intracranial pressure.   An intravenous drip had to be given on the fourth day with considerable reluctance on account of de-hydration resulting from the vomiting.   Bloody cerebrospinal fluid and later xanthochromic fluid was repeatedly withdrawn by lumbar puncture.   There was gross retardation of motor development, but I was impressed by the fact that at 7 weeks she was beginning to take notice of her surroundings and she began to smile. At 9 weeks her head control corresponded to that of a newborn baby.   At 16 weeks it corresponded to that of a 6 weeks old baby and at 24 weeks to that of a 13 weeks baby.   At 28 weeks she began to go for objects with her hands and get them, and her head control was that of a 24 weeks old baby.   She was able to sit for a few seconds without support at 8 months, to pull herself to the standing position at 10 months, and to feed herself (with a cup) at 14 months.   She walked without help at 18 months and put words into sentences at 21 months.   At 6 years her I.Q. was 100 and there was no mechanical disability.   It is interesting to note that an epileptic fit occurred at the age of 8 years.

Case 5.—This girl was born normally 6 weeks before term, weighing 1960 g. She began to smile at 4 months, to grasp objects voluntarily at 6 months, to imitate noises at 8 months and to cast objects at 11 months.   At this age she could say one word with meaning.   At one year she could say 3 words with meaning, but her head control was equivalent to that of an average 4½ months old child.   At 17 months she was examined by an expert in another city with a view to admission to a centre for cerebral palsy, but the diagnosis of simple mental deficiency was made. At 22 months she could stand holding on to furniture.   I wrote that her I.Q. was 'only slightly below the average'.   At 23 months she could sit without support, and at 25 months she began to walk, holding on to furniture.   She began to walk without help at 4 years and two months.   Her I.Q. at the age of 8 was 118.   She was running about well, but not really nimble on her feet.

Case 6.—After seeing an 18 month old boy on account of uniform backwardness in development, I wrote to the family doctor as follows:–
'I think that he is a normal boy, but I am not quite sure and will see him again in six months.   The difficulty is that he has been backward in everything.   He did not sit till a year.   He is not walking or nearly walking.   He was late in reaching out and getting things (nine months), in playing patacake (16 months), in waving bye bye (18 months), and in helping his mother to dress him (he has not started yet). Yet he is a bright little boy, alert and interested.   He would not cooperate in tests, but I saw enough to know that he is certainly not less than 10 or 11 months in development of manipulation.   His head is of normal size (18⅞ ins.).   I think that he is merely a late starter.   It is always a difficult diagnosis to make and time will tell whether we are right'.

At 2 years he began speaking in sentences; his performance on the simple formboard was like that of a three year old.   At 4 years he was well above average in developmental tests, and was normal.

Case 7.—Below is another extract from a letter to a family doctor about a child referred to me at 22 months for uniform delay in development:–

'The immediate impression on seeing this girl was that she was normal mentally and showed normal concentration and interest in her surroundings.   Yet she has been backward in all aspects of development.   She is not walking or talking.   She has no sphincter control.   She can't feed herself.   She has only recently started to hold her arm out for a coat.   She can't point out any objects in pictures on request. When I gave her one inch cubes she cast the lot on to the floor like a child of 13 to 15 months.   She is therefore, uniformly retarded.   Her head, however, is of normal circumference, and this together with her normal interest and the story of the sibling's lateness in walking and talking makes one extremely cautious about the prognosis.   I told the mother that I cannot say whether she will catch up to the normal or not.   Time alone will tell, but there are grounds for hoping that she will. I shall see her again in six months'.

She walked without help at 25 months, began to join words together into sentences at 33 months, and at that age her performance on the simple formboard was that of a three year old.   At 49 months she was normal, with advanced speech, and could count up to 130.   There was no disability.

Many workers have remarked about the unexpected improvement seen in some mentally retarded children.

In our follow-up of 135 infants at Sheffield who were thought to be mentally retarded in the first 2 years,[5] 4 proved to have a lower I.Q. than expected, while 16 fared better than expected.   Unless deterioration occurs in association with epilepsy (especially infantile spasms), and unless there is a familial degenerative condition, or certain rare syndromes already described, deterioration is rare: but unexpected improvement is not uncommon.

More commonly one sees children who were grossly retarded in the early weeks, but who make rapid progress and reach a much higher level than expected, remaining, however, below the average. Below are some brief summaries of examples of these:

Case 1.—Clinical diagnosis: 'minimal birth injury'.   Birth weight 2800 g.   She had grade 2 asphyxia after a difficult forceps delivery.   Breathing was established in 10 minutes.   On the fifth day she became very lethargic, there was no Moro reflex, and she was severely hypotonic.   Subdural taps were negative.   Marked retardation was suspected.   The subsequent course was as follows:

6 weeks	no head control, but smiling had begun.
8 weeks	no head control.
13 weeks	head control less than 6 weeks.
17 weeks	tonic neck reflex and grasp reflex present.
	I wrote, 'I am still not sure whether she has mental retardation or cerebral palsy, but she is interested in objects'.
21 weeks	head control equivalent to 18 weeks.
6 months	grasping rattle.
7 months	roll, prone to supine.
8 months	sit, no support. Mature transfer. Diagnosis of minimal birth injury made, with good prognosis.
10 months	creep. 5 to 6 words.
16 months	walk, holding on. Managing cup. I.Q. thought to be normal.
18 months	walk, no help.
24 months	sentences.
5 years	I.Q. score 87. No disability.

Case 2.—This boy was born at term, weighing 3515 g.   He was normal in the newborn period.   Below is a brief summary of his development:

9 months	first smile. Grasp object voluntarily.
13 months	sit, no support. Onset of major convulsions.
18 months	no sphincter control. Unable to feed self. General level is that of 8 months old baby. Petit mal and grand mal epilepsy.
5 years	I.Q. score 77. No physical disability.

Case 3.—This boy was born at term, weighing 3062 g. He was well in the new-born period. Below is a summary of his development:

4 months	taking no notice of surroundings.
14 months	unable to pull self to standing position
19 months	creep.
24 months	walk, no help.
35 months	5 words. Able to creep up stairs, but cannot get down stairs.
48 months	Unable to dress self, but tries to pull on trousers.
7 years	I.Q. score 92. No physical disability.

Case 4.—This boy was born at term. Below are some essential milestones:

3 months	smile.
12 months	sit, no help.
24 months	walk, no help.
29 months	able to manage cup. Dry by day.
33 months	odd words only.
6 years	I.Q. score 87.

Case 5.—This boy was born at term, weighing 3175 g. Below is a summary of the subsequent course:

2 days	major convulsions. Subdural tap negative.
3½ months	smile.
4 months	vocalise.
6 months	began to follow with eyes.
9 months	no voluntary grasp. No chew. Won't hold object in hand: just drops it. Very defective head control. General level that of 3 months baby. Still having major convulsions.
14 months	nearly able to grasp objects.
2½ years	words in sentences.
3 years	able to walk without help.
9 years	I.Q. test score 88. No disability.

Slow Maturation in Association with Cerebral Palsy: Unexpected Improvement

Below are some further examples of slow maturation, this time in association with cerebral palsy.   In each case early development was grossly retarded, while the eventual level of intelligence reached was quite good.   These cases indicate how easy it is to give an unduly bad prognosis when retardation is found in early infancy.

Case1.—This girl, born at term, began to smile at 6 months.   She began to grasp objects voluntarily at 9 months, to acquire sphincter control and say single words at 23 months, to feed herself, walk unsupported and to help to dress herself at 29 months. She put words together at 3 years.   Her I.Q. at 5 years was 90.   She had a mild cerebral palsy of the ataxic type.

Case 2.—This boy was born at term, weighing 2385 g.   Below is a summary of his development:

1st 12 months	took no notice of anything. Lay almost still. Did not kick. No response to overture.
1 year	began to take notice. Tried to reach objects.

26 *months*   major convulsions began.

39 *months*   single words only.   Cerebral palsy of spastic type diagnosed.

7 *years*   I.Q. score 81.   Diagnosis spastic quadriplegia.   Interested, alert, occasional convulsions.

Case 3.—This boy was born by Caesarian section 9 weeks prematurely, weighing 907 g.   The mother had toxaemia.   Below is a summary of his development:

1st 8 months   Just lay in pram, taking no notice of surroundings.

8 months   first smile.

35 months   words in sentences.   Unable to sit. Good concentration.   Athetosis diagnosed.

5 years   I.Q. score 75.

COMMENT

I have described these cases at some length because of their great importance.   It seems that on rare occasions one sees a child who is retarded in all fields of development in the early weeks, and who then reaches a normal level of intelligence.   It is possible that this picture may occur when there is a 'birth injury' using the term in its broadest sense, the brain having been previously normal, and that full functional recovery may then occur.   The picture may alternatively be due to delayed maturation of the nervous system for reasons unknown, perhaps familial.   The problem is discussed by Edith Taylor in her book on the appraisal of children with cerebral defects.[8]   She described an athetoid child who at 15 months was unable to sit, could hardly use the hands at all, could not chew, and had to have a semi-solid diet because of difficulty in swallowing and of regurgitation. The child had an expressionless face, but was said to be alert and observant.   At the age of 12 years the I.Q. score was 103.

It follows that in developmental prediction the possibility of delayed maturation and unexpected improvement must always be borne in mind, and in all cases *the rate of development* must be observed and assessed.   This is based partly on the history of previous development and partly on the findings on repeated examination.

Unexplained Temporary Cessation of Development

Lulls in development of certain skills, such as speech, have already been described.   Very occasionally one sees a much more general slowing down or cessation of development, without any apparent reason.   The following are examples:

Case Report.—This girl was born at term by normal delivery.   She developed normally until 8 weeks, having begun to smile at 5 weeks with good motor development.   At 8 weeks she had a cold, and then became drowsy, inactive and disinterested in her surroundings.   She was admitted at 10 weeks.   She took no notice of her surroundings and was suspected of being blind.   She was drowsy and apathetic. There were no other abnormal physical signs.   A subdural tap and tests for toxoplasmosis were negative.   An air encephalogram was thought to show cortical atrophy.   The electroencephalogram was normal.   The following letter was written to the family doctor: 'I am afraid that the outlook for this child is extremely poor; although she appeared to develop normally till the age of 8 weeks, she is now obviously mentally retarded; her mental retardation is likely to be of severe degree'. She was discharged, to be followed up as an outpatient. At 14 weeks she was smiling and alert. At 7 months she was a normal happy smiling baby, vocalising well. At 3 years and 9 months in developmental tests she was above the average in all respects.

COMMENT

There is a possibility that the unexplained lull in development was due to encephalitis, but there were no neurological signs and there was no other evidence of that condition. In retrospect there seemed to be every reason to give a bad prognosis. The case shows the need for caution.

Case 2.—This baby was born by breech delivery at term, weighing 3175 g. Owing to a clerical error blood group incompatibility was not expected. She developed mild haemolytic disease of the newborn, responding to 3 simple transfusions. She began to smile at 6 weeks, and shortly after to vocalise. She developed normally until the age of 3 months. She then refused the breast, stopped playing with her toes, and just lay, with no interest in her surroundings for 4 months, without moving her arms or legs. She then appeared to waken up, began to go for objects with her hands at 9 months, and to sit up without support, to walk without support at 16 months, saying 2 words with meaning. At 2 years she was well up to the average in all developmental tests and was speaking in sentences. At just under 7 years she was doing well in an ordinary school.

COMMENT

These are important cases, for they indicate further pitfalls in prognosis. In both cases the period of non-development gave occasion to considerable parental alarm, and there was good reason for an expert to feel the same anxiety about the future of these children.

Severe Microcephaly with Initial Normal Development

I believe that sometimes a child with microcephaly may be relatively normal for the first few weeks, but that slowing down of development then occurs. I have seen several examples of this. I have cinematographic records of 2 such children, giving permanent evidence of the normality of early development.

Case 1.—This girl (Fig. 154) was born at term, weighing 3375 g. There was gross microcephaly, and it was impossible to obtain a proper measurement of the head circumference: it was probably between 11 and 12 inches. X-ray studies eliminated craniostenosis. I followed her up at frequent intervals and recorded her progress by cinéphotography, because of the advanced development. At 26 days her motor development was equivalent to that of an average 6 to 8 weeks old baby. She was smiling and vocalising at 4 weeks. The subsequent history was as follows:

10 weeks	laughs frequently. Tries to grasp objects.
6 months	sitting well without support. Chewing for a month.
8½ months	creeping. Imitating.
10 months	playing patacake; waving bye-bye.
11 months	pulls self to stand. Casting. Helping to dress.
	Very active, interested.
	Head circumferences 14⅞ inches (37·5 cms)

13 months   standing alone.   Walking, holding on to furniture.
15 months   walking.
16 months   domestic mimicry.   Head circumference 15¼ inches (38·7 cms)
              Managing cup.
18 months   3 words with meaning.
33 months   head circumference 39·4 cms.   5–6 words.
              D.Q. now 45.

The subsequent progress was one of gradual falling off in the rate of development.
A sibling was subsequently born with microcephaly.   She showed
a similar pattern of development.   Both children at school age had an
I.Q. score below 50.

Case 2.—This prematurely born boy was seen at the age of 6 months on account
of the smallness of his head.   At the age of 1 month it measured 31 cms in circumference, 32·6 cms at 3 months, and 35·6 cms when seen by me.   There was no
radiological evidence of craniostenosis.   He began to smile at 7 weeks.   Ophthalmoscopic examination revealed a gyrate atrophy of the retina, with nystagmus and
defective vision.   An air encephalogram showed marked cerebral atrophy.   Tests
for toxoplasmosis were negative.   At that time I wrote, 'The degree of microcephaly is surprising, in view of the relatively good head control and satisfactory
development of manipulation.   I do not suppose, however, that much further
advancement will occur, and think that the developmental prognosis is thoroughly
bad.   It remains to be seen'.
The situation was reviewed when he was 13 months old.   I wrote then that
'His level of development is exactly what one would have expected from previous
tests.   His D.Q. is about 75.   I cannot help feeling, however, that in view of the
marked microcephaly, it will be surprising if this relatively good level of development is maintained'.
The boy began to walk without help at 33 months, but when seen at 56 months
he was grossly retarded.   There was no sphincter control, poor concentration, poor
speech, and a complete inability to dress or undress himself.   He cast cubes and
blocks of the formboard, like a child of 12 to 15 months.   He was now well below
the 'educable' level.   At the age of six years his I.Q. score was 40.

Case 3.—Another child, 24 months old at the time of writing, was born weighing
3290 g, with a head circumference of 12⅛ inches (31·0 cms).   She began to smile at
her mother at 7 weeks.   She sat unsupported at eight months, her head circumference at this age being 14 inches, with a weight of 6420 g.   She walked alone at 13
months; her weight was now 8620 g and the head circumference was 15 inches;
she was saying two words with meaning.   I wrote then that I expected her to be
considerably retarded when older, though she was then within normal limits.
Domestic mimicry began at 13 months.   She was able to manage a cup and drink
from it without help at 15 months.   At 24 months she was saying numerous words,
and was beginning to join words into sentences (saying, for instance, 'Shut up' when
her mother sang).   She could get her pants and some other clothes on, and had
bladder and bowel control by day.   Her head circumference was now 15·4/8
inches.   Time will tell what her eventual I.Q. will be.

Mental Deterioration

Slowing down in development, or worse still mental deterioration,
occurs in a wide variety of conditions, of which the following are the
chief examples and causes:–

Malnutrition in infancy.
Severe emotional deprivation: insecurity.

Hyperbilirubinaemia.
Metabolic diseases (e.g. phenylketonuria, other abnormal amino-
acidurias, lipoidoses, mucopolysaccharidoses).
Thyroid deficiency.
Hypoglycaemia.
Hypernatraemia.
Lead poisoning.
Epilepsy, including effect of drugs, effect of severe fits, under-
lying brain disease, perceptual difficulties, learning disorders,
emotional and educational problems.
Degenerative diseases of the nervous system.
Meningitis, encephalitis, cerebral tumour.
Cerebral vascular accidents.
Severe head injury.
Drug addiction.
Psychosis.
Severe personality disorders.
Bad teaching.

**Normal development, followed by slowing and cessation of
development, due to hypothyroidism.   Rapid response to
treatment.**

Case Report.—This boy was interesting because of the slowing down and then
cessation of development of motor control.   He was born at term and was followed
by me from birth to the age of 8 years.   At one month of age his head control was
average: at 6 weeks I described it as almost average: at 11 weeks it was defective,
corresponding to that of an average 6 weeks old baby.   I realised that he had
probably developed hypothyroidism.   His total serum lipoids were 1,100 mg.
per cent, and the skeletal maturity was retarded.   He was given thyroxin.   At 15
weeks his head control was greatly improved, corresponding to the 9 to 10 weeks'
level.   At 6 months he was normal in all respects.   Subsequent progress was
normal.   At 13 months he was walking without support and saying more than a
dozen words with meaning.   He could manage a cup without any help.
At the age of 7 years his I.Q. score was just over 100.

COMMENT
   The absence of the typical appearance of cretinism in children like
this who develop thyroid deficiency after some weeks or months
makes the diagnosis easy to miss.   Cessation of growth in height is
commonly the first feature to draw attention to the condition.

**Normal development for 4 months, followed by sudden men-
tal deterioration with the development of infantile spasms.**
Below is a summary of a typical case.

Case Report.—This child was born at term, after a normal delivery:

  6 *weeks*   smile.
  8 *weeks*   vocalising.
  12 *weeks*   would hold rattle placed in hand for several minutes.

16 weeks	would hold bottle. Raising head spontaneously from supine.
20 weeks	began to look vacant and stopped showing interest in surroundings.
	A week later he had his first infantile spasm.
6 months	full head control. Able to sit like 6 months old baby.
	No interest in surroundings. No smile.
	All investigations negative except E.E.G. (hypsarrhythmia).
	Very bad prognosis given.
8 years	ineducable, in institution.

A similar picture is seen in some children who are moderately retarded from birth.   Infantile spasms develop usually at about the age of 6 months, and there is then immediate and severe deterioration. The condition has been described in Chapter 16.   A bad prognosis was given because of the deterioration in social behaviour.   When one first sees a child of this type the motor development may be up to the average, because he had previously developed normally, but there is a striking lack of interest in the surroundings, and the child has stopped smiling.   I regard a history that smiling has stopped (in the absence of an obvious febrile illness) as a symptom of great importance and bad prognostic significance.

Normal Development, Followed by the So-called 'Acute Infantile Hemiplegia' and Mental Deficiency.

Another cause of normal initial development followed by mental deficiency is a cardiovascular accident.

Case Report.—This girl weighed 4310 g at birth, and delivery was normal.   She was normal in the neonatal period.   Her development was normal.   She began to smile at 5 weeks, to grasp objects voluntarily at 5 months, to chew at 6 months and to sit without support at 7 months.   At the age of 11 months she had a right-sided convulsion, followed immediately by status epilepticus which continued for 12 hours. ¬
When we first saw her 9 days later she was in coma.   There was a right hemiplegia.   The fundi were normal.   The cerebrospinal fluid was normal.   An air-encephalogram showed excess of air over the left hemisphere but no other gross abnormality.   She was discharged home with a bad prognosis, the diagnosis being acute infantile hemiplegia.   At the age of 6 years her I.Q. was too low to score. She was taking no interest in her surroundings.   The hemiplegia was unchanged.

Severe mental deficiency may develop suddenly, usually in association with convulsions, during the course of gastroenteritis or dehydration for other reasons.   It may be due to hypernatraemia or to a cerebral venous thrombosis.

I have already mentioned the way in which mongols slow down in development after the early weeks.

Conclusions and Summary

The case histories indicate the importance of not only being thoroughly conversant with 'normal development' but with the variations which may occur.   Knowledge of such cases is essential for one who assesses the development of infants.   Unexpected slowing down of development, such as that described in several children, can never be anticipated. One must remember the fact that some children have unexpected lulls in development, followed by normal progress thereafter: and more important still, that even severe retardation in the early weeks may be followed by relatively normal or normal levels of intelligence later. Hence the importance of observing the rate of development by taking a proper history and observing the child at intervals.

I have cited examples to illustrate the danger of diagnosing mental retardation when a child, though backward in all aspects of development, has a head of normal size and is responsive, alert and interested in surroundings like a normal child should be—even though there is no helpful family history of delayed maturation.

REFERENCES

1. BAKWIN, H., BAKWIN, R. M. (1972) *Behavior Disorders in Children.* Philadelphia: Saunders.
2. GESELL, A., AMATRUDA, C. S. (1947) *Developmental Diagnosis.* New York: Hoeber.
3. GESELL, A., AMATRUDA, C. S., CASTNER, B. M., THOMPSON, H. (1939) *Biographies of Child Development.* London: Hamish Hamilton.
4. HOLLINGWORTH, L. S. (1942) *Children above 180 I.Q.* New York: World Book Co.
5. ILLINGWORTH, R. S., BIRCH, L. B. (1959) The Diagnosis of Mental Retardation in Infancy. A Follow-up Study. *Arch. Dis. Childh.*, **34**, 269.
6. ILLINGWORTH, R. S., ILLINGWORTH, C. M. (1966) *Lessons from Childhood. Some Aspects of the Early Life of Unusual Men and Women.* Edinburgh: Livingstone.
7. MICHAL-SMITH, H. (1957) *Management of the Handicapped Child.* New York: Grune and Stratton.
8. TAYLOR, E. M. (1959) *Psychological Appraisal of Children with Cerebral Defects.* Cambridge Mass.: Harvard Univ. Press.
9. TERMAN, L. M., ODEN, M. H. (1947) *The Gifted Child Grows Up.* Stanford: Stanford Univ. Press.

CHAPTER 12

HISTORY TAKING

I have already indicated that in my opinion the history is a vital part of the developmental diagnosis. Without a good history which I have taken myself, I am most reluctant to give an opinion about a child's development. It is in this matter that I disagree most strongly with those psychologists who attempt to make their developmental diagnosis and predictions purely on one objective examination. In my opinion this attempt to be really scientific by using nothing but objective methods leads to considerable inaccuracy. They ignore vital information which has a profound bearing on the child's assessment.

It is of interest that in the books written by Bühler,[1] Cattell[2] and Griffiths[3] on developmental testing in infants, nothing or virtually nothing is said about history taking. In marked contrast to these is the excellent book by Hauessermann[4] concerning developmental testing in handicapped children. In that book there is a good account of the way in which the history should be taken.

The Importance of the History

The history is an essential part of the developmental diagnosis for the following reasons:

1. *A history of prenatal and perinatal factors may be relevant to the diagnosis.* With regard to prenatal factors, their importance must not be exaggerated. For instance, it must be constantly borne in mind that a history of mental retardation in parents, toxaemia, bleeding during pregnancy, premature delivery, anoxia on delivery, or genetic conditions such as phenylketonuria, do not imply that the child in question will be abnormal. It merely means that the risk that the child will be abnormal is greater than usual. This is particularly important in the case of the examination of babies for adoption, especially if one of the parents was known to be mentally retarded. It would be a tragedy if children born of such mothers were automatically excluded from adoption, for the majority are mentally normal.

The history of prematurity is essential because of the allowance which must be made for premature delivery in assessing the early milestones.

A history of conditions known to be associated with kernicterus—hyperbilirubinaemia in the premature baby, excessive dosage of Vitamin K and improperly treated haemolytic disease, is important in developmental assessment. In the same way a history of severe anoxia at birth in a child subsequently found to be backward would make one particularly careful to look for athetoid movements.

Of all the prenatal and perinatal factors, one of the most important would be the history of perinatal convulsions in the baby, especially if they are due to hypoglycaemia. Even if that history is obtained, it will be remembered that the odds are that the child will be normal, though one cannot exclude the possibility that epileptic fits will occur later.

With regard to hereditary neurological disorders, one needs to know the age at which those disorders manifested themselves in siblings.

2. *The environmental circumstances*. The importance of environmental circumstances in relation to a child's potentialities has been discussed in Chapter 4. Amongst other relevant factors are the social and educational status of the parents and the opportunities which they are likely to give to the child.

With regard to the assessment of motor development, the opportunity given to the child to bear weight on the legs is important. Defective weight-bearing may be due merely to the mother's fear of allowing the baby to bear his weight.

In the case of the older infant, the mother's attitude has to be determined before an assessment of the baby can be made. If the mother leaves the 12 to 18 months old baby howling in the pram outside the house for most of the day, one would expect his developmental achievements to be less than those of a baby treated more imaginatively.

If a child has been brought up in an institution, the age at which he was placed in a foster home is relevant. The longer the period of institutional care, and the shorter the period in the foster home, the greater would be the retardation to be expected. A history of recent prolonged illness might well be relevant in assessing motor development.

With regard to skills such as feeding and dressing, the opportunities given to the child to attend to these needs himself must be assessed from the history. With regard to sphincter control, the parental management is relevant to the child's development.

3. *The assessment of the rate of development*. This vital piece of information must be obtained from the mother at the time of the first interview. A careful history of the milestones of development gives one a good idea of the course of development. This history is particularly important in the case of those children who develop normally up to a point and then deteriorate.

4. *An account of the rate and mode of development in siblings*. The importance of the familial factor in the age of walking, talking, and acquiring clean toilet habits, has already been discussed.

5. *Other family history*. A family history of sinistrality or ambidexterity, or of specific reading disability, is important.

6. *The history of achievements to supplement and confirm one's own*

observations. The observant mother may observe many skills which one cannot necessarily see in a short examination oneself, particularly if the child is being unco-operative on account of sleepiness or other factors. For instance, when showing a child a picture card, I usually ask a mother whether she thinks that her child would know the objects in question.

It is useful to determine whether the mother's account of the child's development tallies with one's own assessment. It does not always do so. One occasionally sees a child who, after careful questioning of the mother, is said to have been able to go for objects and grasp them for months, and yet who, on examination, has such an immature grasp that one does not believe the mother's story. On the other hand, one sometimes sees a child who is said to be unable to sit, yet who can sit steadily like an 8 or 9 months old child.

Essentials in History Taking

The first essential is that each should understand what the other means. The details of the child's development are asked in simple language, and the questions are put in a precise manner. The choice of questions will depend on the child's age and the doctor's rough estimate of his mental age. For example, when taking the developmental history of an apparently average 10 month old baby, it would not be useful to ask about the age at which the child began to smile and to vocalise, because the mother would not remember. But if the 10 month old baby were obviously defective, the child may have begun to smile only recently, so that the mother's story would be more likely to be accurate.

I suggest that the following questions should be asked, where relevant.

1. *Has he begun to smile at you when you talk to him? You mean* when you talk to him? or—*when did he begin to smile when you were talking to him? You mean when you were talking to him?*
It is not enough to ask 'When did he first smile?' Mothers may interpret as a smile any facial movement in sleep, or a wince of pain from wind, or facial movement as a result of tickling the face with the finger. The early smile must be the result of social overture. If the mother says that he has not begun to smile, one asks *Does he watch you carefully when you talk to him?* A baby watches his mother intently as she speaks to him, opening and closing the mouth, bobbing the head up and down, long before the smile begins. The average full term baby begins to smile at 4 to 6 weeks.

2. *Does he make little noises as well as smile when you talk to him?* or *When did he begin to make little noises as well as smiling when you talked to him?* Vocalisation usually begins a week or two after the smile.

3. *Does he smile much? Is it only an occasional smile?* This question is relevant in the case of defective children. Whereas a normal child

who begins to smile at 4 weeks smiles a great deal by the age of 8 to 10 weeks, a defective child who begins to smile at 3 months may smile only occasionally by six months.

4. *Does he hold a rattle or toy when you put it into his hand, and does he play with it?* or *When did he begin to* . . . .? The average full term baby will hold a rattle placed in the hand and play with it by about 3 months of age.   It is not enough to ask when he first began to grasp.   She may be confused by the grasp reflex, which has to disappear before voluntary grasping can begin.

5. *Does he turn his head when he hears things?   When did he begin?* (Average age 3 to 4 months).

6. *Will he go for a toy and get it without it being put into the hand? You mean without your putting it into the hand?* or *When did he begin to* . . . .?   *You mean* . . . .?   The average age is five months.   It is essential to be sure that she is not referring to the age at which he will play with a rattle or toy only when it is put into his hand.

7. *Does he pass a toy from one hand to the other?* or *When did he begin to* . . . . ?   The average age is 6 months.   (It may be argued that it is unnecessary to ask the mother whether he transfers objects, because the examiner can observe this himself.   As with several of the other questions, it is often useful to compare the mother's version with one's own objective findings).

8. *When did he first sit without support on the floor for a few seconds without rolling over?*   (Average age 6 to 7 months).   It is useless to ask 'when did he sit?'   A newborn baby can be held in the sitting position.   An average baby can sit propped up in a pram at any age after 2 or 3 months.   He can sit 'unsupported' in the pram—with support, however, around the buttocks—several weeks before he can sit on a firm surface without support.

9. *Does he chew things like a biscuit?   I don't mean does he suck things but does he really chew, moving his jaws?   When did he begin* . . . .? Mothers inevitably think of teeth when this question is asked.

10. *Does he creep on hands and knees?   When did he begin to* . . . .? The mother has to distinguish the crawl, whereby he pulls himself forward by his hands when lying flat, the legs trailing behind (average 9 months), from the true creep on hands and knees (average 10 months).

11. *Does he say any words meaning something?*   (Average age one year).   *What does he say?*   It is useless merely to ask when he began to talk.   Mothers are likely to interpret the 6 months old baby's Mummum in crying as a word of meaning.   When the 7 month old baby begins to combine syllables such as 'dada' these sounds are interpreted as words.   In the case of 'dada', one wants to know whether the word is spoken only in the father's presence, or when he is not there.   It is difficult to know when a 'word' is a word.   A child may say 'g' for

'dog' or 'og' before he can say the full word, but he is given the benefit of the doubt when he has obviously attempted to say the word.

12. *How much does he understand of what you say to him? Can he point out objects in books? For instance when you show him a picture book, can he point out the dog, horse, house etc?*

13. *Does he imitate anything which you do—making little noises laughing or putting the tongue out for instance? When did he ....?* (Average age 7 or 8 months).

14. *Does he help when you are dressing him? When did he begin? How does he help you?* The average 10 month old baby holds an arm out for a coat, a foot out for a shoe, or transfers a toy from one hand to another to allow the hand to go through a sleeve.

15. *Does he play patacake (clap hands)? When did he begin? Does he wave bye bye? When did he begin?* Average age 10 months.

16. *Does he join any words together to make little sentences? When did he begin ....?* This is different from imitating phrases like 'oh dear'. One needs to know when the child spontaneously began to join words together. (Average age 21 to 24 months).

17. *Does he walk holding on to furniture? When did he begin?* Average age 10 months.

18. *Does he walk without any help at all? When did he begin?* Average age 13 months. A child of 9 months or so can walk with hands held.

19. *Does he tell you when he wants to use the pottie? When did he begin?* Average age 18 months.

20. *Is he reasonably dry by day if you catch him? When was he reasonably reliable in the day?* Average 2 years.

21. *Is he normally dry at night? When did he become dry at night?* Average 3 years.

It is essential to distinguish conditioning the child to use the pottie, anytime from 3 to 4 weeks of age, from voluntary control, which only begins at about 18 months, when the child tells the mother that he has wet himself, then that he is just about to, and later tells her in time.

22. *Can he manage a cup, picking it up, drinking from it and putting it down without much spilling? When did he begin?* (Average age 15 months, but there is much variation depending on how much chance he has been given to learn. One must be sure that the mother is referring to an ordinary cup, and not a special closed one with a hole in it.)

23. *Does he imitate you doing things about the house like sweeping, dusting or washing up? When did he begin?* (Average age 15 months.)

24. *Can he dress himself fully, apart from back buttons? When was he able to do that?* (Average age 3 years if he has been given a chance to learn to do it: otherwise it is greatly delayed.)

25. *How long does he play with any one toy?* This is an estimate of the child's powers of concentration, but it must be distinguished

from the obsessional play of the defective child with one particular toy, or the refusal of a psychotic child to part with a favourite toy.

26. When mental subnormality is suspected—

How does he compare in general understanding with his brothers (or sisters) when they were his age, apart from his speech (if he is backward in speech)? What are the others like? If at school. *How are they doing at school?* It is obvious that in asking this question one must determine whether the siblings are apparently normal.

A particularly useless question is—When did he first begin to hold his head up? Any answer means nothing. A baby can hold his head up momentarily in the sitting position when a few days old. He can spontaneously lift his head off the couch in the supine position when he is about 5 to 6 months old.

Less important questions are the following:

Is he interested when he sees a feed being prepared?

How much does he sleep? This is relevant in mentally retarded infants who are apt to sleep excessively.

Can he roll completely over from his tummy to his back—not from his back to his tummy? You mean completely over? A clear distinction must be made between rolling from the prone to the supine (average five months) and from supine to prone (average six months). It is even more important to be sure that the mother refers to rolling completely over—not merely on the side, an arm getting in the way and preventing the full movement.

When did he begin to hand you a toy and give it to you (as distinct from handing it to you but not letting it go)?

Can he pull himself to the standing position? When did he begin? (Average age about 8 to 9 months.) It depends partly on how much chance he has been given to do this.

In taking a history about a child who is suspected of having defective hearing, one asks

Can he hear? Why do you think that he can hear?

Does he like being sung to?

Does he respond to music?

Has he favourite nursery rhymes?

Does he hear the telephone, aeroplane, father's footsteps?

Will he come from another room when you call him without his seeing you? seeing you?

I do not think that other questions are relevant or important except in a particularly difficult exceptional case.

The Reliability of the History

I disagree with those who consider that a mother's developmental history is totally unreliable. It is obvious that the further back one goes, the less reliable a history will be, but one does not usually need to go a long way back. When faced with a mentally defective boy of

10 years, minutiae of developmental history are irrelevant.   One does want to know details, however, in a baby.

It is always the doctor's task to assess the reliability of a story about anything, whether an illness or otherwise.   One has to form one's own opinion about a mother's memory.   One has to form one's own conclusion as to whether she is fabricating a reply, as to whether she is trying to make one believe that the child was 'normal' when he was not, and as to whether she is merely basing her replies on the age at which she thinks a child should achieve the skills in question.

In order to check a doubtful reply one comes round to the question in a different way after an interval in order to see if the answers tally.   One checks the answer about one milestone by that about another.   For instance, one can readily check the likelihood that a mother's reply about the age of smiling is correct by asking when he began to vocalise as well.   If she said that the baby began to smile at 3 weeks, but did not begin to vocalise until 3 months, one will know that one or other answer is almost certainly incorrect.   Babies usually begin to vocalise 1 or 2 weeks after they have begun to smile.   One constantly checks one milestone against another, and one will also check the mother's story against one's own findings on objective examination.

Summary

1. It is essential to ask whether he was prematurely born, in order that one can make the necessary deduction from his chronological age and so compare him with an average child of his corrected age.

2. A full developmental and environmental history is an essential part of the developmental diagnosis.   One must determine any factors which may have affected his development.   One must enquire about his previous milestones so that one can assess his rate of development.   One must compare the mother's version of the child's present developmental status with one's own objective findings.

3. Each must understand what the other means.   Questions must be precise.   The mother's memory and veracity must be assessed.

REFERENCES

1. BÜHLER, C. (1935) *From Birth to Maturity*. London: Kegan Paul.
2. CATTELL, P. (1947) *The Measurement of Intelligence of Infants and Young Children*. New York: The Psychological Corporation.
3. GRIFFITHS, R. (1954) *The Abilities of Babies*. London: Univ. of London Press.
4. HAUESSERMANN, E. (1958) *Developmental Potential of Pre-school Children*. London: Grune and Stratton.

CHAPTER 13

THE EXAMINATION OF THE OLDER INFANT AND CHILD

PART I.—THE DEVELOPMENTAL EXAMINATION

In Chapter 9 I have outlined the normal development of the infant and young child. In this chapter I shall discuss the technique of testing.

EQUIPMENT REQUIRED. The following equipment is required for developmental testing in the first 5 years:

10 one-inch cubes.
Hand bell.
Simple formboard.
Goddard formboard.
Coloured and uncoloured geometric forms.
Picture cards.
Scrap book.
Cards with circle, cross, square, triangle, diamond drawn on them. These can be made at the time of examination out of sight of the child.
Patellar hammer.
Paper.
Pellets (8 mm). These can be made at the time of examination from cotton wool or paper.

The relevant items are illustrated in figures.

The various structures made from the cubes are also illustrated (Figs. 132–136).

Examination after the Newborn Period

This section is based on the work of Arnold Gesell and has been modified for use in a busy paediatric out-patient clinic. It is obvious that the more one digresses from the exact technique of examination for developmental tests, the less valid is the statistical basis of one's tests. I regard the modifications suggested as so small that they do not invalidate the result; and a follow-up study already described (Ch. 2) and many hundreds of other personally observed cases, has shown that the tests as outlined are of predictive value.

For further details of developmental tests the reader should refer to Arnold Gesell and his colleagues in *Developmental Diagnosis* and *The First Five Years of Life*, and books by Charlotte Buehler and Psyche Cattell. The latter's tests were based on those of Gesell.

For the purpose of the developmental examination, and to a lesser extent for the purpose of the physical examination, it is important to have the infant or small child in as good a temper as possible.   In the Yale Clinic of Child Development, under Gesell, social workers visited the home in order to determine the baby's normal play time, and the developmental examination was arranged accordingly. Unfortunately the busy paediatrician cannot work under such ideal conditions, but he can at least see that the infant is not hungry at the time of examination.   If he is sleepy, a note to that effect is made and he is re-examined before an opinion can be given.

I see no need for a special room for developmental examination. Most paediatricians will of necessity have to examine infants and young children in the course of ordinary out-patient duties, in the usual room reserved for that purpose.   I have not found the presence of students or doctors a disadvantage.   The child should not be within sight of a window through which he can see objects and people passing.   Irrelevant toys must be out of reach and sight.   I always conduct my examination of the child in the mother's presence.   This seems to be the normal and natural arrangement.   Occasionally a mother is unable to resist trying to help a child to perform a test, but she can be asked to leave the test to the child.   She is also apt to tell a child that he is making a mistake (in the formboard test, for instance), but she has to be asked not to do this.   Sometimes the mother may help by asking the child to carry out a test, such as building a tower of cubes, when he shows no sign of doing it for the examiner.   When one is not sure whether he has really done his best, it is useful to ask the mother if she thinks that the child could do the test in question, or would be able to recognise the objects shown, so that one's findings can be confirmed.

The developmental examination of young children should always be performed before the physical examination, because the child may cry during the physical examination and he would then be unlikely to co-operate in developmental tests.   It is often advisable to carry out the developmental examination before taking the history, for a young child, and particularly a retarded one, will soon become bored and restless and so co-operate less well.

In all tests one observes the child's interest, distractibility, degree and duration of concentration, social responsiveness, alertness and rapidity of response.   The child is watched intently throughout the examination.   One particularly looks for abnormalities of movement (e.g. athetosis, ataxia, spasticity or tremor).   One also listens and notes the vocalisations—their nature and frequency, and later the quality of speech.

All tests are carried out as quickly as possible in order to preserve interest and co-operation.   If a child does not seem to be interested in one test, another is substituted.   In developmental testing of young or retarded children there is no place for long tests.   I cannot agree with those who say that developmental testing in infancy is very time-consuming. It must not be.

Babies and young children readily begin to cry when undressed or when placed in the prone or supine position. Accordingly one begins by acquiring as much information as possible as soon as the child comes into the room, when he is fully dressed. After that he is completely undressed for the rest of the examination and the nappy must be removed.

Summary—Essential Observations

1. Observe and watch baby on his mother's knee. If possible observe him when his mother talks to him, to see whether he watches her, smiles, vocalises. One notices his interest in his surroundings. Note shape and size of head. The heart is auscultated for abnormal murmurs.
2. Palpate the anterior fontanelle. If doubtful, feel the sutures for craniostenosis.
3. Hold in ventral suspension. Observe head control and limb position. In the normal child there is some extension of the hips, with flexion of the elbows and knees. In the abnormal child the arms and legs hang down lifelessly, and there is poor head control. Inspect eyes for opacity or nystagmus which suggests a visual defect. If the eyes are closed, he will usually open them if one swings round.
4. Place in prone position. Note elevation of chin off couch. Note whether pelvis is high off couch or flat. Observe for congenital dermal sinus.
5. Supine position. Note if hands unduly tightly closed.

   The umbilicus is inspected for infection and the abdomen is palpated.

   Examine hips: estimate hip abduction.

   Assess dorsiflexion of ankles—for tone. Test for ankle clonus.

   Shake limbs and assess resistance to passive movement for tone. Test knee jerks.

   Pull to sitting position—to compare head control with that in ventral suspension and prone: and note resistance to pulling to sit position: all to eliminate excessive extensor tone.
6. Measure head circumference. Relate it to weight. Possibly— check response to sound by crinkling paper etc., on a level with ear but out of sight: note cry, startle, quietening, blink.

The whole of the above normally occupies 1 to 2 minutes: it will take longer if doubt about normality arises. It is assumed that the Guthrie or similar test has been performed to eliminate phenylketonuria.

FIG. 128. — Uncoloured geometric forms. Similar to above, but uncoloured and more difficult.

FIG. 129.—Goddard form-board.

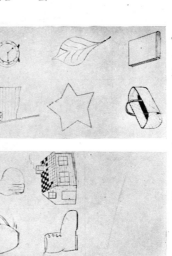

FIG. 131.—Incomplete man.

FIG. 130.—Pictures of common objects for picture identification.

FIG. 132. Tower of cubes.
FIG. 133. Train of cubes
    with chimney.

FIG. 134. Bridge.
FIG. 135. Gate.
FIG. 136. Step.

FIG. 137
Position for first stage of examination of young baby—before he is undressed.

A eirL

FIG. 138.—4 years 3 months.
FIG. 139.—4 years 3 months. (Girl with toy cupboard.)
FIG. 140.—5 years 3 months. (In colour.)
FIG. 141.—6 years 0 months.

FIG. 142   FIG. 143

FIG. 142—7 years 5 months.

FIG. 143—8 years 11 months. (In colour.)

FIG. 144—9 years 9 months. (In colour.)

FIG. 144

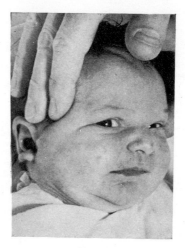

FIG. 145
The doll's eye phenomenon.

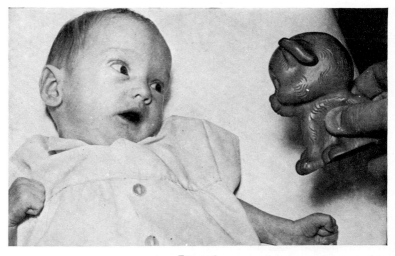

FIG. 146
Fixation and following with the eyes.

FIG. 147
Test of visual acuity with small toys.

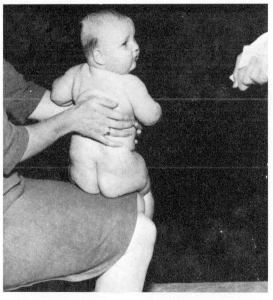

FIG. 148
Testing hearing: paper crinkled behind
baby, on a level with his ear. Four
month old baby turning his head to the
sound.

Three to Six Months

The mother sits at the side of the desk, holding the baby on her knees.

1. Observe the size of the baby's head in relation to his weight, and the shape of the head. Note the facial expression, vocalisations. Note if both hands are largely open. (The hand is likely to be closed more if the child is spastic.)
2. Test the hearing by crumpling paper etc. (out of sight, on a level with the ear, about 18 inches from it). Look at eyes for opacity or nystagmus.
3. If he is 3 to 4 months old, place a rattle in his hand: observe whether he plays with it.
4. Place a one inch cube on the desk in front of him. Note whether he gets it, and how long he tries to get it.
   If he gets it, note whether he transfers it to the other hand. Note how soon he drops it—as a sign of maturity of the grasp. Note—put a date to his manipulative development. If for instance, he cannot get hold of a rattle but will hold it when it is placed in the hand and play with it, his manipulative development is not less than 3 months, but not that of a 5 month old baby. This gap is narrowed by observing whether he merely shows a desire to get it, without reaching for it, like a 3 or 4 month old baby, or whether he reaches for it without actually getting it, like a 4 month baby. If he can get it without it being placed in the hand, his development is not less than 5 months. If he transfers it, he cannot be less than the level of a six month baby. One confirms this by watching the maturity of the grasp—the younger baby holding the cube in an insecure palmar grasp, dropping it promptly, the older one by a more secure grasp, using the fingers more.
5. Place him without clothes in the supine position. If he spontaneously lifts his head off the couch, his motor development cannot be less than that of a 6 month baby. He may not have reached that point: he may merely lift his head up when he sees that he is about to be pulled up.
6. Examine the hips for the degree of abduction, in order to eliminate subluxation or abnormality of muscle tone. Test knee jerks, ankle dorsiflexion, test for ankle clonus.
7. Watch for hand regard—a developmental trait seen in a narrow period of 12 to 20 weeks. It should not continue after that in a normal baby.
8. Pull him to the sitting position, to determine the amount of head lag, if any. If there is head lag, one can say immediately that his motor development is less than that of a 5 month baby. Note whether there is a feeling of resistance when he is pulled up

as in cerebral palsy, and with the hand in the popliteal space as he is pulled up note whether there is spasm of the hamstrings. When he is leaned forward, note whether he persistently falls back, as in the spastic form of cerebral palsy. When he is in the sitting position, his body is swayed from side to side. There should be little head wobble by the age of 5 months. (This test corresponds to the test for 'passivité' when one shakes the limbs in order to assess muscle tone).

9. Pull him to the standing position to assess weight bearing, but remember that success in this depends largely on the opportunity which his mother has given him to stand.

10. If the baby is 3 to 5 months old, assess him in the prone position.

11. Measure the head circumference and relate it to his weight.

12. Throughout note responsiveness, interest, alertness, concentration on toy.
    Always be sure that you have elicited the maximum performance. It is not enough to determine whether he can reach out and get an object: one has to determine the maturity of the grasp—how far he has developed in that skill.
    It is assumed that phenylketonuria has been eliminated.

Seven to Twelve Months

The baby sits on his mother's knee at the side of the desk.

1. Observe his face, skull size and shape, interest, alertness, quality of vocalisations.   Observe eye for opacity, nystagmus.

2. Offer a cube and observe maturity of grasp.
   Observe particularly the index finger approach.   If this is seen, his manipulative development cannot be less than 9 to 10 months.   In the case of the younger baby in this age group, note transfer from hand to hand.
   As soon as he takes one cube, offer another.   The younger child drops the first, the older one retains it.
   Note 'matching'—the baby bringing one cube to the other as if to compare the two (average age 9 to 10 months).   If he is around 9 months or more, offer a small pellet of paper.   Note the index finger approach which dates his level of development immediately.

3. Note whether he can pick up the pellet between the tip of the thumb and the tip of the forefinger.   (Finger thumb apposition: average age 9 months to 10 months.   If he has the index finger approach he will almost certainly show finger thumb apposition).   If he cannot get the pellet between the finger and thumb he will probably 'rake' with his whole hand.

4. Test for hearing by crumpling paper out of sight, on a level with ear, about 18 inches away.   Try other sounds.   ('oo', 'ps').

Note particularly the rapidity of the response on each side.   The retarded or deaf child is likely to be slow in responding.

5. Place him in the sitting position to assess his motor development: observe whether he needs his hands forward as props or whether he can sit steadily.   See whether he can pivot round for a toy when sitting.

6. Place in the prone in order to see whether he goes into the creep position (9 to 10 months), or places the sole of the foot on the couch when in the creep position (average age 11 to 12 months).

7. Pull to the standing position and assess weight bearing.

8. Place in the supine position.   Examine the hips, assess the range of ankle dorsiflexion, briskness of knee jerks, and test for ankle clonus.

9. Measure the head circumference and relate it to his weight. Possibly—ask him to hand a toy to you to determine whether he will release it into your hand (11 to 12 months).

One to Two Years

1. If he is walking, watch his gait as he walks into the room and assess its maturity.

2. When he is on his mother's knee, offer him the ten one inch cubes.   If necessary, show him how to place one on top of another to build a tower.   Note how accurately he places one on top of another and record the number forming the tower. Note tremor or ataxia.   Observe his interest, alertness, concentration, speech, cooperativeness.

3. Make a train of 9 cubes and place one on top of the first to make a train.   Ask him to imitate the process.   Observe whether he adds the chimney.   If he makes a train, show him how to make a bridge of three cubes and ask him to imitate the process.   If you build the bridge when he is watching, he 'imitates': if you build a bridge out of his sight (shielding by a card or hand), he 'copies'. The two are scored differently.

Note particularly whether he takes a cube to his mouth (he should have stopped this by 13 to 15 months), or whether he 'casts' one brick after another to the floor (he should have got out of this by 15 to 18 months).

4. Give him the simple formboard.   Decide on a rough guess about his maturity whether to give him the round block only or all three.   If he gets the round block in, take it out, say 'watch me carefully' and rotate the board slowly.   See if he gets the round one in with or without error.   If he can get the round one in, offer all three: if he can get them in, rotate as above. If necessary, as it commonly is, repeat the process two or three times, so that one can be sure that one has elicited the maximum performance.

5. Show him the picture card. Ask him 'where is the cat?' or 'show me the cat, basket, clock' etc. This is picture identification. If you ask him 'what is that?', pointing to the cat, this is termed 'picture naming', which is more difficult.
6. In the latter part of the period give him a pencil and paper. Ask him to 'imitate' the drawing of a vertical stroke, horizontal stroke or circle, according to maturity. If he is more mature, ask him to 'copy' these strokes (which were made out of his sight behind a hand or card). Note—all tests of drawing depend largely on the opportunity which he has been given to learn. If he has never been shown how to hold a pencil, he is unlikely to do well in the tests. All test objects must be given rapidly, one after the other, before interest flags.
7. Test his hearing.

Age 2 to 5 Years

Note his gait as he enters the room and his head shape, interest in surroundings and responsiveness.

In the case of the younger child in this age group, or of a retarded older child, it is important to carry out the developmental tests as soon as the child comes into the consulting room, before he becomes bored with waiting while a long history is being taken.

There can be no rule as to the order in which tests are given. The essential thing is to maintain the child's interest and to carry out each test quickly, changing to another if signs of boredom appear. If there is a complaint of clumsiness, or if a neurological abnormality is noticed, and he is over three years of age, he is asked to stand on one foot—without holding on to anything. (Normal age for standing for seconds on one foot—three years.) This is quite a sensitive test for a neurological abnormality such as a hemiplegia.

It is often convenient to begin with the cubes. Usually the child in this age group spontaneously begins to build a tower. One watches the hand movements for tremor or ataxia and tries to persuade the child to grasp with each hand, so that one can be sure that cerebral palsy is not present. One notes the accuracy of release, assessed by the accuracy with which one cube is placed on another. The child is then asked to build a train, bridge, gate or steps, according to one's rough assessment of the level he has reached, so that one can determine his maximum ability. In the case of the bridge, gate and steps, these are constructed behind a card or paper, so that the child cannot see the process of construction. He is then asked to copy the structure.

The child may then be given a pencil and paper. He is asked to imitate a vertical stroke, horizontal stroke, circle, cross, square, triangle or diamond, according to the level he is likely to have reached, being asked to draw these after the examiner, or he is asked to copy them.

Show him the picture card and ask him to identify or name objects, according to his maturity.

In the early part of the period he will be shown the simple formboard (as described above) and after about the third birthday, or before in a highly intelligent child, he is timed in his performance on the Goddard formboard, the score being based on the best of 3 trials. If he can place the blocks correctly in the simple formboard, he should be tried with the coloured geometric forms, and if he is successful with these he is tried with the uncoloured forms. In each case he is asked where the shapes fit, being handed one after the other. On no account is he told that he has made a mistake. It is always my practice to give the child another chance with those which he has placed wrongly.

The child is then asked to repeat digits. For instance, he is asked, 'Say after me, nine, seven, eight', and he is given 3 trials. If he can repeat these, one tries 4 digits, and if he can repeat these, 5 digits, in each case giving 3 trials of different numbers. He is also asked to identify colours in a picture.

By the age of 3 or 4 years he is given a Goodenough 'draw a man' test. One gives the child pencil and paper, and asks him to draw a man. The scoring is described on page 229.

In each case one must obtain the maximum achievement for each test. For instance, one must determine how many digits he can repeat.

Throughout the test one observes his powers of concentration, distractibility, interest, and alertness, and listens to and assesses his speech. One notes and records his degree of cooperativeness in tests.

In the section to follow I have named the test recorded with the average age at which success is achieved.

One Inch Cubes (Total needed—10)

16 weeks	Tries to reach cube, but overshoots and misses.
20 weeks	Able to grasp voluntarily. Bidextrous approach.
24 weeks	More mature grasp. Drops one cube when another is given.
28 weeks	Unidextrous approach. Bangs cube on table. Transfers. Retains one when another is given.
32 weeks	Reaches persistently for cube out of reach.
36 weeks	Matches cubes.
40 weeks	Index finger approach. Release beginning. Holds cube to examiner but will not release it.
44 weeks	Begins to put cubes in and out of container.
52 weeks	Beginning to cast objects on to floor.

15 months	Tower of 2. Holds 2 cubes in one hand.
18 months	Tower of 3 or 4.
2 years	Tower of 6 or 7.
	Imitates train; no chimney.
2½ years	Tower of 8.
	Imitates train, adding chimney.
3 years	Tower of 9. Imitates bridge.
3½ years	Copies bridge.
4 years	Imitates gate.
4½ years	Copies gate.
5 years	Cannot make steps.
6 years	May make steps.

Additional information is given by the cubes—the detection of mechanical disability in the hands, such as spasticity, athetosis, ataxia, tremor or rigidity.

Simple Orders.   (Take ball to mother, put it on chair, bring it to me, put it on table.)

18 months	2.
2 years	4.

Common Objects.   (Penny, shoe, pencil, knife, ball).

18 months	Names one.
2 years	Names 2–5.
2½ years	Names 5.

Picture Card

18 months	Points to one ('Where is the . . .?').
2 years	Points to 5. Names 3 ('What is this?')
2½ years	Points to 7. Names 5.
3 years	Names 8.
3½ years	Names 10.

Colours

3 years	Names 1.
4 years	Names 2–3.
5 years	Names 4.

Drawing

15 months	Imitates scribble or scribbles spontaneously.
18 months	Makes stroke imitatively.
2 years	Imitates vertical and circular stroke.
2½ years	Two or more strokes for cross. Imitates horizontal stroke.
3 years	Copies circle. Imitates cross. Draws a man.
4 years	Copies cross.

$4\frac{1}{2}$ years   Copies square.
5 years   Copies triangle.
6 years   Copies diamond.

The Goodenough 'Draw-a-Man' Test

The examiner asks the child to draw a man.   He is urged to draw it carefully, in the best way he knows how and to take his time.   The test is reasonably reliable, correlating well with the Binet tests.   The test is most suitable for children between 3 and 10 years of age.

The child receives 1 point for each of the items which is present in his drawing.   For each 4 points 1 year is added to the basal age which is 3 years.   Thus if the child's drawing shows that 9 items are present in his drawing he scores 9 points and his mental age score is 3 plus $\frac{9}{4}$ — $5\frac{1}{4}$ years.

Method of Scoring the Goodenough★ 'Draw-a-Man' Test:[17]
1. Head present.
2. Legs present.
3. Arms present.
4. Trunk present.
5. Length of trunk greater than breadth.
6. Shoulders indicated.
7. Both arms and legs attached to trunk.
8. Legs attached to trunk; arms attached to trunk at correct point.
9. Neck present.
10. Neck outline continuous with head, trunk or both.
11. Eyes present.
12. Nose present.
13. Mouth present.
14. Nose and mouth in 2 dimensions; 2 lips shown.
15. Nostrils indicated.
16. Hair shown.
17. Hair non-transparent, over more than circumference.
18. Clothing present.
19. Two articles of clothing non-transparent.
20. No transparencies, both sleeves and trousers shown.
21. Four or more articles of clothing definitely indicated.
22. Costume complete, without incongruities.
23. Fingers shown.
24. Correct number of fingers shown.
25. Fingers in 2 dimensions, length greater than breadth, angle less · than 180 degrees.
26. Opposition of thumb shown.
27. Hand shown distinct from fingers or arms.
28. Arm joint shown, elbow, shoulder or both.

★From Goodenough, F. L. *Measurement of Intelligence by Drawings*, New York: World Book Company.

GOODENOUGH 'DRAW-A-MAN' TEST

Age shown is actual age of child at time of drawing.

The series illustrates the drawings of a man made by one child at different ages.

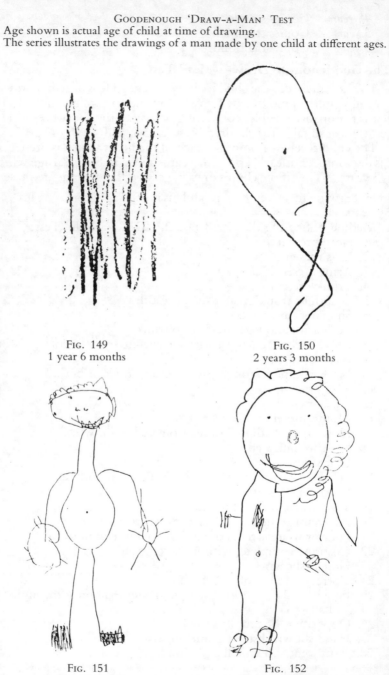

FIG. 149
1 year 6 months

FIG. 150
2 years 3 months

FIG. 151
2 years 11 months

FIG. 152
3 years 4 months

29. Leg joint shown, knee, hip, or both.
30. Head in proportion.
31. Arms in proportion.
32. Legs in proportion.
33. Feet in proportion.
34. Both arms and legs in 2 dimensions.
35. Heel shown.
36. Firm lines without overlapping at junctions.
37. Firm lines with correct joining.
38. Head outline more than circle.
39. Trunk outline more than circle.
40. Outline of arms and legs without narrowing at junction with body.
41. Features symmetrical and in correct position.
42. Ears present.
43. Ears in correct position and proportion.
44. Eyebrows or lashes.
45. Pupil of eye.
46. Eye length greater than height.
47. Eye glance directed to front in profile.
48. Both chin and forehead shown.
49. Projection of chin shown.
50. Profile with not more than 1 error.
51. Correct profile.

It is said that the score tends to be unduly low in children who suffered anoxia in utero and to be unduly high in children with schizophrenia.

Gesell 'Incomplete Man' Test

3 years	1–2 parts.	5 years	6–7 parts.
4 years	3 parts.	6 years	8 parts.
$4\frac{1}{2}$ years	6 parts.		

Simple Formboard

15 months	Inserts round block without being shown
18 months	Piles 3 blocks, one on top of another.
2 years	Places all 3. Adapts after 4 errors.
$2\frac{1}{2}$ years	Inserts all 3, adapting after errors.
3 years	Adapts, no error, or immediate correction.

Goddard Formboard.   (Best of 3 trials)

$3\frac{1}{2}$ years	56 seconds.	6 years	27 seconds.
4 years	46 seconds.	7 years	23 seconds.
$4\frac{1}{2}$ years	40 seconds.	8 years	20 seconds.
5 years	35 seconds.		

Coloured Geometric Forms

$2\frac{1}{2}$ years	Places 1.	4 years	Places all.
3 years	Places 3.		

Uncoloured Geometric Forms

3 years	Places 4.	$4\frac{1}{2}$ years	Places 9.
$3\frac{1}{2}$ years	Places 6.	5 years	Places all.
4 years	Places 8.		

Digits

$2\frac{1}{2}$ years	Repeats 2, 1 of 3 trials.
3 years	Repeats 3, 1 of 3 trials.
$3\frac{1}{2}$ years	Repeats 3, 2 of 3 trials.
4 years	Repeats 3, 3 of 3 trials.
$4\frac{1}{2}$ years	Repeats 4, 1 of 3 trials.
5 years	Repeats 4, 2 of 3 trials.
6 years	Repeats 5.
7 years	Repeats 3 backwards: ('Say these figures backwards').
8 years	Repeats 6 digits, 1 of 3 trials.

Simple Orders.   (Put the ball under the chair, at the side of the chair, behind the chair, on the chair.)

3 years	Obeys 2.	4 years	Obeys 4.
$3\frac{1}{2}$ years	Obeys 3.		

Book

15 months	Interested.
18 months	Turns pages 2 or 3 at a time.
	Points to picture of car or dog.
2 years	Turns pages singly.

The Developmental Assessment of Handicapped Children

The assessment of the developmental potential of handicapped children can be a matter of great difficulty, but it is also a matter of great importance because of the necessity of selecting the right form of education for them.   A comprehensive account of the method of testing children with cerebral palsy was given by Hauessermann.[9] The book by Edith Taylor[25] provides further valuable information. Parmelee et al.[15] found that Gesell tests were entirely suitable for testing blind infants.

Tests have to be modified for children with mechanical and other handicaps, and any departure from the exact method described by the authors of the tests must inevitably to some extent invalidate the results. This problem is covered in Hauessermann's book. That it was possible to form a reasonably reliable assessment of developmental potential in infants with cerebral palsy was shown by a study in Sheffield, to which reference has already been made (Chapter 2). In that study we followed children with cerebral palsy who had been thought to be mentally retarded in infancy, and assessed the I.Q. at 5 years or later. Of 35 children in whom mental retardation was diagnosed in the first 6 months of life, 20 survived, and 19 proved to be mentally retarded later. Of 40 considered to be mentally retarded when seen at 6 to 12 months of age, 29 survived, and 26 were found on follow-up examination to be retarded; and of 59 considered to be retarded when seen between 12 and 24 months, 52 survived, and the diagnosis of retardation was confirmed in 51.

Allowance must be made for the particular difficulty which the handicapped child has to face. Tests depending on vision, for instance, cannot be used for the blind child, and tests depending on hearing or speech cannot be used for the deaf child. Tests of manipulative development cannot be used for the child with severe spastic quadriplegia. In this case, however, one presents the test toy and observes the child's interest and desire to get hold of it. For instance, a 9 months old athetoid or spastic child with good intelligence will try really hard for a prolonged period to get hold of a brick or bell, and although he may fail to grasp it, he can be given a rough score for his determination to try to get it. In contrast a mentally defective child with cerebral palsy would show little or no interest in the object. One has to confine one's tests to those which are applicable to the child in question.

In examining children with cerebral palsy it is particularly important to remember the sensory and perceptual difficulties which some of these children experience. It should also be remembered that late maturation is more common in these children than in those with uncomplicated mental retardation, so that they may fare much better in the future than one would dare to expect when examining them in infancy. The difficulty of prediction, especially in the case of athetoid children, is considerable, but our findings have shown that only occasional mistakes will be made, and one must be constantly aware that these mistakes *may* be made.

THE REMAINING PART OF THE PHYSICAL EXAMINATION AND INVESTIGATION

A full physical examination is always necessary when assessing a child's developmental level, and there is no need to describe the routine examination here. One is particularly interested in detecting any of those conditions which may be related directly or indirectly to the child's development.

Testing of Hearing

Before discussing methods of testing hearing, it is useful to consider the factors which increase the risk that a child will have a defect of hearing. The factors are as follows:–
Family history of congenital deafness.
Genetic conditions associated with deafness.
Waardenburg's syndrome (White forelock, difference in the colour of the iris of the two eyes, deafness).
Pendred's syndrome—goitre and deafness.
Treacher Collins and First Arch Syndrome.
Klippel-Feil syndrome.
Congenital nephritis in males.
Hyperprolinaemia.
Retinitis pigmentosa.
Syndrome of deafness and anomalies of cardiac rhythm.
Various hereditary skin and hair conditions (e.g. multiple lentigines: Albinism, Pili Torti).
Conditions in pregnancy.   Rubella in the first three months.
Cytomegalovirus infection.   Severe toxaemia.   Administration of streptomycin, gentamicin, neomycin, kanamycin, quinine to mother.
Severe anoxia or cerebral damage at birth.
Prematurity.
Hyperbilirubinaemia in newborn period.
Congenital syphilis.
Meningitis.
Recurrent otitis media.
Mental subnormality.
Fibrocystic disease of the pancreas.
Cerebral palsy, especially athetosis and kernicterus.
Cleft palate.   (About half of all cases).
Delayed or defective speech.
Effect of drugs—intrathecal dihydrostreptomycin, vancomycin, neomycin, kanamycin, gentomicin.
Deafness suspected by the parents.
Gesell and Amatruda[8] have described the early clinical signs of deafness in infants, listing the main features as follows:
1. *Hearing and Comprehension of Speech.*
    General indifference to sound.
    Lack of response to spoken word.
    Response to noises as opposed to voice.
2. *Vocalisation and Sound Production.*
    Monotonal quality.
    Indistinct.
    Lessened laughter.
    Meagre experimental sound play and squealing.

Vocal play for vibratory sensation.
Head banging, foot stamping for vibratory sensation.
Yelling, screeching to express pleasure, annoyance or need.
3. *Visual Attention and Reciprocal Comprehension.*
Augmented visual vigilance and attentiveness.
Alertness to gestures and movement.
Marked imitativeness in play.
Vehemence of gestures.
4. *Social Rapport and Adaptations.*
Subnormal rapport in vocal nursery games.
Intensified preoccupation with things rather than persons.
Inquiring, sometimes surprised or thwarted facial expression.
Suspicious alertness, alternating with co-operation.
Markedly reactive to praise and affection.
5. *Emotional Behaviour.*
Tantrums to call attention to self or need.
Tensions, tantrums, resistance due to lack of comprehension.
Frequent obstinacies, teasing tendencies.
Irritability at not making self understood.
Explosions due to self-vexation.
Impulsive and avalanche initiatives.

Collins,[1] in a symposium on the deaf child, wrote that deaf babies gurgle and coo in a normal fashion, and that from 9 to 18 months they appear to be developing speech, saying 'mumum', 'dadada', but that no further progress in speech is then made.   It is important to note this fact.   Congenitally deaf babies do vocalise, and their vocalisations undergo changes leading up to spontaneous and playful sounds. This indicates the importance of maturation in speech development. Tape recordings of infants of congenitally deaf parents and of normal parents showed no differences.   The vocalisations, cooing and crying were identical, and were regarded as developmental.[14]

Part of the routine examination of all babies, certainly after the age of three months, includes a test of hearing.   It is probable that only severe deafness can be diagnosed in the newborn period.   The response to sound at this age includes quietening if crying, crying if quiet, the startle reflex or a blink.   After the age of three months the child should turn his head to sound: and thereafter one notes not just whether he turns his head to sound, but the rapidity with which he does it.   Sheridan[19] and Fisch[5] have described simple screening tests.

Sheridan described the appropriate tests for different ages from 6 months onwards, using the voice, soft paper, rattles, squeaking dolls, a cup and spoon, toys* and common household objects.   The sounds PS, PHTH are high pitched, and the sound OO low pitched.   One must be careful not to blow into the ear when making the sounds.

*STYCAR test—chair, doll, car, plane, spoon, knife, fork.

Frequent repetition of the sounds leads to habituation, so that he no longer responds. He must not be tested when he is tired, hungry or preoccupied with some other interest.

She emphasised the importance of the examiner not being too far from the child: he should be well to the side but outside the field of vision. When the baby is 6 months old, the sound is made 18 inches from the ear, on a level with the ear. When he is older, it may not be desirable to make the noises behind him; but if one is in his sight and covers one's mouth with the hand, one must avoid giving him clues by elevating the eyebrows or other facial expression. Sheridan found that clinical testing of the young child is more accurate than audiometry.

More sophisticated tests are the electronic tests described by Douek et al.,[3] consisting of cortical evoked response audiometry, electrocochleography and the crossed acoustic response. If there is deafness these tests indicate the site of the lesion.

Fisch[5] made the following comments on hearing tests:

1. There is no single form of testing which will give a complete picture of the total hearing capacity of an individual.

2. Hearing tests are subjective tests requiring co-operation. There is no mechanical device which would enable us to test a child without gaining his confidence or co-operation. The handling of the child is decisive.

3. One should not draw any far-reaching conclusions or make final decisions on the basis of observations carried out on one single occasion.

4. A test should not be of such a nature that it would be associated with unpleasant or frightening experiences.

5. The child's obvious reaction to certain sounds or his understanding of familiar speech sounds in *tete-a-tete* conversation does not mean that the child could not have a hearing loss. When deafness is suspected, only a complete test is conclusive.

Wedenberg[26] described methods of testing the hearing of newborn babies. The hearing tests included a study of the sound required to cause blinking and to awaken a child from sleep, using a pure tone audiometer connected to a loudspeaker. One ear at a time was tested.

For the older child the Peep-Show technique of Dix and Hallpike[2] may be used, in association with pure tone audiometry. Fisch's method[5] depends largely on the establishment of conditioned reflexes—training the child to make a particular movement, such as putting a brick into a cup—when a sound is made. Full audiometry can be carried out from the age of three.

When it is found that the child can hear, it is then necessary to determine whether he can understand what he hears. He may suffer from congenital auditory imperception. As Sheridan has said, hearing is the reception of sound by the ear, and involves the cochlea, 8th nerve, brain stem and primary auditory area of the cortex. Listening is paying attention to sound in order to comprehend what is heard. This may involve coding, memory, emotion and previous experiences.

More recent tests include measurement of acoustic impedance, which test the activity of the ossicular chain, and evoked response audiometry. Psychogalvanic skin reactions have not proved to be reliable.

Vision Testing

Before considering methods of testing vision, it is as well to be aware of the factors which increase the risk that a child will have a defect of vision. The factors are as follows:

Family history of blindness.
Prematurity (retrolental fibroplasia, myopia, cataract).
Rubella in first trimester of pregnancy.
Severe toxaemia in pregnancy.   (Myopia in the child.)
Mental deficiency.
Cerebral palsy.
Hydrocephalus.
Craniostenosis.
Ophthalmia neonatorum.
Neglected squint.

In the older child the chief causes of blindness are trauma, rheumatoid arthritis, various causes of cataract formation, and the effect of drugs (such as chloroquin). For complete list see my book, Common Symptoms of Disease in Children (1975).

The method of inspecting the eye of the newborn baby has been discussed on pages 112 and 116. Ophthalmoscopic examination is essential if a defect of vision is suspected, but the findings are not necessarily easy to interpret. When a baby is mentally defective, and therefore late in development of the usual responses, it can be extremely difficult to decide whether he can see or not. On ophthalmoscopy one sees the pale disc which is normal in the early weeks, and it is difficult to determine whether the pallor of the disc is within normal limits.

Dr. Mary Sheridan has described the method of screening young or handicapped children for vision,[20,21] and reference should be made to her papers. From the age of 21 to 36 months she tests with miniature boys★, the child having one set and the examiner, having an identical set, holds up one after another at 10 feet from the child, who is asked to match the examiner's toy with his own. The Snellen letters can be used after the age of three. The Sheridan test depends on the fact that the first letters to be learnt by a child are usually the V. O. X. H. and T., and later the A. U. L. and C.: the child matches letters from

★STYCAR test—chair, doll, car, plane, spoon, knife, fork.

his own set with those held up 10 feet away by the examiner.

As Sheridan has pointed out, there is an important difference between seeing and looking.

'Seeing' is the reception of patterns of light and shade by the eyes and the transmission of this sensory information in some form of neurological activity to the occipital region of the brain. 'Looking' is paying attention to what is seen with the object by interpreting its significance. It depends upon the ability to integrate the sensory information received into meaningful messages. Everyday visual competence involves seeing and looking and presupposes previous adequate opportunity to learn from experience.

It should be noted that hypermetropia, which involves difficulty with near vision, is more common than myopia, which involves difficulty in distant vision. It is often difficult to diagnose a mild degree of strabismus, but it is of great importance to do so. When in doubt, one must consult an expert. The epicanthic fold so commonly seen in normal infants may give an appearance of a squint. The diagnosis is best made by observation of the eye movements up and down and side to side. The cover test is useful but not always easy to perform. One eye is covered with a card while the infant is encouraged to fix upon a nearby object. The eye is then uncovered. If the eye has to move to fix upon the object, there is strabismus. Another test consists of directing a light onto the eyes from a distance of 12 to 14 inches. The light reflection should be centred in both pupils; if there is imbalance, one point of reflection may be off centre. Tests for squint were described in detail by Stanworth.[24] Usually when a baby has a defect of vision, there is nystagmus.

Testing for colour is a matter for the expert. According to Peiper[16] colour blindness can be ruled out completely by the start of the third year. A useful screening device has been described by the Gallachers.[6] Their description is as follows:–'This simple brief evaluation employs the H.R.R. pseudoisochromatic plates which distinguish red green blindness, total colour blindness and blue yellow blindness. Graded colour symbols (triangle, circle, cross) with increasing saturation of the critical hues allow both a qualitative and quantitative evaluation of the defect; the child need only trace the symbol with a brush'.

There are several modifications of the ISHIHARA tests to make the tests suitable for children. About 8 per cent of boys and 0·4 per cent of girls have red green colour vision.

Speech Assessment

Speech assessment is a matter for the expert who will investigate verbal comprehension, vocabulary and word structure. Those interested should consult the publications by Ingram and Reynell. The non-expert should observe whether the child is saying single words only or is joining words together into sentences: and whether he is speaking as distinctly as usual for his age, or whether infantile substitutions are persisting beyond the usual age. For instance, the common central lisp, the substitution of 'th' for 's' as a result of protrusion of the tongue between the front teeth when pronouncing the 's', should disappear around four, and persistence thereafter should be treated by a speech therapist before he starts school. Likewise a slight stutter is acceptable at $2\frac{1}{2}$ years of age, but if it is persisting and marked, it should be treated by the age of four.

When there is retardation in speech, it is most important to determine whether the child understands spoken language. Understanding of language precedes by a long time the ability to articulate. Language is best provoked by talking to the child (e.g., about toys), or by showing him pictures in a picture book.

Handedness or Laterality

The child's lateral dominance can be tested in a variety of ways. Handedness can be diagnosed by asking the child to rub with a duster, brush his teeth, throw a ball, thread a needle, use a broom, draw, cut paper with scissors, pick an object up from the ground, wind a clock, grip a dyanmometer, place counters in a tin or hammer nails. The dominant foot is diagnosed by asking the child to kick a ball. The dominant ear is determined by asking the child to listen to a watch. The dominant eye is determined by asking the child to look at a distant object through a rolled piece of paper. The ability to mirror-read may be tested, because of the unusual facility with which some children with specific reading disability can achieve this.

Other Features

Other features of the physical examination include the palpation of the fontanelle in the young infant for bulging, the palpation of the sutures for undue separation, suggestive of hydrocephalus, or the rim over the suture line in craniostenosis, and the examination of the eyes for optic atrophy, choroidoretinitis or other lesions.

Congenital anomalies, such as cleft palate, congenital heart disease or skeletal anomalies, which are known to be associated with mental retardation, must be looked for.

Special Investigations

Investigations which may be needed include the Kahn and Wassermann reaction, tests for toxoplasmosis, protein bound iodine and x-ray for skeletal maturation and examination of the urine for phenylpyruvic acid, galactose, abnormal amino-acid excretion, metachromatic material and inclusion bodies, and estimation of the motor nerve conduction time.

Apart from these investigations in special cases, and certain other investigations for metabolic conditions (such as hypercalcaemia) it is surprising how infrequently special investigations are necessary in developmental diagnosis. The examination is essentially clinical. With regard to electroencephalography, I have little personal experience of the value of this in developmental diagnosis, except in the case of infantile spasms and other forms of epilepsy. Air encephalography is not often indicated in developmental diagnosis. It is easy to be misled by the findings. Amatruda attempted to relate the findings in air encephalograms to the behaviour of 53 children. She wrote 'in the presence of normal behaviour development 'cortical atrophy' does not necessarily cause a bad prognosis, and may, indeed, be almost without significance'. She added that 'behaviour is the final criterion of the functional integrity of the central nervous system'. Knobloch et al.[12] described an interesting study on 50 patients. A radiologist and a neurosurgeon graded air encephalograms on the basis of ventricular dilatation and cortical markings. A paediatrician carried out Gesell tests and assessed the intellectual potential. There was no evidence of correlation between adaptive or gross motor development and the air encephalogram, or between the presence or absence of mental retardation and the degree of abnormality in the encephalogram. The severity of cerebral palsy was not related to the degree of abnormality in the X-ray.

REFERENCES

1. COLLINS, V. L. (1954) The Early Recognition of Deafness in Childhood. Med. J. Aust., 2, 4.
2. DIX, M. R., HALLPIKE, C. S. (1947) The Peep-Show. Brit. med. J., 2, 719.
3. DOUEK, E., GIBSON, W., HUMPHRIES, K. (1974) The crossed acoustic response and objective tests of hearing. Develop. Med. Child Neurol. 16, 32.
4. EWING, A. W. G. (1957) Educational Guidance and the Deaf Child. Manchester. Manchester University Press.
5. FISCH, L. (1964) Ed. Research in Deafness in Children. London. Blackwell.
6. GALLACHER, J. R., GALLACHER, C. D. (1964) Colour Vision Screening of Preschool and First Grade Children. Arch. Ophthalm., 72, 200.
7. GARDINER, P. (1973) A colour vision test for young children and the handicapped. Develop. Med. Child Neurol. 15, 437.
8. GESELL, A., AMATRUDA, C. S. (1947) Developmental Diagnosis. New York: Hoeber.
9. HAUESSERMANN, E. (1958) Developmental Potential of Preschool Children. London: Grune and Stratton.
10. ILLINGWORTH, R. S. (1975) Common Symptoms of Disease in Children. 5th Edn. Oxford. Blackwell Scientific Publications.
11. INGRAM, T. T. S., ANTHONY, N., BOGLE, D., McISAAC, M. W. (1971) Edinburgh Articulation Test. Edinburgh: Churchill Livingstone.
12. KNOBLOCH, H., SAYERS, M. P., HOWARD, W. H. R. (1958) The Relationship between Findings in Pneumoencephalograms and Clinical Behaviour. Pediatrics, 22, 13.
13. KONIGSMARK, B. W. (1972) Hereditary childhood hearing loss and Integumentary system disease. J. Pediatrics 80, 909.
14. LENNEBERG, E. H., REBELSKY, F. G., NICHOLS, I. A. (1965) The Vocalisations of Infants Born Deaf. Human Development, 8, 23.

15. PARMELEE, A. H., FISKE, C. E., WRIGHT, R. H. (1959) The Development of Ten Children with Blindness as a Result of Retrolental Fibroplasia. *Amer. J. Dis. Child.*, **98**, 198.
16. PEIPER. A. (1963) *Cerebral Function in Infancy and Childhood.* London: Pitman.
17. PHILLIPS, C. J., SMITH, B. BROADHURST, A. (1973) The draw-a-man test: a study in scoring methods, validity and norms with English Children at 5 and 11 years. Clinics in Developmental Medicine. No. 46.
18. REYNELL DEVELOPMENTAL LANGUAGE SCALES (1969) Slough: National Foundation for Educational Research.
19. SHERIDAN, M. D. (1958) Simple Clinical Hearing Tests for Very Young or Mentally Retarded Children. *Brit. med. J.*, **2**, 999.
20. SHERIDAN, M. D. (1960) Vision Screening of Very Young or Handicapped Children. *Brit. med. J.*, **2**, 453.
21. SHERIDAN, M. D. (1969) The development of Vision, Hearing and Communication in babies and young children. *Proc. Roy. Soc. Med.*, **62**, 999.
22. SHERIDAN, M. (1973) The Stycar graded-balls vision test. *Develop. Med. Child Neurol.* **15**, 423.
23. SHERIDAN, M. (1973) The Stycar Panda test for children with severe visual handicap. *Develop. Med. Child Neurol.* **15**, 728.
24. STANWORTH, A. (1974) Squint in the first two years. Medicine No. 27. p. 1614.
25. TAYLOR, E. M. (1959) *Psychological Appraisal of Children with Cerebral Defects.* Cambridge Mass.: Harvard Univ. Press.
26. WEDENBERG, E. (1956) Auditory Tests in Newborn Infants. *Acta otolaryng. (Stockh.)*, **46** 446.

CHAPTER 14

INTERPRETATION

Allowance for Prematurity

In developmental assessment it is essential that allowance must be made for premature delivery (see Chapter 2).

Relative Importance of Different Fields of Development

Some fields of development are more important for assessment purposes than other fields. Below is a summary of my opinions on this.

Gross Motor Development

It is unfortunate that the aspect of development which is the most easily scored is the least valuable for the overall assessment of a child's development and capability. It would be wrong to suggest that gross motor development is useless as part of the developmental examination. It is of great value, but its limitations have to be recognised. Defective motor development, as determined by head control in ventral suspension and the prone position, is commonly the first sign of abnormality in a child who is mentally retarded from birth or before birth. The majority of mentally retarded children are late in learning to sit and to walk, but the exceptions are so frequent that the age of sitting and walking is of only limited value in assessing intelligence.

In Table 8 I have analysed the age at which mentally retarded children, seen by me at the Children's Hospital, Sheffield, learnt to sit for a few seconds without support and to walk a few steps without support. None had cerebral palsy or other mechanical disability. None had a degenerative disease, so that there was no deterioration. Mongols are kept separate from the others. The gradings 'seriously subnormal' and 'educationally subnormal' were based on I.Q. tests at school age.

It will be seen that the age at which unsupported sitting began was average (6 to 7 months) in 8·3 per cent of the seriously subnormal children, in 6·7 per cent of the mongols, and in 10·7 per cent of those who were educationally subnormal. On the other hand the skill was not acquired until after the first birthday in 73·3 per cent of the seriously subnormal children other than mongols, 35·4 per cent of the mongols, and 42·9 per cent of the educationally subnormal children. The age of walking without support was average (12 to 17 months) in 15·2 per cent of the seriously subnormal children other than mongols, and in 29·5 per cent of the educationally subnormal ones. No mongols walked as soon as this. On the other hand the skill was not acquired until the second birthday or after in 65·9 per cent of the seriously subnormal children, 75·6 per cent of the mongols and 52·3 per cent of the educationally subnormal ones.

TABLE 8
Age of Sitting Unsupported

Age in months	Seriously subnormal Total 48 Percentage	Educationally subnormal Total 28 Percentage	Mongols Total 45 Percentage
6 to 7	8·3	10·7	6·7
8 to 9	14·5	39·3	31·1
10 to 11	2·1	7·2	26·6
12 to 17	35·4	39·3	22·0
18 to 23	15·0	3·6 ⎱	13·4
24 +	22·9	0 ⎰	

Age of Walking Unsupported

Age in months	Seriously subnormal Total 59 Percentage	Educationally subnormal Total 42 Percentage	Mongols Total 37 Percentage
Under 12 months	0	4·7	0
12 to 14	5·1	9·5	0
15 to 17	10·1	14·3	0
18 to 23	18·6	19·0	24·3
24 to 35	37·2	40·5	51·4
36 to 47	13·5	4·7	10·7
48 to 59	10·1	2·4 ⎱	13·5
60 +	5·1	4·7 ⎰	

It has already been mentioned that there are great variations in the age of sitting and walking in normal children, some learning to walk without support by the age of 8 months, and some not until the age of 3 or 4 years. Early locomotion does not indicate a high level of intelligence. On page 168 I described a boy who had uniformly advanced gross motor development but his I.Q. score subsequently was only 88. All that one can say about unusually early motor development is that it probably excludes mental deficiency.

The main clinical importance of delayed locomotion lies in the fact that it should make one careful to look for signs of cerebral palsy or hypotonia, though delayed locomotion may occur without discoverable cause. The main importance of unusually early locomotion is that it almost excludes mental deficiency and certainly excludes cerebral palsy.

Fine Motor Development (Manipulation)

Though I have no figures with which to prove it, I feel that the development of manipulation is a better guide to the level of intelligence than is gross motor development.   I have not seen notable delay in manipulative development in normal children.   The only children in whom I have seen unusually early development of manipulation have proved to have a high I.Q. later.   Some children have certain aptitudes, irrespective of intelligence, and some children are better than others in the use of their hands.   I believe that this may sometimes be detected in the latter part of the first year.   If one sees good finger-thumb apposition and a definite index finger approach at 10 months, one is fairly safe in saying that the child is not mentally defective.   I have not seen a mentally defective child with average manipulative ability, provided that he was defective from birth or before, and has therefore not acquired normal manipulation before the development of mental deficiency.   I believe that the relationship of fine motor development to subsequent intelligence would repay further study.

Speech

The words speech and language are often used as synonyms, whereas they should really be distinguished from each other.   By speech one denotes the use of words, but by language one means the expression of thought in words.   The assessment of language from the developmental point of view is difficult, but the use of 'speech' as an indication of developmental level is relatively easy, the two chief milestones being the age at which words are first used with meaning, and the age at which words are first joined together spontaneously.

It is the experience of many workers that the early development of speech is a most important sign of a good level of intelligence. Terman wrote that 'Earliness of onset of speech is one of the most striking developmental characteristics of intellectually gifted children'.   Spiker and Irwin[6] found a good correlation between speech sounds and the level of intelligence, and between subsequent speech and the I.Q.   Catalano and McCarthy[2] described work by Fisichelli, who made a phonemic analysis of tape recordings of the vocalisations of 23 infants in an institution at the mean age of 13·3 months.   They followed these children up and conducted Stanford-Binet tests on them at the mean age of 44·8 months.   There was a strongly positive correlation between the infant sounds and the subsequent Stanford-Binet tests, especially with regard to consonant types, the frequency of consonant sounds, the number of different kinds of consonant sounds, and the consonant-vowel frequency and type ratio.   The correlation between the I.Q. and the number of different kinds of consonants gave a coefficient of 0·45 with the Stanford–Binet tests.

Ausubel wrote that 'intelligence is perhaps the most important determinant of precocity in speech, since it affects both the ability to mimic and to understand the meaning of verbal symbols'. In my opinion the greatest importance should be attached to speech development as an index of intelligence. It has already been stated that the development of speech may be delayed in children of average or superior intelligence, so that it follows that delayed speech in itself can never be used as an indication of mental retardation. Advanced speech, however, is in my experience always an indication of superior intelligence. I should be most surprised if I heard a child speaking well in sentences at 15 months and subsequently found that his I.Q. was 100 (unless there was subsequent emotional deprivation or other retarding factor).

The understanding of words far outstrips the ability to articulate them. I should be just as impressed with a child who was able to point to a large number of objects in a picture book as an indication that he understood the meaning of words. I believe that there is a need for a new developmental test for children aged 12 to 18 months, based on their understanding of the meaning of words.

Just as advanced speech can be regarded as a sign of superior intelligence, average speech can be regarded as a sign of at least average intelligence, though a child of 12 to 24 months with average speech may also prove to be of superior intelligence. This is important, because one sees children with delayed motor development, with or without some mechanical disability, in whom an assessment of intelligence is required. The presence of average speech immediately tells one that his intelligence is normal, even though he is also retarded in another field, such as sphincter control.

In the same way speech is important in the assessment of retarded children, and especially those with a physical handicap such as cerebral palsy. If, for instance, a child were severely retarded in all fields but speech, in which retardation was only slight, I should give a good prognosis with regard to his intelligence, because I would think that his I.Q. would be only slightly below the average. I have only once seen a possible exception to this.

Smiling and Social Behaviour

The age at which a baby begins to smile is of considerable importance in the assessment of a child. The mentally retarded child almost invariably begins to smile long after the age of 4 to 6 weeks, the average age. The mean age of smiling in a consecutive series of 62 mongols seen by me was 4·1 months. It is vital to make due allowance for prematurity in these early milestones. I do not know whether unusually early smiling presages superior intelligence, or whether it is affected by the child's personality. I suspect that it usually presages superior intelligence.

There is some disagreement as to what the baby's early smiles signify. Bowlby[1] regarded the smile as a 'built-in species specific pattern'—a view with which I agree. Bowlby implied that the smile is not merely a learned conditioned response, as has been suggested by some. It has been shown that the essential stimulus for the early smile is the face.

Whatever the psychological explanation of the smile, the age at which the baby begins to smile at his mother in response to her overtures is an important and valuable milestone of development, in that this is bound up with the child's maturity and therefore with his mental development. I agree with Soderling[5] that smiling is in some way dependent on maturation, though environment must play a part.

It is important to note the age at which babies begin to laugh, to play games, to imitate, to draw the attention of their parents (e.g. by a cough), and their general social responsiveness. More important still are those features like the alertness, the power of concentration, the degree of determination of a baby (e.g. to obtain a toy out of reach, or to grasp a pellet when he is not quite mature enough). 'The child speaks with his eyes'. It is very difficult to convert many of these into scores: but they can be observed and used in a child's assessment. They are far more important than the readily scored sensorimotor items, which have been the basis of most of the tests used by those psychologists who found that developmental tests have no predictive value.

Sphincter Control

This is of relatively little value for the assessment of a child. Mentally retarded children are usually late in acquiring control of the bladder, but not always, while many children of superior intelligence are late in acquiring control. Apart from constitutional and anatomical factors, the parental management has considerable bearing on the age at which control is learnt, and this is irrelevant in the assessment of a child's intelligence.

Chewing

I find that the age at which a child begins to chew is of considerable value in assessing a child. Mentally retarded children are always late in learning to chew. It is my impression that babies who begin to chew unusually early (the earliest being about $4\frac{1}{2}$ months), are bright children, but I have no figures to support this.

It has already been said that an extraneous factor has to be considered (and eliminated by the history) and that is failure of the parents to give the child solid foods to chew. This would delay the development of chewing—or at least the age at which it is observed.

The Relationship of One Field of Development to Another: Dissociation

In assessing the value of the history for diagnosis and prediction, it is important to balance one field of development against another. The development in one field normally approximates fairly closely to the development in another. For instance, most children at the age of 6 to 7 months are nearly able to sit on the floor without support: they are able to grasp objects easily and they have recently learnt to transfer them from hand to hand: they have recently learnt to chew: they have just begun to imitate: they are making certain characteristic sounds when vocalising. In assessing any child one automatically assesses his development in each field. Gesell remarked that the developmental quotient can be specifically ascertained for each separate field of behaviour and for individual behaviour traits.

The development in one field is sometimes out of step with that in other fields. It has already been explained that there are great individual variations in various fields of development, children learning some skills sooner or later than others, though they are average in other fields. For instance, some children are late in single fields, such as speech or walking, and yet are average in other aspects of development. I have termed this 'Dissociation'.[4] It is important for enabling one to determine the likelihood that the mother's story is correct, and it draws one's attention to variations in development, such as lateness in one field, which require investigation. The following case history may be cited as an example:

Case Report.—This girl, born at term, reached important stages of development at the times below:

6 weeks Smile.
5 months Grasp objects voluntarily.
6 months Chew.
1 year Casting. Saying 3 words. Good concentration and interest. Very defective weight bearing, equivalent to that of average 3 months' old baby. Knee jerks normal. Marked general hypotonia.
Diagnosis Benign congenital hypotonia.
She walked without help at 5 years. Her I.Q. was 100.

Whenever one finds that a child is notably retarded in one field as compared with his development in others, a search should be made for the cause. Often no cause will be found, but the cause will be found in others. Below is an example of dissociation.

Case Record.—Diplegia in an infant with minimal neurological signs.
This boy was referred to me at the age of $5\frac{1}{2}$ months for assessment of suitability for adoption. He had been a full term baby. He began to smile at 7 weeks and to vocalise 2 weeks later. It was uncertain when he had begun to grasp objects. He had not begun to chew. It was said that he was very interested when his feed was being prepared.
On examination he did not grasp an object. The head control was not full, being that of a 4 months old baby. He bore very little weight on his legs—being no better in weight bearing than an average 2 months old baby, though it was said that he had been given a chance to do so. I thought that the knee jerks were normal.

The baby seemed alert.   I advised the foster parents to let me see the boy in three months, and not to clinch the adoption until I had done so.   I saw him at 9½ months.   He had begun to chew and to sit without support at 6 months.   At that age he had begun to cough to attract attention, and to shake his head when his mother said 'No'.   He could not nearly grasp the pellet between finger and thumb, but his grasp of a cube (with each hand) was average for the age. He was alert, vocalising well and sitting securely.   He had begun to play patacake. Yet his weight bearing was seriously defective.   I now realised that both knee jerks were definitely exaggerated and there was bilateral ankle clonus.   The knee jerk was more brisk on the left than on the right.   When I discussed this with the foster parents they remarked that he had always kicked more with the right leg than the left.   The diagnosis was spastic diplegia, with a normal level of intelligence. The full implications were explained to the parents, who unhesitatingly decided to adopt him in spite of his physical handicap.

This case was interesting because of the minimal signs of spastic diplegia, discovered on routine developmental examination.   There were no suggestive symptoms and the only developmental sign pointing to the diagnosis was defective weight bearing.   It may be that the inability to grasp the pellet was the only sign of minimal involvement of the upper limbs, for judging from his developmental level in other fields he should have acquired finger-thumb apposition.

Below is another case report which illustrates the importance of balancing one field of development against another.

Case Report.—Mental retardation with anomalous features.

This girl was referred to me at the age of 14 months because the parents were unable to accept the gloomy prognosis given to them by a paediatrician in another city.

She was born a month after term by Caesarian section as a result of signs of fetal distress.   The birth weight was 4340 g.   Pregnancy had been normal throughout. There were no other children.   She was asphyxiated at birth and had 'several' convulsions in the first 3 weeks.   She was kept in an oxygen tent for 5 days.   The condition in the newborn period was such that the parents were given a bad prognosis with regard to her future development.

The subsequent history was somewhat confusing.   She had never picked any object up.   Both parents were uncertain whether she could see.   She had been examined on that account by an ophthalmologist when she was under an anaesthetic, and no abnormality was found in the eyes.   She was said to turn her head to sound at 3 months.   She had begun to smile at 4 or 5 months, and to vocalise at 6 or 7 months.   She was said to laugh heartily now.   At 6 months she had begun to hold a rattle placed in her hand.   She had begun to imitate sounds (a laugh, a song) at 8 months and to imitate the rhythm of songs.   She said 'dadada' from 8 months. She had just begun to play with her hands, watching them in front of her face (hand regard).   She had begun to chew at 11 to 12 months, and at that age would eat a biscuit.

On examination she was a microcephalic girl with a head circumference of 42·8 cms, which was very small when her weight at birth was considered.   The fontanelle was closed.   She was obese, weighing 14·5 kg and tall for her age.   She showed no interest in test toys, but was seen to smile at her mother when she talked to her.   She was heard to make vocalisations (complex sounds with 'ch' and 'dada') such as one would expect to hear at 10 months.   The grasp of a cube placed in the hands was immature.   Her head control was that of a 3 months old baby.   In the prone position her face was held at an angle of 45 degrees to the couch.   There was head lag when she was pulled to the sitting position, with considerable head wobble when she was swayed from side to side. There were asymmetrical creases in the thighs. She played for a prolonged period with a rattle placed in the hand, but would not go for an object. She bore virtually no weight on her legs. It was difficult to assess muscle tone owing to the obesity, but the impression was one of hypotonia rather than hypertonia; and abduction of the hips was greater than usual. The knee jerks were normal, but there was bilateral unsustained ankle clonus. The optic fundi were normal. The X-ray of the hips was normal, and the X-ray of the skull showed normal sutures. The urine did not contain phenylpyruvic acid.

There were difficulties about giving a confident prognosis here, and these difficulties were explained to the parents, who were intelligent. The developmental history and examination indicated dissociation. She was severely retarded in manipulation and motor development, and there was no evidence that she could see—though it is difficult to be sure whether a severely retarded baby can see or not until he is old enough. On the other hand, in chewing, imitation, and vocalisation she was only moderately retarded and her I.Q. in these respects would indicate that she should fall into the educable range later. This strongly suggested a mechanical disability, and the unsustained ankle clonus suggested that she might prove to have the spastic form of cerebral palsy. Subsequent athetosis, however, could not be excluded. The relatively good development in speech and imitation suggested that the I.Q. would not be as bad as it appeared on the surface.

The second difficulty was the question of blindness. I was unable to say whether the child could see or not. Blindness would explain some of the features of the history and examination; and in particular the complete lack of interest in surroundings was out of keeping with the fact that the girl turned her head to sound from about 3 months.

The third difficulty was the history of convulsions. There was a considerable possibility that convulsions would occur later, possibly with mental deterioration.

I gave my opinion that the prognosis was bad, and that she would probably prove to be seriously subnormal, but said that in view of the difficulties mentioned above she might prove better than expected—though possibly with the complication of cerebral palsy and perhaps with blindness. I arranged to see her in a year. She was then backward, but not seriously so.

The significance of the development of speech in relation to other fields has been mentioned. In general the finding that speech development is relatively more advanced than motor development would make one look particularly carefully for a mechanical disability, such as hypertonia or hypotonia, though the occasional late walker has also been discussed. Assessment can be particularly difficult when a child is retarded in more than one field of development.

Case Report.—Boy aged 36 months: opinion asked because he was not talking: he said mum only. Hearing was normal. His father had died in the boy's infancy, and there was no available history of the age at which his father began to talk. The boy had not begun to walk alone until 18 months—but his mother had begun to walk at the same age.   He had no control of the bladder, but the bladder was distended and there was dribbling incontinence—ascribed to urethral obstruction. The boy was therefore retarded in speech, motor development and sphincter control.

With the 10 one inch cubes he rapidly made a neat tower, a train with chimney and a bridge; with the simple formboard he made no error on 'adapting': he immediately identified all 10 pictures on the card.   He neatly copied the O and +.   He was alert, responsive and co-operative.   His overall developmental quotient was 100 to 115.

This child was retarded in three major aspects of development, and yet had an above average developmental quotient.   This was confirmed on follow-up.

The Calculation of a Score

Though it is a matter of opinion, I think that it is usually unwise to calculate a single figure for the D.Q. or I.Q. in the preschool child. The reason is that some fields of development are more important than others, so that a single figure is apt to be fallacious.   Ruth Griffiths used an interesting method.   She used the term G.Q., meaning the general intelligence quotient, and to obtain this she worked out the quotient for each of 5 fields of development (the Q.A., locomotor quotient; Q.B., personal social; Q.C., speech; Q.D., hand and eye quotient; Q.E., performance quotient—which includes the ability to reason, or to manipulate material intelligently).   She then added up all five quotients, divided by 5, and termed this the G.Q. I consider that the method of working out the quotient in each field separately and showing a 'Profile' (Fig. 153) is excellent; but I disagree entirely with the idea of obtaining a G.Q. from the product of these 5 quotients, because that would imply that all fields of development are of equal importance.   They are not.   Such a scoring method fails to take into account physical, mechanical or even environmental causes for retardation in individual fields—factors which have no bearing on the child's intelligence.   If one were to calculate one overall score for a child with paralysed legs due to meningomyelocele, his score would be lowered by the fact that he could not walk.

Below is an example of the difficulty of assessing a child on the basis of one overall score.

I saw the girl for the first time at the age of three years five months. The following are extracts from the letter which I wrote to the family doctor:–

'There are several difficulties about giving a confident prognosis here.   One is that there is a family history of late walking in both mother and father, and it would not be surprising if the children were to take after them.

There was delayed motor development.   She began to sit without help at 14 months and walk without help at 22 months.   I have seen quite a few normal children who were unable to walk until after the

second birthday.   On the other hand her speech was good.   She
was saying single words under a year, and sentences at 18 months.
I have never met a mentally subnormal child who could do that.
Furthermore sphincter control began at 12 months.   She has, however, been late in learning to manage a cup, and she has only just begun
to do so, and she is not very good at dressing herself, but I am not sure
whether the parents have given her a chance to learn these things.

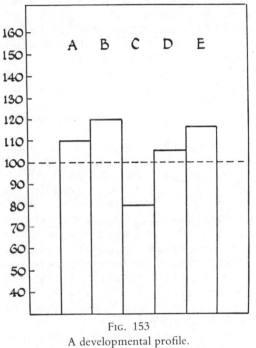

FIG. 153
A developmental profile.
(*After Ruth Griffiths*).
A to E represent five different fields of development.

This is a difficult age at which to carry out developmental testing, but
I have come to the conclusion that in one or two tests she was average,
but in others she was retarded.   There is, therefore, considerable scatter in her performance which makes a confident opinion about the
future impossible.   She looks normal.   She concentrated well on a
doll's house when I was talking to the mother.   Her head is of
normal size.   Her gait is normal.   I explained that when a child has
learned to walk as late as this, you must expect her to be unsteady in
walking for quite a long time afterwards.
    On the whole I think that Mary will prove to be normal, and not
below the average, but one cannot be sure at this stage.   I shall be

seeing her again in about a year in order to re-assess progress.'
I followed her progress with interest. By the age of four years
she was reading well, and at five years she was assessed as having a
reading age of $9\frac{1}{2}$ years. Her manipulative, creative and physical
ability were described by her teacher as excellent.

I would certainly decry the conversion of any scores into one figure
to denote the I.Q., because that would imply that the I.Q. is a static
figure which the child will always have. It has been amply shown
that it is far from static, and that it may be profoundly affected by a
wide variety of factors.

Gesell's term 'The Developmental Quotient' seems to be as good
as any: it indicates how far the child has developed in relation to the
average level of development at that age: and no implication is made
that it will not alter as future years go by. By observing the rate of
development and changes in the D.Q., one can form a good conclusion as to how far the child is likely to develop, given good environmental circumstances. One assesses, in other words, his developmental potential.

I personally prefer to say in my letters to family doctors that a child
has developed as far as an average child of x months: but I always
qualify that by commenting on the individual fields of development,
emphasising where relevant that one is particularly concerned with
his interest, powers of concentration, alertness and speech, and is
much less concerned with his gross motor development. I might
say, for instance, that a 36 months old boy has in general only developed as far as an average 24 months old boy but the fact that his
speech is much better than the 24 months old level, even though he
appears to be below the 24 months old level in other fields, indicates
that there is real hope that he is well above the 24 months level in
potential growth, and that he may well do much better than super-
ficially appears likely at present.

In some cases the difficulties of assessment are such that it is impossible to forecast the child's future without further observation. When
a child who has suffered a severely adverse environment, such as
prolonged institutional care, or has had a serious disease, and is found
to be uniformly retarded, it is impossible to predict his future development. A period of observation after correction of those adverse
factors is essential before a sensible opinion can be expressed. I was
asked to assess the development of an ill six month old baby with
coeliac disease. I refused. I was asked to assess a six year old with
severe renal failure which was first diagnosed in the newborn period:
partly because of prolonged hospital management he was rejected
by his parents who did not want to take him home. He was unable
to walk, partly because of his severe renal rickets. I refused to
attempt to assess his intelligence.

I was asked to assess the mental development of a 21 months old child with nephrogenic diabetes insipidus. He had not thrived, weighing only 15 lbs at the time. He had had repeated admissions to hospital. His general level of development was that of a 12 months old baby with little scatter in different fields, though he showed good interest in his surroundings and in toys—an important observation suggesting that he might prove to have a normal level of intelligence. It was impossible to assess this child's developmental potential without serial observations of his rate of development. He has been followed up since then. At the age of 6 years 4 months he is progressing normally in an ordinary school. Physically he is small, weighing 27 lbs. 6 ozs. (12·4 kg.) and measuring $39\frac{3}{8}$ inches (100 cm.).

The experienced paediatrician will resist the temptation to attempt to give an accurate figure for the child's developmental quotient. He is merely deceiving himself if he thinks that he can distinguish a developmental quotient of 70 from one of 71. He can and should be able to place the child into an approximate position in the developmental range. Any attempt to be more accurate will only lead to inaccuracy.

Summary

Some fields of development are more important than others for the purposes of developmental assessment.

Gross motor development, which is the easiest field of development to assess, and which was the field used more than any other in many studies, is the least useful for the purposes of prediction. Severely retarded children may learn to walk at the average age. Advanced motor development in no way presages a high I.Q.

Manipulative development and the age of chewing are useful for predictive purposes.

The most valuable of all fields for prediction is speech (and pre-speech vocalisation), provided that it is recognised that retardation in speech development does not in itself portend a low I.Q.

The age of beginning to smile and social behaviour are valuable fields for study. The age of acquiring clean toilet habits is of only slight value for prediction.

More important than any of the above are the baby's alertness, interest in surroundings, powers of concentration and determination—all items which are difficult to translate into scores.

In all cases the development in one field should be compared and contrasted with that in another. If a child is notably out of step in one field of development ('dissociation') the cause should be looked for.

Because of the relatively greater importance of some fields of development than of others, it is usually unwise to express the whole of a baby's development in one score.

REFERENCES

1. BOWLBY, J. (1957) Symposium on the Contribution of Current Theories to an Understanding of Child Development. *Brit. J. med. Psychol.*, **30**, 230.
2. CATALANO, F. L., MCCARTHY, D. (1954) Infant Speech as a Possible Predictor of Later Intelligence. *J. Psychol.*, **38**, 203.
3. GRIFFITHS, R. (1954) The Abilities of Babies. London. Univ. of London Press.
4. ILLINGWORTH, R. S. (1958) Dissociation as a Guide to Developmental Assessment. *Arch. Dis. Childh.*, **33**, 118.
5. SÖDERLING, B. (1959) The First Smile. *Acta Paediat, (Uppsala)*, **48**, Suppl. 117, 78.
6. SPIKER, C. C., IRWIN, O. C. (1949) The Relationship between I.Q. and Indices of Infant Speech Sound Development. *J. Speech Dis.*, **14**, 335.

CHAPTER 15

MENTAL RETARDATION

This is only a brief chapter, because the diagnosis of mental retardation has been mentioned directly or indirectly in almost every preceding chapter.

In the sections below I shall bring together the main points about the early diagnosis of mental retardation and add something about the prognosis.

The Child at Risk.   The History

As implied in previous chapters, the following conditions place a child at greater risk of being mentally subnormal than others.

Prenatal—Family history of mental deficiency or degenerative disease of the nervous system.

Low birth weight in relation to the duration of gestation.

Prematurity, especially when extreme.

Multiple pregnancy.

Relative infertility before the pregnancy.

Maternal toxaemia, antepartum haemorrhage.

Maternal infections in early pregnancy, especially rubella.

Cytomegalovirus and toxoplasmosis.

Severe congenital deformities and the many conditions described in Chapter 16.

Cretinism.

Cerebral palsy.

Natal—Convulsions, especially if due to hypoglycaemia, severe anoxia, cerebral haemorrhage, hyperbilirubinaemia, cerebral palsy.

Postnatal—Meningitis, encephalitis.

Severe hypoglycaemia.

Hypernatraemia.

Head injury.

Lead poisoning.

Epilepsy (really prenatal) and drugs used for its treatment.

Emotional deprivation.

Clinical Features

The essential principle in the early diagnosis of mental retardation is the fact that the mentally retarded child who is retarded from birth or before birth is backward in all fields of development, except occasionally in gross motor development and rarely in sphincter control. He is relatively less retarded in gross motor development than in other fields unless there is a superimposed mechanical difficulty, such as cerebral palsy; he is relatively more retarded in speech, and in the amount of interest which he shows in his surroundings, in concentration, alertness and promptness of response.

The situation is different in the case of a child who develops normally for a time, and then develops a degenerative disease, or infantile spasms with mental deficiency. In the case of the latter condition one may see a child of 7 months who has learnt to grasp and to sit and who therefore appears to be up to the average in motor development, but who is totally disinterested in his surroundings and has stopped smiling and who, in fact, has a grave degree of mental deficiency.

As in the case of any developmental assessment, one takes the history of prenatal factors which may be relevant and of the perinatal history. One also takes a history of mental defectiveness in the family. As with any other developmental assessment one remembers that most children born with this background or who have such conditions as anoxia in the perinatal period prove to be normal in intelligence.

As in any other assessment, one must note the history of any possible extenuating factors, such as illness or adverse environmental circumstances, which may have affected his development.

The Early Weeks

As the mentally retarded child is retarded in all fields of development except occasionally gross motor development, it follows that the mentally retarded child at birth is in many ways in a similar position to the premature baby who has a normal level of intelligence. He is apt to sleep excessively, and to have feeding difficulties such as failure to demand feeds, drowsiness, difficulty in sucking and easy regurgitation. The excessive tendency to sleep may persist for several months. Below are some comments by mothers about their severely defective children in the early weeks:

1. He didn't move much when a baby. He didn't seem to live until he was 8 months old.
2. She was a good baby. She never cried.
3. She seemed to live in a world of her own.
4. She was good all the time. She never cried. She just lay.
5. He was a marvellous baby. He was very good. He lay without crying.
6. He just lay in his pram. We didn't know we had him.
7. He just lay in his pram without moving for 6 months. He used to sleep nearly all the time.
8. He was like a cabbage for the first 2 years. He would just sit in his pram.
9. He was a very good baby, and no trouble at all; his brother was a lot more trouble. (The older brother was normal).

The developmental history after birth is nearly always one of lateness in everything, except occasionally in learning to sit and to walk. There is no need to recapitulate the various milestones here except to mention certain special points.

1. The first obvious sign of mental retardation is likely to be lateness in smiling and taking notice, with delayed motor development, as seen in the ventral suspension, the supine and prone position. One can detect many cases of mental retardation in the first 6 to 8 weeks if one is in the habit of performing rough developmental tests on all babies in a well baby clinic.

2. The lateness in following with the eyes is apt to lead to an erroneous diagnosis of blindness. The child appears to take no notice of his surroundings, so that blindness can be readily suspected.

3. The lateness in responding to sound is apt to lead to a mistaken diagnosis of deafness.

4. The lateness in learning to chew leads to feeding difficulties. If the retarded child is given solid foods (as distinct from thickened feeds) before he can chew, he is apt to vomit, and if he is not given solids when he has recently become able to chew, he may pass the critical period and refuse solids or vomit them.

5. The reciprocal kick, which disappears normally when a child is beginning to walk, persists in a retarded child until he can walk. One may see it in a retarded child 2 or 3 years of age.

6. The persistence of hand regard. The normal baby between 12 and 24 weeks of age can frequently be seen lying on his back watching the movements of his hands. This can frequently be seen in retarded children much older than 24 weeks of age.

7. Mouthing—the taking of all objects to the mouth, characteristic of the 6 to 12 months old child, persists in retarded children. It normally stops when the child has become proficient in manipulation. One sees, therefore, a 2 or 3 years old retarded child taking cubes and toys to the mouth.

8. Casting—the deliberate throwing of one object after another on to the floor—normally stops by 15 or 16 months. It continues long after that in defective children.

9. Slobbering normally stops by the age of about a year, but it persists in defective children.

10. Toothgrinding (Bruxism). Toothgrinding when awake is almost (but not entirely) confined to mentally defective children.

11. Altered Vocalisations. Karelitz and Rosenfeld,[3] in their study of infant vocalisations, found that there were striking differences between the cry of the abnormal baby and that of the normal one. In the abnormal child there was a much longer latent period between the application of the stimulus and the cry. He needed repeated or almost constant stimulation to elicit the cry. The voice quality was different in the abnormal child, and was often guttural, in some it was

258 THE DEVELOPMENT OF THE INFANT AND YOUNG CHILD

piercing and shriek-like, and in some high pitched, weak or thin. The normal increasing variety of sounds found in the developing normal infant was greatly delayed in the abnormal one.

As with all developmental assessments, the diagnosis is only made after a careful consideration of the history, the clinical and developmental examination, and a judicious consideration of the evidence, taking full account of any possible extenuating factors which may have caused retardation, and of any glimmer of hope in the way of better than expected vocalisation or interest or concentration.

12. Lack of interest and concentration. Of all features of the retarded child, these are the most important. There is a noticeable lack of interest in surroundings. There is a fleeting interest in toys, or else he does not seem to notice them at all. If given a toy, he will not do anything constructive with it. It does not hold his attention. If he drops it he makes no effort to recover it. If it is out of reach he makes little or no effort to obtain it. He lacks an alert expression and is easily distracted. He is usually less responsive than a normal child. He is slower at responding to test situations.

I have repeatedly seen children who were average in motor development, but whose defective interest and concentration indicated marked deficiency. For instance, a full term child learnt to sit without support at 8 months and to walk without support at 17 months. She was dry by day at 18 months and dry by night at 2 years. At 1 year her interest and concentration were defective. She began to say single words at 3 years and sentences at 5 years. At the age of 9 years her I.Q. was 20. There had been no deterioration.

13. Aimless over-activity. Many children who were sleeping excessively and 'so good' as babies undergo a remarkable transition as they grow older, to aimless over-activity, concentrating on nothing.

Physical Findings

These include in particular the presence of major congenital abnormalities, cerebral palsy, abnormalities in the size or shape of the skull or facial features of disease. It was noted in Chapter 16 that any significant congenital abnormalities carry an increased risk of mental retardation. In Chapter 8 I emphasised the extreme importance of the measurement of the head circumference in relation to the child's weight, adding that certain important features of the shape of the skull are commonly found in mental subnormality. The frequency with which cerebral palsy is associated with mental subnormality was noted in Chapter 17.

Below are two typical case histories of children followed up from birth, in whom a very early diagnosis of mental retardation was made.

Early Diagnosis of Mental Retardation: Confirmation on Follow-up

Case 1.—This full term child was admitted to hospital at the age of 3 months on account of laryngotracheobronchitis. She showed no interest in her surroundings. She would not hold a toy placed in her hand. Head control was defective. A diagnosis of mental retardation was made.

At the age of 15 months she learned to sit without support and to chew. At 30 months she began to walk without support and to say odd words. She could not manage a cup. She could build a tower of four cubes. Concentration was poor. At 5 years and 8 months the I.Q. was 60.

Case 2.—This boy was prematurely born, weighing 1814 g. The mother had toxaemia of pregnancy. Delivery was normal. He had two convulsions on the second day and had head retraction. On the third, fourth and fifth days he had a series of cyanotic attacks. A diagnosis of cerebral oedema was made. The lower limbs were thought to be flaccid. The subsequent history in the follow-up clinic was as follows:

6 months	Hand regard seen.
9½ months	Began to chew.
11 months	One word with meaning. Able to grasp objects.
1·0 year	Sits without help. Beginning to transfer objects.
22 months	Walks, no help.
24 months	D.Q. 70.
3 years	Sentences.
6 years	I.Q. 61.

The Prognosis of Mental Defectiveness

The unexpected improvement seen in some mentally retarded children has already been described. I think that this improvement is chiefly confined to the first years of life. I have not seen a mentally defective child of 5 years improve rapidly and reach a near-normal level of intelligence.

As for the ultimate prognosis in mentally retarded children, it is roughly true to say that a child with an I.Q. of over 50 is likely to be able to earn his living, unless there are associated handicaps.

In Fairbank's well known study 122 subnormal children were followed up for 17 years; 95 were self-supporting, two-thirds of them in manual labour. Compared with normal controls there was more juvenile delinquency, a higher marriage rate, more children and more divorces.

Ferguson and Kerr[2] followed 400 boys and girls from special schools in Glasgow for mentally handicapped children and re-examined them in the early twenties. Seventy-five per cent of the girls with an I.Q. of over 50 had at least 5 years' continuous employment. Only 8 boys were unemployed. Thirteen of the 162 boys were skilled craftsmen. Half the girls and a fifth of the boys were in semi-skilled jobs. By the age of 22, 30 per cent had one or more convictions in law. In a follow up study of 1,000 boys for a 10 year period, 75·8 per cent of those with an I.Q. score of more than 60 were self-supporting.

Some mentally defective adults have acquired remarkable facility in certain skills, such as arithmetic. Others have shown remarkable talents in music and feats of memory.

In attempting to give a prognosis, we must remember not only the possibility of unexpected improvement, which has already been mentioned, but the possibility of deterioration, especially if epilepsy develops.

Much depends not just on the level of intelligence, but on his behaviour. If he is a hyperkinetic, destructive type he is likely to achieve less than a quiet, easily managed child of the same level of intelligence. He is likely to achieve more if brought up at home, than if he is placed in an institution.

A child may have to be graded seriously subnormal even though his I.Q. is well over 50. I saw one child with an I.Q. of 77 who was so intensely hyperkinetic that he could not be managed in a special school and he had to be certified as seriously subnormal. A child with cerebral palsy may have to be certified as subnormal on account of his physical handicap, even though his I.Q. score is well over 50.

Differential Diagnosis

It is a tragedy to diagnose mental subnormality when the child is normal, for the mistake will cause untold anxiety and suffering. On the other hand it is important for many reasons not to miss the diagnosis.

Many of the sources of confusion in the diagnosis have been discussed by writers under the heading of pseudofeeblemindedness.

The following are the main conditions which have to be distinguished from mental subnormality.

1. DELAYED MATURATION. This has been discussed in Chapter 11. An occasional child is backward in the first weeks and subsequently catches up and becomes normal. If there is microcephaly, such a course of events is unlikely to occur: but if the head circumference is of normal size, one should be particularly cautious in giving a definite prognosis without follow-up study.

2. CEREBRAL PALSY. It is easy to confuse some forms of cerebral palsy with mental deficiency. The two conditions are commonly combined. A child with athetosis, particularly before the athetoid movements become obvious, can be thought to have simple mental deficiency, whereas in fact his I.Q. level is normal.

3. SENSORY DEFECTS. Failure to recognise a visual defect or a defect of hearing may well lead to an erroneous diagnosis of mental subnormality. In an older child, the specific problems of dysphasia, dyslexia, difficulties of spatial appreciation and allied conditions, are important pitfalls.

4. THE EFFECTS OF EMOTIONAL DEPRIVATIONœ The retardation which can result from severe emotional deprivation was described in

Chapter 4. It is especially important to remember in assessing children for suitability for adoption when they have been in an institution, or have been moved from one foster home to another. When retardation in such a child is found, one must never suggest that there should be a further period of institutional care, in order that his progress can be assessed, for a further period would retard his development still further. The correct procedure is to place him in a good foster home, and then observe his development after a period of say 3 months in that home. Sometimes a retarded child has had such an unfavourable environment that it is unwise to express an opinion about his potentialities at all. One must always be prepared to postpone judgment if in doubt, or to withhold one altogether.

5. SCHIZOPHRENIA AND INFANTILE AUTISM. There is disagreement as to the diagnosis of autism. I prefer to adhere to the original description by Leo Kanner of Baltimore, but others have extended the original description to include large numbers of mentally defective children. It is found that many seriously defective children show some features of autism: but I have seen many children who have been termed by some autistic, and whom I considered to be typical mental defectives. The lack of interest in people (or anything else) has led some to call these defective children autistic.

Rutter[4] listed the principle features of the autistic child. As a baby, he is likely to show no interest in being picked up by his mother. He may cry only rarely, while others scream almost continually unless rocked. Later there is profound delay in language development, and if speech does develop, it is largely inappropriate. There are 'stereotyped mannerisms, ritualistic and compulsive phenomena, abnormal interpersonal relationships and aloofness, lack of interest in people, the avoidance of eye gaze (gaze aversion), little variation of facial expression, relative failure to exhibit feelings or appreciate humour, and lack of sympathy for others. He may spend hours in ritualistic occupations like scratching the pram cover or flicking his fingers in front of his eyes, rocking himself or whirling objects. The autistic child prefers toys to persons, ignoring the latter, but he may show little interest in toys either, except when feeling their surface and spinning them. Most autistic children have a normal shaped head, and commonly an intelligent appearance. Most of them look normal.

I was asked to see a boy of 4 with a diagnosis of mental retardation. My immediate impression when he walked into the room was that the diagnosis was correct, for he took no notice of anyone in the room. I gave him a Goddard formboard to keep him occupied for a few minutes, and was immediately impressed by the way in which he rapidly fitted the blocks in their correct places. I knew immediately that he was a case of autism. Autism has to be distinguished from schizophrenia. Autism manifests itself in early infancy, or at least within the first two years, while schizophrenia rarely manifests itself before the age of four. There is probably no genetic factor in autism, but there is a family history of schizophrenia in 40 per cent of cases. Hallucinations occur in schizophrenia but not in autism.

A working party in London suggested the following criteria for the diagnosis of schizophrenia.[7]

> Gross and sustained impairment of emotional relationships with people: including aloofness, impersonal attitude to them, difficulty in mixing with other children.
>
> Apparent unawareness of his own personal identity to a degree inappropriate to his age. Abnormal posturing, scrutiny of parts of the body. The confusion of personal pronouns.
>
> Pathological preoccupation with particular objects or certain characteristics of them without regard to their accepted functions.
>
> Sustained resistance to change in the environment and a striving to maintain or restore sameness.
>
> Abnormal perceptual experience (in the absence of discernible organic abnormality) is implied by excessive, diminished or unpredictable response to sensory stimulants—for example visual and auditory avoidance, insensibility to pain and temptation.
>
> Acute excessive and seemingly illogical anxiety.
>
> Speech may have been lost or never acquired or may have failed to develop beyond a level appropriate to an earlier stage. There may be confusion of personal pronouns, or mannerisms of use and diction. Though words or phrases may be uttered they may convey no sense of communication.
>
> Distortion in mobility patterns—excess (hyperkinesis), immobility (katatonia) or bizarre patterns, or ritualistic mannerisms such as rocking or spinning.
>
> A background of serious retardation in which islets of normal, near normal or exceptional intellectual function or skill may appear.

Sometimes psychoses are superimposed on mental deficiency and this increases the difficulty of assessment.

It can be difficult to distinguish schizophrenia from mental subnormality. The lack of response, delayed or absent speech, and peculiar behaviour, can readily lead to errors in diagnosis. It is commoner in boys than girls. The differential diagnosis was discussed by Schachter et al.[5] on the basis of the history, psychological tests, play observation and response to therapy.

Summary

The mentally retarded child, who is retarded from birth or before birth, is backward in *all* fields of development, except occasionally in gross motor development and less often in sphincter control: he is relatively more retarded in speech, alertness, concentration and interest in surroundings than in other fields, and relatively less retarded in motor development.

The diagnosis is made on the basis of the history, physical examination and interpretation of the results.   The history includes that of 'risk factors'—factors increasing the risk of mental subnormality. It includes a detailed developmental history.   The examination includes physical examination for cerebral palsy, congenital abnormalities, facies of disease, and in particular for abnormalities of skull shape and size.   The developmental examination in the light of other findings establishes the diagnosis.

Mental deficiency must be distinguished from blindness, deafness, autism or other psychoses, learning disorders or environmental retardation.   The possibility that a retarded child is merely a 'slow starter' must be remembered.

There may be unexpected improvement in some mentally retarded children, though there were no undesirable environmental factors. As a rough guide, one can say that a child with an I.Q. of over 50 is likely to be able to earn his own living, unless he has a severe physical handicap.

REFERENCES

1. BENDER, L. (1960) Diagnostic and Therapeutic Aspects of Childhood Schizophrenia. In Bowman, P. W., Mautner, H. V. *Mental Retardation*. New York: Grune & Stratton.
2. FERGUSON, T., KERR, A. W. (1958) After Histories of Boys Educated in Special Schools for Mentally Handicapped Children. *Scot. med. J.*, **3**, 31.
3. KARELITZ, S., KARELITZ, R. E., ROSENFELD, L. S. (1960) In Bowman, P. W., Mautner, H. V., *Mental Retardation*. New York: Grune & Stratton.
4. RUTTER, M. (1968) Concepts of autism: a review of research. *J. Child Psychol. Psychiat.*, **9**, 1.
5. SCHACHTER, F. F., MEYER, L. R., LOOMIS, E. A. (1962) Childhood Schizophrenia and Mental Retardation: Differential Diagnosis before and after One Year of Psychotherapy. *Amer. J. Orthopsychiat.*, **32**, 584.
6. TREDGOLD, R. F., SODDY, K. (1956) *Textbook of Mental Deficiency*. 9th ed. London: Bailliere, Tindall and Cox.
7. WORKING PARTY. (1961) Schizophrenia Syndrome in Childhood. *Brit. med. J.*, **2**, 890.

CHAPTER 16

THE ASSOCIATION OF MENTAL SUBNORMALITY WITH PHYSICAL DEFECTS AND DISEASE

It would be impossible in one chapter to discuss all the many diseases and congenital abnormalities associated with mental retardation, because the number of relevant conditions is so vast. But it is a good general rule that any major congenital abnormality, such as cleft palate, congenital heart disease, polydactyly, syndactyly and especially congenital abnormalities of the eye, are indications that the child is 'at risk' of mental retardation—that is, he is more likely than children without those abnormalities to have a lower than average level of intelligence. Most chromosomal defects are associated with mental retardation—as are many examples of abnormal aminoaciduria. The mean I.Q. of children with Turner's syndrome or Klinefelter's syndrome is less than the average for the whole population.

In a series of 1068 personally observed mentally subnormal children at Sheffield, excluding mongolism, cretinism, hydrocephalus and cerebral palsy, 312 had major congenital anomalies (29·3 per cent). They included 89 children with serious eye disease, of which 23 had optic atrophy, and the remainder had cataracts, colobomata, retinal changes, buphthalmos or anophthalmos: 43 children with congenital heart disease, and 13 with cleft palate. This study was based on children seen in hospital, to which many children with severe congenital anomalies are sent, and it is not therefore completely unselected.

It is interesting to note that in a series of 702 personally observed children with cerebral palsy, only 53 had congenital anomalies (7·5 per cent).

It would be profitable to discuss each of the numerous congenital defects separately: but I have picked out a few of the more important conditions associated with mental subnormality, including certain features of physical growth.

Physical Growth and Other Features

Mentally defective children tend to be small in stature. Sexual development is often delayed and hypogenitalism in boys is common. In some cases the stunting of growth is extreme. A child under my care weighed 11·8 kg at the age of 11 years and was 94 cms in height, but no cause could be found after the fullest investigation. Jones and Murray[23] studied the heights and weights of 126 educationally subnormal children. Seventy-three per cent were below the average

264

weight and 68 per cent were below the average height. There have been many other studies to the same effect. I would say that when an infant fails to thrive and remains unusually small, when the food intake is adequate and the fullest investigation has failed to reveal a cause, the diagnosis of severe mental subnormality should be considered and examined for by means of developmental testing.

Approximately 20 per cent of the mentally subnormal children seen by me were low birth weight babies, weighing $5\frac{1}{2}$ lbs. (2,500 g) or less at birth, whereas the incidence of low birth weight in this country is between 6 and 7 per cent. Many of these were 'small for dates', meaning that they were unduly small for the duration of gestation. It seemed that defective physical and defective mental growth had both commenced *in utero*.

The age at which the *anterior fontanelle* closes is of little importance in the study of mental subnormality. Though it may remain open unduly long in some mentally defective children without hydrocephalus, the intelligence is normal in the great majority of children in whom it has remained open longer than usual. In microcephalic infants the anterior fontanelle closes unusually early, but it often closes unusually early in normal infants.

The teeth in mentally defective children are more liable to show caries than those of normal children. This may be due to poor nutrition, defective chewing or other factors. In a study of 319 mental defectives significant structural alterations were found in the teeth of 84.[54] It was thought that the abnormalities were of prenatal origin. The dental changes in association with kernicterus are well known.

Many workers have studied the *skin markings* on the hands of mentally defective children. The frequency of whorls in the palms of the feeble-minded and imbeciles is said to be less than that in the general population.

A single palmar crease is common in mongols and other mentally defective children[11] but is common in normal children. A single palmar crease was found in 3·7 per cent of 6,299 newborn babies. It was more common in boys than girls, in premature babies, and in infants with congenital anomalies. It is a useful pointer to a prenatal cause of a defect, such as mental subnormality or cerebral palsy. An incurving little finger is not confined to mongols, being common in normal children.

Some pay much attention to low-set ears. It is difficult to define these. Robinow and Roche[48] noted that ears appear to be low-set when the neck is extended or short, or when the cranial vault or the mandibular ramus is high. There is a high cranial vault in hydrocephalus and the Treacher Collins Syndrome; a short mandibular ramus in the Cornelia de Lange syndrome, the bird-headed dwarf, the cri du chat syndrome, the Pierre Robin syndrome, trisomy 13-15 or

trisomy 18, and in renal agenesis.   There is a short neck in the Klippel
Feil syndrome and in certain mucopolysaccharidoses.   Abnormality
of the shape and structure of the ear is a feature of some defective
children.

Mongolism

Mongols are developmentally at their best in the first few months
of life.   I have seen several mongols who were able to sit without
support on the floor at 7 or 8 months, though the average age at which
mongols learn to sit is 1 year.   Development then seems to slow
down, so that they become seriously mentally defective.   I saw a full
term mongol who began to smile at 4 months, to grasp objects
voluntarily at 7 months, to roll from prone to supine at 7 months, and
to sit without support at $7\frac{1}{2}$ months.   When he was 8 months old,
however, I was interested to note his defective concentration and the
persistence of hand regard—a sure sign of retardation.   He walked
without help at 34 months, and joined words to form sentences at 69
months.   His I.Q. test score at 6 years was 28.   Relatively advanced
development in early months should not, therefore, lead one to suppose that one is dealing with an unusually intelligent mongol.   In one
study Gesell tests in the first year did not correlate with subsequent
development, but tests in the second year did.[51]   According to Gesell,
the average mongol learns to sit at one year, to walk at two years, to
say single words at three years, to feed himself at four years, to acquire
clean habits at five years and to join words to make sentences at six
years.   In a study of 612 mongols brought up at home, it was shown[41]
that the average age at which mongols passed certain milestones was as
follows:–

	Boys	Girls
	(months)	
Sit unsupported	12·5	11·1
Walk	26·1	22·7
Toilet trained	34·8	34·8
First word	26·6	21·8
Sentences	41·8	52·1

I feel unable myself to predict that a given mongol will prove to
have a higher or lower I.Q. score than other mongols.   I do not think
that the relatively advanced motor development which one occasionally sees is indicative of a better than usual level of intelligence.
I feel that one's estimate of the home environment, with the amount
of love and stimulation which is likely to be given to the child, provides the only clue as to the possibility that an individual mongol will
fare somewhat better than other mongols.   Conversely, placement
in an institution would suggest that he will fare less well than others
more fortunately placed.   I know of no study in which the head cir-

cumference of infant mongols has been related to their eventual level of intelligence. The degree of facial stigmata provide no clue as to future I.Q. (Øster).[43] There are numerous papers concerning the I.Q. scores of mongols. The mean I.Q. is around 28. Opinions differ as to the number who achieve an I.Q. of over 50: Engler in his study of 100 mongols gave a figure of 2 per cent and Brousseau in a study of 206 mongols gave a figure of 1 per cent. Wunsch found that 13 per cent of 77 mongols had a score over 50, and Quaytman found the same figure in 75 mongols. I feel that the lower figure of 1 to 2 per cent corresponds with my own experience. The highest I.Q. found by Øster[43] in 526 mongols was 74. Øster[43] found that practically all mongols over 10 understand when spoken to, and that most adult mongols speak intelligibly. Speech, however, is retarded, with a husky voice and poor articulation. One or two had been known to learn to read and write, but probably without understanding it. No mongol, he said, had been found to be able to add sums. I have seen a 12-year-old mongol who, as a result of prolonged and probably misguided teaching, could read simple books (at the 5 to 6 year old level) and make simple additions. On investigation, however, it was found that she had no idea what she had read, and the figures meant nothing to her. Her I.Q. test score was about 30. In a study of 293 mongols[22] the mean I.Q. of 18 mosaics was the lowest, of 254 trisomies was intermediate, and of 21 translocation mongols the highest. The stigmata were the same in all groups, but the translocation mongols were the most active and aggressive.

Although one still hears or reads the comment that mongols are docile, easy to manage and musical, there is no evidence to that effect.[3,6,57] Convulsions are extremely rare; I have not yet seen a mongol with cerebral palsy.

The mortality continues to be high, about half dying by the fifth year.

Convulsions and Epilepsy

There is a strong association between epilepsy and mental deficiency, due to the frequent association between epilepsy and underlying brain disease. In any institution for mental defectives, convulsions are likely to be common. Kirman wrote that of 777 mental defectives in the Fountain Hospital in 1953, 185 (25 per cent) had fits while in hospital. Of 218 mongols, only two had fits.

In my series of 444 mentally retarded children without cerebral palsy, and excluding mongols, the overall incidence of convulsions was 31·3 per cent. In those slightly to moderately retarded the incidence was 16·3 per cent; in those severely retarded the incidence was 46·8 per cent. None of 87 mongols had fits.

In 285 mentally retarded children with cerebral palsy, the incidence of fits was 37·5 per cent. In the slightly or moderately retarded ones the incidence was 22·8 per cent as compared with a figure of 53·7 per cent in the severely retarded ones. In all groups, cases of postnatal origin were excluded.

The prognosis of neonatal convulsions depends on the cause. A follow-up study of 137 infants[49] indicated that 86 per cent of infants with neonatal convulsions with a normal E.E.G. were likely to develop normally, irrespective of the cause. Those with a flat, periodic or multifocal E.E.G. had a 7 per cent chance of normal development, and those with a unifocal lesion were uncertain. The overall result was normal—50 per cent: died—20 per cent. Rose and Lombroso analysed the result in relation to the cause, those with hypocalcaemia having the best outlook. In another study of 151 infants with hypoglycaemia[27] those who had symptoms and fits had a poor prognosis: asymptomatic cases showed no brain damage.

There is a strong relationship between the type of epilepsy and the level of intelligence. The so-called infantile spasms (akinetic seizures, 'salaam spasms, myoclonic jerks'), with the E.E.G. picture of hypsarhythmia are usually associated with severe mental deficiency. This kind of epilepsy is associated with a wide variety of diseases, including serious brain defects, phenylketonuria, neurodermatoses, sequelae of severe hypoglycaemia, toxoplasmosis and pyridoxin dependency. It may follow immunisation procedures. Jeavons and Bower in their review[21] found that three per cent of their cases became mentally normal. Livingston et al.[32] described 622 cases, all followed for at least 3 years. A total of 142 were in an institution. Twenty-three had died. Only 11 of the remaining 457 had a normal I.Q. The others were retarded, the majority severely so. I have emphasised the striking fact that those children who appear to develop normally until five or six months and then develop infantile spasms, become mentally defective immediately the fits begin, but do not undergo progressive deterioration. After a period of some weeks they commonly improve and may occasionally become normal. In view of the multiplicity of causes of infantile spasms, it is hardly likely that any particular treatment will have a significantly beneficial effect on the child's intelligence.

Petit mal does not lead to mental impairment, though frequent attacks during school lessons may cause a child's performance to fall off. Temporal lobe epilepsy is liable to lead to mental impairment.

Mental deterioration in epileptics may be due to the underlying brain defect: anoxia or multiple petechial haemorrhages; repeated head injuries: psychological factors—exclusion from school: learning difficulties, and the effect of medication, especially of barbiturates.

When assessing the mental development of a child with epilepsy, the mere measurement of the I.Q. score is inadequate. Epileptic children may have a variety of cognitive difficulties. Stores[55] reviewed their problems. Children with damage to the left hemisphere if dominant for speech tended to have defective verbal abilities: those with damage to the right hemisphere had visuospatial or perceptual-motor defects. Epilepsy in the dominant temporal lobe was apt to be associated with defects of memory or learning. Centrencephalic epilepsy was associated with impairment of sustained attention. Phenobarbitone overdosage may cause drowsiness and defective concentration. Stores wrote that 'the assessment of the intellectual capabilities of a child with epilepsy in terms of I.Q. alone can be most misleading, for hidden in this global assessment may be specific defects which if unrecognised might adversely affect learning in various spheres of life.'

The psychological difficulties of epileptic children are well known. Ounsted described a syndrome of epilepsy with hyperkinesis, usually but not necessarily associated with a low I.Q. It was common in boys, and made them intolerable at school.

Hydrocephalus

Now that operative procedures are commonly carried out on these children, it has become more important to know the natural history of untreated cases, in order that one can assess the results achieved by various surgical procedures. Laurence[30] followed up 179 of 182 unoperated cases seen in London. Eighty-nine (49 per cent) had died. Nine remained progressive, and 3 were not traced. Eighty-one (47 per cent) had become arrested, and of these 75 per cent were in the educable range, 33 of them having an I.Q. of 85 or more, and 26 having an I.Q. of 50 to 84. Twenty-seven of the 81 had little or no physical disability. There was little relationship between the I.Q. and the circumference of the head or the thickness of the cortex as measured in the air encephalogram. A child with a cortical thickness of 0·5 cm was found to have an I.Q. of 85, and another child with a similar measurement had an I.Q. of 100. Laurence's figures may be too optimistic. His case material consisted of children who were referred to a neurosurgeon who did not operate on children with hydrocephalus and therefore the patients referred were already to some extent selected. Even so, only about one-third of the survivors had an I.Q. of 85 or over at the time of the survey. Results indicate that with a ventriculocaval shunt, the outcome is likely to be much better. It is known that children with arrested (untreated) hydrocephalus tend to be facile in behaviour, happy, pleasant and talkative, with a tendency to clumsiness and slight ataxia.

In a prospective study of an unselected series of 475 newborn babies born with spina bifida and hydrocephalus,[36] and assessed by a psychologist at the age of 5 to 9 years, the following were the I.Q. scores:–

I.Q.		Hydro-cephalus with Spina Bifida	Spine Bifida Without Hydrocephalus	Hydrocephalus Without Spina Bifida	Total	Per-centage
Superior	120 +	3	5	4	12	2·5
High Average	110–119	13	19	7	39	8·2
Average	90–109	73	54	35	162	34·1
Low Average	80–89	47	18	25	90	18·9
E.S.N.	51–79	83	14	18	115	24·2
50		21	3	33	57	1·2
		240	113	122	475	

Table 9 shows the I.Q. scores in a study of 136 children with meningomyelocele and hydrocephalus followed to the age of 6 to 11 years of whom 68, the milder cases, had no shunt, and 68 had a ventriculocaval shunt—usually the more severe ones.

TABLE 9
I.Q. scores in hydrocephalus

I.Q.	68 unoperated	68 operated
120–129	5	—
100–119	19	8
80–99	32	29
50–79	9	26
below 50	1	4
unknown	2	1

Table 10 shows the I.Q. scores in a later study of 31 children of school age who had no hydrocephalus, 28 with hydrocephalus of slight degree not requiring a shunt and 75 children who had hydrocephalus and a shunt.

TABLE 10
I.Q. of children with spina bifida, with or without hydrocephalus

I.Q.	No hydrocephalus (31) and hydrocephalus with no shunt (28)	Hydrocephalus and shunt
	n=59	n=75
Average	87	79
	Per cent	Per cent
100+	31	10
80–99	52	33
60–79	12	30
Below 60	5	18

Table 11 shows the relationship between the prognosis with regard to mental development and the pre-operative thickness of the cerebral mantle, as determined by air studies.

TABLE 11
Relationship between thickness of cerebral mantel and I.Q. scores

Preoperative Mantle	Number	Survivors	14 over 80	Percentage
10 mm or less	32	16	5	31
11–35 mm	235	125	79	63
(a) Unoperated	177	91	53	58
(b) Unoperated	58	34	26	76

Owing to the frequent association of hydrocephalus with meningomyelocele, one would expect that the mean I.Q. level of children with meningomyelocele would be rather low. In the absence of hydrocephalus, however, the mean I.Q. would probably be little below the average.

Out of 19 children who suffered from neonatal meningitis and survived with gross residual hydrocephalus, treatment by ventriculocaval shunt resulted in prolonged survival in 14 children. Seven of these were of normal intelligence, but 7 others were retarded.

The prognosis of hydrocephalus following subdural effusion and other intracranial haemorrhage was described by Lorber[35]. Of 32 survivors who were assessed at 18 months to 16 years of age, following intracranial haemorrhage in the newborn period, 16 had a normal intelligence (I.Q. 80 to 114), 9 of them with no physical sequelae; 16 were retarded, 12 grossly so.

Tuberculous Meningitis

Lorber[33] followed up 100 children who survived tuberculous meningitis, which had been treated at the Children's Hospital, Sheffield. Seventy-nine were followed for 5 years or more. Six had an I.Q. below 50; 14 had an I.Q. of 71 to 80; 24 had an I.Q. of 81 to 90; 25 had an I.Q. of 91 to 100; 16 had an I.Q. of 101 to 110; 6 had an I.Q. of 111 to 120; 3 had an I.Q. of 121 to 130; 2 had an I.Q. of 131 or more. It was guessed that the I.Q. of the 4 not tested ranged between 81 and 100. The importance of early treatment was emphasised. Those with a low I.Q. were all under 3 years of age at the onset, and all had come to hospital in a late stage, while those treated early fared well with regard to future intellectual level.

Sequelae of Meningitis and Encephalitis

Wolff studied the intelligence of children who had had meningococcal meningitis two or more years previously. Out of a total of

179 cases occurring at Birmingham, 138 were followed up. The mean I.Q. of 26 who developed meningitis before 6 months of age was 76·3; 4 were idiots. The mean I.Q. of 27 who developed it between 6 and 12 months was 90·8; and the mean I.Q. of those developing it over 1 was 96·8.

Miller et al.[42] wrote a comprehensive review of post-infectious encephalomyelitis. In all cases coma and convulsions tended to carry a bad prognosis. The incidence of sequelae after postinfectious encephalitis was as follows: After rubella—2 to 5 per cent: chickenpox 20 per cent: mumps 30 per cent: pertussis 35 per cent: measles 35 per cent and scarlet fever 45 per cent. In only a small proportion of these did the sequelae include mental defectiveness. In measles intellectual deficits occurred in children only. Intellectual sequelae were relatively more common in the case of whooping cough and scarlet fever.

Severe neurological sequelae, including mental retardation, have followed encephalitis in association with roseola infantum.[8] They may also follow post-immunisation encephalomyelitis.

Neonatal pyogenic meningitis is almost universally regarded as having a bad prognosis: but Lorber[34] showed that of 12 children with neonatal meningitis without spina bifida, now aged 1 to 5 years, 9 fully recovered, and 3 were mentally and physically normal but had a valve in place.

Megalencephaly

This term describes a generalised hypertrophy of the brain, with a cytological defect in the nerve cells. A full description of the condition was given by Kinnier Wilson. According to Ford it is commoner in males, and may be familial. The cranium is large, but the child lacks the facial appearance of hydrocephalus. The diagnosis is in part established by ventriculography, which demonstrates the absence of ventricular dilatation. There are varying degrees of mental deficiency.

Craniostenosis

The level of intelligence found in children with craniostenosis depends in part on the extent of the premature fusion of the sutures. In some of the mildest forms children appear to develop normally at first, but drop behind when it becomes impossible for the brain to enlarge further owing to the fusion of the sutures. In more severe ones, in which the skull is already severely deformed at birth, mental development seems to have been retarded before operation was possible.

I have the impression that the level of intelligence is lower when there are other associated congenital anomalies (as in Apert's syndrome).

Hypertelorism

MacGillivray[38] described the association of various anomalies with hypertelorism. They include shortening of the digits, amyotonia and congenital heart disease. He stated that there is no correlation between the extent of skull deformity and the degree of mental deficiency. The intelligence may be normal, but it is usually defective.

Cleft Palate

As there was little literature on the level of intelligence found in children with cleft palate, we studied[19] 112 consecutive cases of cleft palate with or without hare lip, taken from an alphabetical and entirely representative list. The mean I.Q. of 80 on whom we were able to carry out Stanford–Binet tests was 95·4; 47 had an I.Q. test score of less than 100, and 33 had an I.Q. over 100. School reports obtained on a further 17 gave comparable results. It appeared that the mean I.Q. was slightly lower than that of the population as a whole.

Achondroplasia

MacGillivray[38] found that 5 of 16 cases were mentally defective. He added that the mental defect in achondroplasia and Morquio's disease is static, while in gargoylism it is progressive. Jervis wrote that 'a certain degree of mental impairment is often present'. Ford stated that the I.Q. is in inverse relation to the size of the head. In three quarters the head is abnormally large. This is mainly due to megalencephaly, though in some there is dilation of the ventricles.

In contrast the intelligence is usually normal in DYSCHONDROPLASIA, a condition which probably includes conditions termed multiple bony prominences, multiple exostoses, diaphyseal aclasia, chondrodysplasia, multiple congenital osteochondromata, Ollier's disease, and multiple enchondroses; and in PROGRESSIVE DIAPHYSEAL DYSPLASIA (Englemann's Disease), in which there is enlargement and cortical thickening in the diaphyses of long bones.

Neuromuscular Conditions

Mental retardation of slight degree is more often seen in children with muscular dystrophy than in other children. In a group of 30 children with progressive muscular dystrophy, the mean I.Q. was 82.[1] In a study of 38 boys, one third of the children had mental retardation.[59] It was suggested that there was a combined genetic and environmental factor. In a group of 36 children, half had an I.Q. score of less than 90—an incidence three times greater than that of the normal population. Worden and Vignos[58] found a mean I.Q. of 83 in 38 patients aged between 4 and 17 years. There was no progressive deterioration. It was suggested that children with muscular dystrophy tend to have special difficulties in reading and mathematics. Dubowitz[14] has described intellectual impairment in children with muscular dystrophy before there were any signs of physical handicap. He thought that there might be an associated sex linked genetic mechanism causing intellectual impairment, or that some metabolite of degenerating muscle might damage the central nervous system. A similar view was expressed by Cohen, Molnar and Taft.[9] They found mental subnormality in 20·9 per cent of 211 children with the Duchenne type of muscular dystrophy, but no increased incidence of subnormality in their siblings. In 39 families with two or more affected children, there was complete concordance with respect to the I.Q. in 94·9 per cent.

Hypotonia may be due to a variety of pathological conditions, and many mentally subnormal infants, including all mongols, are hypotonic. The intelligence in children with benign forms of hypotonia is likely to be normal. Dystrophia myotonica is often associated with a severe degree of mental subnormality.

Cerebral Palsy

I have reviewed the literature concerning the intelligence level in children with cerebral palsy elsewhere[20] and will summarise it below. Putting together 6 important papers on the subject, I calculated that the I.Q. of 55 per cent of 2,480 children was less than 70. Twenty per cent of the normal population have an I.Q. of 110 or more, as compared with 3 per cent of 1,768 affected children described by four workers. It seems to be the general opinion that the intelligence level of children with athetosis is little different from that of children with the spastic form of cerebral palsy.

With regard to the relation of the I.Q. to the distribution of spasticity in the spastic form, the I.Q. of those with spastic quadriplegia is likely to be the lowest, and of those with spastic diplegia to be the highest. The mean I.Q. of those with hemiplegia is about 77. There is probably no difference in the I.Q. of those with left and right hemiplegia, though there is a difference of opinion on this point.

The I.Q. of children with the rigid form of cerebral palsy is almost invariably extremely low. They are all in the seriously subnormal class. The same applies to the I.Q. of those with the rare 'atonic' form of cerebral palsy.

I have no figures for the I.Q. of children with congenital ataxia. My clinical impression is that the mean I.Q. of these children would be considerably below 100.

It is generally agreed that the more severe the cerebral palsy, the lower is the I.Q. likely to be, though this does not necessarily apply to athetoid children. It is usually the case that the I.Q. tends to be less in children who have convulsions.

Neurodermatoses

1. *Sturge Weber Syndrome*

Greenwald and Koota found mental changes varying from mild deficiency to profound idiocy in 60 per cent of 50 cases of the Sturge Weber syndrome. Mental retardation, when it occurs, is more often mild than severe. A good review of the subject is found in the paper by Peterman *et al*. Thirty-one of 35 cases had convulsions. There was mental retardation in 19 (54 per cent). Eye changes (glaucoma or buphthalmos) were found in 13. The essential part of the disease is a venous angioma of the leptomeninges over the cerebral cortex, which is usually associated with a portwine naevus, often in the area supplied by the trigeminal nerve. Circulatory changes resulting from the lesion of the leptomeninges subsequently lead to the other manifestations—hemiplegia, fits and mental retardation.

2. *Tuberous Sclerosis*

Complete forms of this disease are rare. The manifestations include adenoma sebaceum, rhabdomyoma of the heart, hamartoma of the kidney, phakomata of the retina, epilepsy, periungual fibromata and bone changes. Incomplete forms are much commoner. Mental retardation is usual but not invariable.[50] Some show little defect in the early years but deteriorate later.

3. *Neurofibromatosis*

Mental retardation is a relatively infrequent manifestation of this disease. In one series of cases the mean I.Q. score was 85 to 90.[24]

Blindness

In order to make a meaningful assessment of the relationship of blindness to I.Q., one must know the cause of the blindness. There have been several studies of the I.Q. of children with retrolental fibroplasia[5,10,45]. They indicate that the mean I.Q. is considerably less than that of the normal population: but the babies were almost all prematurely born, and prematurity, often with associated hyperbilirubinaemia or hypoglycaemia, is a factor in mental retardation. In all studies of blindness in relation to I.Q. the psychological effect, particularly in relation to management, has to be considered.

Parmelee[44] studied the development of blind premature children, and found that they tended to be later than others in learning to sit and walk. They were not later than other children, however, in beginning to smile, to take objects to the mouth, to pull themselves to the standing position, or to walk while holding on to furniture. Gesell and Amatruda found that blind children were no different from others in their development except in visual pursuits.

In my series of 1068 mentally retarded children seen in Sheffield, excluding hydrocephalus, cretinism, mongolism and postnatal cases, 89 (8·3 per cent) had major eye defects, such as optic atrophy, choroidoretinitis or cataract. Hilliard informed me that among 1,720 patients from all Units in the Fountain Hospital Group over a period of 11 years, 108 (6·3 per cent) were known to have optic atrophy. Microphthalmia, anophthalmia and other serious congenital defects of the eye are liable to be associated with mental subnormality.

Deafness

A study of the intellectual level of deaf children was carried out by Kendall in Professor Ewing's department at Manchester. He found that when children whose deafness resulted from the rubella syndrome, tuberculous meningitis or kernicterus were excluded, there was no significant difference in test score at any age level when the performance tests were administered to representative groups of deaf and ordinary children, balanced for socio-economic status.

Foale and Paterson found a higher incidence of hearing loss among the mentally defective boys at Lennox Castle, aged 10 to 19, than is known to be present in the school population of England, Wales and Scotland. The authors mentioned the importance of remembering that high frequency deafness causes symptoms resembling those of mental retardation, and that impaired hearing may be a factor in the low test scores in backward children.

Kodman et al. tested 189 children and adults in institutions. Hearing loss was defined as one of 30 dB or more. The incidence of hearing loss in the group aged 7 to 19 years was 19 per cent.—almost four times that found in American public school children.

According to Lindenov deaf mutism is only associated with amentia when there is retinitis pigmentosa. As in the case of blindness, when assessing the significance of a low I.Q. in handicapped children one must always consider the psychological effect and the effect of normal management with overprotection and suboptimal stimulation.

Phenylketonuria

When assessing studies of the I.Q. scores achieved by children with phenylketonuria, one must know that the diagnosis was correct, the age at which treatment commenced and the quality of the management with the level of serum phenylalanine maintained. The younger the child when treatment is commenced the better the results to be expected.

It is known that the brain is damaged by too low or too high a serum phenylalanine. A few untreated older children or adults with a normal I.Q. in spite of phenylketonuria continue to be reported.[2,56]

Wright and Tarjan reviewed 362 cases from the literature. Sixty-three per cent had an I.Q. of 1 to 20, 32 per cent an I.Q. of 21 to 50,

4 per cent an I.Q. of 51 to 70, and 1 had an I.Q. of over 71. Paine reviewed 106 cases; 70 per cent had an I.Q. of under 20, 84 per cent an I.Q. below 30, 93 per cent an I.Q. below 40, and 98·1 per cent an I.Q. of under 50. The usual age for learning to sit was 12 to 15 months. Twenty-six per cent had fits, and only a few were spastic, but 79 per cent had abnormal electroencephalograms. Associated anomalies included congenital dislocation of hip, congenital heart disease and undescended testes.

Partington[46] found the following I.Q. scores in 75 patients aged two or more with untreated phenylketonuria.

I.Q. Score	Percentage
0–20	61·3
21–40	26·7
41–60	5·3
61–80	5·3
81+	1·3

These findings corresponded closely with those of Knox.[17,18] According to Hsia et al.[17,18] all that one can expect to achieve by dietary means is to preserve the status quo and to prevent deterioration. They based this opinion on 24 cases, 12 of which were treated, 12 serving as controls. The test period was one of 12 to 15 months. They emphasised the importance of keeping the serum phenylalanine down to normal levels. Berry et al. in a discussion of 3 cases, found no notable improvement in intelligence, but there was an improvement in behaviour, motor ability, manual dexterity, and attention span with a reduction of tenseness and irritability. On the other hand Woolf et al. in a study of 10 cases, described 'a sharp and significant rise in I.Q.' in almost every case. They said that the I.Q. continued to rise, the mental age plotted against chronological age showing a point of inflexion at the time the diet was started.

Berman et al. compared eight treated cases with three untreated siblings and eleven unaffected ones. The intelligence quotient was significantly greater in the treated than the untreated cases, but less than that of the unaffected ones in spite of careful treatment. It should be noted, however, that there may be important features unrelated to the I.Q. In one study 13 children with phenylketonuria were matched for age, sex, I.Q. and race; affected children were more clumsy, talkative and hypersensitive.[52] Others have found overactivity and defective concentration in these children, not related to a low level of intelligence. We need a full psychological and psychosocial assessment of affected children.

In a comprehensive review by Dobson et al., relating the I.Q. score achieved to the age of onset of treatment, the following were the findings:–

Age of starting treatment (months)	Number	I.Q.
Birth–1	11	89
1–4	9	77
5–10	11	68
11–17	19	67
18–24	21	73
25–36	13	65
37–47	16	63
48–72	14	57

Many investigations are now in progress to determine how soon the special diet can safely be discontinued.   It is yet too soon to provide a reliable answer.

A study of six children with *transient neonatal tyrosinaemia* of high degree showed normal development at 25 months.

Others have shown that infants who had a high tyrosin level in the blood in the newborn period subsequently scored significantly less well in verbal and cognitive abilities and fine motor skill.

Congenital Heart Disease

Ross described the association of congenital heart disease with mental retardation in 21 cases at the Johns Hopkins Hospital, Baltimore.   She suggested that the intelligence quotient in congenital heart disease tends to be lower than the average.   This corresponds with the findings of Bret and Kohler in their study of 88 cases; but Landtmann et al.[29] found no significant lowering of the I.Q. in children with congenital heart disease.

In two studies of 98 children with cyanotic and 100 with acyanotic congenital heart disease, compared with 81 normal siblings and 40 normal children, the cyanotic children fared significnatly less well than acyanotic or normal children.[31,47]   The factors responsible may be reduced manipulative and motor experience, less opportunity for exploration, overprotection and psychological problems arising from the handicap.

Mautner found that 30–40 per cent of mongols have congenital heart disease.   He mentioned the well-known association of rubella during pregnancy with the subsequent finding of pulmonary stenosis and mental deficiency in the fetus.   He suggested that anoxia in the cyanotic types might cause pathological changes in the brain.

Ireland et al. found that the incidence of congenital heart disease in 723 mental defectives in institutions was 2·4 per cent.   This is 7 times higher than that found in comparable ages in the general population. When mongols were excluded the figure was still much higher than in normal people.   It is interesting that in my series of 1068 mentally retarded children (excluding mongols as before), 43 had congenital heart disease (4·0 per cent).

Thalidomide Babies

In a detailed study of 22 'thalidomide' babies it was found that the mean D.Q. was 90. The effect of institutional care was duly considered. In view of the known association between congenital anomalies and a lower than usual level of intelligence, this result was to be expected. McFie and Robertson[37] studied 56 affected children: 4 were mentally subnormal. They emphasised the difficulties of assessment if there were upper limb deformities and dependence on others. When the upper limbs were normal there was a tendency to a higher performance on verbal tests—perhaps because of stimulation by the parents. In another study[16] of 33 Canadian children, a third had a D.Q. below 90.

Galactosaemia

Komrower and Lee[28] reviewed as many cases as they could find of galactosaemia in Great Britain, in order to assess their clinical, psychological and emotional state. They traced 22 boys and 38 girls, all treated cases. Eight had cataracts, one had portal hypertension, but the others were healthy. The mean I.Q. was 80, with a scatter from 30 to 118. The I.Q. decreased with age: the mean I.Q. for 0–5 years was 90, at 5 to 10 years 79, and over 10 years it was 70. They tended to show depression, timidity, withdrawn behaviour and hostility.

Cretinism

It is often said that the younger the child when treatment is instituted, the better are the results to be expected. This is not altogether true because if cretinism is diagnosed in early infancy, there is the possibility that there has been damage to the brain in utero. Control of treatment is not always satisfactory, and so it is not easy to determine from several studies whether the I.Q. score achieved could have been better with improved medical care. Nevertheless one's conclusion from one's own experience, and from reading the literature, is that the mean I.Q. of children treated early would be around 90. The paper by Smith, Blizzard and Wilkins[53] is important, for it reviewed 128 cases of hypothyroidism. Their results can be summarised as follows: Ten of 22 with no thyroid function treated adequately before 6 months of age, and 12 of 29 treated adequately before 12 months, attained an I.Q. greater than 90. In contrast none of 50 inadequately treated or treated after 12 months attained such an intelligence quotient.

Lead Poisoning

Lead poisoning is known to lead to a reduction in a child's intelligence. Byers and Lord followed 20 children who had been admitted to hospital in early childhood on account of lead poisoning, without much evidence of lead encephalopathy. Nineteen were subsequently retarded at school. Jenkins and Mellins studied 46 Chicago children with pica, mostly from poor families. Thirteen died. Twenty-seven of 33 survivors were mentally defective, and in 20 this was ascribed to lead poisoning. Bradley and Baumgartner[7] compared the subsequent mental development of 9 children treated with B.A.L. and 9 treated with E.D.T.A., following them up for 2 to 5 years after their stay in hospital. Mental development was normal in all, but those treated with E.D.T.A. had fewer visuomotor sequelae.

Mentally subnormal children are likely to continue taking objects to the mouth long after normal children have stopped doing so, and they are more likely to eat dirt. Hence they are especially liable to suffer lead poisoning and further mental deterioration.

Summary and Conclusions

1. A wide variety of diseases and malformations, especially those involving the skull, eyes and skin, are associated with varying degrees of mental retardation. Though certain anomalies, such as deformities of the ears, are often associated with mental retardation, these so-called stigmata of degeneration can never be used as an aid to diagnosis because they are often found in normal children. Nevertheless, the finding of severe congenital deformities of any kind should make one look particularly carefully at the level of mental development which the child has reached and follow his developmental progress.

The anterior fontanelle is of little value for the assessment of a child's development. Physical growth is apt to be defective in retarded children.

More and more metabolic defects and abnormalities are being found in association with mental deficiency.

2. Though between a quarter and a third of all mentally retarded children have or have had convulsions, epilepsy *per se* is not usually associated with mental retardation. Mental retardation in epileptics is due to the underlying brain disease, or to the effect of frequent convulsions, to psychological causes in relation to epilepsy, or to some extent to the drugs used for treatment.

Infantile spasms are usually associated with severe mental deficiency.

3. Although mental retardation is found in varying degrees of frequency in the above conditions, each child has to be assessed individually and never assumed to be mentally defective without a full developmental examination being performed. Nevertheless,

the final assessment will be made against the background of the known facts concerning the intellectual level likely to be found in the various conditions described.

REFERENCES

1. ALLEN, J. E., RODGIN, D. W. (1960) Mental Retardation in Association with Progressive Muscular Dystrophy. *Amer. J. Dis. Child*, **100**, 208.
2. ALLEN, R. J., GIBSON, R. M., SUTTON, H. E. (1960) Phenylketonuria with Normal Intelligence. *Amer. J. Dis. Child.*, **100**, 563.
3. BARON, J. (1972) Temperament profile of children with Down's syndrome. *Develop. Med. Child Neurol.* **14**, 640.
4. BENDA, C. E. (1960) *The Child with Mongolism.* New York: Grune and Stratton.
5. BJEKLHAGEN, I. (1952) Retrolental Fibroplasia in Sweden. *Acta Paediat. (Uppsala)*, **41**, 74.
6. BLACKETER-SIMMONDS, D. A. (1953) An Investigation into the Supposed Differences Existing between Mongols and other Mentally Defective Subjects with Regard to certain Psychological Traits. *J. ment. Sci.*, **99**, 702.
7. BRADLEY, J. E., BAUMGARTNER, R. J. (1958) Subsequent Mental Development of Children with Lead Encephalopathy, as Related to Type of Treatment. *J. Pediat.*, **53**, 311.
8. BURNSTINE, R. C., PAINE, R. S. (1959) Residual Encephalopathy following Roseola Infantum. *Amer. J. Dis. Child.*, **98**, 144.
9. COHEN, H. J., MOLNAR, G. E., TAFT, L. T. (1968) The genetic relationship of progressive muscular dystrophy (Duchenne type) and mental retardation. *Develop. Med. Child Neurol.*, **10**, 754.
10. DANN, M., LEVINE, S. Z., NEW, E. V. (1958) The Development of Prematurely Born Children with Birth Weights or Minimal Postnatal Weights of 1000 g or less. *Pediatrics*, **22**, 1037.
11. DAVIES, P. A. (1966) Sex and the single transverse palmar crease in newborn singletons. *Develop. Med. Child. Neurol.*, **8**, 729.
12. DÉCARIE, T. G. (1969) *A study of the Mental and Emotional Development of the Thalidomide Child.* In Foss, B. M., Determinants of Infant Behaviour. Vol. IV. London: Methuen.
13. DOBSON, J., KOCH, R., WILLIAMSON, M., SPECTOR, R., FRANKENBURG, W., O'FLYNN, M., WARNER, R., HUDSON, F. (1968) Cognitive development and dietary therapy in phenylketonuric children. *New England J. Med.* **278**, 1142.
14. DUBOWITZ, V. (1965) Intellectual Impairment in Muscular Dystrophy. *Arch. Dis. Childh.*, **40**, 296.
15. FULLER, G., SHUMAN, G. (1971) Treated phenylketonuria, intelligence and blood phenylalanine levels. *Am. J. Ment. Def.*, **75**, 539.
16. GOUIN-DÉCARIE, (1969) A study of the mental and emotional development of the thalidomide child. In Foss, B. M. (Ed.) Determinants of Infant Behaviour. Vol. 4. London, Methuen.
17. HSIA, D., KNOX, W. E., QUINN, K. V., PAINE, R. S. (1958) A One Year Controlled Study of the Effect of Low-Phenylalanine Diet on Phenylketonuria. *Pediatrics*, **21**, 178.
18. HSIA, DAVID YI-YUNG, O'FLYNN, M. E., BERMAN, J. L. (1968) Atypical phenylketonuria with borderline or normal intelligence. *Amer. J. Dis. Child.*, **116**, 143.
19. ILLINGWORTH, R. S., BIRCH, L. B. (1956) The Intelligence of Children with Cleft Palate. *Arch. Dis. Childh.*, **31**, 300.
20. ILLINGWORTH, R. S. (1958) *Recent Advances in Cerebral Palsy.* London: Churchill.
21. JEAVONS, P. M., BOWER, B. D. (1965) Infantile Spasms. *Clinics in Develop. Med.* No. 15. London: Heinemann.
22. JOHNSON, R. C., ABELSON, R. B. (1969) Intellectual behavior and physical

characteristics associated with trisomy, translocation and mosaic types of Down's syndrome. *Am. J. Ment. Def.*, **73**, 852.

23. JONES, A. P., MURRAY, W. (1958) The Heights and Weights of Educationally Subnormal Children. *Lancet*, **1**, 905.

24. JONES, F. A. (1961) Clinical Aspects of Genetics. London: Pitman.

25. KENDALL, D. C. (1957) in Ewing, A. W. G. (1957) *Educational Guidance and the Deaf Child*. Manchester Univ. Press.

26. KOCH, R., SHAVE, J., WEBB, A., GRALIKER, B. V. (1963) The Predictability of Gesell Developmental Scales in Mongolism. *J. Pediat.*, **62**, 93.

27. KOIVISTO, M., BLANCO-SEQUEIROS, M., KRAUSE, U. (1972) Neonatal Symptomatic and asymptomatic hypoglycaemia: a follow-up study of 151 children. *Develop. Med. Child Neurol.* **14**, 603.

28. KOMROWER, G. M., LEE, D. H. (1970) Longterm follow up of galactosaemia. *Arch. Dis. Childh.*, **45**, 367.

29. LANDTMAN, B., VALANNE, E., PENTTI, R., AUKEE, M. (1960) *Ann. Paediat. Fenn.*, **6**, Suppl., 15.

30. LAURENCE, K. M. (1958) The Natural History of Hydrocephalus. *Lancet*, **2**, 1152.

31. LINDE, L. M., RASOF, B., DUNN, O. J. (1967) Mental development in congenital heart disease. *J. Pediat.*, **71**, 198.

32. LIVINGSTON, S. EISNER, V. PAULI, L. (1958) Minor Motor Epilepsy. *Pediatrics*, **21**, 916.

33. LORBER, J. (1959) The Follow-up of Children with Tuberculous Meningitis with Special Reference to Psychiatric and Neurological Aspects. *Proc. roy. Soc. Med.*, **52**, 269.

34. LORBER, J. (1974) Neonatal Bacterial Meningitis. Medicine No. 27, 1579.

35. LORBER, J. (1974) Post-haemorrhagic hydrocephalus. *Arch. Dis. Childh.* **49**, 751.

36. LORBER, J. (1971) Results of treatment of myelomeningocele. *Develop. Med. Child. Neurol.*, **13**, 279.

37. McFIE, J., ROBERTSON, J. (1973) Psychological test-results of children with thalidomide deformities. *Develop. Med. Child Neurol.* **15**, 719.

38. MACGILLIVARY, R. C. (1957) Hypertelorism with Unusual Associated Anomalies. *Amer. J. ment. Defic.*, **62**, 288.

39. MAMUNES, P., PRINCE, P. E., THORNTON, N. H., HUNT, P. A., HITCHCOCK, E. S. (1974) Tyrosinemia. *Pediatric Research.* **8**, 345.

40. MARTIN, H. P., FISCHER, H. L., MARTIN, D. S., CHASE, H. P. (1974) The development of children with transient neonatal tyrosinemia. *J. Pediat.* **84**, 212.

41. MELYN, M. A., WHITE, D. T. (1973) Mental and developmental milestones of non-institutionalised Down's syndrome. *Pediatrics.* **52**, 542.

42. MILLER, H. G., STANTON, J. B. GIBBONS, J. L. (1956) Para-Infectious Encephalomyelitis and Related Syndromes. *Quart. J. Med.*, **25**, 427.

43. ØSTER, J. (1953) *Mongolism.* Copenhagen: Munksgaard.

44. PARMELEE, A. H. (1955) The Developmental Evaluation of the Blind Premature Infant. *Amer. J. Dis. Child.*, **90**, 135.

45. PARMELEE, A. H., FISKE, C. E., WRIGHT, A. H., CUTSFORTH, M. G. (1958) Mental Development of Children with Blindness due to Retrolental Fibroplasia. *Amer. J. Dis. Child.*, **96**, 614.

46. PARTINGTON, M. W. (1962) Variations in Intelligence in Phenylketonuria. *Canad. med. Ass. J.*, **86**, 736.

47. RASOF, B., LINDE, L. M., DUNN, O. J. (1967) Intellectual development in children with congenital heart disease. *Child Development*, **38**, 1043.

48. ROBINOW, M., ROCHE, A. F. (1973) Low set ears. *J. Am. Med. Ass.* **125**, 482.

49. ROSE, A. L., LOMBROSO, C. T. (1970) Neonatal seizure states. *Pediatrics.* **45**, 404.

50. SCHEIG, R. L., BORNSTEIN, P. (1961) Tuberous Sclerosis. *Arch. intern. Med.*, **108**, 789.

51. SHARE, J., WEBB, A., KOCH, R. (1961) A Preliminary Investigation of the Early Developmental Status of Mongoloid Infants. *Amer. J. ment. Defic.*, **66**, 238.

52. SIEGEL, F. S., BALOW, B., FISCH, R. O., ANDERSON, V. E. (1968). School behaviour profile ratings of P.K.U. children. *Am. J. Ment. Def.*, **72**, 937.
53. SMITH, D. W., BLIZZARD, R. M., WILKINS, L. (1957) The Mental Prognosis in Hypothyroidism of Infancy and Childhood. A review of 128 cases. *Pediatrics*, **19**, 1011.
54. SPITZER, R. MANN, I. (1950) Congenital Malformations in the Teeth and Eyes in Mental Defectives. *J. ment. Sci.*, **96**, 681.
55. STORES, G. (1971) Cognitive function in epilepsy. *Brit. J. Hosp. Med.*, **6**, 207.
57. SUTHERLAND, B. S., BERRY, H. K. (1960) A Syndrome of Phenylketonuria with Normal Intelligence and Behaviour Disorders. *J. Pediat.*, **57**, 521.
57. TIZARD, J., GRAD, J. C. (1961) *The Mentally Handicapped and their Families*. London: Oxford University Press.
58. WORDEN, D. K., VIGNOS, P. J. (1962) Intellectual Function in Childhood Progressive Msucular Dystrophy. *Pediatrics*, **29**, 968.
59. ZELLWEGER, H., HANSON, J. W. (1967) Psychometric studies in muscular dystrophy Type 3A (Duchenne). *Develop. Med. Child Neurol.*, **9**, 576.

CHAPTER 17

THE DIAGNOSIS OF CEREBRAL PALSY

The Difficulties

The diagnosis of cerebral palsy in the first year is regarded by some as a matter of great difficulty. For instance, Skatvedt[11] wrote that 'spasticity in the usual sense, as demonstrated in spastic stretch reflex, is not seen in the infant', and, 'In the course of the second year of life, the diagnosis of cerebral palsy should be possible for the experienced physician'. Scherzer[8] wrote that 'the spastic type of cerebral palsy is not apparent usually before one year to 18 months of age'. In fact cerebral palsy of the spastic type, except in mild cases, can be readily diagnosed in the first few days of life. I have seen an obvious case on the second day of life, and filmed and followed up cases diagnosed on the fourth and fifth day of life. The rigid form can be readily diagnosed in the earliest infancy. The athetoid form cannot usually be diagnosed early, because one cannot be sure of the diagnosis until athetoid movements develop, which may not be for one or two years after birth. Congenital ataxia cannot be diagnosed until about 6 months, because it is dependent on certain purposive movements not found before then: but tremor can be diagnosed early, certainly by the time the baby is able to sit.

It would be profitable to begin by enumerating the main difficulties in early diagnosis.

1. There are all grades of severity of cerebral palsy, from the severe form diagnosed readily in the newborn period, to the mildest form, which is first brought to the doctor's attention at 9 or 10 years.

It can be extremely difficult to diagnose mild degrees of spasticity in early infancy. Signs may be equivocal for several months before it finally becomes clear that disease is present. Brisk knee jerks may be thought to be within normal limits, but with the passage of time it becomes clear that they are pathological. It is always difficult to draw the line between normal and abnormal, and to say, for instance, whether brisk tendon jerks or slight hypertonia are normal or otherwise. Sometimes one has to be prepared to wait and see—in order to determine whether a child is affected or not. In the majority of cases, however, the diagnosis is obvious in the early days or weeks of life.

2. There are several types of cerebral palsy, each with its own features. Using the American Academy of Cerebral Palsy classification these are the spastic form, athetosis, rigidity, ataxia, tremor, atonic form and mixed types.

3. The diagnosis is greatly complicated by the wide range of levels of intelligence, and particularly by the frequency with which mental

retardation is found.   Mental retardation alone has a profound effect on the developmental pattern.

4. The delayed appearance of signs of cerebral palsy, particularly signs of athetosis.   As babies grow older, certain signs become more obvious.

5. The occasional disappearance of signs of cerebral palsy.   One sometimes detects signs of the spastic form of cerebral palsy in early infancy and finds that these signs gradually disappear.   A colleague,[4] saw a boy who was born after precipitate delivery at term, weighing 3175 g, and who was well in the newborn period.   He began to smile and to watch his mother at 2 weeks.   The mother noticed right-sided ankle clonus at the age of 2 weeks, and an experienced doctor confirmed its presence.   It could be triggered by just touching the feet in the direction of dorsiflexion.   When the boy was 5 weeks of age clonus disappeared, and the baby walked alone without help at $8\frac{1}{2}$ months, being normal.   I have many times found exaggerated tendon jerks and defective motor development in the early weeks, and found that the signs disappeared as the child grew older. Some of these fall into the category termed by Gesell 'minimal birth injury'.

I have been able to follow an example of this condition from birth to the age of 14 years.   In the newborn period and subsequently in the first year of life the boy had an obvious left hemiplegia.   The left upper limb was not used at all for the first few months.   The arm improved as he grew older, and by the age of 5 or 6 years the sole remaining sign of cerebral palsy was a left extensor plantar response. There was no spasticity of the leg.   The hand was normal.   There were no other abnormal signs.

André-Thomas[2] described several examples of the disappearance of signs of cortical injury, especially hemiplegia, and emphasised that on that account prognosis must always be guarded and that examinations must always be repeated.   Minkowski,[7] using the André Thomas method of examination, divided 74 newborn babies into three groups, (a) normal (25 infants), (b) minor neurological abnormalities (43 infants), (c) gross neurological abnormalities (6 infants). On re-examination 2 years or more later, of the 25 who were normal in the newborn period, 19 were normal subsequently and 6 had minor but temporary problems (such as ocular defects and delayed walking): of 43 in Group B (showing minor neurological signs in the newborn period), 22 were normal subsequently: 18 had minor neurological handicaps, but three had serious sequelae.   Of 6 who showed serious neurological signs in the newborn period, three continued to show severe sequelae on follow-up, while the remainder showed trivial and temporary neurological signs.

Solomons, Holden and Denhoff[9] described 12 infants who showed abnormal neurological signs in the first year, and who had been followed for a period of one to three years, during which time all abnormal signs disappeared.

One pays much less attention to single signs than to a combination of signs. For instance, one would pay little attention to some degree of hypertonia alone, but one would pay much more attention to a combination of hypertonia and delayed motor development, or an unusually small head circumference. One pays much less attention to delayed motor development alone than one does to delayed motor development combined with delayed social responsiveness (late smiling), or a small head circumference.

The difficulties in the early diagnosis, the impossibility of drawing the line between normal and abnormal in some cases (with particular reference to the knee jerks and abduction of the hip), and especially the occasional disappearance of signs of cerebral palsy, make it essential not to tell the mother about one's suspicions until one is quite certain about the diagnosis and the permanence of the condition. Continued observation is essential in all but the severe cases.

The Child at Risk

Certain prenatal and natal conditions place a child 'at risk' of cerebral palsy. They include:

Family history of cerebral palsy.

Prematurity, especially extreme.

Multiple pregnancy.

Low birth weight in relation to the duration of gestation.

Mental subnormality.

Severe anoxia, convulsions, hyperbilirubinaemia or cerebral haemorrhage in the newborn period.

Diagnosis of Any Form of Cerebral Palsy

The diagnosis must be made, as always, on the basis of the history, the examination, and the interpretation of one's findings.

The history includes the 'risk factors'. The mother may herself have noticed that the baby feels stiff, or is stiff on one side, or keeps one hand clenched when the other is open, or does not kick the legs properly. The baby may kick both legs together, instead of reciprocal kicking. The mother may have noticed that when the baby creeps, one leg trails after the other. She may notice that the child consistently refuses to use one hand. She may give a clear history of 'dissociation'—meaning in this context that there is severe retardation in gross motor development, such as sitting, while the baby is more advanced in other fields of development. For instance, she may say that the child can readily pick up a currant between the tip of the forefinger and the tip of the thumb, but cannot nearly sit unsupported.   This would immediately suggest an abnormality of muscle tone—hypotonia or hypertonia.   There is likely to be a history of delay in reaching other milestones of development, because of the commonly associated mental retardation.

Spastic Form

The diagnosis is then made on the developmental examination. In summary, the following are the essential points:

First Three Months

1. If newborn, note the quantity and quality of his movement, for the spastic child tends to be relatively immobile.   If he has spastic quadriplegia he is apt to lie with his limbs unduly extended, and his hands unusually tightly closed.   After about three months the hands should be predominantly loosely open.   A hemiplegic child would be likely to have one hand tightly closed and the other open, and there might be asymmetry of movement.
2. Observe the child, his head size and shape, his facial expression, his alertness and interest in his surroundings.   A small head circumference in relation to the weight is common because of the frequency of associated mental subnormality.   Because of the frequent mental retardation, there is often a lack of normal alertness and responsiveness.
3. Hold the child up with your hands in his axilla.   There may be abnormal extension of the hip and knees (or asymmetry), and the legs may cross.
4. Hold in ventral suspension.   There is usually delayed motor development and so there will be excessive head lag.   The arms and legs commonly hang down lifelessly without the flexion of the elbows and knees and slight hip extension seen in the normal child.

   Some infants display excessive extensor tone in ventral suspension and the prone position, and so give the wrong impression of displaying advanced motor development: but on pulling the child to the sitting position from the supine, the gross head lag is obvious. It is incorrect to term the head lag 'hypotonia'.
5. Place him in the prone position, in order to assess maturation. The spastic infant commonly assumes an immature position owing to the mental subnormality, but may show excessive extensor tone, as above.
6. Place him in the supine position.   Note the symmetry or asymmetry of the kick.   Note whether the hands are equally open or closed.   Assess muscle tone by feeling the muscles, assessing the resistance to passive movement, assessing the range of movement, and shaking the limbs (for passivité).   Assess the range of movement especially in the hips (after flexing them to a right angle) and

in dorsiflexion of the ankle. When doing this, test for ankle clonus. Test the knee jerks—beginning to tap over the dorsum of the ankle.
Test the bicep jerks, beginning to tap over the shoulder.

8. Pull him to the sitting position in order to assess head lag. Sway him gently from side to side in order to determine the degree of head control (passivité). When he is being pulled up into the sitting position, have the hand in the popliteal space in order to detect spasm of the hamstrings. When a child is spastic one feels a resistance to pulling him up to the sitting position and the knees may flex: one can see this and feel the spasm of the hamstrings. When leaned forward he repeatedly falls back, because of spasm of the erector spinae, glutei and hamstrings. When he is pulled up to the sitting position, he may rise to his feet, because of excessive extensor tone, and give the wrong impression of advanced weight bearing. The true diagnosis is revealed by the other signs of excessive tone, mentioned above, the exaggerated knee jerks, the ankle clonus, and reduced abduction of the hip and ankle dorsiflexion, with head lag when he is pulled up.

9. Measure his head circumference and relate this to his weight.
At the end of this period, persistence of the Moro reflex, grasp reflex and asymmetrical tonic reflex, point to the diagnosis. They should have disappeared by 2 to 3 months.

4–8 Months

1. Observe the child, as in the case of the younger infant, noting the quality, quantity and symmetry of movement.

2. Give the child a one inch cube to go for. This may reveal the typical spastic approach, unilateral if he has a hemiplegia, with the slow characteristic dorsiflexion of the wrist with splaying out of the fingers as he approaches the object, often with ataxia and tremor. In a mild case this may be missed, but careful observation of the two hands shows the difference in the two sides in a hemiplegic child. It is different from the ataxic approach of the athetoid child, who does not show the wrist dorsiflexion and splaying out of the fingers. One can usually make the diagnosis of spastic hemiplegia at a glance when the child reaches for an object and grasps it: but one confirms the diagnosis by the other tests enumerated.

3. Hold the child up with your hands in his axilla, in order to determine whether there is excessive extension of the legs. Test in ventral suspension and the prone position, as above.

4. Place him in the supine position. Note undue closure of one hand (as in hemiplegia). Note the symmetry of the kick. Test the knee jerks, the degree of hip abduction and ankle dorsiflexion, and test for ankle clonus. Elicit the plantar response. Pull him

to the sitting position, as before.   As before, note the resistance to pulling him up (because of spasm of the erector spinae and glutei) and the repeated falling back when placed sitting forward.   Note shortening of the limb if there is hemiplegia.   See that the child is lying flat and straight on the couch, and bring the malleoli together, to see if one leg is shortened.   From the end of the couch note whether the heels are parallel—or whether one is higher up the couch than the other because of shortening.   The foot of a hemiplegic limb may be smaller than the normal foot.   Unless the child and room are warm, the hemiplegic limb is cold as compared with the normal one: feel with the palm of the hand.   If there is hemiplegia and there is moderate involvement of the arm, the affected arm will be shorter, and except in a warm room, relatively cold as compared with the normal side.

5. Note signs of general retardation.
6. Measure the head circumference.
7. Check the hearing.

9 Months Onwards

1. Observe for the same signs.
2. Offer the child a pellet of paper and one inch cubes and if he is old enough, get him to build a tower.   In trivial cases the ataxia or tremor may be slight and readily missed: there may be merely slight clumsiness in building the tower.   Give him beads to thread: a timed bead threading test may reveal slight neurological involvement.   As in the case of the younger infant, one can frequently make the diagnosis at a glance as he tries to pick up a pellet of paper; if the child has a hemiplegia the difference in the use of the two hands is immediately obvious.   One then confirms the diagnosis by the other tests, such as the estimation of muscle tone by shaking the limb, the tendon jerks and the range of movement in the hip and ankle.   As before, pull him up to the sitting position.
3. Always test the plantar response; this may be difficult.   The most sensitive area for it is the distal half of the outer side of the foot.   One tests with the thumb, and *never* with a pin or key, which hurt.   Never convey the stimulus across the sole of the foot, for this confuses by introducing the plantar grasp reflex, which is flexor.   When in doubt squeeze the calf muscles (Gordon's sign) or stroke firmly along the tibia (Oppenheim's sign): as stated elsewhere these signs depend merely on the fact that in disease of the pyramidal tract the area over which the reflex is obtained is increased (as it was in the young normal baby, prior to myelination).
4. If the child is standing or walking, note toe walking and note the gait.   Note shoe wear.
5. If old enough (over three) get him to stand on one foot.   This is a

sensitive test, in the case of a hemiplegia immediately showing the difference in the two sides.

6. Note signs of general retardation.   Measure the head circumference.

These are the basic signs of the spastic form of cerebral palsy.   In a busy clinic, it would take perhaps two or three minutes to carry out the tests described.

The following is a typical case history of a mentally retarded child with cerebral palsy of the spastic type:

Case Report.—This boy was born at term by normal delivery and was well in the newborn period.   The subsequent course can be summarised as follows:

4 weeks	I wrote, 'Note the immature prone position. Suggestion of spasticity in lower limbs, but hands loosely open'.
6 weeks	'Very primitive in prone position. Poor head control'
9 weeks	Smiles.
14 weeks	Vocalising. Following with eyes.
6 months	Grasping voluntarily.
15 months	Sitting, no support.
18 months	Single words beginning.
2 years	Walk, no help—no sphincter control. Cannot feed self. Concentration defective. Would do nothing with cubes.
3 years	Words together.
5½ years	I.Q. 47.
	Very mild right hemiplegia.

Athetosis

It is virtually impossible to make a definite diagnosis of athetosis until the athetoid movements are seen, and these may be delayed for some years, though I have seen them in the first week.   The condition may be suspected because of one of the conditions known in some cases to be followed by athetosis—in particular, severe anoxia at birth, haemolytic disease of the newborn or neonatal hyperbilirubinaemia.   Athetosis can be expected to develop if there was kernicterus in the neonatal period.

Observation of the development of babies with kernicterus has provided us with useful information concerning its natural history.

Polani[10] described 73 cases.   The kernicterus was due either to haemolytic disease or to the hyperbilirubinaemia of prematurity. The early signs of kernicterus which appear not later than the sixth day in a full term baby, or the tenth day in a premature baby, were opisthotonos, rolling of the eyes, high-pitched cry, loss of the Moro reflex and of the mouth reflexes, jaundice, refusal of feeds, drowsiness or irritability, hypertonia, respiratory difficulties, cyanotic attacks and sometimes fever.   These usually disappear by the end of the second week.   He then described a silent period from the second week to the end of the first or second month, though feeding and sucking difficulties or stridor were common at this time.   After the second month, neurological distrubances were obvious in 9 out of 10 babies.

In 8 the only abnormality was delay in development. The infant often characteristically extends the elbows and pronates the wrist. In 37 there were attacks of opisthotonos following stimulation or distress. These attacks became more frequent with the passage of time, and then developed spontaneously. They began to decrease in severity by the age of 9 to 11 months. Between the attacks the children tended to be hypotonic. In half the children this phase was followed by hypotonia; in the other half it was followed by athetoid movements. In 25 children hypertonia developed after the second month, with relaxation in sleep. In 21 the phase of hypertonia was followed by athetoid movements. In 4 children hypotonia and developmental retardation appeared after the second month.

At the end of the first year 55 children were surveyed. There was marked hypotonia in 23, hypertonia in 11, mere developmental retardation in 19, and athetoid movements in 2. The age of onset of athetoid movements was studied in 56 children. In 39 the onset was before $2\frac{1}{2}$, and in 17 it was between 3 and $3\frac{1}{2}$ years.

Polani's paper is a useful one and has supplied us with valuable information. I am sceptical, however, of any studies of the age of onset of athetoid movements because I know from experience how easy it is to miss them in the early months or to imagine them if particularly looking for this. I believe that careful examination will reveal signs of athetosis sooner than is commonly thought. One of the earliest signs is ataxia in carrying out voluntary movements, such as grasping a cube. I have made the mistake of diagnosing ataxia only to alter it later to athetosis.

I would emphasise the rhythmical tongue thrusting commonly seen in babies who will subsequently prove to have athetosis. I think that this may occur in other babies, but when I see it I regard athetosis as the most likely condition.

The Moro and asymmetrical tonic neck reflexes persist longer than usual. As the infant grows older, retardation in motor development becomes more obvious. After 12 months or so the typical tetrad of athetosis will be found. This consists of difficulty in vertical gaze (present in 90 per cent), enamel hypoplasia of the deciduous teeth, high tone deafness (found in the majority), and athetoid movements.

Not all athetosis is due to kernicterus. In those cases in which kernicterus was not a factor, the signs are usually delayed motor development, often rhythmical tongue thrusting, and then ataxia, followed by typical athetoid movements. The knee jerks and biceps jerks are normal in athetoids, and the plantar responses are flexor.

The athetoid child is by no means always late in development, provided that the I.Q. is average. The following is an example:

A child with known haemolytic disease of the newborn, which had been improperly treated, was followed up carefully because of the possibility of the development of signs of athetosis. At 4 months the motor development was thought to be better than average. At 6 months he began to sit without support. At 11 months he began to walk, holding on to furniture, and he could pull himself up to the standing position. He was saying 2 words with meaning at 16 months. He walked without help at 20 months, and at this time athetoid movements became obvious. The I.Q. at 6 was 86.

I have seen other athetoid children who were able to sit unsupported by 6 or 7 months and to walk without help by the first birthday.

Rigidity

The rigid form is diagnosed by the extreme rigidity of all limbs, in the absence of signs of disease of the pyramidal tract, such as increased tendon jerks, ankle clonus, positive stretch reflex, and extensor plantar response. It is almost always associated with a severe degree of mental deficiency.

Ataxia

The ataxic form is diagnosed by the ataxia in the child's approach to an object, and ataxia in sitting and walking.

Hypotonic Form of Cerebral Palsy

This is a rare form of cerebral palsy which can readily be confused with the hypotonias. Almost all infants with this condition are mentally defective.[6] The circumference of the skull is likely to be small. There is an increased range of movement. Fits occur in a third. The plantar responses are extensor and the knee jerks are exaggerated, so that benign congenital hypotonia, the Werdnig-Hoffmann syndrome and myopathies can be readily excluded.

The Clumsy Child

There are all gradations between the normal and the abnormal, and it is impossible to draw the line between the two. Not all clumsy children should be included in the section on cerebral palsy, but it is likely that many clumsy children are examples of that condition. The intelligence of the clumsy child may be average or superior but it is more often below average.

Clumsy children are usually regarded as normal for several years, and then they begin to get into trouble at school or worry their parents because of their awkwardness. Mothers commonly say that the child 'falls a lot', 'always has bruises on his legs', is 'awkward with his hands', 'cannot pedal a cycle', and say that the teacher complains that 'his writing is bad', or that 'he doesn't seem to hold his pencil properly'.

Ford[3] in his book used the term 'congenital maladroitness'. Annell[1] used the term 'Motorial Infantilism'. Arnold Gesell used the term 'Minimal Birth Injury'—an undesirable term, because it implies knowledge of the causation. Others have called these children 'motor morons'. They are awkward at tying shoe laces or at buttoning their clothes. They tend to misjudge distances, as when passing through a doorway; they break objects more than others; they cannot thread a needle or throw a ball well or jump like normal children of their age. They cannot stand on one foot as well as their contemporaries, though they walk normally. On building a tower of cubes slight unsteadiness or tremor is usually noted. In a few there are minimal signs of athetosis or of disease of the pyramidal tract in the way of an extensor plantar response. Timed tests of manual dexterity—such as the pegboard—reveal that the child is a long way behind for his age. The intelligence quotient may be average or superior, though it is probably more common to find that it is below average.

Clumsiness may be due to hypotonia, congenital myopathy, muscular dystrophy, familial dysautonomia, the Klippel-Feil syndrome, agenesis of the corpus callosum, chorea, degenerative diseases of the nervous system or a cerebral tumour and other organic causes. Older children may be clumsy because of drugs—such as the antiepileptic drugs. Clumsiness is often associated with overactivity and may be a familial feature or a reaction to insecurity.

One begins by asking the child to build a tower of one inch cubes. One may notice tremor or ataxia in the hands as he builds. When he is older he is likely to have difficulty in standing on one foot, in walking along a ledge, in the timed bead-threading test, in the Goodenough draw-a-man test, in the Goddard formboard test, and in right left discrimination. He may be asked to hop on one foot; to screw a bolt; to pat the back of first one hand then the other rapidly; and to copy a circle, square, triangle and later a diamond. He achieves a better score on the Wechsler verbal scale than on the performance scale.

From the point of view of developmental assessment, the condition is important because of the frequency with which these children are wrongly thought to be mentally subnormal. As always, one has to assess a child not on the question of whether he can do a given test, but on the way in which he does it.

Differential Diagnosis

1. MENTAL RETARDATION. By far the greatest difficulty in diagnosis lies in the differentiation of cerebral palsy in association with mental retardation from mental retardation alone. The two conditions are frequently associated. It follows that when signs of mental retardation are found, a thorough search for signs of cerebral palsy should always be made.

2. ISOLATED MOTOR RETARDATION. It is easy to confuse mild diplegia with isolated motor retardation. I have myself made this mistake.

Case Report.—I was asked, by a paediatrician, Dr. R. Gordon, to see a child of 10 months of age on account of defective head control and suspected cerebral palsy. There was no retardation in other fields. Diplegia was suspected, but although the knee jerks were brisk, I mistakenly decided that they were within normal limits. There was no adductor spasm in the thigh muscles. He learned to sit without support at 14 months, to feed himself with a cup at 18 months, and to join words together at 23 months. I saw him at intervals, but it was not until he was over 3 years old that it became obvious that the plantar responses were extensor. He had no deformity.

3. VOLUNTARY RESISTANCE TO PASSIVE MOVEMENT. The child may be thought to be spastic, whereas in fact he is merely resisting passive movement.

4. ABNORMALITY OF JOINTS. Abduction of hips may appear to be limited, so suggesting adductor spasm, when in fact the child is voluntarily resisting the movement. Limited abduction of hips may be due to congenital dislocation of hips. I have myself made the mistake of diagnosing spasticity in a newborn baby who had notable limitation of movements of the joints due to punctate epiphyseal dysplasia. The limited movement of joints in arthrogryposis multiplex congenita might be confused with spasticity. A mentally subnormal or severely hypotonic child who constantly lies in one position may develop a muscle contracture which limits the abduction of the hips and may suggest spasticity.

5. UNSTEADINESS OF GAIT. Children who are late in learning to walk are usually later than others in learning to walk steadily: many such children are referred to me as cases of cerebral palsy.

6. NORMAL MOVEMENTS. It is easy to confuse the normal movements of the arms and legs of a baby with those of athetosis, if he has had some condition such as severe jaundice, which leads one to look carefully for athetoid movements.

7. CAUSES OF TOE-WALKING. Most children with cerebral palsy of the spastic type sooner or later tend to walk on their toes: but toe-walking may be normal, for some children when learning to walk develop this habit. One eliminates the diagnosis of cerebral palsy by determining that there are no other features of cerebral palsy; for instance, the muscle tone, tendon jerks and plantar responses are normal. Toe-walking occurs in the premature baby when held in the standing position at the equivalent of term. It occurs with congenital shortening of the Tendo Achillis, muscular dystrophy, autism and dystonia musculorum deformans.

8. CONGENITAL SHORTENING OF THE GLUTEUS MAXIMUS, GASTROCNEMIUS OR OF THE HAMSTRINGS. This makes it difficult for the child to sit, and delays sitting. The tendon jerks in these conditions are normal, thus eliminating the spastic form of cerebral palsy.

9. WEAKNESS OF MUSCLES DUE TO MYOPATHY, HYPOTONIA OR ERB'S PALSY. In all these cases, weakness rather than stiffness would be detected. Erb's palsy rarely persists, and in the older child the

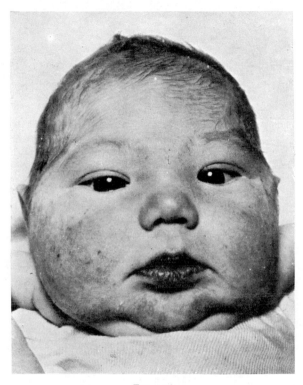

Fig. 154
Child with severe microcephaly.

facing page 294

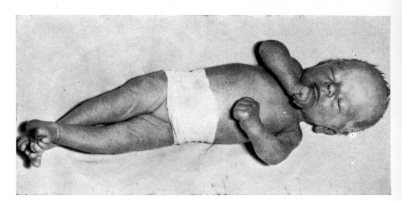

FIG. 155

Abnormal appearance of child aged 8 days. Hands tightly closed. The legs tend to cross and they are unusually extended. Knee jerks normal. Cerebral haemorrhage. Severe convulsions age 3 days. (As FIG. 82.)

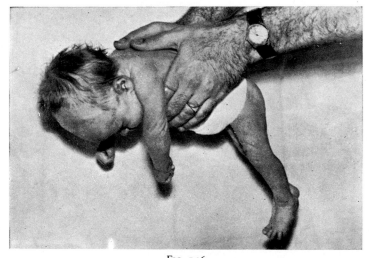

FIG. 156
Same child as Figure 155.
Head held up quite well, but arms and legs not flexed.

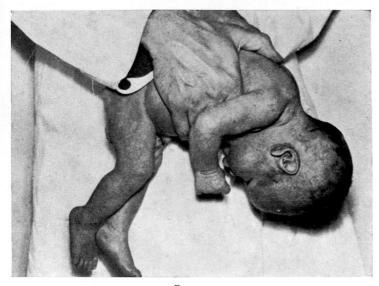

FIG. 157

A case of proved cerebral palsy at 6 weeks.

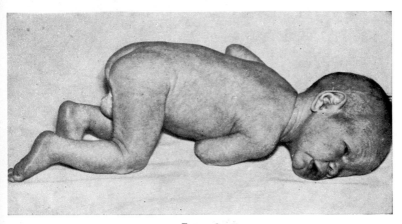

FIG. 158

Defective head control. Inadequate extension of hips and flexion of knees.
Same boy as Figure 154. Pelvis rather high for the age.

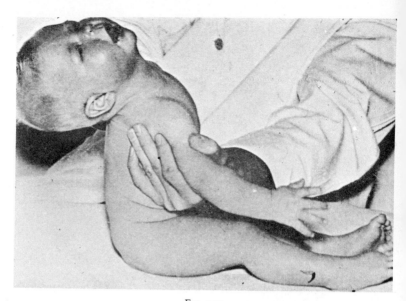

Fig. 159

Severely mentally defective child with spastic quadriplegia, aged 6 months, showing severe head lag on being pulled to the sitting position.

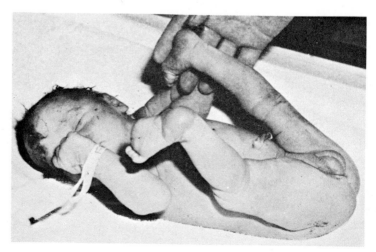

Fig. 160

Breech with extended legs. Age 10 days. Note the posture.

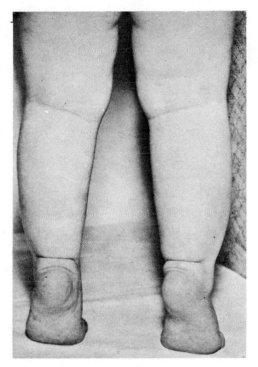

Fig. 161
Toe walking due to congenital shorten-
ing of the Tendo Achillis.
There is also a constriction band.

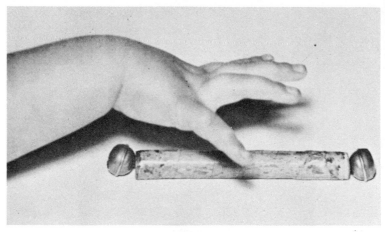

Fig. 162
Typical spastic approach to object, with splaying out of fingers.
(Mild hemiplegia.)

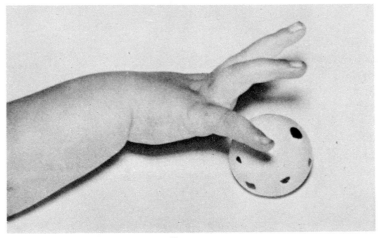

Fig. 163
The same.

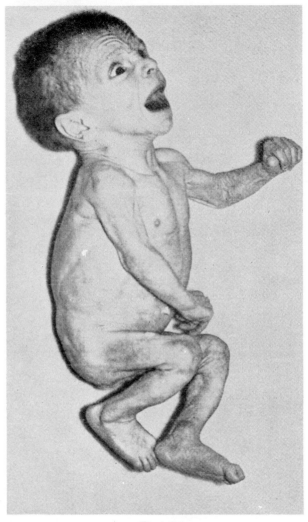

FIG. 164
Kernicterus, aged 2 weeks.

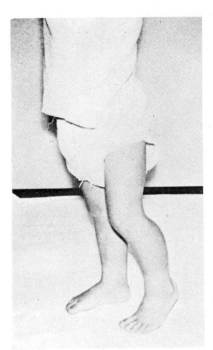

FIG. 165

Child with mild left hemiplegia. Toe walking.

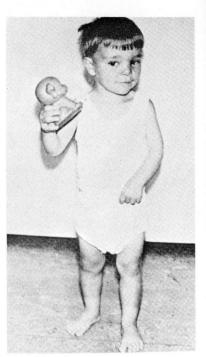

FIG. 166

Child with mild left hemiplegia. Characteristic arm posture.

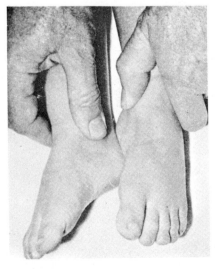

FIG. 167

Child with mild left hemiplegia. Shortening of affected leg, shown by position of left internal malleolus in relation to the right, when the child is lying on his back with the legs fully extended. Thumbs on internal malleoli.

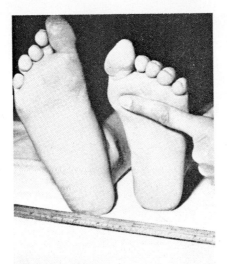

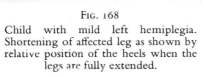

Fig. 168

Child with mild left hemiplegia.
Shortening of affected leg as shown by
relative position of the heels when the
legs are fully extended.

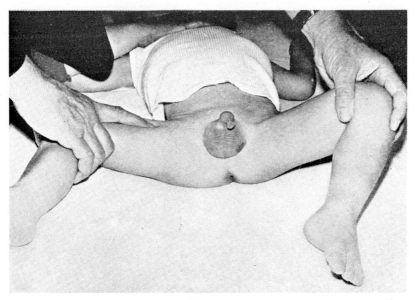

Fig. 169

Child with mild left hemiplegia. Limited abduction of left hip, owing to hypertonia.

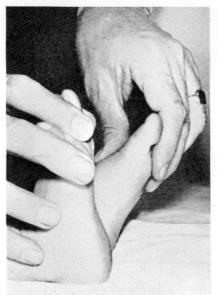

FIG. 170
Child with mild left hemiplegia. Limite
dorsiflexion of left foot, owing t
hypertonia and perhaps some shortenin
of the Tendo Achilles.

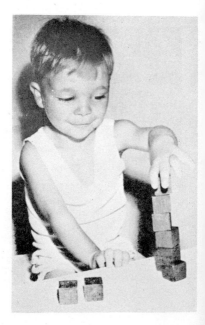

FIG. 171
Child with mild left hemiplegia.
Typical splaying out of affected hand
when building a tower of bricks.

characteristic grasp of the spastic hand, with the slow splaying out of the fingers, is different from the grasp of the child with Erb's palsy. The muscle tone elsewhere is normal.   The knee jerks, hip abduction and ankle dorsiflexion are normal.   It must be noted that a true monoplegia is exceedingly rare; hence if the child had a spastic hand, there will almost certainly be some involvement of the lower limb— but that involvement may be only trivial.

10. OTHER CAUSES OF INVOLUNTARY MOVEMENTS.   These include tremor, torsion spasm, spasmus nutans, chorea and tics.   It is easy to confuse athetosis with ataxia, particularly in the infant, in whom the first sign of athetosis is ataxia, before the characteristic involuntary movements begin.

In torsion spasm the first sign is often hypertonicity of the calf muscles, leading to plantar flexion and inversion with adduction of the foot.   Later torticollis develops, followed later by the typical torsion spasm.

Spasmus mutans can be confused with tremor, but the characteristic head nodding or twitching, with the peculiar habit of looking out of the corner of the eyes, should establish the diagnosis.   The movements are often inhibited by looking fixedly at an object.

Athetosis should not be confused with the more irregular movements of Sydenham's or Huntington's chorea.

11. DEGENERATIVE CONDITIONS OF THE NERVOUS SYSTEM.   It is easy to diagnose these on the grounds that no abnormality had been previously noted, when in fact there were neurological abnormalities which had not been looked for or recognised.   The conditions at issue include the lipoidoses and leucoencephalopathies.   Schilder's disease (encephalitis periaxalis) and multiple sclerosis may be confused with cerebral palsy of prenatal origin.   Toxoplasmosis may cause convulsions and spasticity, the real cause being missed.   Phenyl-ketonuria rarely but occasionally causes spasticity.

12. ABNORMALITIES OF THE SPINAL CORD.   These include diastematomyelia, syringomyelia and spinal dysraphism.   Holman et al.[5] reviewed the conditions known as diastematomyelia.   It is a congenital anomaly in which a spicule of bone transfixes the spinal cord, and leads to progressive paresis of the lower limbs.   In about half of all cases a tuft of hair or congenital dermal sinus reveals the condition.

Syringomyelia may occur in later childhood.   There is likely to be muscular atrophy, arthropathy, weakness or spasticity and dissociated anaesthesia.

Paraplegia may be due to a purely spinal lesion.   Congenital absence of the sacrum causes weakness of the legs with absence of sphincter control.

13. OTHER SYNDROMES.   Cleidocranial dysostosis is character-ised by absence of the middle third of the clavicle, allowing the

shoulders to approximate anteriorly in the midline; it is sometimes associated with spasticity and mental subnormality.

Platybasia and other anomalies of the base of the skull may be associated with shortness of the neck, ataxia or hypotonia.[12]

REFERENCES

1. ANNELL, A. L. (1952) *Disorders of Motor Function in Schoolchildren. The Affective Contact.* p. 367. Amsterdam: Strengholt.
2. ANDRÉ-THOMAS, DARGASSIES SAINT-ANNE (1952) *Études Neurologiques sur le Nouveau-né et le Jeune Nourrisson.* Paris: Masson and Perrin.
3. FORD, F. R. (1960) *Diseases of the Nervous System in Infancy and Childhood and Adolescence.* Oxford: Blackwell.
4. HARVEY, C. C. (1959) Personal Communication.
5. HOLMAN, C. P., SVIEN, H. J., BICKEL, W. H., KEITH, H. M. (1955) Diastemato-myelia. *Pediatrics*, **15**, 191.
6. LESNY, I. (1960) The Hypotonic Forms of Cerebral Palsy. *Cerebral Palsy Bull.*, **2**, 158.
7. MINKOWSKI, A. (1960) Personal Communication.
8. SCHERZER, A. L., (1973) Current concepts and classification of cerebral palsy. *Clinic. Proc. Children's Hosp. Nat. Med. Center.* **29**, 143.
9. SOLOMONS, G., HOLDEN, R. H., DENHOFF, E. (1963) The Changing Pattern of Cerebral Dysfunction in Early Childhood. *J. Pediat.*, **63**, 113.
10. POLANI, P. E. (1959) The Natural Clinical History of Choreoathetoid Cerebral Palsy. *Guy's Hosp. Rep.*, **108**, 32.
11. SKATVEDT, M. (1958) Cerebral Palsy. *Acta Paedia. (Uppsala)*, **46**. Suppl. 111.
12. SPILLANE, J. D., PALLIS, C., JONES, A. M. (1957) Developmental Anomalies in the Region of the Foramen Magnum. *Brain*, **80**, 11.

CHAPTER 18

ASSESSMENT OF SUITABILITY FOR ADOPTION

When assessing a child's suitability for adoption it must be constantly remembered that the interests of the child are the primary consideration. Nevertheless, the interests of the adopting parents have to be considered, for they have a considerable bearing on those of the child. One has to try to prevent a mentally defective child being unwittingly adopted, in order to protect the adopting parents from a tragic disappointment, and to protect the adopted child from possible rejection by the adopting parents. An important aim of the doctor is therefore the detection of a severe mental or physical handicap. It may be argued that one should attempt to match the child's developmental potential with that of the intelligence and social status of the adopting parents, as was done in Arnold Gesell's clinic in New Haven. This is a debatable aim, but it is difficult to deny that a child who is thought to be of slightly below average developmental potential would fit in better in the home of a manual labourer than in the home of professional parents.

Gould[8] in his book on 'Stress in Children' wrote that ideally it would be most desirable to match the abilities and temperament of the child to those of the adoptive parents. I am not sure that it would. I am not sure that it would be better for a neurotic mother to adopt a neurotic child. Knowing the importance of environmental factors in schizophrenia, it might well be better to try to place a child of a schizophrenic parent in a particularly calm and stable home.

I am not sure that we are right in saying that a baby who is thought to have a rather low developmental potential should be placed in the home of a manual labourer rather than in a professional home. A child a little below the average at six months might well prove to be above average if placed in a good loving stimulating home; if placed in a less good home, he may become further retarded. In the same way a mentally superior baby might not be expected to achieve his best if placed in a poor home. Admittedly, it is not the function of the paediatrician to chose the home for a baby; but in deciding whether a baby is suitable for adoption, he may be influenced in his decision by observing the sort of foster parent who wants to adopt.

My constantly reiterated warnings about the difficulties and fallacies of developmental prediction should be remembered. It is a tragedy if a doctor wrongly diagnoses mental subnormality or cerebral palsy, so that the baby cannot be adopted; and it is most unfortunate if he passes a baby as normal, when in fact he is a microcephalic spastic idiot. I have seen a good many examples of both mistakes.

Current adopting practices now raise new problems—that of religion, that of the coloured child and that of a child with mental or physical handicap.

The Limitations of Developmental Assessment

It is important that a doctor who is attempting to assess a baby should be conversant with the limitations of developmental assessment.   He should know that by proper assessment one can diagnose mental subnormality, and one can detect cerebral palsy of moderate or severe degree.

The assessment is made, as always, on the basis of the history, the examination and the interpretation.

The History

The importance of a full history, prior to any developmental examination, has already been described.   It would be wrong to agree to any child being adopted without a proper history concerning the real parents, the pregnancy, birth weight, duration of gestation, the delivery and the condition of the child in the newborn period. One must know whether there is a family history of hereditary diseases and particularly of degenerative diseases of the nervous system or of psychosis.   One must know whether there is a history of illnesses during pregnancy, such as toxaemia or antepartum haemorrhage, which increase the risk of abnormality in the child.   One must know about any factor making the child 'at risk', or more likely than others, to be abnormal.   The greatest 'risk' factor of all is probably extreme prematurity or a marked discrepancy between the birth weight and gestational age ('small for dates'), but it is essential that none of these factors should be given an exaggerated importance.   For instance, a history of mental subnormality in a parent should certainly not be regarded as contraindicating the adoption of the child.   A history of epilepsy in a mother should not prevent a child being adopted. I find a constant tendency to exaggerate the importance of these factors.   The doctor who assesses the baby should note the factors carefully and keep them in proper perspective.   He should then concentrate on assessing the child, and except in the case of degenerative diseases of the nervous system and psychoses he should be careful not to give the 'risk' factors more importance than they merit.   For example, if the doctor is asked to assess a 6 months old baby whose mother was mentally defective, it would be wrong for him promptly to conclude that the baby was unsuitable for adoption.   He should assess the baby, as he would any other, and if he found that he was in all respects up to the average or above average, he would pass the baby as suitable.   If, however, the baby were a little below average, he would take the family history into account, and postpone a decision until say 10 months, when he would reassess the baby, and consider the rate of development in the intervening period.

As in the case of any assessment, one must obtain a history of previous milestones, in order that one can estimate the rate of development, and of factors which might have affected the development, such as illnesses.

The paediatrician may be asked for advice as to whether a normal child can be adopted into a home containing a mentally or physically handicapped child. There is no easy answer to this. If he is adopted it is likely that he will suffer in various ways. He may grow up to be embarassed by his handicapped 'sibling': the mother is apt to suffer physical, emotional and financial stress as a result of having a severely handicapped child, and so the adopted child may suffer: and there is likely to be favouritism for the handicapped child. The normal child may be held responsible for the handicapped child after the death of the parents. The decision must depend on the severity of the handicap and other family circumstances.

The Examination

Grossly defective infants, such as mongols and those with severe microcephaly, will already have been sifted out, and are not likely to reach the doctor who is assessing babies for adoption.

The age at which the assessment for adoption is made is of the greatest importance. It has already been stated that we are not able as yet to assess a baby seriously before he is about four weeks of age (and at a similar corrected age in the case of premature babies). In my opinion the earliest age at which one should attempt to assess a full term baby is six weeks. This is because it is relatively easy to assess the motor development at this age, and normal full term babies have begun to smile at the mother's overtures and probably to vocalise. They will watch her intently as she speaks to them. It is the normal practice in Britain to place an infant at the age of one or two weeks in a foster home in which the foster parents are likely to adopt; and the age of six weeks would be a convenient one for assessment, giving the foster parents a little time in which to become acquainted with the baby. If one is doubtful about the development at this age, he should be reassessed at six months, but not sooner.

I have no doubt that it is much easier and safer to assess a baby at the age of six months, if this can be arranged. The difficulty lies in the foster parents' natural desire to clinch the adoption, and the fear that the real mother may change her mind and demand the return of the baby. At the age of six months one can readily assess the gross motor development, particularly in the sitting position; the child has begun (at four or five months) to reach out and grasp objects without their being put into the hand, and the maturity of the grasp can be assessed at six months. He begins to transfer objects from one hand to the other at this age.   He begins to chew.   He may have begun to imitate (e.g. a cough or other noise).   His interest in his surroundings and determination can be observed.   The maturity of his response to sound can be determined.   For instance, he should immediately turn his head to sound.

If one is doubtful about the baby's development at six months, the best time to see him again is at ten months.   By this age he should be able to stand holding on to the furniture, and perhaps to walk, holding on to it; he may be able to creep; but much more important than this is the index finger approach to objects and finger thumb apposition. He should be able to wave bye bye and play patacake, and he should be helping his mother to dress him by holding his arm out for a coat or his foot out for a shoe.

In the first year the most difficult age for assessment is two to four months, and the next most difficult age is eight to nine months.   This is because there are so few significant new milestones at these times. It is easy to make a mistake at two to four months in the assessment of motor development, and there are no useful new developments in manipulation or social behaviour.   The same applies to some extent to the age of eight to nine months.

There is much to be said for a doctor assessing adoption babies at the same age—so that he becomes really conversant with the developmental features of that age.   There is not usually any difficulty about arranging this.

The disadvantage of placing a child at two to three weeks in a foster home in which adoption is desired is the possibility that he will turn out to be defective.   The great advantage, however, is that the infant does not suffer emotional trauma by being changed from one home to another.   If the child should turn out to be defective, the foster parents will be bitterly disappointed; but one must remember that if they adopt earlier and he subsequently turns out to be defective, they will suffer much more.   It is wrong to keep him in an institution for a long period, such as six months.   In that case he will suffer emotional deprivation, which apart from anything else will retard his development and make assessment more difficult.   It must be remembered that in this country a period of three months must elapse between the institution of adoption proceedings and their finalisation.

If the final verdict is that the child is backward, one has to try to assess the degree of backwardness.   It is important to try to predict whether he will be educable in an ordinary school or a school for educationally subnormal children, and still more important to predict that he will not be suitable for education at school.   Such predictions are fraught with great difficulties, and one must take the head circumference into account.   The additional finding of cerebral palsy may simplify matters, if it is severe, or make it more difficult, if it is less severe.   In all cases one has to state the position to the parents, making it clear, if one thinks it to be the case, that the child may make an unexpected improvement and even turn out to be normal. This will depend in large part on the head size.

Many foster parents, on being told that the child is thought to be backward, state unhesitatingly that they will adopt in any case. In one way this is desirable, because it would be a tragedy for the child if he were not adopted. In that case prolonged stay in the foster home is the best substitute for adoption. On the other hand, it is impossible for parents who have never had a mentally subnormal child to know all the implications of adopting such a child. They cannot possibly know all that it involves. They cannot know what it is like to have a mentally defective child in the home, and have to watch him all the time for his own safety. They cannot really know the physical, social, emotional and financial stresses to which they will be exposed. At least they will not feel the guilt, disappointment and other attitudes which real parents feel when they find that their own child is defective. They will have little sense of shame when their neighbours and relatives see the child. They may be respected for their courage for knowingly adopting such a child. They will not expect too much of him, and yet they may always hope for some improvement. It is reasonable to suppose that a couple would not deliberately adopt a defective child unless they were the sort of people who would be likely to be able to cope with him.

If a child is of normal intelligence, and yet is found to be handicapped, there is no objection to the child being adopted, provided that the parents understand the implications as far as possible. Again, it would be a tragedy for the child if he were not adopted.

I feel strongly that developmental prediction is so difficult, and it is so vitally important that for the child's sake no unavoidable mistake should be made, that children should be assessed for adoption only by someone who is especially interested and experienced in the problem. This may be a child welfare clinic doctor who has specialised in the subject, or a paediatrician who is specially interested in it. I am certain that *no child should be rejected as being unsuitable for adoption without an expert seeing the child and agreeing with the diagnosis. It is a dreadful tragedy for a normal child to be rejected for adoption because someone has mistakenly thought that he is retarded or spastic.*

The doctor who assesses the suitability of a baby for adoption frequently has to give genetic advice. Only an expert should do this. The common problems are as follows:–

1. Incest. This is said now to be more common than cousin marriages. The difficulty is that the child is at risk of inheriting one of the serious recessive diseases.[5] According to Roberts[14] there is a 1 in 8 chance that a first cousin will be heterozygos for any individual gene carried by oneself and the risk to the child of an incestuous conception is at least 4 times greater than that to a first cousin. He quoted

two studies of incest; of 31 children 6 died, and 13 of the 25 survivors were normal. The overall risk of abnormalities in incestuous unions is probably somewhere between 30 and 60 per cent.

2. Schizophrenia. The genetic factor probably acts by predisposing to schizophrenia under the influence of additional environmental factors. There is probably a 10 per cent risk of the child developing it if a parent had it. The risk is much greater if both parents have schizophrenia. The difficulty is that if the grandparent had schizophrenia, the mother may not be old enough for one to know whether she has developed it. I have met a similar problem in the case of Huntington's chorea.

3. Manic depressive psychoses. The risk of the child developing it is 10 to 15 per cent. Again, the mother may not develop it until the age of 40 or 50.

4. Epilepsy. The genetic factor is only a small one. The risk of the child being affected is about 2·5 per cent. The risk is much greater if both parents have epilepsy.

5. Degenerative diseases of the nervous system. If a sibling has a degenerative disease of the nervous system, or has had infantile spasms (which can be due to a wide variety of causes), the risk for the child who is being assessed for adoption is greatly increased. If a parent has a degenerative disease of the nervous system, again the risk to the child is considerable. The opinion to be given must depend on the exact diagnosis in the parent.

6. Mental deficiency. It is impossible to give sound genetic advice concerning a child being assessed for adoption who has a defective sibling unless a full investigation has been carried out on the defective child: one has to do one's best to eliminate the recessive and dominant conditions, because of the high risk to siblings.

7. Neurosis or alcoholism. These are probably in the main environmental in origin, and so there is no added risk of the child developing it.

It is the practice in this country for adopting parents to be informed of the background of the real mother and father. Discretion must be shown in this matter. It is certain that the adopting parents must not hear for the first time in court about diseases such as syphilis in the real mother or father.

In conclusion, there are many difficulties in assessing a child for adoption. The assessment should on no account be made by a doctor who has no interest or special experience in such work. The difficulties are considerable, and experience can only be obtained by examining a large number of babies, and by following them all up in order that one can learn from mistakes. In my opinion all children assessed should be followed up at school age.

One must do one's best to prevent foster parents unknowingly adopting a defective child. However careful one is, some children, for reasons stated, will turn out to be defective when they were thought to be normal at the time of assessment.   Yet one must remember that parents having their own children have no certainty that their children will not be defective, and unlike adopting parents they cannot even choose the child's sex.   There will always be some risk in adoption.   Unless adopting parents are willing to take some risk, they should not adopt at all.

REFERENCES

1. ADAMS, M. S., NEEL, J. V. (1967) Children of Incest. *Pediatrics* **40**, 55.
2. BAKWIN, R. M., BAKWIN, H. (1952) Adoption. *J. Pediat.*, **40**, 130.
3. BLACK, J. A., STONE, F. H. (1958) Medical Aspects of Adoption. *Lancet* **2**, 1272.
4. British Medical Journal (1953) Adoption. I Supplement P. 240.
5. British Medical Journal (1968) Inbreeding and Adoption. Leading Article. **2**, 257.
6. EDWARDS, G. (1954) Adoption. *Proc. Roy. Soc. Med.*, **47**, 1044.
7. ELLISON, M. (1958) *The Adopted Child*. London: Gollancz.
8. GOULD, F. (1968) *Stress in Children*. London: Churchill.
9. KARELITZ, S. (1957) Adoption. *Pediatrics*, **20**, 366.
10. KARELITZ, S. (1958) Adoption. *Ann. Ped. Fenn.*, **4**, 1.
11. KORNITZER, M. (1959) *Adoption*. London: Putnam.
12. KORNITZER, M. (1968) *Adoption and Family Life*. London: Putnam.
13. NORMAN, A. P. (1960) The Problem of Adoption. *Practitioner*, **185**, 175.
14. ROBERTS, D. F. (1967) Incest, inbreeding and mental abilities. *Brit. Med. J.* **4**, 336.
15. ROWE, J. (1966) *Parents, Children and Adoption*. London: Routledge and Kegan Paul.
16. WITTENBORN, J. R. (1957) *The Placement of Adoptive Children*. Springfield: Charles Thomas.

CHAPTER 19

MISTAKES AND PITFALLS IN DEVELOPMENTAL DIAGNOSIS

Although it may be felt that I have said enough about the difficulties of developmental diagnosis, I feel that the matter is of such importance that it would be profitable to summarise what has been said by putting together the common mistakes and pitfalls in developmental prediction. In doing so one will bear in mind the many warnings of Arnold Gesell. He wrote: 'So utterly unforeseen are the vicissitudes of life that our common-sense will deter us from attempting to forecast too precisely the developmental career even of a mediocre child'. 'Diagnostic prudence is required at every turn'. He quoted a saying of William James, that 'Biographies will never be written in advance'.

The main mistakes and pitfalls are as follows:

1. Failure to Take a Proper History

In view of the importance of prenatal factors and perinatal events, such as convulsions, for the development of the child, a history of these is important. One must know about hereditary conditions, such as mental deficiency, degenerative diseases and psychoses. One should ascertain whether there are any particular developmental patterns in the family, such as delayed speech.

Failure to take a history of the milestones of development makes it impossible to assess the previous rate of development. This is vital, for the history may suggest that although the child was backward at first, he is showing signs of catching up to the average. Conversely the history may show that the child's development is slowing down, or that he is actually deteriorating. Apart from this, the developmental history serves as a useful check against one's own objective findings. One always compares one's own findings with the mother's statements about the child's abilities.

Of particular importance is the effect of emotional deprivation. It is especially important in the assessment of suitability for adoption, when the child in question has been in an institution or has been moved from one foster home to another. When retardation is found, one must never suggest that there should be a further period of institutional care so that his progress can be assessed, for a further period would retard his development still further. The correct procedure is to place him in a good foster home and then observe his development after a period of say 3 months in that home. Sometimes a retarded child has had such an unfavourable environment that it is most unwise to express an opinion about his potentialities at all.   One must always be prepared to postpone judgment if in doubt, or to withhold one altogether.

Failure to take a proper history may lead to the regrettable mistake of considering that retardation is due to inborn factors when in fact it is environmental in origin.   Insufficient attention may be paid to a history of severe illness, emotional deprivation, institutional care or lack of opportunity to practise.   For instance, the age at which a child bears weight on the legs, chews, feeds himself, dresses himself or attends to his own toilet needs, depends on the domestic environment.

In the case of mentally retarded children, there is particularly liable to be an unsatisfactory environment, so that they may function at a level lower than that of which they are really capable.   If the environment is improved, they make an unexpected advance in their level of functioning.

2. Undue Reliance on the History

I have sometimes felt that when children are being examined for the purposes of adoption, too much reliance is placed on the history. With this in mind I have emphasised in preceding chapters that although certain adverse prenatal factors such as bleeding during pregnancy, maternal toxaemia, hydramnios or premature delivery, are associated with a somewhat high incidence of abnormalities in the fetus, the majority of babies born of mothers with these conditions are normal.   The same applies to perinatal morbidity in the baby: although perinatal anoxia, cerebral irritability and even convulsions are associated with a higher incidence of abnormalities, the great majority of children who survived these adverse conditions in the newborn period grow up to be normal.   In the same way undue attention should not be paid to the fact that one of the parents was mentally backward, or that one of the siblings had some anomaly of the central nervous system.   In the former case, the great majority of children will be normal.   In the latter case, the incidence of anomalies in the child depends on the disease in question.   I have seen it suggested that adoption should be postponed if any of the above adverse factors are found in the history.   This, I am sure, would be wrong.

3. Failure to Allow for Prematurity

A disastrous mistake in the assessment of a young baby is a failure to allow for premature birth (Chapter 2).   Particularly in the early weeks failure to allow for prematurity will lead to gross errors of assessment.

4. Errors in the Timing of the Examination

The timing of the examination in relation to the child's normal play time has been described in Chapter 13.

Mistakes can readily be made in the case of epilepsy. One should never attempt to assess an epileptic child who has had a fit on that day, or who is still in a confused state after a fit even a few days previously, or who is having frequent petit mal attacks. In the same way one must not examine him when he has toxic symptoms from drug therapy which may make him drowsy, ataxic or irritable and unco-operative.

The ideal age at which a developmental examination should be made, if one can choose the age, is of importance. For the purposes of adoption I would feel that the age of 6 weeks or 6 months is ideal for the purpose. In some ways I would rather give an opinion about a child when he is 6 to 8 weeks of age than I would when he is 3 or 4 months old. This has been the experience of others, including Cattell.

The age of 10 months is a good one at which to assess a baby, and if I am in doubt about the development of a baby at 6 months, I try to see him again at 10 months. At ten months one has available various new milestones of development—the index finger approach to objects, the finger thumb apposition, the child's co-operation in dressing (holding an arm out for a sleeve, a foot out for a shoe, trans-ferring an object from a hand which is about to be put into a sleeve), the creep, the ability of the child to pull himself to the standing position, and to cruise (walking, when holding on to the furniture). There is the imitation of the mother (byebye, 'patacake', 'so big',) and the possibility of words with meaning. The age of ten months is an excellent one for assessing a baby. By the age of 12 to 24 or more months, children are apt to be coy and non-cooperative, and difficult to test.

Wherever possible I would avoid testing a child between 8 and 16 weeks of age and between 8 and 9 months of age.

5. Unsuitable Choice of Test

Binet Simon tests indicated that 60 per cent of canal boat children were mentally defective, while other tests gave a figure of 7 per cent. The modification of tests for children with cerebral palsy has been discussed by Haeussermann.[2]

In my opinion some of Ruth Griffith's tests are unsatisfactory.[1] Most of her tests are modified Gesell items, but some are not, and some are in my opinion seriously misleading. For instance, the score for the personal social quotient in the first 3 months consists of the following 8 items: smiling: regarding persons momentarily: enjoying his bath: quieting if crying by being picked up: vocalising when talked to: recognising mother visually: returning examiner's glance with smiling back or cooing: following moving persons, es-pecially the mother, with his eyes. It is impossible to bunch these items together in this fashion. In the first place, the item 'enjoys his bath' is hardly a good sign of intelligence. Many intelligent babies

scream violently when bathed.   Secondly, quieting on being picked
up is hardly a sign of intelligence.   A newborn baby responds in this
way.   An average baby begins to smile at 6 weeks and to vocalise at
about 8 weeks, and one cannot score them together.   The important
thing is not *whether* a child smiles, but *when* he began to smile in response to his mother's overtures, and with what degree of maturity he
does it: i.e. how readily and frequently he smiles.   If a full term child
had only just begun to smile at 3 months, I should say that he is almost
certainly mentally defective; but on the Griffiths' scale he scores his
his point.   The whole scale is far too coarse at this age.   One must
remember that a performance of a 3 month baby at a 2 month level
may mean that at 10 years he will be in the educationally subnormal
class.   Small variations from the average are important, and really
coarse methods of assessment add greatly to the inaccuracy of infant
testing.

One may criticise many other of her items.   For instance, she
included the grasp reflex as a sign of motor maturity at 1 month, but
the grasp reflex is not a sign of intelligence.   The loss of the grasp
reflex may be a sign of maturation, but that is the opposite of what she
appears to mean.   Other items which I would feel are unsuitable
include: friendliness to strangers (fourth month): stopping crying
when talked to (fifth month): holding on to spoon (fifth month):
drinking from a cup (seventh month): being able to be left sitting on
floor.

The first two of these do not require comment.   As for the third
'he holds on to a spoon' one has to assess not just the occurrence of the
act, but the maturity of the act   As for drinking from a cup, newborn
babies have been known to do this.   As for the item 'can be left
sitting on the floor', this is far too coarse for a test: there is much more
to the assessment of the maturity of sitting than the fact that he can be
left sitting on the floor.

6. Errors in the Performance of the Tests

It is wrong, as stated in Chapter 13 to conduct the physical examination of the infant before carrying out the developmental tests.   He
is likely to be much more co-operative if given test objects before he
is undressed for his physical examination.

It is usually a mistake to examine the child in the absence of the
mother.   I was reminded of the importance of having the mother
present during the test when I nearly made a mistake in assessment.
I was testing the child's ability to copy strokes made with a pencil.   He
had successfully imitated a vertical, horizontal and circular stroke,
and I made a cross, asking him to do the same.   He made a circle
close to the cross.   I assumed that he could not make the cross, but
the mother said, 'He is playing noughts and crosses; he likes it'.

Slowness in presenting the tests, or failure to modify the sequence of testing if a child is showing signs of boredom, will lead to errors.   The importance of carrying out the testing before a long history is taken when assessing a young child has been mentioned in Chapter 13.

7. Errors in Respect of the Physical Examination

The vital importance of the measurement of the head circumference has been mentioned in Chapter 8.

Even though a head is smaller than usual, a normal rate of growth should prevent one making the mistake of diagnosing mental subnormality on the basis of smallness of the head.   On the other hand an abnormal rate of growth of the head circumference, especially the slowing down in the growth, would make one strongly suspicious of mental subnormality.   It is vital not to forget the fact that the head size must be related to the size of the baby.   A little baby can be expected to have a little head, and a big baby a big one.   No child should ever be suspected of mental subnormality merely on account of physical features such as a small or large head, or even because of gross abnormalities such as hypertelorism or craniostenosis.   The developmental diagnosis can never be presumed: it must be made on a full developmental examination.

Napoleon, on account of the ugly shape of his head, was thought to be the least likely in his family to achieve much.   Mirabeau was regarded as the ugly duckling of the family, and had a disproportionately large head.

Hydrocephalus is not necessarily incompatable with a good level of intelligence.   In the first place, it may be arrested at birth.   I well remember seeing a seriously disturbed mother who had been told that her baby had hydrocephalus and would be spastic and mentally defective.   The diagnosis was undoubtedly correct, but I told the mother that the prediction given, though likely, was by no means necessarily correct.   Within a month it was obvious that the hydrocephalus was arrested, and the child proved to be normal.

Bakwin described the dreadful tragedy which resulted from a wrong diagnosis of mental deficiency in a child with hydrocephalus and spina bifida.   The father was given a bad prognosis and was given the extraordinary advice that he should tell his wife that the baby had died.   The girl was then transferred to an institution, but as she grew older it became clear that her intelligence was within normal limits.   The father was then advised to tell his wife that the girl was in fact alive; but he would not do so.   The mother was then told by another person.

Hydrocephalus may cause difficulty in two ways.   In the first place, the process may become arrested at any stage, so that development may be normal.   In the second place, it is difficult to assess head control, when the sheer weight of a large head may cause undue head lag.

8. Failure to Diagnose Sensory Defects

Sensory defects, such as visual or auditory ones, are obvious factors which profoundly affect development. Visual defects will affect the age of smiling, following with the eyes and manipulation. When the child is older, specific reading disability or congenital auditory imperception may be missed.

The fact that sensory defects, such as visual or auditory impairment, may lead to emotional deprivation and reduced manipulative and other experiences, should not be forgotten: one defect may lead to another, so that development is retarded by a combination of factors. The combination of retarding factors in cerebral palsy has been described elsewhere.

A failure to detect mechanical factors, such as hypotonia or cerebral palsy, will cause gross errors in assessment.

9. Failure to detect Other Signs of Organic Disease

Minimal neurological signs may be missed, so that the organic reason for a child's lateness in motor development may not be recognised. There may be an organic basis for the child's lateness in feeding himself, dressing himself or acquiring sphincter control.

It would be foolish to attempt a developmental assessment of a child who has a physical illness which would reduce the level of his performance.

CEREBRAL PALSY. Cerebral palsy and so-called 'birth injury' interfere with the assessment of a child for a variety of reasons. Cerebral palsy causes mechanical difficulties which interfere with the use of the hands and with gross motor development; it is frequently associated with visual and auditory defects, with mental retardation, with poor attention span even in the absence of mental retardation, with emotional problems and with perceptional difficulties such as defects of body image, space appreciation, and form perception, so that tests with formboards are misleading; and there may be other defects arising from cortical damage. Speech is usually defective. The child's environment has not been conducive to a good level of achievement in tests commonly employed, he may have been kept indoors, and had little contact with other children, and be unable to speak. Haeussermann[2] emphasised the fact that brain lesions 'penalise' a child. She wrote that: 'While the actual ability to comprehend and reason may be well within the normal range, in some cases the level of adaptation may be disproportionately lower'. 'Children with cerebral palsy will be more readily understood and their attempts to communicate more alertly observed and accepted by an examiner to whom it has become evident that while a child may be non-speaking, he may be far from non-communicating'.

Of all forms of cerebral palsy in which mistakes can be made in the assessment of intelligence, I would think that athetosis has the pride of place. Perlstein has made the same comment, when referring to kernicterus. I have myself made such a mistake. The following is a brief case history:

Case Report.—This boy was born at term, by a difficult forceps delivery, weighing 3860 g. There was a severe degree of asphyxia, but he was well in the neonatal period. I saw him at 1 year because of lateness in sitting and walking. The milestones were confusing. He had learnt to chew at 8½ months, and to roll from supine to prone at 6½ months. He had begun to say single words just before I saw him. He was interested, and laughing at the antics of his sibling. There was no sign of the spastic form of cerebral palsy. The grasp was a little ataxic, like that of a 5 month old baby. There were no abnormal movements. In my letter to the consultant who referred him to me, I wrote, 'I find it difficult to reconcile the fact that in the development of speech and chewing he is at the level of an 8 month old child, while in the use of hands and of sitting he is only at the level of a 5 month old child. This would suggest a mechanical difficulty. There is no doubt at all that he is quite considerably mentally retarded, apart altogether from his mechanical difficulty. Further observation is essential over a period of some months, in order to see how he develops'. (In retrospect, the diagnosis of mental retardation was obviously wrong, because of the normal speech development).

At 18 months I wrote: 'There is a mechanical difficulty, which is not spasticity. The point I made before about the lack of correlation between his locomotor development and speech is particularly obvious now, for he can say a lot of words and still cannot sit. This must represent a mechanical difficulty, and not mere mental retardation, for no child who is unable to sit on account of severe mental retardation is nevertheless able to talk'.

He began to put words together and to walk a few steps at 2 years. At 4 years athetoid movements became obvious. His I.Q. at 5 years was 100.

Another difficulty in the assessment of infants with cerebral palsy is the delayed maturation which is sometimes seen, and to which reference has already been made.

10. Undue Attention to the Results of Special Investigations, such as Air Encephalograms

The relative lack of correlation between these and performance has already been described.

Case Report.—I saw a child at the age of 2 months, who was admitted to hospital with a history of frequent convulsions in the previous 3 weeks. He was found to be backward in development. He had been born at term, but had only begun to smile at his mother at 8 weeks. On examination there was complete head lag in ventral suspension and when pulled to the sitting position. A subdural tap was negative, but an air encephalogram showed a large amount of air on the surface of the brain, indicating cortical atrophy. He was discharged in 2 weeks, with a diagnosis of epilepsy and mental retardation. On follow-up examination he was soon found to be making rapid progress. His head control was full at 5½ months, he grasped objects voluntarily at 7 months, and began to transfer them at 8 months. At 10 months he was considered to be mentally normal. His I.Q. score at 9 years was 122, and there was no physical disability.

11. Errors in Interpretation caused by the Child's Failure to Co-operate

It is easy to diagnose mental subnormality in a child who is behaving badly and who will not co-operate. His behavior may be due to fatigue, hunger, shyness or other reasons.   If a child arrives tired and will not co-operate, he must be given a rest before he is examined or the opinion must be withheld altogether until he can be examined under more favourable circumstances.

One can make the mistake of considering lack of co-operation or interest to be a sign of low intelligence, when in fact it is merely a feature of the child's personality.   One must also avoid the mistake of confusing the obsessional perseveration of the mentallly defective child—who not uncommonly plays with one toy for hours on end—with true good concentration, such as one sees in an intelligent child.

12. The Difficulty of the Sleepy Baby

Errors in the assessment of motor development in the young baby are readily made if a child is sleepy or asleep.   The sleeping 6 weeks old baby, for instance, often assumes the fetal position in the prone, with his knees drawn high up under the abdomen; in the wakeful state his pelvis is lower and legs often extended.

13. The Interpretation of Prone Development

It is easy to underestimate a young baby's development in the prone position, particularly between 2 and 8 months of age.   He is apt to lie without attempting to raise his head from the couch, when if he tries he can raise it to a considerable extent.

14. Examiner Regard

The 5 or 6 month old baby may look at the examiner so closely that one makes the mistake of thinking that he shows no interest in the test objects.

The child may be so interested in other objects around the room that one wrongly thinks that he has poor concentration.

15. Errors in Assessment of Maturity of Responses

Though the rapidity with which a baby drops a cube gives some indication of the maturity of the grasp, a child may drop the brick accidentally.

One must distinguish the accidental dropping of a cube from true casting—a feature which usually commences at about 12 months of age.

When the child is older, one may fail to observe the maturity with which an act is performed.   For instance, a child who has only learnt to walk 2 or 3 days before the examination may show a mature gait, indicating that he could have walked alone weeks earlier if he had had the desire or confidence.   In the case of speech, when a child is said not to be able to talk at all, one may fail to observe the vital fact that he knows the meaning of numerous words.   The excessive head lag due to the mere size of the head in hydrocephalus can lead to errors in assessment.

In several of the studies on child development, the score is based on an all or none achievement: for instance, a 7 months old baby can either sit without support or he cannot. In one case he obtains a mark, and in the other he does not. This completely ignores the maturity of the act; one child who can sit without support may sit like an average 7 months old baby, and another like a 9 months old baby. The score should obviously be different.

16. Errors due to the Attractive Appearance of an Infant

The absence of shyness, the presence of good looks, a pleasant personality and charm, may lead to an erroneous diagnosis of mental superiority. It is easy to make the mistake of giving a higher assessment to a bouncing active baby than to a sleepy placid one, without good justification. The facile behaviour and talkativeness of older children with hydrocephalus is apt to give an exaggerated idea of their intelligence.

Some of the features of a child's behaviour, good or bad, may be related purely to his personality, and not to his intelligence.

17. Error Due to Unattractive Appearance

One must never be misled by this. Amongst famous people of history who were renowned for their ugliness were Socrates, Mirabeau, Napoleon Bonaparte and Leo Tolstoy.

18. Failure to Realise that some Aspects of Development are Vastly More Important for Assessment than Others

Some have placed far too much reliance on motor items of development, because they are readily scorable, and far too little on the more important features of a child's behaviour—the alertness, the rapidity of response, the interest in surroundings, the degree of determination, persistence and concentration. Gesell called these 'Insurance factors' and paid great attention to them.

A child may have average motor ability and yet show grossly defective concentration, indicating mental subnormality. Aimless overactivity or defective concentration in a child who appears to be normal in other respects should make one suspect mental retardation and follow up closely for confirmation of that suspicion.

19. Ascribing Retardation to Laziness

I am frequently told that a child's general retardation or delay in speech or sphincter control is due to mere laziness. This diagnosis is always wrong.

20. Failure to Assess the Rate of Development

A common mistake is to fail to assess the rate of development—by taking the developmental history, and seeing the child again, repeatedly if necessary, before a conclusion as to his developmental potential is reached. I regard this as of the utmost importance. For instance, in the case of assessment of suitability for adoption, the over-confident and inexperienced doctor will make a practice of assessing babies on a single examination. In many cases one can do this: in many others it is impossible, and the child must be seen again before a confident opinion can be given.

21. Failure to remember the Different Patterns of Development

Lulls in development cause confusion. A child's apparent failure to progress in speech development may cause anxiety if the frequency of this in normal children is forgotten.

22. Difficulties with Regard to Deterioration

It has already been noted that mongols and children with untreated phenylketonuria slow down in development. This feature should not be termed deterioration: it represents a slowing down of the process of development. I have several times heard that an unusually good intelligence level had been predicted for a mongol on account of good early development.

True deterioration may occur as a result of readily diagnosable conditions, such as lead poisoning, hypoglycaemia, head injury, meningitis or encephalitis. These cannot usually be anticipated: in the absence of a family history of a degenerative disease it is almost impossible to predict most other forms of deterioration. The deterioration associated with epilepsy has been described in Chapter 16. I am always mindful of the possibility of deterioration in a retarded child who is having uncontrollable fits. It is well known that deterioration may occur in severe forms of cerebral palsy. Quite marked deterioration can be expected when a mentally defective child is placed in an institution.

One cannot expect to predict an unusual course of development, whether due to known extraneous circumstances or not. There may be unexpected and unexplained deterioration, or merely failure to fulfil early promise: or more commonly there may be unexpected improvement.

The improvement sometimes found in retarded infants has been described in Chapter 11. One is much more likely to under-estimate a child's potential than to over-estimate it. The possibility of unexpected improvement will always be borne in mind, but the likelihood of such improvement must not be over-estimated. In my opinion unexpected improvement is rare.

23. Failure to Assess the Child as a Whole

As described in Chapter 14 one balances the development in one field with that in other fields. When there is 'dissociation' one must look for the cause—which is often organic disease.

The whole child has to be assessed with regard to prenatal and perinatal conditions, environment, physical abnormalities, the rate of development and the developmental examination. A proper assessment cannot be made on the basis of purely objective tests.

Safian and Harms in a discussion of 4 cases of mistaken diagnosis of mental retardation wrote: 'We hope that in the future we shall become somewhat less dependent on these testing methods and shall rely more and more on a totalitarian aspect on the one hand, and on the other, the individualisation study of any child whose fate is given into our hands'. Charles wrote: 'The overall impression one gains from the literature on diagnosis is that the soundest approach depends upon clinical judgment reinforced by social data and test results interpreted in the light of all the evidence'.

24. Confusion by Schizophrenia and Autism

These are described on Page 261.

It must be remembered that psychoses can be superimposed on mental deficiency.

25. Failure to Withhold Judgment in Case of Doubt

In some children, owing to the presence of confusing factors, prediction is impossible without further prolonged observation. The following is an example of a combination of difficulties of this nature.

Case Report.—Unusual Skull, Developmental Retardation and Difficulties in Prediction.

I was asked to see this boy at 11 weeks because of suspected hydrocephalus. The circumference of the head at birth was 37·5 cm, his weight then being 3800 g. On examination at 11 weeks the circumference was 42·5 cm, but the fontanelle and sutures felt normal. There was a slight antimongoloid slant of the eyes, and there was a prominent forehead, but I thought that the head could be within normal limits. The head was unlike that of either parent. The boy was said to have begun to smile at 7 weeks and to vocalise at 8 weeks. The head control was that of a 6 weeks old baby. There were no other abnormal physical signs.

He was seen at intervals. He was said to hold a rattle placed in the hands at 3 months. At 4 months the head control was that of a 3 months old baby.

At one year the head circumference was 49·5 cm. I thought that the clinical picture was that of megalencephaly. He showed hand regard. The head control was that of a 3½ months old baby. He was unable to grasp objects, though he 'grasped with the eye'; he did not hold on to an object placed in the hand. I wrote that 'In no way can I see development beyond the 4 month level'. I thought that his development had slowed down.

At this stage a full investigation was carried out with a view to possible operation for the hydrocephalus by insertion of a valve. Ventricular studies and an air encephalogram showed that there was no hydrocephalus, and the appearance was consistent with a diagnosis of megalencephaly. The E.E.G. was normal. The interpupillary distance was large—55 mm. While in hospital he was able to sit like a

7 month baby (at the age of 13 months), and he was seen to wave bye-bye.   This had just begun.   He bore virtually no weight on the legs.   Voluntary grasping began at 14 months.

At 20 months the head measured 50·8 cms.   I was immediately impressed by his incessant jargoning, and his responsiveness to his parents.   He had begun to jargon at 18 months.   He said 8 or 9 words clearly.   He was unable to crawl or roll, but he could bear almost all his weight on his legs momentarily.   He could not stand holding on to furniture.   He was said to play only a short time with individual toys, usually merely throwing them to the ground.   He would not grasp cubes or other test objects.   His mother said that he would be unable to point out objects in pictures. He would not feed himself at all with a biscuit or spoon, and there was no sphincter control.   He held his arms out for clothes from 18 months and played patacake at the same age.   I thought that in view of the speech he had developed as far as a child of 14 or 18 months, though in all other respects he was much more retarded.   I gave as my opinion that his I.Q. would be not less than 60 or 70, and that it might well turn out to be well up to the average.

The family developmental history was interesting.   An older child had been a 'slow-starter'.   I had seen him at 2 years, when he had just begun to walk a few steps.   He was then very advanced in speech, speaking in long mature sentences. In all respects he was a normal child of advanced intelligence.   The parents thought that the youngest child (with the megalencephaly) had throughout compared well with his older sibling in speech and all other aspects of development.

I have described this case at some length to show the difficulties which are sometimes encountered.   Firstly, he had a peculiar head. Secondly, his development appeared to slow down and he took less interest in his surroundings.   Thirdly (at 20 months), his speech had made remarkable progress, and was far in advance of all other fields of development.   (No physical disability, such as spasticity, had ever been found).   One rarely sees a child with uniform retardation except in speech, in which retardation was only slight.   Fourthly, there was the family history of severe motor retardation in a sibling, who was now normal and of superior intelligence.

In such a case a prognosis must be guarded, and only prolonged observation could give one a clear picture of the developmental potential.   At the time of writing (when he was 20 months old) he was still under observation.   The parents, who were highly intellig- ent, had been given a full explanation of my difficulties in assessment, and I gave them hope that the child would be normal.   I promised that he would not be severely defective (unless he developed some unforseen complication like encephalitis).

One must always be prepared to withhold a prognosis altogether, sometimes even for 2 or 3 years in particularly difficult cases.

26. Unwise attempt to assess ill child

When a child has a debilitating illness, such as coeliac disease, it would be foolish to attempt to make a developmental assessment. He should not be assessed until he has recovered and until any effects of his illness on his development have disappeared.

27. The Problem of the Possible Effect of Future Environment or Illness

It is impossible to predict certain variables which may affect the child's development in future, even though one has assessed his developmental potential. One cannot predict changes in environment which will profoundly affect the child's progress: one cannot predict illness, epilepsy or degenerative diseases of the nervous system, or other conditions which will affect his development.

28. Difficulties with Regard to the Prognosis of Infantile Spasms

Case Report.—A boy of 8 months was seen with the recent onset of infantile spasms. He showed no interest in one-inch cubes or other test objects. Air studies and an electroencephalogram were carried out.

Two months later he was taking a little more interest in his surroundings, but he was sleeping nearly all the twenty-four hours every day. At 13 months he was still making no attempt to reach out for objects or to chew. I thought that he was severely mentally defective.

Two months later he had begun to hold his arm out for clothes and to wave bye-bye. He walked without help at 19 months, joined words together at three years, but had no sphincter control. At 43 months he had reached the level of a 24-month child.

At 69 months he had reached the level of a 60-month boy, and at seven his I.Q. score was 100.

Comment

It is not easy to give a confident prediction of the future in cases of infantile spasms in which there is no obvious cause, such as tuberous sclerosis, severe hypoglycaemia or phenylketonuria. The majority do badly and remain defective, though some degree of improvement is usual. Occasional children, however, make an almost complete recovery. I saw a child with this condition who later had an I.Q. score of 100, but had troublesome visuospatial difficulties.

29. The Difficulty of Assessing the Effect of Acute Infections or other Disease of the Nervous System

It is impossible to predict the outcome of encephalitis or severe meningitis until sufficient time has elapsed to observe the rate of improvement.

The following is a remarkable case history which well illustrates the error which can be made in assessment of such a child.

Case Report.—Unexpected Recovery from State of Decerebrate Rigidity in Tuberculous Meningitis.

This girl was admitted to the Children's Hospital, Sheffield, at the age of 2 years and 5 months. The clinical and bacteriological diagnosis was tuberculous meningitis. She was drowsy and irritable on admission, and in spite of full intrathecal and intramuscular antibiotic treatment, she deteriorated progressively, until she became more and more deeply unconscious. 3 months after admission she was in deep coma, and in a state of decerebrate rigidity. There was no evidence that she could see or hear.   She had bizarre movements of the limbs, bruxism, and extreme spasticity, with opisthotonos and severe emaciation.   An air encephalogram showed a moderate degree of hydrocephalus.   After consultation with the parents, treatment was abandoned and she went home.

She unexpectedly made remarkable improvement at home, so that 5 months after discharge it was decided to resume treatment in order to ensure that she did not relapse.   She made a complete recovery, both physically and mentally.

At the age of $7\frac{1}{2}$ years she weighed 38·1 kg and was 129·5 cms high.   Her fundi, vision and hearing were normal, and there were no neurological signs.   The X-ray of her skull showed calcification above the sella.   Her school progress was excellent, and her I.Q. was 101.   The E.E.G. remained abnormal.

COMMENT

There was every reason to give an extremely bad prognosis here, and yet she made a complete recovery.   This is a perfect example of the extreme caution needed in predicting development in the early days after an attack of meningitis or encephalitis, even though at the time the future seems as black as it could be.

I gave a bad prognosis in the case described below:

Case Report.—Cerebral Venous Thrombosis with Recovery.

This boy, born at term, developed normally until 4 months, having begun to smile at 4 weeks.   He then developed an upper respiratory tract infection, perspired profusely and became severely dehydrated, developing keratitis and broncho-pneumonia.   He was admitted with diarrhoea, vomiting and major convulsions. He passed into coma and had several further convulsions.   When he emerged from coma he was spastic, with grossly exaggerated knee jerks, tightly clenched hands and opisthotonos, and took no notice of his surroundings.   The cerebrospinal fluid was normal and all virus studies were negative.   A diagnosis of cerebral venous thrombosis was made.

At 13 months, the boy was a bright, normal boy without any abnormality.   He was walking without support, helping his mother to dress him, and saying words with meaning.

COMMENT

It was easy to give an extremely bad prognosis with regard to his subsequent development.

Case Report.—A girl aged 22 months was admitted with advanced tuberculous meningitis after unsuccessful treatment of some weeks' duration in another hospital. She was deeply unconscious, with left sided spastic hemiplegia, bilateral optic atrophy and convulsive movements on the right side of her body.

She was treated with intrathecal streptomycin, isoniazid, prednisolone and pyridoxine.   She recovered consciousness, but was found to be blind.   Her eye-eyesight after two months began slowly to recover, and at the age of 4 years the vision on the right was 6/12 and on the left 6/60.   A year later the vision was 6/9 on each side.   The left disc remained pale, but the right disc was almost normal.

COMMENT

It is easy to give a bad prognosis in such a case, particularly with regard to eyesight.   Caution should be used at all times in giving a prognosis.

30. Failure to Recognise the Difficulty of Diagnosing Mental Superiority in Infancy, and still more, the Impossibility of Predicting Future Eminence

I have said enough to indicate that the developmental quotient merely indicates how far the child has progressed in his environment, under the circumstances of his health, good or bad.   On the basis of his D.Q., in the light of all possible factors which might have affected it or might be going to affect it, and in the light of the evidence concerning his rate of development, one makes a judicious guess as to the potential which he has for the future.

I am not competent to enter the numerous arguments amongst educationalists and psychologists concerning the meaning or definition of intelligence, and the significance of the intelligence quotient, particularly in relation to backwardness at school.   As Stoddard wrote, I.Q. tests show what the child knows, but they do not show how far he can go in pursuit of ideas, or determine his originality or ability to concentrate on his tasks.

Pidgeon and Yates warned against the idea that a score on an intelligence test provides an indication of a child's inmost intellectual capacity and therefore sets a limit to the level of attainment that he can be expected to reach.   They wrote: 'We can say that the child's level of attainment is likely to fall within a specified range of scores above or below the level of his intelligence test performance'.

31. Failure to Learn from Mistakes, because of Failure to Keep Proper Records, to which Reference can be and is Constantly Made

Developmental diagnosis is fraught with difficulties, and he who is over-confident, makes 'spot-diagnoses', and fails to follow up the children whom he has assessed, will inevitably make unnecessary mistakes.   A careful follow-up system is essential for anyone hoping to become proficient in this field.   Mistakes made must be examined in detail, the reasons for the mistakes being determined, so that the mistake can be avoided in future.

If children are assessed for the purposes of adoption, they should be re-examined (preferably by a different person) when they are of school age, so that the accuracy and usefulness of one's assessments can be determined.   If mental retardation or cerebral palsy is diagnosed in other infants, they should be followed up so that one's opinion can be confirmed or disproved.   A punch card system, which enables one to determine in a moment the names of children who are due for follow-up examination, is invaluable.   I find that repeated cinematographic records of infants with suspected abnormality is useful not only for self-instruction, but for the teaching of others.

If one is to learn from mistakes, and become reasonably proficient in developmental assessment, a really adequate follow-up scheme is absolutely essential.

32. Failure to recognise the Difficulties of Developmental Prediction, and its Limitations: The Idea that Developmental Diagnosis is Easy

This is a suitable note on which to end this book.   The more one learns about the subject, the more one realises what the difficulties are and how great they can be.   He who thinks that developmental diagnosis is easy is making a serious mistake.   Developmental diagnosis can only be made on the basis of a careful detailed history, a full developmental, neurological and physical examination, and interpretation of the results in the light of one's own experience and particularly in the light of the experience of others who have warned everyone that developmental diagnosis demands the greatest diagnostic acumen, common-sense and caution.

I was once asked to see a boy because of behaviour problems. These turned out to be due to dyslexia and allied difficulties.   Two psychiatrists who had seen the boy on previous occasions had assessed his I.Q. score as 79 and 79·1 respectively.

In a clinical meeting I saw a demonstration of the treatment and results of treatment of phenylketonuria.   I read the following 'The Intelligence Quotient on the . . . scale at the age of 5 weeks was 89'.

Perhaps one day such accuracy will be possible.   I doubt it.

REFERENCES

1. GRIFFITHS, R. (1954) *The Abilities of Babies.* London: Univ. of London Press.
2. HAEUSSERMANN, E. (1958) *Developmental Potential of Preschool Children.* London: Grune and Stratton.

INDEX